Alan Brett

And know they love you
memoirs of a teacher who really cares

Betsy Graham

And know they love you

Published by The Conrad Press in the United Kingdom 2020

Tel: +44(0)1227 472 874
www.theconradpress.com
info@theconradpress.com

ISBN 978-1-913567-28-6

Copyright © Betsy Graham, 2020

The moral right of Betsy Graham to be identified as author of this work has been asserted in accordance with the Copyright, Designs and Patents Act 1988.

All rights reserved.

Typesetting and Cover Design by:
Charlotte Mouncey, www.bookstyle.co.uk

The Conrad Press logo was designed by Maria Priestley.

Printed and bound in Great Britain by Clays Ltd, Elcograf S.p.A.

You who are on the road
Must have a code that you can live by
And so become yourself
Because the past is just a good-bye.
Teach your children well,
Their father's hell did slowly go by,
And feed them on your dreams
The one they pick, the one you'll know by.
Don't you ever ask them why, if they told you,
you will cry,
So just look at them and sigh
And know they love you.

'Teach Your Children'

Crosby, Stills and Nash

Preface

I'm hating something I wanted to love. This book was written over a period of two school years: September 2016 to July 2018. I'm not sure how it began. Nor am I sure I can explain it to you, but I'll try. I used to be so proud to be a teacher, but after eleven years in the trenches, I began to feel like I was at the end of my rope. I couldn't breathe. I cringed whenever I was out on a Saturday night and the inevitable question arose- 'what do you do?' I hated having to say the words out loud 'I'm a teacher.'

I began to feel embarrassed, self-conscious even, and felt as if despite the conversations to the contrary, people would be quietly horrified to hear that I had boxed myself into a public sector profession so willingly. It was never the children that got me down, but it was pretty much everything else.

Then, when too many events had conspired to make the chaos no longer bearable, I did what every thirty-something girl does, and went to therapy. And I began to unpick the way I felt, and, explored my feelings about the job in great detail, even at one point feeling like the only option for my sanity was to find a new career. I fantasised about working as a lawyer one week, a PA in London the next, whatever was the polar opposite of everything I knew how to do.

But slowly, I began to acknowledge all the good things that I do, and all the reasons why I'm extremely good at helping small people to learn and feel great about themselves. I found new strength to go on. My lovely therapist, Karen, used to comment that my face lit up when I spoke of the hilarity I experienced with the children day to day, and darkened whenever I expressed my frustration and discontent with the system. I began to realise that I wanted to carry on, and I was in fact, very proud of what I do, but I didn't have to pretend I aligned with the views of the many.

So late in the summer of 2017, as passion mixed with anger bubbled up inside my chest, I took out my laptop and began to tap away, not knowing where I was going. Suffice to say that this book sort of wrote itself, as I beavered away during the rainy summer holidays, and then once school began again, during the evenings, if I wasn't too knackered. After all, I was never short of material. So here it is. My feelings and my experiences.

While they are truly my own, I suspect that some of the educational twaddle and nonsense may indeed resonate with many teachers far and wide. We can't always change those things we don't agree with, but we don't have to remain silent and quietly conform either.

Before you ask, I am still working at my school, and I hope to keep my job, thus all names and identifying details have been changed so that hopefully you should have no idea where this fine institution is or who its inhabitants are.

I'd be lying if I didn't hope that you will really enjoy this book, because a teacher (and teaching assistant's) wages aren't much to write home about. Plus Mrs Wright (my beloved teaching assistant and partner-in-crime who you'll hear about continuously through this book) is getting on a bit, and I've sort of promised her that if we hit the big time, then we'll set sail to the Bahamas with the profits. We might even take a few bottles of Sauvignon Blanc along for the trip, Mrs Wright's favourite tipple. Either that or we'll hopefully be invited to go on *Lorraine*, or maybe *Loose Women*, although come to think of it, that might blow our cover.

If we're not that lucky, and if you think you do know who we are, then please don't tell, or there's a good chance we might be fired, being that we've given away most of the family secrets.

And to Bebe Duke, if you're reading this, then, while I couldn't stand the bloody sight of you at school, I do thank you for the endless source of material you have inadvertently provided, and wish you every happiness as you continue to belittle, humiliate and deride the small children entrusted to your care. Peace out.

1

Early days

As she sat on my lap, her tiny shoulders heaving and face streaked with tears, it hit me smack in the face; this is not how it is supposed to be. What are we doing to these children?

I was in our little side room between our two Year One classrooms, mid-way through the year, with the three small people deemed to be 'below average' in phonics, as we tried in vain to prepare them to pass a silly national screening test the following month. As Lola, Oliver and Ashlyn sat around the tables watching the little YouTube video about the 'sh' sound, morale was high, or so I thought. As soon as it came to having a go, at putting pen to paper, or whiteboard in this case, one of them began to misbehave.

As Ashlyn and Oliver beavered away, practising writing the letters in their best handwriting, Lola dawdled, and lazily trailed her pen across the board doing anything but what she had been asked. The educator in me tried to jolly her along, and to remind her that she was just as capable as the others. 'Come on Lola!' I chirped, eager for her to up her game and practise her letters. 'You can do it! Have a go, come on.'

Lola looked up at me, her little glasses always inching their way down further towards her nose, as the morning wore on, before her eyes filled with tears and the floodgates opened. She began to sob, and I mean really sob. Great gasping sobs that rendered her breathless and barely able to speak. The sad part was, that before she even opened her mouth to explain, I knew exactly what she was going to say. 'It's just so hard!' she sobbed loudly, tears rolling down her face. 'My mummy wants me to read and she won't help me. She just says I have to do it myself and I can't!' she wailed.

I'd never felt so sad in all my life. For this was not a child playing up to her teacher in a last-ditch attempt at getting out of doing her work. This was an expression of genuine and sincere distress, the culmination of months of being tutored after school, interrogated daily by her mother as to what she hadn't learned that day, and aged five, being forced into a pressure cooker in the pursuit of academic glory by her panicked and extremely pushy parents.

Ashlyn reached over and began to rub Lola's back as she cried, while I tried hard to remain quiet and allow her the space to get it all off her chest. And then, after I decided it was warranted and that she needed comfort, I picked her up and sat her on my lap, before sending Ashlyn off in search of tissues. As her sobs began to subside, and Ashlyn duly returned with a handful of tissues, Lola took them and removed her little pink glasses so that she could dab her teary eyes. I don't think I've ever seen a sight that warmed my heart and simultaneously broke it at the same time, than Lola holding her tiny glasses and wiping away salty tears.

This is exactly the kind of situation I've tried to avoid all of my teaching life. That children, feel the pressure caused by the system that forces every child into boxes, regardless of any other factors that exist. And Lola was a sad casualty of the broken and damaging educational system of our country.

In the beginning, I found it hard to comfort the small people if they were upset. Back when I started, we were told not to comfort children unless they were, absolutely, beside themselves. Loosely translated it means no cuddles, no picking up, no consoling. Nothing involving physical contact, period.

They were four years old. Four. Now I know that over the years, and due to the hysteria, that has developed since some terrible breaches of trust between teachers and pupils, people have become less trusting of adults towards children, and rightly so. You only have to do a quick google search of major headlines involving children, to realise that times are changing, and not for the better. But unfortunately, over the years, this has resulted in an almost bizarre interpretation of the rules, and while they were put in place to protect children, it has also spectacularly backfired. So, I've always tried, to keep children at arm's length if you like, to remind them that I'm '*The Teacher*'. However, I was fortunate enough to work with an older, lady teacher, before I even started formal training. She used to hug all of her charges goodbye at the end of each day, and wisely told me 'you should never push them away.'

Day after day I watched her give them a cuddle as they lined up at the door in their brown tweed blazers and wide-brimmed school hats. This was a private school, and I marvelled at the stark contrast that I'd already seen, between two largely similar institutions.

How lovely to be hugged by your teacher every day. The class were largely girls, in fact I think there was only one little boy, and he was not the slightest bit perturbed to be, entirely, surrounded by females all day, every day. As far as I remember, he was a nice little chap, and rather popular among his classmates.

Once I began my teaching practices and began to watch other teachers, all, very different in their approaches, I usually followed their lead, as that's what any good student would do, right? I think it wasn't until I got my own class, my first class, that I began to develop my own way of working with such tiny children, and over the years, I have found my own niche if you like. I don't often blow my own trumpet, but as my scepticism, about all things education-related, grew, I started to notice lots of things, not least that I was being hugged a lot by my class, and much more so than the other teachers.

2

September song

It used to start late in the year, maybe by the summer term. By this point, you've already spent the best part of thirty-nine weeks together, and bonds and relationships have been made.

They feel comfortable, secure, and essentially, they know where they are with you. And slowly but surely, little hands started to wrap around my waist unexpectedly. Closely followed by another, and another. And I always rub their back. And ask them if they're ok. And thank them for my hug. They smile, happy that their kindness has been recognised, but also because it made them feel a little bit special, even if it was just for a moment.

I didn't used to loathe teaching. Loathe is perhaps the wrong word, I'm not sure I can choose any word to accurately describe it. Teaching is, by its very nature, comprised of lots of different elements, all housed under the 'umbrella' term. But it is made up of so many parts, not all of which I have begun to tire of. It's a complex mix; part parent; part behaviourist; part educator. Some days you smooth so much conflict the United Nations would be proud.

I love the children. There is no question about that. It is the one shining light in the otherwise, sometimes, bleak experience. It can be such good fun. Such a fantastic way to spend one's working day, in the great company of no less than thirty, five and six year-olds, who never fail to amuse, as we navigate the path of learning together.

It's September, and I am greeted with thirty little people who have just arrived back after the long summer break. Their, faces, are sun-kissed and tanned, they have smart back-to-school haircuts. Their shoes are shiny, jumpers are neat, and hopefully, labelled, and my classroom is filled with the chatter and excitement at seeing each other after an enforced hiatus from their close friendships. Sixteen lovely girls and fourteen lovely boys are now my sole responsibility from 9am to 3pm every day, and they will be for the next thirty-nine weeks. I am very fortunate to be able to work with a fantastic, worth-her-weight-in-gold teaching assistant, who over the years has become a close friend.

We're a good team. She is older than me, far wiser, and has already reared two boys of her own and passed the parenting finishing line with a gold medal in hand. 'Don't worry my dear, we'll whip them in to shape,' she whispered to me after we met them in July, when they visited us for a morning. When the day of meeting the little cherubs finally dawned, I was filled with the usual whisper of unease, masked by cheerful optimism. By the end of the trial morning, let's just say, I was relieved that they didn't belong to me. At least not yet anyway.

That's not entirely true. They were lovely, but had been described lovingly by their reception teacher as 'a bit lively.' I wasn't surprised. Said teacher was also part of the leadership team, and spent quite a bit of time out of class to meet her larger responsibilities, leaving her young charges in the hands of her teaching assistant and, usually, a parent volunteer. Unfortunately, lovely as they were, the lack of consistency had played its part, and it would be Mrs Wright and I who were now tasked to undo all of the 'unsettlement' that this has caused.

They descended upon us that morning, the girls all playing nicely, drawing pictures, and whirling around the room in their princess dresses. And then there were the boys. Oh, my lovely boys. Shrieks of 'hey!' and 'that's mine!' echoed around the room, making the merely three hours that they spent with us seem just the opposite. A disproportionate amount of time was spent refereeing over toys, encouraging them to share and not to shout at each other. In my eleven years of teaching, I've had classes that were much harder, but I sensed that this might take some work and might not be as easy as it often is.

We would have to do the donkey work, in fact, for the majority of the autumn term. As we chivvied them off to lunch that day, we were both silently sizing up our plan of action, and working out exactly how we were going to unite and tame this motley crew of individuals that we'd been handed. 'I think this is going to be hard work' I advised Mrs Wright after they'd gone. 'Don't worry, we'll soon get them round to our way of thinking,' she says cheerily, as she reapplies her 'lippy', and heads off to eat her lunch in the delightful haven that is the staffroom.

Back to September. We welcome them with open arms, all, of these little darlings we thought we had begun to get the measure of in July. We start to feel our way, we get to know them. Who doesn't get on with who, who wears glasses, can't hear, has allergies, needs to sit here, needs to sit there. And those, who can't sit altogether.

'Carpet places!' I threaten on day four. I'm not even kidding. A tried and trusted formula that we just, keep on coming back to. I don't shout, I'm not a shouter. In fact, I have a reputation for being the kindest, calmest and most gentle teacher in the school, and I'm not even blowing my own trumpet here. Well, maybe a little bit. I don't believe in shouting, as I can communicate exactly what I need to without ever raising my voice. Maybe it's a gift. Maybe it's not. I wish others would learn it.

So 'we' (I) decide carpet places might be best. A large world map carpet lies right in front of my chair and occupies the majority of the floor space. Four rows, each with seven or eight. We assign them a place. And yes, before you ask, they are strategically placed. Anyone who can't see too well or who wears glasses, they're in the front row. The 'carpet rollers,' a name coined for those that prefer to be supine instead of upright, are also at the front, lest they be too far away for us to 'remind' them how we behave on the carpet. Good looking, good listening, good sitting, lips closed, just in case you were wondering. Then we scatter the 'model' pupils in between. 'You'll show Jacob how to sit nicely, won't you?'

And how could we forget the prestige that comes from being allowed to sit at the back of the mat? And the last person at the end of the back row, who has the much-coveted job; for they are, in charge of turning the lights on and off and opening and closing our door, a bazillion times each day.

3

The three R's

We let them settle in for a few weeks. There's a lot of free play, just as there should be. Some of these children only just turned five a few short weeks ago and they are now beginning their second full year at 'big school.'

In their groups of six, we slowly begin to introduce them to the concept of formal work, i.e. sitting down in your seat and attempting to write sentences and record sums. It sounds simple, but to some of them, it comes as a big shock to the system. 'I just want to go and play in the sand' whines one little boy, as despite all the encouragement that we give him, he is reluctant to even hold his pencil let alone copy the sentence we/I wrote on the whiteboard.

Another uncomfortable feeling is evoked in me. I want to say to him that it's ok, sure, go ahead, go play in the sand, but I can't. You see, I'm not supposed to. I'm supposed, to make him write. I'm supposed to pretty much work a miracle, so that by December, when the first lot of data is handed in, he is able to dazzle us with his performance and produce something that looks vaguely coherent and resembles a proper sentence of writing that I can actually read. With a capital letter and a full stop too y'all. In a mere three month's time. You see, there's no time for him to develop, no time for him to learn at his own pace. At least not in the government's mind, or the school's.

We also begin our phonics groups. I used to love teaching phonics. It was one of my favourite subjects. I've always been good at reading and writing, it came naturally. As the daughter of an accountant, you'd have thought I'd be more of a maths whizz, (see what I did there, teacher folk! It's an ageing maths programme, but still rather useful), but that is not the case. Reading and writing is much more my thing, which is probably why, teaching the first steps of reading, i.e. phonics, floated my boat, so to speak.

Phonics, a fancy name for letter sounds. We all learned to read in different ways. When I was at school, I don't remember being taught the sounds, just reading whole word, flashcards that my mum practiced with me at home occasionally, and reading those *1,2,3 and Away!* books. Who didn't delight in the simple happenings of Roger Red-Hat, Billy Blue-Hat and the rest of the gang? I don't remember learning any letter sounds at all, at least not at school. My sister, two years younger, got herself a very fine education, courtesy of *Sesame Street*, before she even went to school. Although, she remembers being a might confused later on, when she was told the last letter of the alphabet was in fact z, and not zee....

I beavered away at *Biff, Chip and Kipper* books. Perhaps you know who I'm talking about? The brothers and sister whose names not only resemble food, you might find in the local 'chippy' but whose names very considerately can be decoded so easily. My own children are reading them now, I feel like I've never been parted from any of them. We can't forget Floppy the dog, or their pals, Wilf and Wilma. They'd all get excited when the magic key began to glow, and off they went into another world, albeit a lot smaller than their actual size.

I enjoyed these books, and perhaps at six, it was the sense of satisfaction that mastering this newfound skill had brought. If you can read, you have opened the door to a whole world, one of fantasy and imagination, and, also, of expression and opinion. I do remember having a debate with my mum when I was about six, when I was frustrated that the pronunciation of a word was contrary to how it was spelled. 'I don't care if it's pronounced oars, it's oars,' I whined, emphasising the letter 'O' rather than the sound.

We spend the first few weeks assessing which sounds the children know, and don't know, and then somehow begin to collate this and make some sense of it all. Those that know loads, are in the top group. Those that have acquired most of what they should have been taught in reception, are in the middle. Then there's the few who didn't make the cut. They are poor. They have retained very, little, and, will need the most intensive support. We're not allowed, to take into account that English is not their first language, that their home life is far from stable, or even admit that they just aren't ready for formal learning yet. We decide to place them into two groups of three, each with an adult. I take the top group, the other teacher (we have sixty children, across two classes and we work together; well, in spirit and on paper, but, in reality, not even close to it) takes the middles. Off we go.

So now, having settled into our new rhythm, we're about to mess that all up, by trying to squeeze yet one more thing into our already tightly packed, 'there's-no-room-for-fun,' schedule. And, not only that, it's probably the most important subject that we need to teach this year. So, every day, for twenty-five to thirty minutes, they will be taught phonics. They need it to help them read. There's no question that it's useful, but the real reason? We are teaching them to pass the phonics test next June. Because our school's success depends on it. It helps us keep Ofsted from beating on our door. And come to think of it, so does my job.

We have our little data meeting with the Big Guns, aka The Boss, in September. These are done termly. She loves data with a passion. She excitedly hands me a bundle of papers for my perusal. They are a haze of little coloured boxes and spreadsheets, highlighting who falls where, where they should be, where they need to get to etc. It's enough to make your eyes glaze over. Mine inevitably do. I'm just, not that interested really. I want to get to know who they are, what makes them tick.

Coloured boxes on spreadsheets, don't tell me that. They don't tell me that Lola and Niamh are brilliant gymnasts. They don't tell me how Sophia lives and breathes for art. They don't tell me how selfless and kind Matthew is. And I should know that stuff, that should be the most important thing. Nevertheless, we look at who did not meet the Good Level of Development in reception, and we discuss how we are going to help them to progress.

As a result of this meeting, the lovely Mrs Wright, now has four new best friends, who as soon as they walk into the room every day, she will whip out their book bag at the speed of light and listen to them read. It's the only way they're going to improve, and if the parents pitch in and play their part at home, then we're in with even more of a chance. It's decided that she will also need to do a maths intervention group, with said four children, and some from the other class. She will also do some speech therapy work with another child. This will be from a photocopied material page sent to us from the local authority speech therapist who popped in for ten minutes last year, when the child had been on the waiting list since he was three.

Phonics, shmonics. 'I want eighty-eight percent pass rate this year,' demands the boss. It was eighty-three percent last year. Righty ho then. I'll just wave my magic wand. She types this target into its little box on her computer. It's actually, my target for data. And if I don't meet it, it's not really going to help me to creep up the next step on the pay ladder. Well, even if there was a possibility of anybody's salary increasing at all, what with the miserable budget and the wage freeze. Schools are in dire straits, financially. They've, been on a downhill slope in general, for years, only now the finances have waved the white flag and joined them. People think we're kidding, when we say we don't have a glue stick between thirty of us. It's true. Pencils too. We've never been so poor.

Every day, little legs dangle from chairs, happily chattering away, arguing, about how the only glue shall be passed around their table of six. 'But Layla's my best friend, and she said she's going to give it to Jessie, and I have to be last!' shrieks Lola, blue-lipped with grief. 'No, I didn't say that' replies Sam, quickly backtracking now his underhanded methods and own interpretation of sharing have been rumbled. 'How about you go after me?' he negotiates with her, as she reluctantly sits back down in her seat. And, so it goes.

I clap. Not in applause, no. It's a, well-rehearsed, routine, and one that they all know. I clap the pattern, and they repeat it.

When everybody is clapping, and little heads have looked up, I stop and pause for a moment. 'Right, which table doesn't have any glue?' I ask. They all start clamouring at once. I quickly assign one person from each table to take charge and tell me what's needed. I don't have any more glues. Exasperated, I sigh. 'Mrs Wright, could you, please, go to the office and tell them I can't run a classroom without any glue sticks?' I ask her. We wait, and I encourage them to try to start their work, despite, the fact that they haven't got any glue, to stick the blasted paper, in their now, rather battered-looking books.

A few painful minutes pass, and then like a beacon of hope, Mrs Wright appears in the doorway, a couple of glue sticks in each hand, like pistols ready for the draw. 'They said that's all we can have,' she dryly informs me. Another sigh emanates from my now irritated form. You see, it's all got a bit pathetic. There's a large stash of the bloody things in a cardboard box under one of the office lady's desks. We know they're there. She knows we know they're there. But we can't just help ourselves, oh no. They have to be rationed. Where once they were just a glue stick, something we didn't really care about using in such wasteful abundance, now they are held hostage in the office, deemed such a precious resource that we are encouraged to really question whether we in fact need them at all.

With ever-increasing frequency I send Mrs Wright to go and beg for mercy, so that they can get their work done and life can go on. It's another, albeit small, irritant that makes this job just that little bit harder. Especially when it's coupled with the dressing down from the office busybody, who makes it her mission to be as obstructive and difficult as she can be when it comes to the dispensing of school supplies.

'We can't give you any more, you'll just have to make do with those,' she usually says, referring to the neatly levelled out and clearly empty glue that no amount of turning the tube will magically conjure any more. Maybe she thinks we have magical powers. Maybe, I wish I did too.

They're 'encouraged' to stay in their seats, in order to get them ready for Year Two, where learning is 'ramped up' in preparation for national testing (SATs) at the end of the year. By the end of the year we've all but ditched the free play, using it as the pot of gold at the end of the rainbow, for if, rather than when, they've finished their work.

It works very well. Some work hard and are quickly rewarded with such delights as the Art Station (let's not even go there), the sand tray, the Duplo, the dressing up, and best of all the bikes. Some are distracted, and despite copious reminders, languish at their desks and rarely make it to free play much more than five minutes before we tidy up.

Three scooters and three mountain bikes that were donated to us live chained up outside the classroom. They serve as a little visual reminder of the prize. They represent the, by now very well-known message; get your work done and they will be yours. They love them. Some can't wait. They fly through the door in their race to get there, nearly knocking each other out in the process. They don't really notice, or care, come to think of it. They grab the helmets and struggle to get them on, they don't care if they're on the right way, let alone done up properly.

They've got far bigger fish to fry. They mark their bike by placing a hand on the handlebars and start to pull. Against somebody else who's got the same idea. Largely we leave them to sort out these little tiffs by themselves, but usually every afternoon is fraught with the shrieks of 'I'm telling!' and a stampede of children all trying to reach us at the same time. When we ask what the matter is, they all speak at the same time, desperate to get their point of view across. We listen, we solve the problem, we send them out again. I am also marking a book, listening to somebody read, refereeing another disagreement in a different part of the classroom, and dealing with them at the same time. That must be a skill, right?

4

The motley crew

They are characters that's for sure. There's Amy, whose reputation preceded her. 'She'll be prime minister one day, won't you Amy,' Mrs Wright informs me in front of her. She's a little bit like hard work in September, but she's grown on me, and now she's our right-hand man. Or right-hand woman, if you want to be PC. She loves to be first and is one of life's leaders.

'Amy, you're like a bull at a gate,' Mrs Wright says to her frequently, exasperated, as she nearly takes out other children in her quest to be first to line up. She tripped and nearly knocked herself out by hitting her head on the corner of the table which rather frightened us once. I thought there would be tears, but oh no, up she jumped declaring she was fine. One eye pointing in the direction of the doorway wondering if first place was still up for grabs no doubt. One of the eldest, she is a stereotypi-cal high achiever and all-round 'good girl'. She helps others, and has an on and off love affair with Pieter, a little Swedish boy half her height, and miles behind everybody else in his speech development.

With his beautiful blue eyes adorned with gorgeous long eyelashes, squeaky voice and casual manner, he's a cutie, and he knows it. He's won her heart, and the feeling seems very mutual. They look like little and large, complete polar opposites in terms of size, as she leads him to activities and 'helps him' with his work.

Or rather completes it for him as they are at complete opposite ends of the spectrum as far as academia is concerned. He's learned a lot from her though, and she's thoroughly enjoyed taking the role of guiding him. She sees herself as far higher up in the pecking order than him, but he's not complaining. Peer tutoring is the official term and it's done wonders for him.

While their affection knows no bounds, it resembles the behaviour of some of the great romantic couples of history - can't live with him, can't live without him. Hey, we've all been there. It reminds me of Burton and Taylor, or maybe Den and Angie, minus the glass-throwing. She gets cross with him a lot. He argues with her. 'Amy is being rude to me!' he squeaks. 'No, I wasn't!' she shrills indignantly, her face streaked with angry tears. Their volatility is never ending. We've had to split them up a few times.

All good marriages go in peaks and troughs, and their marriage of sorts is resplendent of this. They have a lot of good times. Amy comes up to my desk one afternoon and brings me a picture. 'Oh, Amy, that's lovely!' I say, and unlike a lot of the array of rubbish, that regularly hits my desk and then gets 'filed' at the end of the day, I am genuinely pleased with her offering.

A bright yellow triangle shape adorns most of the page. I'm told it's the church. 'Who are they?' I enquire, pointing at the two figures underneath the triangle. 'That's me and Pieter, we're getting married.' 'Amy, that is so lovely!' I reply. I decide to ask her a few questions, scope her out on her views on the subject. She's a bright girl and knows her own mind. Maybe she can give me some tips. 'Do you think that you'd like to get married one day?' I ask. 'Yes, I would, but my daddy won't let me,' she replies, with great seriousness. I laugh. 'What do you mean your daddy won't let you?' 'He said he doesn't want me to get married ever. He wants me to stay at home with him!'

She giggles, and we talk about how funny it is that daddy thinks that. In her family, daddy is indeed a stay-at-home dad, who works part-time and looks after her baby brother. And her mum? Well mum is the head of HR at a large multi-national corporation. 'Mum said I'm going to change the world' she declared breezily to me on the way to lunch one day a few months back. She's a smart cookie, Amy, and one thing's for sure, she won't be anybody's doormat. I could learn a thing or two from her.

As a teacher, you're not allowed to have favourites, but I'd be lying to you if I said we didn't. Everybody has favourites. The trick is to treat them all the same, so that even though I know that there are some that make me smile more than others, they should never notice any differences in the way that they are treated.

One little girl, particularly, stood out to me, this year. We were warned that she was a bit of a whirlwind, somebody with a strong personality and perhaps, dare I say it, a little spoiled. 'Marches to the beat of her own drum', is more like it. We got glimpses of all of them last year, through sitting in assemblies and other whole school activities together, so were reasonably au fait with who they were. But this one particularly scared me. In truth, I was a little afraid of her. With her larger than life personality, and penchant for throwing a few tantrums, I was, more than a little, concerned, as to how she might deal with the word 'no'. Honey, I'm going to be saying it a lot in the first term, so you'd better get used to it.

She was delightful on the move up day in July, and when we set off in September for real, I began to get a feel for the little thing, and also for her rather pushy parents. Half Spanish, half British, with beautiful dark skin and curly hair, she's a beauty, and she knows it. Physically, she's pretty petite, much smaller than many of the others despite being one of the eldest.

She's short-sighted, so a pair of round pink glasses adorn her cherubic little face. Well, when she remembers to bring them to school that is. She's bilingual, speaking Spanish and English fluently, and her English is filled with Spanish pronunciations. I'd imagine it's no mean feat speaking two languages fluently from two years old, but she's brilliant, and her grammar is better than poor Matteo, who continually muddles his pronouns and thinks everyone is called he.

Lola's assertiveness and say-it-how-it-is attitude is quick to set him straight. They sat next to each other on the carpet for a bit, and I watched one day as she shrilled at his misuse of the word 'he', when referring to Holly, who was seated next to him. 'She is a girl! Not a he! He is a boy!' she gesticulated at him, waving her arms around in irritation. As her face leaned forward closer to his to emphasise her point, she was no doubt frustrated at his ineptitude with regards to something, seemingly, so simple. I don't think he really had a clue what she was talking about, but she seemed satisfied to have got her point across to this oik, set on butchering the English language. Poor Matteo, God love him.

Lola was delightful, and her enthusiasm and excitement seemed limitless. I began to really like her, and instead of my polite requests to cooperate falling on deaf ears as I'd feared they would, they were met with a cheery, 'ok Miss Graham!'

She is a fidget. Oh, my goodness, she could not sit still for more than a minute on the carpet before she was turning around to fondle Ella's long plaits, or debate whose marker pen worked best with her old flame, Sam. Lola's fidgeting and inability to sit still for more than ten seconds at a time was a continual source of both amusement and frustration for Mrs Wright and I. It's actually really hard to teach a lesson and oversee all of the little things that occur, on the carpet as well, so I frequently had to ask Mrs Wright to abandon doing a reader, and come and do crowd control for me.

Over the nine or so, months together, we tried everything. First, I had Lola in the, aforementioned, front row, by my feet. You remember who sits in the front row, right? Only she was like a meerkat, continually up on her knees, leaning on my lap and stroking my legs and feet. Not to mention giving me a running commentary on what everybody else was doing. She's always seen herself as a little bit more important than her classmates, and she doesn't hesitate to bend the rules to fit her needs. She's me, in a nutshell, really (the rule-bending part).

Always one to ignore and flout the rules, instead of raising her hand to tell me something like everybody else, she gets up from her carpet space, and I use the term carpet space loosely, for she is really in multiple spaces, and comes and stands next to my chair. She usually then, ignores my gentle suggestions of returning to her seat, and carries on with whatever it is that she just can't wait to tell me.

She leans into me, nuzzles her face into my arm or chest, and really seems to crave the cuddles, perhaps more so than most. In Spain and Latin American countries, babies and young children are smothered in baby cologne for that ultra-fresh, just-stepped-out-of-the-shower smell, and Lola's mum clearly relishes this tradition. It's an unusual thing in a classroom, to have children that smell like a breath of fresh air, rather than quite the opposite. So, as she cuddles into me, her clothes and hair reeking of Nenuco, I always say to her, 'Lola, you smell yummy!' and I give her wrist a little sniff. Her smile beams from ear to ear, happy for the attention, but no doubt, mystified as to why I like the smell so much.

So, then we kept her on my side of the class, but this time at the end of the second row, so she only had Ella, who is a good role model, to chat to, rather than one on either side. Nope, that didn't work either. At the instruction of the SENCo (special educational needs coordinator), we tried a weighted lap cushion, but whereas it was there to try to pin her down, all she did was declare it was too heavy and kept folding it up. She took a liking to Jacob's wobble cushion, that he quickly tired of, but it actually had the reverse effect on Lola.

It's supposed to help children self-regulate; i.e. they have something to move around on but it helps them stay in their own space rather than lopping onto someone else. Lola enjoyed it at first, and it became a bit of a novelty. Then she rolled around more than ever before so 'we' both agreed she might be better to just try to sit nicely on the carpet.

She's a kind soul though, and her empathy and compassion are something I wish every child had. As a parent, I would be so proud of some of the things I've witnessed both her and others do this year. Surely these qualities are more important than academic achievements? Millie, a tiny little thing whose confidence really soared by the end of the year, but who certainly lacked it at the beginning, sat in front of Lola on the carpet. One day Millie had had an upset, and like all little tiffs that happen here, there's not a hope in hell of keeping it private. Here the dirty laundry is very much aired in public, to their great enjoyment, as we sit quietly and talk through what's happened. It's the only time they'll actually sit in silence on the carpet, when there's a playground drama and the prosecution and defence's cases are being heard. They take great delight in this little ritual, hanging on every word as the delinquent tries in vain to defend themselves, while simultaneously being slandered by an ever-increasing number of people who 'saw' what happened and have jumped on the bandwagon of accusation. Talk about fickle. Best friends one minute, the next they can't wait to throw each other under a bus. Oh, to be five again!

Millie was upset about something, and began to cry as we talked. She's a sensitive, little soul, and doesn't do well with conflict. Without any direction from us, Lola, now on her knees, having long abandoned sitting on her bottom like everybody else, turned and gathered Millie's hands in her own and gently held them.

She then cupped Millie's face in her hands and stroked her cheeks, while softly speaking words of comfort. It was one of those moments when I was just so proud of her, and I got that fuzzy feeling in my chest. I think my ovaries began to ache; I mean, who wouldn't want a child, as compassionate and as loving as this?

She's a whirlwind though, but like many teachers, I secretly quite like the non-conformists. I'm drawn to them. Probably, because they reflect my own feelings and mirror my own behaviour. If we don't want to do something, we won't, and no amount of cajoling, negotiating or begging will alter our mindset, or our decision. Some might call us stubborn, wilful, unique. Whatever.

5

The games we play

They're a lovely bunch, and as autumn slips into spring, we begin to gel, and by now we normally have a close bond with them. We have a lot of fun with them too, and it shows.

One of their favourite pastimes is a game concocted years ago by Mrs Wright. It's called 'The Superhero Challenge', and they love it. It's pretty useful too, especially for those afternoons where nobody can remain quiet without uttering a word for more than thirty seconds, and it's only two o'clock. I clap and remind them that we need to work more quietly. They work quietly for about twenty-five seconds before the noise level rockets back up to deafening volume and the cracks in our armour begin to show.

Just as my stress levels begin to rise, Mrs Wright swoops in to save the day. She knows that I'm trying to crack on with the readers, as we've already hit midweek and we've read with two children out of thirty. At this rate, we'll have the parents beating down our door. 'Come on children, Miss Graham's got to hear Scarlett read. Shall we do the Superhero challenge?' 'Yes, yes!' they all shriek, delighted that today it's been offered up to them on a plate, rather than them having to beg for it. The game is quite simple in its design, it's not even, officially a game. Basically, it's a clever way to keep them quiet, but in a fun, rather than miserable way.

Mrs Wright, sherbet lemon for the afternoon sugar-low tucked into her cheek, locates her wheely chair and gets comfy. Her eyes flit around the room, looking for the first player, and they watch avidly, pencils in hand, waiting in anticipation to see if it's going to be them who's chosen. She selects her first victim.

'Lucy' she muses, sidling up alongside Lucy's chair like a detective hoping to crack a case. Lucy's and her classmates' eyes all hold Mrs Wright's gaze. They hang on her every word. 'I hear you're off to ride an elephant after school is that right?' The smiles are all from ear to ear. Lucy looks down, smiling, her lips firmly pressed together to keep her from laughing. There are a few titters in various parts of the classroom, as Mrs Wright gets creative and looks for her next victim.

'Harry, mum told me she was going to dye your hair pink tonight, I think it will really suit you.' Harry looks surprised and delighted, and then he too remembers the vow of silence, and knows that his lips must stay shut and he must remain silent, if he's in with a chance at a win. If they respond, they know it's game over and victory belongs to Mrs Wright.

They utterly delight in this little ritual, and it takes place at least once or twice a week. A firm favourite in their minds, but also in ours. For while, it does provide some blessed, albeit temporary, relief from the noise created by thirty children, it also lifts our spirits. They do say that laughter is the best medicine after all.

Another little gem, created by Mrs Wright, involves a crying baby. I'm making myself look inept here, as she is the one who's responsible for the majority of the joviality. She is by nature a comedian, a quick-thinker who could talk the hind legs off a donkey. She's played her part, having worked in sales in the corporate world for the majority of her career. An enviable salary, a company car, quarterly bonus as well as champagne and fine dining as the reward for making a big sale, there's not a lot she hasn't done. She's lived all over the world, including on the Mexican border, dated a Texas oil baron; she's lived it large and has the scars to prove it. Which is why she's so brilliant at this game we call teaching; this, to her really is child's play.

Around Christmas time we acquired a plastic baby doll, wearing a white baby-gro, which I think we might have used in the Christmas Play, (brace yourself for that chapter). It now resides in the mess that is the depths of our class cupboard, forgotten and unloved. But they can see it, they know she is in there. I was working one-to-one with a child, at the back of the class, one afternoon, while Mrs Wright supervised their handwriting session. She's fab at getting the best out of them, and they share lots of jokes. When the noise level inevitably creeps up, she's quick to bring them back down.

So, it was with some bemusement that I heard her say with mock seriousness that day 'children, ssh, you'll wake the baby in the cupboard!' 'What baby ?' they all shrieked. 'Ssh!' says Mrs Wright, 'can't you hear it? It's crying, you've woken her up now.' They took great delight in this little game, and we continued it for the rest of the year. Every time the noise level accelerated, one of us would remind them; 'you'll wake that baby in the cupboard, then we'll never get her back to sleep.'

We make a great team, there's no doubt about that. While next door, in the other class, we're stuck with '*Hinge and Bracket*', there could not be a greater contrast on our side of the wall. Think *Absolutely Fabulous*, minus the afternoon boozing and fags I suppose. If you were to pop in, you'd surely get a sense that 'Ed' and 'Pats' were running the show, and a bloody good one at that. Actually, that doesn't make us sound a very responsible pair at all does it? Not the sort of people you'd be happy to leave your most precious and treasured little people with for six hours a day, but I can assure you we're pretty good at keeping them safe from harm. Despite all our moans and groans, we really do love them all. Mostly.

Eddie and Patsy are probably my favourite characters ever created by Jennifer Saunders, and our daily double act resembles their dynamic. She once described their friendship as one where Patsy continuously backs up Eddie, no matter what ridiculousness they might be dealing with and however absurd the situation might be. And this is true for us. We present a united front. And not just when it comes to the children, oh no, but also against all of the other staff, most notably '*Hinge and Bracket*', next door. When push comes to shove, you need a teammate who will take one for the team. Who, when your back's against the wall, will lie, lie and lie again, to protect you. This is no place for the faint hearted, it's 'dog eat dog' in here.

The myth that work ends when they go out of the door at 3pm is just that, a myth. By my own choice, I choose to tie up any loose ends at home in the evening, from the comfort of my living room, sweatpants on, etc. rather than slog it out until 6pm like a lot of them do. Personal choice is everything.

By 3:15pm, when that bell rings, it is like Christmas has come early. Every day. Six hours of noise, moderate levels of stress, and lots of fun later, we all need a break from each other, well, at least until 9am tomorrow. It's the golden hour, as that clock slowly, wends its way past the magical time, of half-past two. This marks tidy-up time, and we know we're on the home stretch. As the clock inches its way towards home-time, we start to get twitchy in anticipation. They finally depart, not before returning multiple times to gather lost articles, jumpers, and water bottles, and we head off to make a cup of tea and digest the day's events.

Oh sweet, blessed relief. Some days, I'll stay for a little bit. It's what's expected really. On a bad day, Mrs Wright and I are out of the door soon after them. But it's not a job that you leave at the door until tomorrow morning.

Those thirty are for the year, in some ways, like our own children. Each night, thoughts of the day linger in my mind. I wonder how Harris is feeling, I must remember to talk to Lola about that tomorrow, I need to read with Millie etc.

It never leaves you. It's the same in the mornings. No matter how hard it is to get going, by the time I'm in full-on morning mode, I'm thinking about them and what I need to do with them that day, usually while whizzing the electric toothbrush round my mouth. I'm, at my most, optimistic, first thing in the morning, well, until I actually get there.

6

Don't make us go

It was a few weeks in when were presented with our first mission to accomplish, our first mountain to climb and the most dreaded event in any school calendar; a school trip. My not-so-lovely year partner, there's a whole history on that, decided that having been granted her first choice of year group back in the summer, she would start the year off with a bang and single-handedly orchestrated a trip to a large city zoo. Our topic for the autumn term was animals, and as she breezed past me one afternoon, she casually dropped it into the conversation. Her mission for the children to experience the animals of the Serengeti, while still only an hour and a half from school, was very clear.

It was less of a suggestion and more of a definite plan. We were going to the zoo, and there wasn't a damn thing I could do about it. And the date for this joyous occasion? The end of September. Yes, you read that right. We've had the children for less than a month and we're going to take them far away from the carefully manufactured safety and containment of our own four walls.

The only problem was that I had barely registered just how awful this was going to be. Now back in July when teacher placements were decided, my year partner Bebe, sealed her place in the school history books for managing to snag, not only a change to a new year group as per her request, but also the go ahead to take both her TA, and her own class with her.

Now this is virtually unheard of, to have the same teacher two consecutive years in a row. It's an unwritten rule that children should, wherever possible, have a change of teacher every year during their primary school years, and it rarely deviates from this. So, it was met by the rest of us with some bemusement, that she had in fact succeeded in pulling such a coup, and seemingly been handed everything she wanted on a plate. Hell, they even stuck a big, shiny bow on it to seal the deal.

So it was no surprise that, having already spent the previous twelve months getting the feel for her charges, she was entirely confident in her ability to take them into the wilds of the city not four weeks after we started the school year.

Unfortunately, as the date drew closer, the same could not be said for us. The date started to creep up on us, and we began to dread its arrival with increasing fervour. For they had thirty little robots who would happily behave, mind themselves and be genuinely delightful for the duration of both the travel and the visit, while we, certainly in September, did not.

Now I've already waxed lyrical about how much I genuinely adored and continue to adore this lovely group of children, but the early days and weeks were far from easy. We had a group of individuals, and some rather lively and non-conformist ones at that. Could they really be trained enough for us to brave, en masse, the big wide world, unprotected by the confines of the classroom? We began to suspect not.

I've led lots of school trips in my eleven years as a teacher, so it's not as if I lack confidence in delivering them safely from A to B, with hopefully a little education and fun thrown in for good measure. But there was just something about going so early in the school year that made my blood run cold.

School trips in the early years of primary school are generally in the summer term for a reason, that reason being that the children are suitably trained and well behaved enough for us to safely venture away from the premises. We know them better than they know themselves, and this works to every teachers' advantage. Talk to any teacher in Key Stage One about their feelings about a school trip in September and I can guarantee their answer will echo my own feelings. Hell. No.

There is one thing that every teacher prays for in the days leading up to a school trip- good weather. Please God, just let it be dry! There really is nothing worse than a trip in inclement weather.

We check the weather channel constantly, hoping and praying that the gods will smile upon us, and grant us the one thing that will make the day just a little less torturous. School trips are rarely enjoyable for anyone over school-age, and the prospect of it pissing with rain, the entire day, makes us want to curl up and bury our head in the duvet. Game over. Wave the white flag. We're, done. But, we can't be done, at least not until 5pm.

And sure enough, when I awoke on the dreaded day, it was raining. As I peeled back the curtains that morning, the sky was dark and fine drizzle filled the air. Sigh. On days like this there's no point in wishing it were different, you have to adopt a positive mentality in order to get through the day.

Stress levels are always high on any trip day, and they begin to rise as my car pulls into the car park. I know I only have a short window of opportunity to make sure we're good to go, and to make sure all of our bases are covered before we steer the ship into unknown territory.

There's the lunches to collect, the first aid kit to bring, the various medicines that some unfortunately may need during the day. Not forgetting, of course, the spare pants, Edward's basket of, over-the-counter moisturising creams, that we are sure are highly unnecessary, but yet, we continue to prescribe. And, of course, the piece de resistance; the vomit bucket, carefully lined with a plastic bag for easy disposal. You didn't think we'd get away without schlepping all this crap around with us, did you?

When you're the teacher, despite being the leader, the one with whom the responsibility for everybody's safety, education and enjoyment rest heavily on your shoulders, in the grand scheme of things you are left in a heap at the bottom of the pile. You are the one who will forfeit lunch, a trip to the toilet. You will be the one that stands in the road in the face of oncoming traffic while the small people are carefully shepherded across busy roads by the army of parent helpers you've had no choice but to reluctantly bring. We suffer.

Mrs Wright arrived a little bit late that day, and I'll admit, it rattled me. The very suggestion of doing a day, THIS day without her by my side, was unthinkable. The bell went, and thirty overexcited little people shuffled their way into the classroom, wrapped tightly in waterproofs and clutching their little plastic bags with their lunch in.

It's really hard as we still have to go through the motions of our regular start to the day, but with time pressure and anticipation to contend with. The, aforementioned, parent helpers, have unfortunately, sneaked into my classroom and now stand awkwardly at the back ready to watch my every move. They've now got, akin to what essentially is VIP access, a behind the scenes look at Mrs Wright and I in action. Only she's not here yet, it's just me.

Luckily, Mrs Hancock, a valued helper of ten years, who gives up her time every week to come and read for a morning, has kindly answered my pleas for her to accompany us today. Wherever possible, I prefer to take trusted volunteers rather than nosy parent helpers, as I really don't want to endure any extra stress on an already crazy day. Does an aneurism hurt?

Although there were lots of factors that contributed to our supreme lack of enjoyment that day, one small person certainly caused some excitement. For all the wrong reasons. Ever heard of a squirrel brandishing a nerf gun and slaying all the inanimate objects in your house, at night, under the cover of darkness? Nope, I thought not. Meet Sam. If you want to know more about weapons, he's your man. If you want something turned into a weapon, he's your man. If you want to know how to use any object as a weapon, well, you guessed it, he's most certainly your man. I have never met a child who was so in to play fighting. Every conversation, no matter how mundane and completely unrelated somehow inevitably turned into a bloodbath. There is no weapon he doesn't know about, no toy that can't be used as an alternative weapon... you get the idea.

I realise, I may be portraying him as a socially deviant tinker, but actually, he was a really lovely little boy who just became too embroiled in his own rich fantasy world of heroes and villains. Try as we might, he just could not seem to tell any story without straying down that path of violence. But I'm not talking about dark things, I'm talking about a mixture of hilarity and comedic situations that somehow involved lightsabers, nerf guns, bows and arrows etc. There was simply nothing the boy didn't know about.

He holds his audience captive, does Sam. He's German, with quite a strong accent and yet very articulate. Right from the get-go, Sam loved to talk, and he took great delight in entertaining and enthralling his audience with his fictitious and highly unbelievable stories that usually ended in death and/or destruction. It became a bit of a challenge to get him to stop talking, and he just never seemed to let up. He reminded me of a passage I read once during teacher training, when we were learning about the stages of children's development; 'Four year-olds tell long stories, often confusing fact and fantasy'. Well this was Sam to a T, and yet he was nearly six at the start of the year.

Every story became more and more elaborate, and for the adults, utterly unconvincing. As the rest of them dissolved into giggles, his face lit up at the very sight of the power he held over his audience, who waited with bated breath, for the next instalment. His grin was from ear to ear as he told of such tales as squirrels, seemingly breaking into his house, and holding everybody hostage during the night. Or that time when his dad supposedly climbed up on to the roof in the middle of the night wearing only pyjamas and brandishing a lightsaber to defend them. They lapped all of this up, and as they predictably squealed at the hilarity, Mrs Wright and I were no longer able to keep a straight face either. Mrs Wright often played into his delusions, and it was a great source of amusement. He thoroughly enjoyed the extra attention, and absolutely revelled in the chance to try to create answers to her questions.

'So, Sam, how did that squirrel get into your house then?

You know, when he grabbed that Nerf Gun and held you all to ransom that night?' chirps Mrs Wright, winking across the classroom at me as she goes in for the kill. 'Uh, well, um, he goed into the garage and then he sneaked into the back door and then he finded the nerf gun when he sawed my dad in the kitchen so he quickly ran up the stairs to my bedroom...' Like I said, he never even draws breath as his eyes light up while telling his fantastic tales. Mrs Wright, pauses for thought, as she listens carefully to this new chapter in the story, and absorbs the details. She swallows the sherbet lemon she's been sucking, it's coming up to 2pm you know, and brings her index finger to her lips as if she's about to say something profound. All the little eyes are on her, as they wait for her response.

'Sam, that's pretty scary, oh my goodness!' she says, playing into his delusions. 'But I was thinking, and shall I tell you what I wonder?' she asks, not waiting for his reply. 'I don't think that squirrel had to sneak in through the garage. I think that squirrel's got a key!" she laughs, as we all, me included, erupt into voracious laughter at this utterly ridiculous yet delightful little foray off topic. You don't get any weirder than this. And I think what started us down this path of insanity, was trying to teach a lesson on baby animals.

Sam's inability to clearly distinguish the difference between fantasy and reality was unending. After one half-term we did the post-week off telling of news once they all arrived back to school. It's a good way to settle us all back in as we're all a bit out of sorts and still in mourning for the nine glorious days off we just had. When I chose Sam to talk, it was with some trepidation - who know's what torment and misfortune might have befallen his family this week? As it turned out, Sam had gone skiing for a week, and claimed his mum had broken her leg. We indulged him, and told him how that must have been terrible, not for a moment expecting it to be true. After a couple of days of this, I caught his dad at the door one afternoon and explained the rumour Sam had mentioned. As it turned out, Sam's mum had actually had a really nasty accident on their first day of skiing in France, and, had to be flown to the nearby hospital. Oops!

Unfortunately, Sam's behaviour that day was far from amusing. I think it was about mid-way through the day, when miraculously, those hands on the clock began to move closer towards our departure time, that we had an unfortunate incident with a very irate zookeeper.

We had found our way past the giraffes and through the rhino enclosure when we wended our way to an indoor exhibit containing some lemurs. I don't know much about lemurs, save for the fact that they live in a semi-covered environment, and that under no circumstances should one pull their tail. Yes, that's right. Somehow, as I steered the ship and led the group through the wooden doors and into the darkness of the interior part of the enclosure, we collectively oohed and aahed at the lemurs climbing above us on their netting. The children were, captivated, and spent quite a bit of time admiring them, before we were shepherded along the exhibit.

The children and parent helpers followed me and the guide as we headed to the next display. As the final part of the group came through the doors, I turned around to check that we were all still together, and was presented with a very stony-faced Mrs Wright, marching Sam towards me holding his hand. 'I am so cross, Miss Graham,' she whispered sternly to me. 'The zookeeper is absolutely furious with him. He's just PULLED the tail of one of the lemurs.' Sam looked extremely uncomfortable, not least because his mum was one of our helpers and was also a witness to his crime. Suffice to say that words were had, and Sam had no choice but to remain with me for the rest of the trip.

Mrs Wright, in a quiet moment out of earshot of the children, did explain that the zookeeper was truly appalled, and obviously very protective of his animals. I think it's fair to say that we've blotted our copy book here, plus it's both unfortunate and yet a blessing that Sam's mum has seen firsthand how much of a handful he can be, as if she didn't already realise.

I couldn't wait to get home. Finally, as the exit time neared, we made our way back to the toilets before beginning the long trip back down the road towards the car park where the coach would be waiting. Communication, however difficult with Bebe, was necessary today, so as we piled back on the coach, I texted her to let her know that we were ready to go. Thirty minutes passed. THIRTY LONG, BLOODY, MINUTES and she finally trails back towards us with her crew. I could kill her.

She's spun it out on purpose, just because I had wanted to leave at our earlier and planned time, not least because it took so painfully long to get here earlier. Oh and just to round things off nicely, our parent helpers have been feeding some of the children muffins and crisps from their own supplies, ignoring the rule of not feeding other people's children because of the all too real allergy risk. Great.

As we finally get underway, I stare silently at the motorway in front of us, vowing never, ever, to do this again. Predictably it takes nearly two hours to get home, all in rush hour traffic thanks to good old Bebe, who's claiming to have had a lovely time. Mrs Wright glances over at me and hisses into my ear 'when we get back to school, you hold her down and I'll hit her.' It's a very tempting thought, but I think I'll go for the safer option and settle for a glass of wine and a hot bath.

Pieter, the little boy I mentioned earlier, thoroughly delighted in absolutely every aspect of the trip, and although he was a bit of a live wire, he was far from being our biggest problem that day. He excitedly called out all of the animal names, some of which I suspect he had never really heard of, and repeatedly dashed along to each enclosure in search of the next creature. He managed to claim one of my maps, littered with pictures to show us where to go, and I let him lead the group, his little friends in tow as we journeyed through this foreign land. He still remembers this months later, telling me in his broken English: 'Miss Graham, remember I read the map!'

Yes Pieter, you sure did! He couldn't do a lot, back in September, but he clearly relished the praise that came from the small things that he could do, and this was a definite fond moment for me. Actually, that was probably the only glimmer of enjoyment for me the entire day.

'Zoo again this time next year?' Mrs Wright chirps at me the following morning with a wink. 'What do you think? 'Jog on', is my reply.

7

Meet the parents

The parents; they can be our biggest champions or our fiercest critics. Unfortunately, while a good, ninety percent support our cause, and help us work together for the good of the children, there are also the other ten percent who make it their mission to sabotage us. It happens with ever-increasing regularity, and year after year it seems to somehow outdo the previous one.

They are nutters. Nut-jobs, kooks, weirdos, whatever you want to call them. We look at them in collective awe, as we wonder just how they've managed to produce their delightful children, given that for the most part they seem scarily unstable. It's bizarre. We've seen it all, there's just nothing that can really surprise us anymore.

Every July, all of the teachers gather in pairs to prepare the next teacher for the class they're getting. The class lists come out, pens are grabbed, computers are on, as we prepare to make notes to help us make sense of this, mind-blowing, chasm of information, that's about to hit us. We are a nosy bunch, us teachers. We don't just want to know what Max and Kora can do in terms of their learning, oh no, there's a need for far more intrusive information than that.

We want to know what their home life is like, whether their mum and dad are together, whether they can stand to be in the same room together at parents evening, or whether we should get the boss to feign another appointment, lest things start to kick off. It's hard to call for reinforcements when you're in a classroom on your own, with the door shut. I think they should install a panic button, but instead the boss does make it her duty to wander around and make her presence known. Believe me, this is very, valuable information.

Over the years I've had parents come separately and together, and had the pleasure of seeing how brilliantly they can co-parent for the wellbeing of their child, but also just how deep the old wounds run when it all turns sour. One parent came armed with a clipboard and pen, and spent more than the ten allotted minutes to not only quiz me about just exactly what I was teaching them (we already did a meeting for parents so that we could describe this in detail, which he failed to attend), but wanted me to provide evidence for his upcoming court case where I assume he planned to vilify his soon to be ex-wife and go for the sole custody of his daughters.

He wanted me to back up his claims that the girls were distressed and unhappy and that it was affecting their learning. I refused to make any sort of reference to this, and certainly did not want to sign my name to anything. This went on for the next several years, while one of the girls became more and more emotionally fragile and unhappy, before the courts decided it was not in her best interest to spend time with her father (at her request). It's a sad state of affairs really. The child was far happier in her last few years at primary school, once her equilibrium had been restored, and she was free from the strain of her warring parents.

We wait excitedly, as the first name is read out. As we go through each name on the list, we take heed of any glimmer of information the previous teacher can provide- about the parents that is. And the most important question I ask; which ones are the nut-jobs? Who do we need to watch out for? Who do we need to bob and weave from when we spot them on the playground? Who is going to write the nasty notes and accost us in the queue at Waitrose? The 'nutters' are highlighted in pen, as we are given detailed examples of their 'crimes' this past year. 'She's one to watch.' 'Whatever you do, don't take her on a trip.' 'She's very pushy, she's very anxious, she'll be in every day.' Terrific. I know I'm psyched for the coming year. But believe me, this advice is given in good faith. It'd be foolish not to heed the warnings, I know this from experience.

It doesn't take long for things to start to fray. We've dealt with the problem ones, parents that is, but there are others. Those that slither up like snakes that have been under the radar, and now are ready to test the waters on the two of us. We are two strangers that have now spent the last few weeks in close company with their child, and they've no doubt been told little snippets by them that will help to build up a picture of us. They're ready, to throw their curveball, but are we ready to catch it?

It's the end of the day, in cold, windy October, when Daisy's mum rocks up at the classroom door after we've dismissed them. We've got this routine down now, home-time that is. I stand on one side of the doorway, Mrs Wright takes the other, as we call them a few at a time from the carpet to be safely released into the care of their adult, not before I've held their shoulders and checked that they are indeed being picked up by the right person and not a random stranger who's just rocked up.

We should make a formidable presence standing in the doorway, the two of us. We smile, look cheery and make it seem like we've had a wonderful day, whether we have, or whether it's been the longest six hours of our lives. We've sent most of them out, there's only a few stragglers left sitting on the carpet, or lounging alongside tables, book bags and water bottles in hands. Outside, the parents and their little darlings filter away en masse, and hopefully, it looks as if it's going to be a peaceful finish.

Wrong. 'Can I have a quick word?' she asks, as I feel my neck muscles tense. It's the words at the end of the day that every teacher dreads. We never know. We never know if they're going to just want to tell us some pertinent information, or just have a moan that the sodding reading books haven't been changed yet. We plaster fake smiles on our now uneasy-looking faces. 'Of course! Come in!' we reply, and in they come, to our turf, our territory. We frantically backtrack through our minds, trying desperately to remind ourselves of anything significant that happened today with their child, and just exactly what misdemeanour we might have inadvertently committed. One strategy I've learned, over the years is to let them talk. It buys me some more thinking time, some time to prepare my defence usually.

Mrs Wright takes up residence on the edge of the table, while I busy myself around my desk, pretending to tidy up, as I wait for the monster to be unleashed. 'It's Matteo,' she states, as Daisy stands alongside her mum, looking uncomfortable. 'He's been pushing her around in the playground, hitting her and I'm not happy about it. We had all of this last year in reception,' she continues. 'She's coming home saying she's frightened to come to school, and I'm not having that' she says, with more than an air of irritation. Come on Mrs Wright, you start, I think to myself, but as I'm, technically, the one in charge, it should really fall to me to sort this one out. I'm grateful she's stayed behind after school, for moral support, but I'm going to have to demonstrate some authority here, if I'm going to have any sort of presence this year.

'I get it, I do,' agrees Mrs Wright. She's good at getting parents to see it from both sides, probably because she's a parent herself. She continues 'she's coming home saying she's been upset by Matteo, he's thumped her in the playground and you want to kill him, I get it,' she repeats, letting Daisy's mum know that she understands where she's coming from. Now, I'm caught between a bit of a rock and a hard place. While I sort of want to admit to her that yes, Matteo's behaviour is less than desirable, I can't give her too many details, about why that is, as I would be breaking confidentiality.

Which is why when I try to assure her that we are very aware and are dealing with it, believe me, multiple times every single day, I know my words have done little to convince her. Mrs Wright takes over, and crouches in front of Daisy. 'You, my little pickle, need to make sure you come and tell Mrs Wright when that happens at lunchtime, don't you?' she chirps, Daisy now looking much more relaxed and smiling at Mrs Wright's attention. 'How about we pinkie promise, shall we? That if you're not having a happy playtime, you'll come and find me and I'll make sure that everything's ok, how about that?' she muses. Daisy extends her little finger and interlocks it with

Mrs Wright's to signify the agreement. Daisy's mum seems happier, and it seems we have managed to smooth things over, and dampen the flames of the impending fire, at least for the time being.

'Have a lovely evening' we breeze, as hand in hand they make their way out to the car park, and I close and lock the classroom door, relief beginning to flood through me. The relief seems to be short-lived, when Emma, the PE teacher who seems to know the family quite well, happens to meet them in the car park on their way out. She is quick to come and report back the post-game, wrap-up. 'Was she ok?' I ask, my mind still on overdrive trying to decompress from the stress of it. Plus, I think we did a good job of smoothing it over, and she seemed happy when she left. 'Well, let's just say, I think she's going to be a hard one' smiles Emma, before she reveals all, like some sort of bizarre kiss and tell. 'She just, kind of said, that it was hard to tell who was the teacher there, Miss Graham just stood there, Mrs Wright did all the talking' she relays back, word for word. Sigh. I know, it'll be fine, but it's a bit of a downer. Because she can see that Mrs Wright is the go-to person, and that I step back. But mostly, she's just tapped into my worst fears, that she knows I lack confidence when it comes to dealing with strong characters, and she's just gotten a firsthand look. Roll on July.

Another massive weapon from the parents is the nasty notes. Now, granted, they're not received, too often, but when they are, it's not particularly pleasant. It hurts. And, over the years, I've received a few. Not always awful, but certainly curt and bordering on rude. Last year, when the first one from Alfredo's mum arrived in week three, Mrs Wright suggested we hang on to it and keep it in a box on my desk. Partly so that we could have a chuckle about them later, but also, to keep the beginnings of what we suspected might be a lengthy paper trail.

As our contact with parents is rather limited, thankfully, it's the children that bring us these little pieces of white paper, folded into quarters and proffered at the beginning of the day. Nine times out of ten it's a quick and cheerful note informing us of their different collection arrangements at home time, i.e. 'Lucy's going home with Mila's mum tonight for tea' which is always a relief. But, every once in a while, there's the note that raises my pulse from fifty beats per minute to one hundred and ten in about four seconds, as I quickly scan the page and skim-read the angry scrawl. Usually, it's when I'm sat in my chair, thirty pairs of eyes upon me as we're about to take the register.

One of my, not-so-finer moments, was a few years ago in Year Two. One little girl in my class, Adrienne, had brought me a note, while we were all sitting down, ready to start the day. The note, from her mum was, actually very nice, but kindly asked that Adrienne wear her PE shoes for PE and not her expensive and impractical school shoes. A fairly, innocuous note, you would think. Only Adrienne and I both knew better. For yesterday, Adrienne had informed us that she did not have her PE shoes, and after Mrs Whitmore, my teaching assistant had spent half an hour searching the abyss of the cloakroom, we allowed her to wear her school shoes.

As I questioned her calmly about why she had lied, the rest of the room fell silent, as their ears pricked up to listen. Mrs Whitmore, came and joined us at the front of the classroom, and very kindly and calmly reminded Adrienne of why she did the wrong thing, and how it was wrong to lie to us, although she was pretty annoyed herself. Adrienne, realising, by now, that she, wasn't popular, shifted uncomfortably in her carpet space, pretending to have forgotten that her shoes were indeed at school. No doubt realising, that her error in judgement had now gotten her teachers in a spot of bother.

I didn't shout, I didn't, scream. But the irritation that had built up inside me needed to go somewhere. After all, I had had, in effect, my own telling-off from her mother. Keeping in my mind that this really was a non-event, and she was only seven, I simply spoke quietly, but firmly, as I explained that I was very cross and told her not to lie to me again. And in a final show of my feelings on the subject, I held the letter aloft, all the children looking on as I looked Adrienne right in the eye and quietly tore the letter into tiny pieces.

Like I said, it wasn't the nicest thing to do, but it's hard enough trying to keep all the parents happy without the children inadvertently dropping us in it. But please keep in mind that the likes of Bebe Duke would have lost the plot and gone to town and screamed and shouted, thus making the child feel like they could never do anything right again as long as they lived. I look back on it as not being a very nice moment, but at the end of the day, I did it as quietly and as kindly as I possibly could have, given the circumstances.

Then, there's, the other times, when notes literally come in that leave us mystified and clueless as to what the problem is, despite the three-page essay we've just received. Last year we had a parent who truly was, a bloody nightmare. Every time I saw her at the end of the day, and at parents evenings, she came across as a jolly, motherly, middle-aged and slightly rotund little woman, who if you'd seen her in the street, you'd probably smile and think what a lovely person she was. Not so said the brown turtle. Mrs Wright and I realised, pretty, quickly, through our own observations and from the heads up from Liz Dawson, who had the class last year, that she was going to be a force to be reckoned with. 'Mark my words' affirmed Mrs Wright as we stood in the doorway after sending them out at the end of the day, 'she's a smiling assassin,' as she returned the woman's jolly wave and pushed her son out the door.

She was right. Sometimes, the little notes come directly to us, but sometimes, when parents are really, het up, they bypass us and decided to go straight to the top, to the Big Guns. The office ladies are the usual receivers of such delightful correspondence, as they are, unwittingly, handed the sealed envelopes and have the pleasure of opening and reading them before they pass them on to the boss for her perusal.

And here's what happened, this particular time. A couple of mornings a week, one of the joys of teaching is the shared torture of manning one of the playgrounds, as part of a whole-staff rota. It's not too bad, I suppose. It lasts all of fifteen minutes, and twice a week isn't really, much to complain about, is it? Well, unless it's raining, when every minute ticks by slowly. One of the downsides of everybody playing before school, is that bags have literally been thrown anywhere on the play-ground, and when the bell rings to come in, some seem to be completely oblivious to the fact that they need to collect said articles, and disappear off inside without them. Great.

Which means as you send each class in, there is always a trail of abandoned bags, water bottles, hats, PE bags and jackets that need to be picked up. If the children are still around, it's always a good option, to ask them to pick them up and then redeliver them once we all get in. Be the last class to go in though and it'll be the moral dilemma - pick them up because I should do, or leave them because I can't really be bothered.

The Big Guns, provided she's not soothing parents and their grievances in her office before school, will often wander about and make herself visible and available to parents dropping off, who might want to bend her ear about any matter related to school. And sometimes not. Sometimes it's about them, and as our old boss used to say privately, 'I'm not a marriage counsellor' when parents would inevitably appear at her office in tears, expecting her to be able to offer words of wisdom as to whether to leave their partner or not.

This morning, I wasn't in the playground, and went out to collect my class from their little line and lead them in. As the children disappeared around the corner, happily chatting about their evenings, the Big Guns appeared smiling, and handed me one of the most enormous and over-stuffed backpacks that had been forgotten by Nicholas in my class. After struggling to lift it herself, she handed it to me and we remarked just, how on earth somebody of six was meant to carry all this? We wondered, what in God's name he had in there? She, kindly, asked if either Mrs Wright, or I, might help him sort it out.

As I schlepped, the giant rucksack inside and dumped it on one of the tables, I was immediately distracted by the usual shenanigans that is getting them all in and sat on the carpet. It's noisy, I'd really like a sip of my tea, and Jessica's already pawing at me asking if she can move all of the names back to green on the behaviour ladder. Like an angel, my saviour Mrs Wright, appears, a vision in bright pink, and wearing the exact shade of lippy to match, and after a cheerful good morning to everybody, rams her coffee into its little space beside mine on the shelf in our cupboard as we begin the day. As I, absent-mindedly, respond to Jessica's request, and try again to herd them all away from water-bottle central and over to the carpet, I quickly fill in Mrs Wright about the backpack.

Nicholas, who has just realised he is now bag-less, appears through the doorway grinning like a cheshire cat as Mrs Wright motions to the backpack which now rests beside her on the table. 'I think we need to have a sort out, don't you?' she chuckles, as she heaves the blasted thing upon her shoulder, and exaggeratedly pretends to stagger across the classroom to her brown recliner under the weight of it.

'Good gracious!' she exclaims, setting it down on the floor beside her as she collapses into her chair as Nicholas comes to stand beside her. By this time, all, of the children's attention, has been captured by this little deviation from the norm, and all eyes are on Nicholas and Mrs Wright. Nicholas, doesn't receive, much positive attention at home, due to less than ideal circumstances there, so, he relished his turn to take centre stage.

As Mrs Wright opens the bag, remarking again how heavy it is, she grins and asks Nicholas, 'what on earth have you got in here, Nicholas? Have you got a small child from reception in there? Have you packed your brother and brought him to school?' Nicholas, like all of them erupts into great guffaws of laughter. Laughter is undoubtedly the best way to set them up for the learning later in the day, that's for sure. As Mrs Wright and Nicholas remove one item at a time, there's lots of gentle laughter and squealing, as Mrs Wright and I both marvel at just what seems to be hiding in this receptacle. 'Why have you got a hat, scarf and gloves in here Nicholas?' asks Mrs Wright, mystified. 'It's July, are you planning on taking a trip to the Arctic?' she chuckles, as once again they all dissolve into laughter. Nicholas seems to have everything but the kitchen sink in his bag, and after some discussion, it's agreed that Nicholas will go home tonight and ask his mum to help him to sort his bag out, in future, only bringing in what he really needs. The winter weather gear, the extra trainers, waterproof jacket and endless books and folders can be left at home. As Mrs Wright fastens the bag, before handing it to him, we remind all of the children of the need to travel light. After all, there's plenty of years ahead for carrying hoards, of school textbooks, to and from school.

Now you would think after reading this, that this tiny job was done and dusted, as per the boss's instructions. A little bit of fun and laughter was had by all, and then normal service resumed. It was an event so insignificant that you would struggle to wonder how any problem at all could be created from this, right? Wrong. The next day, mid-way through the morning, the Big Guns popped down to our classroom, just as we were sending them out to play, as the children wandered around opening milk cartons and pleading with friends to help them peel their bananas. Waving what appeared to be three hand-written pages in front of us, the Big Guns smiled, slightly flummoxed and in awe of, what she's just had the misfortune to receive and read. 'I've just had this letter from Mrs Jones,' she explains, offering it to us so we can read. The letter is from Nicholas's mum, and is essentially a three page rant about us sorting through his bag yesterday. She's claimed that we are 'violating his human rights' and that we shouldn't be sorting through his personal property. You get the idea. It went on and on, threatening something, along the lines of how she's going to contact the local MP. The three of us smile in bemusement, surprised at the pure ridiculousness of the letter.

Mrs Wright fills her in, on what we actually did and said to him, as the Big Guns wearily heads off to her office to prepare her written response, as she must respond to the letter within five working days. Mrs Wright pops another piece of satsuma into her mouth before looking at me with a smile. 'You couldn't write a script for this!' It was around this point that I began to realise that I could, and the idea for this book was born.

It's a shame, as I know that there are loads of absolutely fantastic and very appreciative parents, who are always hugely grateful for our work each year. But every now and then there are a few resident 'nutters' who seek to spoil the peace and harmony and upset the equilibrium. And you know what? For those like Mrs Jones, who choose to behave in this way every time a decision is taken that they might not agree with, there is an unfortunate consequence. And it is, that they will forever be known as, 'the parent that wrote THAT note', and consequently placed in the proverbial, 'Turkey File.'

Their child will forever be the one that is handled with extreme care every year, sometimes to the detriment of the rest of their classmates, in a bid to ensure that they don't 'kick-off' and make all our lives a misery for the rest of the bloody year. Is it right? Of course not. But when you know that every time you decide to organise an extra-curricular activity, that every time you organise a school trip, or even just try to literally lighten the load of a child's backpack that you will be leaving yourself wide open for a whole heap of criticism and rude letters, it's not a hard choice to make. To think all we did was sign up to teach kids.

It's a sad time, when parents completely let rip, to their child's teacher, and worse still when they do it in front of their child. At the end of one year, when the children in the Year Two classes were muddled up and re-grouped, ready for a new start in Year Three, one parent was so upset that she blasted the teacher at the end of the day in her classroom, her little girl standing awkwardly beside her. Her grievance? Why, she, simply didn't like the fact that her daughter had been put in a class with Samuel and not with Julia, and demanded that the teacher change it. Now, what she didn't realise, was how much work had gone on behind the scenes, and that sorting out who's in each class is no mean feat.

Each class must be balanced correctly, and there are many factors that need to be considered; gender, special educational needs, extra languages and when their birthday falls etc. Also, you can't have all the brainboxes in one class and leave the rest of the children in the other, can you? Plus, the teacher had already allowed each child to list several of their friends, and, essentially rank them in order, so that they would all be with the person that they most wanted to be with.

I even helped the teacher, as they had been in my class the year before, and I knew the friendships quite well, and, also, I knew who, really, shouldn't be together. We sat down after school and checked that bloody list twice, confident that every single one of those thirty children were with either their first or second choice friend. So, it genuinely came as a surprise when this mother kicked off and claimed we had decided this all on a whim. So incensed with rage was she, that she stalked off, not until after, truly upsetting the teacher who explained that it wasn't possible to just swap classes, however unhappy the mother was.

The next day, one of the office ladies took a delivery from the local florist. A huge bunch of brightly-coloured flowers had been dropped off, accompanied by a card of apology for the teacher. Like I said, it's a sad time when, as a parent you no doubt realise, that you've totally overstepped the mark, and now have to try and grovel apologetically for completely annihilating your child's teacher. When things happen like this, which is, more regularly than you'd think, is it any wonder that nobody wants to be a teacher anymore? Would you? While, I suppose it was a nice thing to do and went some way to repairing the relationship, it's quite sad when you stop and really think about it. Plus, dear parent, if you are reading, then you should know that this sort of behaviour is not kept under wraps. Most of the staff, including your child's next teacher, have read your card of apology and had a good chuckle over it, along with some choice words about you, I can tell you. Your card, no pun intended, has well and truly, been marked. Forget about helping on a school trip, or coming in to read, because, quite honestly, we've, had our fill of you and wouldn't trust you now, as far as we could throw you.

In future, you might want to consider your poor child in all of this, who has to face the embarrassment of knowing that you screamed at their teacher, the person that they actually have a lot of respect and admiration for, spending six hours a day with them, five days a week.

Talk about undermining our decisions. No wonder they're pulling people off the street, begging them to sign up for all this nonsense. Thanks for making our job that little bit more unbearable. But, thank you to those parents who are supportive, and speak to us kindly. You're way up there, and we're grateful that you can treat us as human beings when you'd like to discuss issues. Thank you for setting your child the kind of example that we try to set for them every day, and for helping to make our job more of a pleasure than a painful experience. We salute you.

8

The squirrel

Mrs Wright calls me that. It's a strange thing, being a teacher, but one particular quirk is that you are never, ever really alone at any time of the day. There is zero privacy, zero personal space and absolutely zero, free time. It's just so alien to any office environment.

I have a cupboard, it's my space. It's not much, but it's a place to put my handbag, coat and a few other treasures. There is no coat hook, so it's more that it's folded and squished into a dark corner. I have a couple of pics of me and the ex, tacked to a shelf, a pleasant reminder of happier times. I should take them down, but, I can't bring myself to.

Every morning when I arrive, after carefully noting down my time of arrival, I quickly put my keys away and have a sneak peek at social media. It's really the only time, a sacred two minutes to myself, in the dark, calmness of my prison. I don't really enjoy my perusal of Facebook and Instagram, so I resign myself that the end of the day is when we'll next catch up, and reluctantly put my phone away. I dig around in the cupboard for my laptop. It's a crappy old one, a Dell. The school seem to think they're fantastic, those of us that have the pleasure of using them would beg to differ.

Years ago, I would have taken the bloody thing home each night, now I don't really much care where it spends the night.

I cross the room, laptop in hand, ready to set up for the day.

My poor desk, covered in detritus from the previous day that I couldn't be bothered to deal with, awaits me. Sometimes, when I'm in a good mood, I'll sit in my easy chair, and attempt to make some sense of the piles of paper. Offerings from the children, girls' hair clips that I'm sure I recognise but when I ask them they deny all knowledge of, the marker pens that refuse to work, the notes about who's going to tea with whom. Oh wait, they were yesterday's. When I'm in a bad mood, I swipe my arm across the whole thing and launch everything to the carpet, just so I can set the computer down in a clear space. I usually calm down after a few minutes and tidy the floor, but sometimes I leave it.

And then the children come in and question why there's rubbish all over the floor. It certainly won't go unnoticed. 'Miss Graham!' questions Lola, hands on hips and her head cocked to one side as she stands above the pile of rubbish. 'What is this doing here?' She's less than subtle in giving me a dressing down. She won't pick it up though. Some will. They rush to clear the floor space, they're keen to please.

Lola is always happy to be a non-conformist that way. If I ask somebody to pick something up for me, the expectation is that they will do it, however nicely I ask. A sort of unwritten rule; you do as you've been asked. Well at school anyway. Come to think of it, it's not just an unwritten rule, it's one of our golden rules, carefully plastered all over a wall in the classroom, lest they forget.

Some won't follow the crowd though. At Christmas time, we had one of our Christmas Play performances one Thursday morning, a couple of weeks before the end of term.

After weeks, and I mean weeks of tortured rehearsals - the kind where all of the staff are ready to kill each other and the one hundred and twenty children are delirious with boredom and frustration - we finally made it to the home stretch. After two performances to the parents, our final one was to the Silver Circle. Not a law firm, no, but the elderly in the community still mobile enough to travel into school.

After we had finished and returned to the classroom, the next big challenge is getting thirty overexcited children to remove their costumes and change back into their uniforms. It's usually chaos. The lure of a longer playtime and fruit and milk is enough to motivate them to make it snappy, but there's always a few stragglers.

And a whole host of unidentifiable clothing is up for grabs on the floor. My sister had happened to pop in to see the performance, and she visited the classroom to say goodbye before she left. There were only a couple of children just fastening a shoe or grabbing a banana as we talked about how it went. I always find it a bit hard to carry on as normal when on the rare occasion family come to visit, but I chivvied the last few outside, and there was just Lola left.

As she started to march towards the doorway, having been one of the one's cavorting around in her undies instead of changing as she should have been, she walked right past a piece of clothing lying abandoned on the floor. 'Oh, Lola, could you pick that up for me poppet?' I asked her, and as I described earlier, she didn't put up a fuss and obliged. She held the vest in her hand, turned it round to look at the label, before declaring, 'it's not mine!'

And, with not a care in the world, she tossed it over her

shoulder and carried right on out the door without even a backward glance, leaving us to dissolve into laughter, our faces no doubt a picture of disbelief at her boldness. I told you she was a one of a kind.

9

Boys versus girls

When I began teacher training, one of the first things we were taught was the difference between how boys and girls learn. It was all very technical, and while we thought we knew most of it already, it wasn't until I found myself in the midst of thirty children all day, every day, that I began to realise just how true this was.

Our class this particular year was ever so slightly girl- heavy, and I loved it. Being one of three girls, I've never really had that much experience with boys, so I'm always slightly relieved when the classes are equally balanced or tipped slightly in favour of the girls. Every child is different, but in the early years of school, where girls mature faster than boys, it is very evident that, much of the time, the girls are running the show. This was particularly evident this year. Never expect a boy to be able to find something on his own. Be it a toy, a classroom resource, even a pen, or their own jumper, for God's sake. I can guarantee you they will fail to locate the item without significant assistance.

And who will provide the assistance? Why, the girls, of course. Amy's brilliant in that respect. She's not only willing and eager to please, but rather enjoys the responsibility and sense of trust that I have placed upon her. She won't hesitate to take control, grabbing the poor chap by his wrist and marching him off to the cloakroom in search of the item. The boys never seem to mind either. They're not the least bit inhibited by the fact that Amy's in charge, they couldn't care less. Well, some men do prefer a woman to take control, don't they?

At 3pm every day, we're usually in the throes of utter chaos, as we try to get them ready to go out of the door. They wander in and out of the classroom, dishevelled and lacking any sense of urgency, as we try in vain, to chivvy them along and keep them from killing each other in the cloakroom. Herding cats. Did I mention that the cloakroom is further along the corridor, far away from our line of sight?

Thank God for Mrs Wright, as she is a frequent visitor to the cloakroom, as she treks down there to round up the few that have seemingly disappeared from the classroom without a trace, and are usually mucking around and generally up to no good. I wonder what it is they find to do out there quite honestly, but it never ceases to amaze me just what they do find to get up to. Sliding on their knees when they reach the tile floor is a favourite among the boys, as is crawling under the pillars that divide the cloakroom into allocated bays for each class. Don't think for a moment that the girls are blameless here, oh no, they are just as guilty. Then there's the water fountain.

It always astonishes me that even if we've just had a story all together on the carpet before home-time, and everybody is calm and quiet, that when we send them, a group at a time to go and collect their things, there is nearly always a punch up in the cloakroom that needs to be broken up.

Today is no different. 'Miss Graham!' calls Megan, her voice breathless with excitement as she ploughs through the classroom doorway, her coat on and her oversized backpack slung over one shoulder. They're the bane of our lives those backpacks. 'Sam and Matteo are fighting in the cloakroom!'

I sigh. It has been merely moments since they were under our careful supervision, and now, as soon as they have escaped, having made sure we weren't around, they can't resist a little brawl. It's a bit of sport really. 'Can we not stand in the doorway?' I ask the several who have yet to make it back into the classroom and are still loitering, coats, and giant backpacks blocking the entrance and exit so that nobody else can get in or out. Including myself. 'I'll go my dear,' volunteers Mrs Wright, with a smile. She's good at breaking up fights, and will bring the little delinquents back to me, in due course.

They are just so different, even at such a young age, and I'm afraid you'll never be informed by a child that two or more girls are fighting in the cloakroom, it just isn't done. Boys really are more, black and white, about things, at least in my experience. When difficulties occur in group games, they tend to just thump each other in a surge of testosterone, and then within five minutes, it's all forgotten.

Not so with the girls. Upset one girl and you may have well upset them all, as they close rank and adopt a 'them versus us' mentally. What is it with them? Every upset lingers in the air like a dark sky, where cross faces and purposeful looks are traded back and forth between those at war. Then there's the sniping, the deliberate exclusion of some, and the crowning touch, those words exchanged between the ring-leaders, 'we don't like Jessica do we Ayla?' On and on it goes. Mrs Wright has been in and out of that group room like billy-o, taking them in first one by one, then in a group to try to get to the bottom of what is rapidly becoming a *Nightmare on Sesame Street*.

With the boys, it tends to be more a case of fisticuffs in the playground over lunch, usually over that illegal goal in a football game, but by the time that bell rings, it's almost always forgotten. Which group are easier to manage? Honestly, the boys, hands down. They are generally very workable, simple solutions work best, such as teaching them how to decide which team they're going to be on when they play football next lunchtime, and they just don't bear grudges.

Girls, just like most women, I should imagine, require and seek much more aid from others to solve their friendship problems. And even if they have had hours of Mrs Wright's and my time and conflict resolution management that is almost befitting the UN Peacekeeping Treaty, they're never truly satisfied. If they've been wronged, it takes them far longer to get over it, and I'm convinced that person's cards are forever marked, at least in their eyes. I suppose this sets them up nicely for womanhood really.

10

PE

I really enjoy PE, at least I did until I was tasked with being the PE coordinator. I'm pretty active, in my spare time, and the enthusiasm that my own hobbies provide me is something that I have tried to foster with my own class. A dancer of some years, I finally found the confidence to teach the children five years ago, and never looked back. It's become a staple of our alternative curriculum, with notable success, in particular when my whole class paired up and participated in a School's Got Talent county-wide competition, a few summers ago.

Every year we forget how painful it is going to be. Having taught reception for five years previously, I know that they are in fact very capable and certainly not inept, but there's something about that six week hiatus from all things school-related that makes me question just how ready they will be.

It's the clothing. One should never underestimate the importance of labelling every article that belongs to your child. I can guarantee, if it does not have a label, you will never, and I mean, never, see it again. And yet year after year, we are surrounded with a bazillion unclaimed sweatshirts that seemingly fail to belong to the person who's lost it.

'This year, we've got to be tougher,' Mrs Wright muses as we're on the phone in the summer holidays, lamenting our return to the prison. 'We need to have them all in, that's the parents, day one, and tell them; this is how it is. We need to tell them what's what. I can't be doing with all this faff, searching for jumpers and God knows what else. I've lost hours of my life in that bloody cloakroom, I'd have more luck finding Lord Lucan out there. If they don't label their stuff this year, I'm Ebay-ing it for the homeless.' Mrs Wright volunteers for a charity both locally and in London, supporting homeless people and helping them to get back on their feet, so homelessness and the associated stigma and issues surrounding it are a subject that is close to her heart.

Some are brilliant at looking after their stuff, and yes, you guessed it, it's usually the girls. But while some boys are good at this, equally some are just woefully inept at managing themselves and their belongings. We often end up with items that just bounce around the classroom and seemingly somehow, fail, ever to make contact, with their original owner. Mrs Wright frequently picks up a jumper from the floor, or that has been discarded on my chair, calls out the name of the owner, and asks them to put it into their drawer or their book bag. Job done. Well, you would think, but no, ten minutes later said jumper is found abandoned in a different part of the classroom. How? 'Megan!' cries Mrs Wright in a mixture of exasperation and amusement. 'Come and put this in your book bag, it's like a boomerang!' They all giggle, but then somebody pipes up. 'Mrs Wright, what's a boomerang?' Give me strength.

Over the year, they're trained to meet the target, which is to be able to get changed for PE in five minutes or less. By the end of the year, it's a cinch, and there's really only one or two that haven't been able to grasp this concept, but at the beginning of the year, it's bloody painful. Never underestimate the need for modelling. Not the fashion kind, but the kind of educational modelling, whereby any skill that needs to be acquired is carefully explained and demonstrated multiple times until the children pick it up. And I mean multiple times.

This year, in addition to our outside games session, which is led by a company, one afternoon a week, they also have the pleasure of a PE lesson with me, every Wednesday morning after playtime. We managed to put it off the first week, and delay the torture, but by week two, there's nowhere to run, and nowhere to hide. It's happening. And Mrs Wright does a playground duty on a Wednesday, so she'll need a cup of tea and fifteen minutes of escapism in the staffroom and time to touch up her lippy before she can help me get them changed. Bollocks. And I'll need all the help I can get.

'Right, come on then 1G, in you go,' I call cheerily as I lead them in from their line in the playground. I say a line, but it really resembles a queue at a festival, where nobody follows the rules in their haste to get to the front or find their friends. 'Come and sit down on the carpet' I minister, stepping over the threshold with my cup of lukewarm tea in my hand, while trying to listen to five children tell me different things at the same time. The funny thing is, as they clamour around me, my eyes are looking into the distance at the state of the goings-on in the classroom, and I can't actually see exactly who it is that's pawing at my arm, or tapping my hip, to gain my full attention. 'Miss Graham, can I have a drink?' asks Sam, knowing full well he should have done this at playtime. 'Please can I go to the toilet?' cries Evie-Mae, holding her crotch as she dances about in desperation. I don't really have a choice with that one, do I? I never say no when they ask to go to the toilet, for obvious reasons. I play my part, and do the whole, 'you're supposed to go to the toilet at playtime' routine and 'are you really desperate?' spiel that's been ingrained in me since day one.

But does it really matter when they go? I'll admit, it's disruptive if you're trying to teach and somebody keeps getting up from the carpet and disappearing, but when you gotta go, you gotta go. If you don't let them go, you will pay the price. The consequences are messy, we both know that. It's when they do a two-pronged attack, in a cleverly thought-out plot, executed with typical five year-old sophistication when they fancy going for a muck-about with their best friend. One will sidle up and ask me, the other Mrs Wright. And if we're not both within hearing distance and we say yes, then they've won.

As soon as Mrs Wright returns, it's all hands on deck. There's nowhere really to separate them while they change, so we always end up with everybody in a soup bowl on the carpet on top of each other, which only contributes to the aforementioned lost clothing. There isn't a week that goes by when we're not held hostage from going to lunch, because one of the boys has lost his socks and we can't leave until we've found them. And no, Mrs Wright is not going to look through thirty individual PE bags to locate the missing items.

For the first session, I've decided, I'm going back to basics. Nobody is to even touch their PE bag until I've explained what to do. 'What do you do with all of your clothes?' I ask. 'Put them back in your bag!' they answer in unison. 'What do you do when you've finished?' I ask. 'Hang your bag up on your peg!' they cry.

See, they know the answers, but the problem is, it doesn't happen like this. I've explained what they'll need to wear- t-shirt, shorts, no socks or tights, and their sports shoes. As I send a group at a time to go and get their bag, Mrs Wright takes one more sip of her coffee, and then we brace ourselves for the chaos. The clock is ticking, and to be honest, if we manage to get to the hall and have ten minutes there before we have to come back and reverse the changing process, then it'll be a miracle.

The room quickly fills up with the small people, who scatter themselves around. Some are dressed within about three minutes, others we could wait for until Christmas. And so, begins the sea of clothing. Pairs of shorts and socks, vests, and jumpers, begin to form one large puddle, as the belongings are quickly mixed up, with whoever they're sitting alongside. Some are in their undies and messing about while others are struggling to work out which way out their shorts go or fumbling with the buttons on their t-shirt.

'Can you take my tights off please?' asks Vanya cheerfully. 'Oh Vanya, I'm sure you can do that!' I encourage, as she looks worriedly at me. 'But I can't. My mummy puts them on me in the morning' she explains. I smile, and begin to help her, but she questions me again. 'And can you help me put them back on again when we come back?' she asks. 'I can't do it and I can't get the lines on the feet right and then they're all scratchy' she grumbles, referring to the seams. I chuckle and she smiles at me. 'Oh Vanya! What are we going to do with you! We'll have a go together and I'll show you how to do it' I explain.

After what feels like, a very long time, everyone is finally dressed, even though it's taken over twenty minutes to ensure that everybody is suitably attired. 'Shall we just get 'em changed back again now Miss Graham, and call it a day?' whispers

Mrs Wright hopefully in my ear, as we lead them to line up. It's unbelievably tempting, but like everything here, it'll never get any better if we avoid it. Resigned to her fate, Mrs Wright wends her way to the end of the line to bring up the rear.

As soon as we've walked to the hall, I sit them down on the floor, so I can lay down the rules. PE is like a trip to Disneyland for them, so it's pretty obvious that given free reign, in a large open space, they're going to go nuts. From day one, the law must be laid down. It's very simple, and mostly in the interests of safety. They must not run. They must not scream. They must listen. They must not climb on or off anything unless instructed. Basically, akin to Monica from *Friends* 'rules help to control the fun!' but in this case, they really do!

I took Sensible Sally's class for PE a couple of years ago, and the first thing I said to them before we began was 'we're going to have some fun' as I prepared to explain the new warm-up game idea I'd stolen from my gymnastics club. Mrs Wright suddenly appeared behind me, and dryly said to me in front of our audience, 'you might want to explain what fun is, Miss Graham,' because God knows, up until now, they sure as hell haven't had any! Well, apart from maybe the robot dance, but that's another story.

Right from the get-go, the children need to know the rules, because if they do something stupid, Mrs Wright and my head's, will be on a plate, and that's a scary prospect. In the present culture of suing anybody who wrongs you, it's not surprising that, while we enjoy and want to improve the skills of all of the children, particularly when obesity is a huge concern, it's a constant worry that, should disaster strike, then we could bear the culpability. So it's important that the children learn from day one, that if they misbehave and don't listen, then there is a consequence, and at their age, it will be sitting out at the side of the room for a few minutes.

The next part of the lesson will be the warm-up, so they take their shoes off and rush forth to find a space. Imagine thirty small people standing in bunches of three, their arms outstretched at either side as they wave them around in their attempt to find their own space. 'You're too close to me!' wails Lola. 'I want to be next to Marco!' squeaks Henry, who's so close to Marco it's a wonder he hasn't taken his eye out. Mrs Wright looks at me with a smirk. 'Here we go Miss Graham. Tell me again, what is the life expectancy of a TA?' she chuckles, as she makes her way across the room to move Henry five feet away from Marco.

Oh God, why did I decide to be so conscientious today? Why didn't I just take them out to the playground in their uniforms and have them play on the jungle gym? But I didn't, so I'll have to try and make a go of what's left of the lesson. Own spaces finally found, they stand with their arms by their sides, ready to listen. I explain that we're going to play the traffic light game and remind them of the rules. If I say red, they stop. Green they can jog and amber they can hop on the spot. Simple, effective, and good fun in their eyes, it's also a good first look at how coordinated everybody is, or isn't.

As they launch themselves in different directions, whooping with excitement and the ability to run free, I'm not surprised to look up at the clock to find that we need to go back to class if there's any chance of us getting them to lunch on time. Mrs Wright looks equally relieved to discover that we've run out of time, thus putting an end to the torture. Only now, it's back to reverse the process and go back to the cesspool of abandoned clothing. Much like Patsy and Eddie from *Absolutely Fabulous*, I want to scream the words 'abort, abort!' as we declare the mission null and void.

Somehow, the next twenty minutes pass quickly, as we button buttons, untuck collars and I've helped Vanya back into her tights, my head almost reaching the floor as she lifts each foot in turn, steadying herself by holding on to my shoulders to stop her from wobbling. Then just when it's looking like we've reached a ninety percent success rate and almost everybody is dressed reasonably appropriately, there's the cry that's about to sink the ship.

'Mrs Wright, I can't find my other sock!' cries Matthew, sitting in a pile of clothing on the floor. Mrs Wright looks up at me and dryly offers the words, 'is it July yet Miss Graham?' as she wearily heads over to the now sock-less Matthew. Only thirty-eight more weeks of this. It will get better.

11

Mistletoe, mistletoe

There are moles everywhere in this place, no conversation goes unnoticed. Thank God, there are no CCTV cameras in the classroom, or we'd all be out of a job.

By and large, she's not a bad old girl, the boss. She joined us several years ago, having replaced our old battle-axe who finally, to the relief of us all, retired to the sunny climes of Portugal. Now, she was a force to be reckoned with. A slightly-on-the-larger-side, sixty-five year-old, with a crop of faded red-brown hair, she ruled 'her' school with an iron rod. She hired me way back in 2007. I must admit the first moment I met her, I liked the woman. She came across as kindly, in a caring, grandmotherly sort of way, which was exactly the type of person my twenty-three year-old self wanted to work for. It was comforting I suppose.

But she was a real battle-axe. One whose face would turn blue with rage on many an occasion, and she would literally almost self-combust, as rage about school issues took over. Every morning on my way past the office, I would stick my head in to ask how the land lay, in order to find out whether I needed to keep a low profile and bob and weave, or whether things were status quo.

When work and bureaucracy became too much, she would evacuate her office and wander down to reception where I was based, in order to spend some time with the tiniest learners in the school. A source of comfort and the epitome of a simpler life, she was soothed by watching them crawl around the floor with the puppets, or endlessly filling and emptying little containers in the outside water tray.

When she retired, after I'd been there about five years, we were all a bit trepidatious as to who we were going to get next. When the Big Guns arrived, we were pleasantly surprised with the governors' choice. Far younger, with several young school-age children of her own and a positive attitude to boot, we were cautiously optimistic. For one thing, she smiled every day, never shouted, seemed genuinely interested in getting to know her new team, and kindly reassured us that it wasn't her intention to change everything.

But Mrs Wright clocked her right away, quietly branding her a 'smiling assassin.' I was puzzled, as my only interactions with her thus far had been positive, but Mrs Wright had seen her type before. In the first few weeks she put a stop to a difficult parent who had been collecting her son early every week to go swimming, a battle the previous boss simply didn't have the energy to fight. When she cornered her that day, tempers inevitably flared, but the Big Guns triumphed, and after a very heated conversation with the parent, passed several TA's in the corridor as she walked past, smiling and cheerfully greeted them, 'good afternoon ladies.' A smooth operator indeed.

Consequently, every time she pops her head up like a ninja, we've now adopted a codeword, mistletoe, which has been a useful way to warn the others of her impending and impromptu visits. The back story behind the moniker shall be revealed later, so keep your eyes peeled.

12

The wonders of nature

I've never really been much of a fan of the great outdoors myself. It is too damp, too muddy, and, definitely, too cold. I am partial to a bit of sun, but alas, a sunny day is a rather rare occurrence, living in England. I really hate feeling cold, and I'm usually the first person to start bleating about the need for the heating to go on at school. They're quite miserly though, as in the eleven years that I've worked there, the heating is rarely put on before the arbitrarily set-in-stone date of October half-term. They're desperate to save money, and if that means we freeze, then freeze we do. When I worked down in reception, where the outside doors are open to support such ideals as 'free-flow play', I used to send children to the office in pairs, with little messages written on mini-whiteboards for them to thrust at the office staff the minute their persistent knocks at the hatch were answered, *please can we have the heating on? xxx*. It rarely worked, and thus I spent a lot of time wearing my coat indoors.

Every morning, once we are all seated on the carpet, in assigned carpet places, of course, I pick up the register from its place on my easy chair, and glance upwards at the windows. Where I had left them winched firmly shut, lest any precious heat is lost, they are now open a few centimetres in search of fresh air. Mrs Wright has arrived. Mrs 'Outdoorsy' rather likes, to feel the galing wind in her face, and has the unfortunate habit, of trying to impress her will upon us! Actually, thank God she does, otherwise we'd rarely smell the glorious fresh air, particularly as the room is usually filled in the afternoon with a certain unpleasant 'odour de bottom.'

One afternoon, when I was reading with Lola, she returned from changing her reading books and appeared with a little book from the reading scheme about making a scented cushion. A non-fiction text designed to broaden the children's horizons beyond the usual fiction provided by the likes of *Biff, Chip and Kipper*. Lola's interest was immediately piqued by the glossy photographs giving step-by-step instructions on how to make one's own. She really wanted to make one, and one look at how the spark lit up and excitement literally shone out of her face at the possibility, I knew I couldn't say no. A quick word to Mrs Wright, and we've come up with a plan.

There's a little garden, at the back of the school, filled with overgrowing plants, where we might be able to wade through and gather the necessary items. Well, this sort of going off on a tangent is exactly what Mrs Wright and I breathe for, and we love any excuse to participate in something off-curriculum and child-led. The plan was to go and gather three plants needed; lemon balm, mint and sprigs of lavender, dry them out for a few days, while we scrounged enough material for thirty little cushions and then assemble them, ready to take home on a Friday afternoon.

Mrs Wright was designated the group leader, and this is really where her expertise lies, you know - outdoors. I never knew that moss only grows on the north side of the tree until I met her, nor could I identify a dock leaf if I was covered in nettle rash. The troops were rounded up, one beautiful, spring morning, and excitedly chattered in the line as we grabbed a couple of old school trays in which to place the fruits of our labour. As she led the long line down the playground and round to the back of the school to the garden, I went at the back to bring up the rear.

As we stepped over the overgrown foliage, the dampness from the night before seeping into the soles of my beautiful, new suede boots, Mrs Wright gathered them all around her as she let out a huge sigh of contentment. 'Oh! Children, isn't this lovely?' she exclaimed, inhaling a deep breath of the beautifully fresh air. 'Do you know, when we were small, my sister and I used to spend all our time outside, climbing trees and collecting whatever we'd find.' The children all gathered around her listening carefully, fondling some of the leaves of the plants that were overflowing from the abandoned flower beds.

Mrs Wright moved her band of merry men northwards, as I steered Pieter and Matteo away from the sticks of wood they'd been eyeing up as potential weapons, silently lamenting my choice of footwear this morning. As they followed her along, Mrs Wright did what she does best, and held the lemon balm aloft for all to see. Then she began to explain in great detail what it looks, feels and smells like, as well as informing them where and when it grows.

Jesus, I'm thirty-four and I don't think I could identify lemon balm if my life depended on it. Even though I suppose there's a good chance the smell might give it away. I think I've led a sheltered life, and we can't help but think that given the political correctness that's rife today, that the next generation will likely go the same way, given the perceived dangers of a spontaneous romp through the garden.

So Mrs Wright was in her element, a David Attenborough in the making, as she led the group through their trek through the bushes, stopping to exclaim and display what she'd found, and encouraging the children to go and find some plants as well. As she spoke, I watched their faces, eager to see how they would respond. And, as with any time she's centre stage, whatever the topic, they listened in earnest, utterly captivated by her stories, her knowledge, and her passion for the great outdoors.

In a nutshell, she's a sort of Joyce Grenfell, mixed with Alan Titchmarsh, with a passion for flora and fauna, the wonders of the natural world and having this innate gift of being able to share it among the small people. Job done, we tramped back to the classroom, me hoping my new suede boots would recover from the trek. The plants were smelled, touched, and licked, I believe, by George, before being placed in the trays on a shelf as we waited for them to dry out.

On Friday afternoon, we got cracking, taking a group of six children at a time to construct their little scent bags. The plans deviated slightly as we had no time to sew. Plus the idea of sewing with thirty small people en masse is far too ambitious for the end of the week. Mrs Wright has been out to the art station, and managed to smuggle away some scraps of material from the clutches of Bebe Duke, and I've found a bit of ribbon that'll do us nicely in the depths of our cupboard.

The assembling of the little bags was actually quite quick, as they selected their material, picked up their lovely dried leaves and wrapped them in the material before handing them over to us to tie with a ribbon. It didn't take nearly as long as I feared, and with the two of us, we quickly whizzed through all of the groups and finished the job. While they weren't as exquisite-looking as the one in Lola's reading book, they did look quite lovely and definitely did the job. We stepped back and congratulated ourselves on being able to lead a totally off-curriculum project, that truly came from one child's interests, and managed to get them all completed by 3:15pm. As they wandered around the classroom getting their things ready for home, talk again returned to these little bags, as they held them and showed them to their friends as they sat on the carpet.

About a minute before that bell rang, as Lola returned with her things, I took a moment to look at her little bag in her hand. I suppose I was sort of hoping she'd be absolutely cock-a-hoop about her teachers going to the ends of the earth to make her idea come to fruition, and thrilled we'd made it happen. 'Are you happy Lola? Do you like your scented bag?' I asked her, as Mrs Wright looked on. All of a sudden, Lola's face crumpled, and she burst into tears as she wailed, 'we didn't do it right!' Mrs Wright and I looked at each other incredulously, before bursting into laughter! And then I had to send her out of the door to her mother bawling. Terrific. Well, they do say that no good deed goes unpunished.

Despite Lola's dissatisfaction at our attempts to be creative, our spirits, weren't, remotely dampened, so for the first time this year we decided to create a nature table in the classroom. Back when I went to school, I can remember having one, a little place where 'all things natural' were placed for all to gaze at. After a conversation at home about it, it was my dad, who asked if we still did that, as he remembered from his own school days circa the 1960s. How could I even begin to explain how times have changed so much, that there's simply no time to do any of that anymore, what with every minute of learning time having to be accounted for?

But being the rebels we are, as soon as autumn began to show its face, we decided we'd go against the grain and set one up. A lowly and unused bookcase was covered with a piece of green tissue paper in readiness for receiving the typical autumn treasures. Then the floodgates opened. The children were beyond thrilled that every time they found an acorn, a pine cone or a tiny shrivelled up brown leaf, they were welcomed for our collective enjoyment, rather than being dismissed and asked to go and put them into either their drawer or their book bag.

Whenever by mid-week we judged that things were going south, we decided we would head off on an autumn walk around the playground to clear our heads and delight in the changing of the seasons. Again, Mrs Wright would be the group leader, drawing their attention to the almost leaf-less trees, and explaining why they had lost them and when they'd be back. We stood in a huge circle in the playground, looking at the early autumnal haze of the sky, looking right up at it and inhaling deep lungful's of the crisp and delicious smelling air as we marvelled at the wonders of nature.

Pretty swiftly, the nature table became a mass of different coloured leaves in all shapes and sizes, acorns, pine cones, twigs and sticks found abandoned on the ground, and anything else that could be found. When the chestnuts came, complete with the prickly outer casing, they were given an insubordinate amount of air-time, and were proudly brought to the carpet for closer inspection.

When Christopher delivered his treasures after a long weekend at his father's house in the country, they fawned upon them as if he had just procured the crown jewels. As he stood in front of the class, delighting in explaining just where he had found them, the precious items were passed along the lines for everybody to fondle and poke before they were added to the nature table bearing pride of place.

Talk about bringing them along. In the early days, there's nothing like a project that unites the many and the few, and this shared pursuit to collect all things autumn went down an absolute treat. I don't think I've ever seen so many, genuinely excited faces, thrilled at what they had been able to source from their walk to school and their own playground. And what do you know, I've learned a little in the process myself.

Later on in the year, when there was talk of each class in Key Stage One having the pleasure of watching frogspawn turn into tadpoles via a tank in the classroom, I left it to Mrs Wright to make the final decision. I didn't want to be the 'bah-humbug' that I am, so turned it over to her as I knew there was a good chance she'd say yes. A few days later, we now had a large plastic tank set up in the classroom, and a set of instructions on how to look after them. Mrs Wright began to realise what a huge responsibility this was going to be, but cheerfully remarked, 'well, I'm just going to have to read up on how to care for these little chappies!'

We got off to a good start, as the children spent their every free moment fighting to stand at the front of the tank and peer over the top to see the tadpoles. It was all going swimmingly, as the pungent water and cucumber cubes aided the development of the little creatures. Then, the three-day bank holiday weekend posed a rather serious problem. Given that none of us would be there to keep them from a certain death, we moved the tank away from the direct sunlight, tossed a few more cucumber slices in for good measure, and left that Friday, after saying a quick prayer for their survival.

On Tuesday morning, as she breezed through the classroom door before school, Mrs Wright was eager to learn their fate. As she wandered over to the tank, she tapped the sides a few times to find a distinctly still and unmoving bunch laying floating just at the water line. She turned to me, her face ashen, as she whispered, 'I think they've snuffed it! What are we going to do?' We had about fifteen minutes before the children came in. As Mrs Pegg ambled through the connecting classroom door to visit, and Mrs Beale trailed in through ours, Mrs Wright was quick to fill them in. 'Black armbands, girls, I've killed them all!'

The four of us spent the next ten minutes wondering how on earth we were going to hide this from the children. After all, they were in full-on tadpole mode, and each day the VIP's were on tadpole watch, going back and forth seventy-five times a day to check the tank and make sure the hostages were doing ok. Of course the ones that Bebe Duke had next door had gone from surviving to thriving, but let's face it, it's not like she was going to give us a few of hers so we could save face in front of the children was it? So we hastily decided to temporarily remove the tank from view, and bundled it into the side room and set it on the table, where Mrs Wright tried in vain to rouse the occupants, while I brought the children in.

As Mrs Beale returned from having made her large morning coffee, the children having been mercifully delivered to assembly buying us precious extra time, the two of us stood in the doorway to have a peek. 'Any luck?' I asked Mrs Wright. 'It's over Miss Graham, wave the white flag!' she laughs, as I fill in Mrs Pegg who's sneaked away from Bebe Duke and come to see if she can help. 'How are we doing?' she asks, as I reply, *ER*-style. 'Stand down, no survivors, they're all DOA at the scene.' 'Oh bugger!' replies Mrs Pegg, laughing.

Now, despite trying to pull a fast one on the children and avoid any unhappiness, I decided it was better to just 'fess up' and explain what had happened. Mrs Wright was a little reluctant, but I felt it was an important lesson, that even with the best of intentions, things don't always turn out right. They were disappointed for sure, but we said a few prayers for the dearly departed, and promised them we'd try again. The lady who had originally brought us the frogspawn duly went back to her pond and brought us some more, as we filled the tank again and prepped the water, and then off we went again. It gave us all another opportunity to go one better, and the children were much more vigilant and desperately wanted to have a successful outcome this time. And we did. Three weeks later we bade a fond farewell to them, as one of the other TA's collected them and transported them to her garden pond. 'It might be best if I say no next year, Miss Graham. What do you think?' chuckled Mrs Wright after they'd vacated. We'll see.

13

Christmas play hell

The darkened hall, lit only by four out of the ten remaining stage lights that still work, begins to fall silent. One hundred and twenty children fill the space in a sea of colour, decked out in an array of brightly-decorated Christmas jumpers for the pre-Christmas 'Mufti' day (i.e. wear a Christmas jumper and bring us a bottle of your best bubbly that we can flog on the tombola stall at the school fair tomorrow). Terrific.

Ten of us adults are spaced strategically alongside the rows of benches where the tiny people have been placed, in order of their speaking parts. Just like last year, Year Two, aka the Big Ones, are doing the acting, while we, Year One, quite literally the Little People, will be the musicians. The rehearsals for any performance are always without fail supremely awful for pretty much all involved. But for the one hundred and twenty five and six year-olds, it's a mixture of anticipation and amusement, as well as abject suffering and inevitable humiliation.

We're a year on, and Lola, now one of the Big People has been selected, in addition to her own role as a sheep, to introduce the play. As the chatter dies down and the hall becomes hushed, she clambers up the wobbly little wooden stairs, dressed beautifully in her navy long-sleeved t-shirt and red plaid skirt, clutching the ailing microphone in one hand, a laminated strip of words in the other.

With silence now reigning, she lifts the microphone to her lips and her tiny hands fumble with her word card. 'Welcome to our Christmas Play' she mumbles in her beautiful Spanish accent. 'We hope that you ...' She barely gets through the second sentence.

'I CAN'T HEAR YOU! I DIDN'T HEAR ANY OF THAT.' Bebe Duke's booming monotone voice cuts Lola dead in her tracks. She looks so tiny, all on her own at the front of the hastily erected wooden stage, suddenly dwarfed in the absence of any other children around her. Her face falls, and like the others, she's bracing herself for the tirade of criticism that has claimed many a victim among her peers already.

I've had enough of this. We, the Little People, and the associated staff that make up the Year One 'team,' have only been privy to the rehearsals for the last week or so, but already, I've seen enough. The leader, Stella Stuart decided last year, that it would be better for her to take Year Two into the hall alone so that they could 'work on the acting,' and that we could carry on as normal and sing without having to concern ourselves until nearer to the end when it's all put together. To the naked eye it would seem appropriate, but really, it's just a way of telling us we're, surplus to requirements, and just to piss off and take our delinquent rabble with us.

Mrs Wright and I worked so hard last year. We invested so much of ourselves into these children, that to relinquish them into the hands of others has been perhaps more difficult than usual, particularly for me. We have far less contact with them now that they no longer belong to us, but just enough to see where it's heading. Some have changed, and not for the better. In a continual battle of internal conflict, I try not to interfere, and try to keep a little distance to help to reinforce the bond they need to develop with their new teacher. But sometimes it's too hard to do. I feel very protective of all of them, but there comes a point when a line must be drawn. For, while I may have to collectively collaborate with Bebe Duke and Stella Stuart, I will not allow them to humiliate and destroy the self-confidence of those that we worked so hard to nurture.

Before Bebe Duke or Stella Stuart have a chance to say anything else that might hurt her, I open my mouth and the words fly out before I can stop them. 'Lola' I call, as she turns her head towards me at the side of the stage. 'Lola you have a lovely voice, I know you can say the words really clearly and really well.' Her face immediately brightens, and she gives me one of her huge smiles. She turns back to the front and raises the microphone to her lips once more, this time delivering her lines slowly and with more clarity than before. Her new teacher and I both tell her she did that so well, as she tiptoes down the rickety steps and back to her place next to the other sheep and shepherds on the bench, on the left-hand side of the hall.

The rehearsal schedule trolls on, and we're approaching the finish line. One afternoon, we assemble again for the penulti-mate rehearsal, one Friday during the first week of December. Matteo, one of the aforementioned 'bored and delirious' chil-dren subject to the trauma of all things 'Christmas Play', has taken the decision to spar with Felipe who's sat next to him on the bench for the majority of this time. After copious amounts of shushing and repeated warnings from either Stella Stuart or an increasingly infuriated Mrs Cannon, the poor TA, who happened to have the misfortune of sitting alongside said bench, they finally give it a rest. To the rest of us, it's simply one less distraction to contend with, but by God I feel their pain. I'm clock-watching like billy-o and I've got almost thirty years on them. The play grumbles along as the cacophony of angels cluster around the hard wooden stage, alternately mumbling, or shouting their lines, while Stella Stuart bellows forth from her easy chair of sorts, and my attention is drawn to her rising stress levels.

From the corner of my eye I can see tremendous activity on the back bench, as Mrs Beale reaches over to put her arm around Matteo, who I now realise is crying. He's not one to break easily. Did I miss something? Was it possible he was blasted by Bebe Duke or Stella Stuart while I'd inadvertently slipped into some sort of coma? No. As my eyes search the scene to try to gather the missing pieces of the puzzle, I realise that Matteo has pulled repeatedly on the sleeve of his jazzy Christmas jumper, no doubt to alleviate some of the tedium, and startled himself by rendering himself partially sleeveless, much to his dismay. Something prickles in my chest. To see such huge dark eyes awash with salty tears. Tears of regret. Tears of poor judgement, and, if he's anything like me, tears of exhaustion as we near the end of term. My heart breaks a little inside for him, to be five years old and realise that a problem has arisen that he can't fix alone.

And that's what's so great about all of the TA's. Kudos to them, in the same breath that they can chastise a small child who has done wrong, they are equally quick to embrace and love them, almost as if they were their own child. I love that about them. Mrs Beale, for all of her bluster, is the first to put her arm around him and offer some reassurance that sleeve-less or not, the world shall still keep turning. I can hear her whispering to him in her southern drawl, 'it's ok, sweetheart' as she rubs his back and asks him a few questions. Don't bother with why, it doesn't matter a jot. And as I'm sort of somewhat surplus to requirements, I don't wait for Stella Stuart's permission, as I leave the hall to grab a bunch of tissues from one of the reception classes. As I return, I offer Mrs Beale the box, and she passes a handful to Matteo, who looks up at me as he dabs his eyes. I couldn't give two shits about this play really, it's the little things that matter, and this is one of them.

The sodding instruments. Whose brilliant idea was it to give sixty, five year-olds a variety of percussion instruments to play en masse, tunelessly and at deafening volume? We did, that's who. We had to really. They were given sod all else to do throughout the entire duration of the torturous hour-long performance, so we had to do something that would prove to the audience that it was a combined effort, and indeed a Year One *and* Two Christmas production.

Poor Year One, we're the bottom of the pile really. The useless second-class citizens of the play who are so low on the totem pole we may as well wave the white flag now. Banned from rehearsals for the first five weeks (actually for us it's quite a blessing to be purposefully excluded and have nothing to do with any of it, shenanigans and all) and deemed far too rowdy and unruly that we threaten to scupper their chances of getting the serious work done; i.e. the acting, if we were present.

Stella Stuart loves it. Every year she can't resist getting up on that stage and showing the children how to do it. Sometimes we, and they, have a bit of fun. After all who doesn't love to see one of the teachers make a complete ham of themselves up on that stage and try to steal the limelight from the poor child that's not yet confident and ballsy enough to deliver their lines with gusto? She's a funny one is Stella Stuart. She's the leader of the pack in KS1, and she wouldn't want it any other way. Every year she moans about how she's the only one remotely qualified to run the play, but the plain old truth is that she's a martyr. She likes nothing better than to be in control, and she knows full well that if any of the three other teachers, including me, offered to do it, there's no way in hell she'd ever trust us to do it properly. So, every year we pretend to get the violins out, as she begins her moans and groans about what a huge amount of work it will be. As we come to the end of the long weeks of rehearsals, the hall is filled with her barked instructions. 'Don't turn your head to look at the stage.' 'Who can I hear zipping and unzipping their shoes?' 'Christopher, if I see you poking those maracas near your willy one more time you'll be out!' And so on, and so on.

The day of the performance finally arrives. As well as the weeks of rehearsals, it's taken just as many weeks to get the costumes in! The letters to parents are sent out well ahead of time, asking them to provide something which can either be pulled from the child's own clothes, or a £3.99 job from the local Sainsbury's. While there's occasionally a rumble of discontent on the grapevine, usually the parents come up trumps, and duly deliver their child's costume on time and in a named plastic bag as per our instructions.

As they arrived in dribs and drabs each day, we took great delight as a class in admiring them and then Mrs Wright hauled the little stool from under my chair and hung them on the rail above our windows. As we neared the dangerous time, two days before, we're checking them off on a list to see who the non-conformers are as Mrs Wright prepares once again to make some phone calls. After we've played the game they love 'stand up and sit down when I call your name out' and Mrs Wright has been from left to right among the costume bags, we've nailed the culprit to be George.

He's pretty sure he told his mum about needing a costume, but Mrs Wright wisely hurries off to the office to make the phone call, whereupon his dear mother claims to know nothing about it. Luckily, all she has to provide is a nice shirt and tie- occasion wear- and promises she'll have it in by tomorrow. The next day, we're all sat down on the carpet ready to start the register when dear George wanders in, sheepishly bearing a coat hanger covered with a plastic bag which hides his costume. 'Morning George' I call, as he walks over to my chair before offering his costume to me. 'Oh well done! That's great you've brought it in!' I praise. I've got my lap full, with the register and the assorted treasures that have been delivered along with it, so I send George across to Mrs Wright, who's also sitting comfortably in her brown recliner. The children all look expectantly as Mrs Wright takes the coat hanger from George and peels back the plastic bag, to reveal a beautiful dark purple shirt neatly hung. Around it is a black waistcoat, and a brightly coloured bow tie around the collar of the shirt.

Mrs Wright's face breaks into a huge beaming smile as she marvels at George's outfit. 'This is smashing, you're going to look gorgeous George! Oh, look at the sparkly waistcoat! Did mummy sew those bits on? George, a miracle has occurred! Can you walk on water?' George is delighted at receiving such high praise and attention, and smiles shyly and answers a few of her questions. 'Well' begins Mrs Wright, rising from her chair and heading over to the windows. 'I'm going to hang this up with all the others, and do you know what children?' she asks, as the little faces turn to watch her every move. 'I think we are going to be the best dressed class in the play!'

Finally, the performance day arrives. Getting them all changed into their costumes takes a month of Sundays, but thankfully there are no tea towels to be tied around heads with pairs of tights, although buttoning up twenty-one shirts and affixing bow ties requires all the extra help that we can get.

As we head into the darkened hall, to the hushed chorus of 'oohs' and 'aahs' by the parents, grannies and granddads seated in the audience, we thank God that in about seventy minutes time this will all be over for another year. The music system miraculously fires up, and Stella Stuart takes her place on her cushion on the floor with her back to the audience. I take a deep breath and pray it goes well. Sometimes the hysteria that organising and executing this creates, must be akin to trying to organise the BAFTAs, not an infant school Christmas Play.

As we finally finish, and the parents applaud, we silently congratulate ourselves that somehow it all came together. Nobody bottled it and refused to say their lines, the baby Jesus was located in his cradle and we remembered to put the manger on at the correct time, the microphones didn't fail us and Liz Dawson didn't hit too many duff notes on the piano.

The final hurdle we need to overcome, is getting them out of the hall and back to the classroom. Now you'd think that this was a non-event, but the problem is, the parents quite rightly want to take photos of their beloved, and while it takes a bit of time to give everybody their chance to come up to the stage, the children quickly become overwhelmed and tearful. It's a fine line between celebrating their success, and every child needing counselling afterwards.

We nearly always have to peel somebody away, nearly hysterical at the thought of the rest of the day at school without mum and dad, so as soon as is humanly possible, we get them out and back en route to the classroom. There's always a few tears, but after some consoling and the promise of a longer playtime and moving their name up the behaviour ladder, they're usually ok. Thankfully, this time it's just Darla who cried. During the final song, she was stood alongside her classmates next to me to sing, when I looked up from my script and noticed the tears streaming down her cheeks. I took her hand and pulled her to me, and then picked her up and sat her on my lap as I whispered, 'what's the matter?' 'This song just makes me really sad,' she sniffled, as I offered her a tissue and said she could stay here with me.

When we made it back to the classroom, there was excited chattering, amongst the clothes being tossed in every direction and I made a beeline for the bin, putting the fifteen-page script straight in. 'Praise the Lord Miss Graham' breathes Mrs Wright wearily. 'Shall I go and pop the kettle on?'

14

Extra credit

I'm always in trouble. There. I've said it. Always bottom of the pile. I'm the one who'll be walked over, shouted down in meetings (if I ever contribute), and I take the starring role as the general whipping boy, so to speak.

In any school, it's all about what you can do as 'extra.' I use the term loosely, as, while it sort of relies on the goodwill of staff to go above and beyond the call of duty, sadly, in reality it is quite necessary to work yourself into the ground in order to get the kudos and advance steadily up the pay scale. And don't think that this pay scale advances with any sort of frequency or regularity, oh no. Now the sands of time have shifted south, and we've all been forced into the demoralising and debilitating horror that is, *'Performance Related Pay'*.

Now, you'd think that, naturally, any sort of performance would be related to one's own ability to teach, but oh no, think again. No, it's the performance of the children that counts, and your ability to fiddle the results that will determine whether you are deemed a useful asset to the school and a valuable resource. In other words, are you value for money?

Some like to exist in a cosy little bubble of narcissism, mistakenly believing that they are irreplaceable, and that the school would be lost without them, and couldn't function because of their value, their commitment, and their ability to do all of the above. But they're wrong. Because we're all expendable.

All of us, there's really no distinction, are essentially all the same, despite what the over-confidents among us choose to believe. And in this day and age, there is always someone younger, someone far more energetic, their enthusiasm not yet dampened by years of fighting a losing battle with the powers that be, and here's the deal-breaker, the buzzword, the bottom line; they're cheaper.

Here's how it works. When I began teaching aged twenty-three, doe-eyed and eager to please, I was rather chuffed to be making twenty-one thousand pounds as a starting salary. With pretty much zero concept of salary and progression and how it all works, I was quite delighted for my years of toil to be rewarded in such a way. In fact, I was just relieved and happy that I had any money at all, let alone having a decent starting salary and a fair bit of money just to piss about with. I was still living at home, having had a fantastic final year in my PGCE, where in 2005/06, they were actually paying us to do the course, in the form of a six thousand pound gratuity that was divvied up to us in nice little instalments of six hundred and sixty-six pounds per month. Five years later when a friend of a friend decided to train, she had to pay them nine thousand pounds for the privilege.

I fooled around, when it came to applying for jobs, leaving it until the summer of 2006 when the course was all but finished. Most of my peers had already secured jobs with their placement schools months before. It was symptomatic of my lack of confidence and self-belief. I didn't want to apply for any job, didn't feel like I had a right to, until I had completed the course and held the certificate in my hand. But by then all the jobs had gone, and I returned home to a lazy summer and then the dawning of the fact that I was unemployed and needed to find temp work. It was my dad, a staunch conservative and 'moderate facist', who wanted to get a good return on his taxes, who insisted that I signed on to claim Jobseeker's Allowance while looking for a teaching job. This enabled him to feel like he was getting his money's worth and making a small dent in getting back some of his tax that he sorely resented paying.

So, my sister and I toddled off to the local job centre, one hot day in late August of that year. Both of us, reluctantly admitting defeat and resigning ourselves to the fact that despite being educated, we were now at the mercy of the government facility to provide for us. As it turned out, my sister's prayers were somewhat answered on that very day, when she was offered a position at a graphic design company, her first job. While jealously, I continued with the application to file my claim, and she went home and signed her contract.

I needn't have been too peeved, as while the fruit of her labour brought her newfound financial independence, and later that year for her birthday, a grey, much-wanted, new Toyota Aygo along with it's corresponding finance deal, it also came at a price. She zipped about all year, paying extortionate parking fees but having quite a jolly time, as I watched from the wings. I was mystified as to how things could turn out so well for her, and far less so for me. It was a pattern of thinking that has continued to this day, the comparison between the two of us, one, who, in my eyes, was always succeeding, her, and one always failing, me!

As it turned out, her new boss, a guy who was quite up himself, and a first class jerk by all accounts, showed his true colours pretty quickly, and after a year she happily moved on to a creative agency in a more modern and upbeat environment, with nicer bosses. Meanwhile, I was living from fortnight to fortnight, on the seventy pounds provided by the JSA. I mourned my lack of permanent employment and resisted everyone's suggestions to temp or get 'supply' work. I lurched between hope that things might yet happen for me, and considering suicide.

No joke, it was a really, dark year for me. No money meant no travel, no spending, and no fun. The weather was miserable, and so were my thoughts. How can I have gotten here? Why did I ever bother studying? Will I ever get a job? As well as having my own melancholy to contend with, my dad was always there to remind me just how useless I was, and how I was a waste of space. This, unsurprisingly, did little to lift either my spirits or my bank balance. My, already fragile, self-esteem had taken a nosedive, and I truly questioned whether I really had anything to live for. That sounds a bit dramatic doesn't it? But my dad's frustration that neither he, nor I, were in control of the situation only served to make our already strained relationship that bit more fractious.

My mum and gramps were my staunch supporters, and knew that when the jobs would start popping up after Christmas, I would be sure to find something great that would kickstart me into my chosen career path. But my dad just wanted me to take any teaching job, anywhere. I refused. I didn't want to just work down the road in the less than desirable schools, which Ofsted had rendered in 'Special Measures', and where teachers were running screaming from the building. It just wasn't me. It didn't feel right. I had already had one or two interviews last-minute in July, and one was in a place which I truly hated. 'There's a lot of teenagers and drug addicts that use the green opposite our school after hours, so we often find syringes and things around the premises' chirped one headteacher, not doing a lot to put my over-thinking mind at rest. I knew there and then that I would NEVER work there. If my life depended on it, I would never work there. I am better than this. And I carried on looking.

It took me a total of nine interviews before I hit the jackpot. A lot of those jobs I never wanted, and some I pretty much gave up before the actual interview, after I'd sized up the other candidates and decided they were better than me. When that call finally came, in June of that year, it was from the school I thought I was the least likely to work at, but I was thrilled and excited. A few hours later though and the fear began to set in. It was self-doubt, 'what have I done? I can't do this'. I actually felt quite sick as the panic set in, which put a bit of a damper on things temporarily, but unknowingly the school had spotted something else in me - that I was not currently working and thus available until my position officially started in September.

They offered me lots of supply work, and I agreed. It, actually helped to get the lay of the land before I began, so I spent the next few weeks before the summer vacation filling in for various teacher absences. It was good to be a fly on the wall and work out some of the characters.

For the next five years, I worked happily in reception, save for the four of those years alongside Bebe Duke, and my salary jumped up every year as if by magic, without requiring any extra effort, or being open to scrutiny. By 2014 however, 'Performance Related Pay' had arrived, and having hit the top of the main scale of teachers pay after six years, in order to get the tiny crumb they throw you and make the next increment on the pay ladder, it was now up to me to prove my worth via copious amounts of form-filling. It involves meeting a series of silly targets, proving that you are doing work above and beyond those on the main scale. I was pleased when, after a year of trying to make it happen, it was finally approved. When the next pay cheque went through, I was excited to see my raise.

I needn't have gotten too excited though, it was all of about fifty bucks per month, despite a 3K rise. By the time I made it to my session with Karen, my therapist, that evening, the tears fell. At the bloody injustice of it all! Karen had kindly given me a concession on my weekly therapy fees months ago, and quietly offered to continue to allow me to pay the reduced rate. Therapy was yet one more thing in my life that was just a tad too expensive, meaning I was continually living beyond my means. And now, four years later, my salary remains the same. Oh yeah, and now there's a wage freeze too. It's a constant source of frustration. I mean, in what other job, public sector aside, does one's pay remain the same year after year, despite the responsibilities increasing? It's crazy!

The final straw was when I wanted to make the next jump on the housing ladder, two years later. I'd unexpectedly found a house that was everything I wanted and more - isn't that always the way - but was literally all of ten grand out of my price range. After multiple stressful phone calls with my mortgage advisor, praying I could borrow more, he felt I had two options; put your lower offer in and wait for the inevitable, or get on the phone and start begging your parents for money. Disappointment didn't even cover it. I was close to tears when I gave the bad news to Mrs Wright after school that rainy day in January, as in my eyes, I'd been screwed over once again. Every time I tried to change my circumstances, I'd pour in a whole load of effort and after many tears and heartache, I ended up back where I started.

Now, I know reading this that you're probably thinking what an entitled piece of work I am. After all, I chose to work in the public sector, which generally means a lifetime of low pay, but a reasonable pension. Well, unless you want 'in' on the management side of the job, which many of us just don't. Maybe I was just a bit naive, thinking it would be easy to choose my direction, and not to face financial obstacles due to my job choice. But, I'd argue, of course, that all public service workers should be paid much better. Nurses, the police, the fire service to name just a few. I suppose I just felt increasingly frustrated, and never imagined that by my early thirties I'd have so little control over my ability to better myself and move forwards, as I saw all my friends doing.

And, that's now, where we're at. All teachers being asked to improve their performance, their results, their ability to make real change and move the school forwards, without getting any sort of financial reward for their troubles. It's a dangerous position to be in, that is certain. Like many other professions, overworked and underpaid. Ever wondered why we have a retention crisis?

15

Sharing is caring

'Why can't you hear it? What stops you from believing you're a good teacher?' asks Karen, my therapist, when I visit her. It's the week of October half-term, and I'm sitting on her couch in her cosy brick cottage, lamenting the outcome of my termly observation last week. I'm exhausted, and the dismal weather does nothing to lift my spirits.

'I don't know' I answer, fiddling with the plaster on my index finger while we talk. In fact, I've undone and rearranged the plaster for the entire duration of our fifty-minute session, needing something to fidget with. 'I suppose, I always assume I'm in trouble, and I'm at the bottom of the pile. Of course, it would be too good to be true to be rated outstanding. It's like I set myself up to fail before I've even started' I reflect, sadly. She leans back into the cosiness of the couch as she sits opposite me, as I ramble on incoherently as I recount my tale. 'I wonder if you put yourself there,' she says quietly.

She might have a point there. It was merely six days ago when I was scheduled my turn for the teaching observation of the term. I was the last one to be done, and as the event neared, I found myself becoming increasingly anxious. This was, no doubt, due to the fact that in the days preceding I still hadn't got a clue what I was actually going to do. It had to be maths, and, while I'm not rubbish at it by any means, it's just not a favourite subject of mine. The irony is, I'm the daughter of an accountant, somebody who lives and breathes for numbers. After many days of procrastinating, and then days of trying to locate and squirrel away the textbooks that Bebe Duke has been using, and yet refusing to let me have, I began the task of getting myself together. I like to sail close to the wind, so predictably, I left it until the day before, during my PPA (Planning, Preparation and Assessment) time to get everything prepped and ready to go for the next morning. Why change the habit of a lifetime?

It took me two whole hours. Two hours of thumbing through the textbooks, skim reading to extract the necessary information, and fumbling through reams of plans that Bebe Duke produces every week yet fail to tell me anything that the book hasn't already told me. I've only taught under-sevens for the last ten years, is there really anything different that is pertinent information? I've decided to carry on with our work on subtraction. The pattern that permeates through all of the maths schemes that we've used over the years is broadly similar; a week on addition, a week on subtraction, a week on sharing etc, and then repeat every term or so. It doesn't really work that well in reality, for they need many weeks of consolidation for it to really be mastered. Only the curriculum doesn't allow for that.

More recently there's been a shift in thinking, and the fashion for the older children is to go back to 'blocking,' whereby topics are taught for several weeks at a time to ensure the new buzzword has been met; 'mastery.' It sounds like something to do with *Harry Potter* doesn't it? These phrases are forever being bandied around like they've discovered the magic elixir of life, and it drives me nuts.

I was surprised how long it took me to prepare. Granted, I had to make thirty ten-frames to aid with my subtraction lesson, but I figured we could use them again so my efforts wouldn't be completely in vain. (Ten frames, just in case you were wondering, is just a fancy word for a ten-square grid that we can use to show addition and subtraction methods). But there's just so much more. The visual stimulus for the teaching part of the lesson. A presentation with pictures and questions for me to talk about as we work together on the carpet. Then it's the sheet of subtraction calculations needed for them to complete their group work, plus an extension task for the bright ones. I also needed something to support the one child who is working well below the level of his peers, but whom I still have to include in the main teaching lesson. Normally he would just work through his own programme, but today I will have to try to make the lesson achievable for him, which is rather tricky.

And when Wednesday at 10:45am finally rolled around, I knew all the gods up there had conspired against me, and things were not going to go to plan. For starters, it had been raining continuously all morning, which means no going outside, nowhere to go to let off steam, and no playtime. Instead, they had to settle for another episode of '*Old Bear*' on YouTube, and a little wriggle about in their carpet spaces. I slunk off already feeling rattled, and grabbed a cup of tea to hold while I paced up and down in the office. Have I prepped the powerpoint? Have I photocopied enough sheets? Have I got the extension task ready for the ones that'll finish in ninety-seconds flat? Did I give Mrs Wright and Mrs Beale the heads up so they know what to do? I know the answer is yes to every question, but my mind has gone into overdrive as my pulse rate rises to eighty beats per minute.

The Big Guns is making small talk by the kettle, and when that bloody bell shrieks and signals the end of 'playtime,' I decide to beg for mercy. 'I just need a few minutes to let them have a bit of a move about' I tell her, knowing that the last thing they need is to go straight into the blasted learning after a no-play playtime. 'Oh, of course, no problem' she smiles, giving me an extra five minutes to meet both our needs. Theirs to burn off some energy, and me some time to calm my nerves and shaking hands.

Mrs Wright is back to the classroom before I am. Normally she resists the urge return on time, as do all of the TA's in the staffroom. God, when I used to sit there every break time, so did I. How dare that inconvenient bell disturb our all too short conversations? But today she knows we're under pressure, and she will do her absolute best to help me in whichever way she can. She's my right-hand man, and I know she wants me to relax and do what we both do so well every day behind closed doors. As the children put away their water bottles and apple cores are flung idly in the general direction of the bin, Mrs Wright chivvies them back to the carpet while I put a song on. By song, I mean a guided dance tutorial from the free program I subscribed to earlier in the year.

It's full of such delights as 'The Chicken Dance' led by dear old Maximo, the Gumby-esque latin dancer who leads them through the dance. His other favourites are also notably awful too, with 'The Macarena' and 'The Electric Slide.' They love it though and I'd be lying if I said there wasn't a tiny part of me that enjoys it too. Mrs Wright and I always join in with them, as it really does lighten the mood and it's good to be active and share a bit of fun with them to break up the monotony. Today I've chosen another favourite of theirs. As the beat picks up, and they quieten in response, my eyes glance nervously towards the open doorway, trying to catch a glimpse of the Big Guns when she arrives. The children dance about, copying the dance moves by the lively crew, blissfully unaware that anything untoward is about to happen. Just as they should be. They should never have to feel the way I do right now, and should feel that this day, this lesson is no different to any other.

But it is for me, because they're allowed to observe every teacher once a term, just to check we've still got it I suppose. The NUT (National Union of Teachers) has very clear directives on this. So in theory, we've only got to suffer this three times a year and unless there's any glaring holes in your knowledge and the ability to transmit this effectively to your charges, then you're all good. But if you don't get it right, then there's a good chance you'll be given a one-way ticket to Observation City, where all manner of scrutiny may be unwittingly bestowed upon you, whether you like it or not.

Just as the song finishes, and the children are breathless with enthusiasm, the Big Guns appears and pulls up one of our tiny wooden chairs and seats herself at the back of the room. Shit. Time to get this show on the road. Somehow, I remember I already had the foresight to get them to collect the whiteboards and pens (instruments of torture) from their drawers earlier, to eliminate World War Three and the resulting casualties, and place them in their carpet spaces ready for the lesson. Now this doesn't remotely guarantee that it'll be a peaceful start to the lesson, but observations are all about damage control, and this is a prime example.

'Ok, pens and boards down everybody' I call gently across the classroom, as the noise begins to die down, and Mrs Wright pulls up her wheely chair next to the table, waiting for me to send her new best friends over to her. 'George, sit up nicely. Matthew, get a tissue! Herb, leave your shoes alone please' I instruct, as while it is highly important to have complete focus when you're teaching, the powers that be, and Ofsted, are also big on low-level disruption and the impact on 'the learning'. 'Right, have a little look at my Smartboard' I ask them, bringing my chair around my desk to sit nearer to them. 'What do you think we're learning about today?' I ask. My first question (open-ended of course) tossed out to them, I give them a moment to talk with their talk partner (the child sat next to them) to discuss what they think we'll be doing. It's actually written up there for them (the bloody 'LO- learning objective,' and a little subtraction sentence), so figuring out the puzzle shouldn't be that tricky. Hands fly up in the air, and the chorus of 'ooh, ooh!' begins. It's looking good, they're in to it, and I begin to relax a little. Now, my eyes flit around the room scanning quickly the sea of hands raised in the air. I need to pick a smart child to answer.

There's a reason for this; pick someone who you know is ninety-nine percent likely to have both understood what you asked and can explain it, and you're quids in. Pick someone who hasn't got a Scooby-Doo, and who when asked to explain will go off on a completely different tangent, and you're stuffed. The observer will likely scribble in their running commentary something such as 'pupil was confused and did not understand what was being asked' = no learning. The whole class teaching part of the session went great, and as we split up into groups to work with them, it was looking good. At this time of the year, when they've barely settled in, we only work with three groups as we have three adults, and the other two groups are given an activity which they should be able to do by themselves. So in a nutshell, there's independent learning as well as taught sessions.

As we settled in to the task, ten frames laid out and little plastic bears being put in each square for counting, things were looking good. Mrs Wright and Mrs Beale are in full flow, as they model how to use the frames to subtract a number. The bright ones who have already mastered this are onto the formal methods- completing subtraction sums set out in the usual format. But one group threaten to ruin the whole show.

As is the fashion for outdoor learning, I chose to put one group outside under the shelter as it was raining, with the task of writing their numbers in chalk on the dry part of the asphalt. It's all very reception-y, but truly this is what they should be doing in the early days of Year One, and God knows half of them couldn't orient their numbers correctly if their lives depended on it. I look up from my group to cast my eyes through the window to make sure they're on task, only to find George and Eric having a game of chase. As I abandon my group to intervene and remind them what they are supposed to be doing, I warn the boys that they need to do what they've been asked. Back with my group at the table, I'm quickly drawn into their struggles, and unsurprisingly I forget to check on the group outside. The Big Guns is watching though, and she's scribbling away furiously on her little clipboard, noting down that George, Eric, and to my surprise, the whole entire group except for Vanya, have spent their time chalking all over the coloured metal posts that hold the shelter up. Good grief.

It's all over, curtains for me. This time it's Mrs Wright who deals with it, striding outside and demanding they all come in. She shows incredible restraint as she quietly reads them the riot act, before sitting them all down at the front of the room by our chairs, leaving Gracie-Lou sobbing and Vanya now alone outside, the sole survivor of the numerical and chalky disaster. Suffice to say, when the verdict's in and I have my de-brief with the Big Guns and Liz Dawson at the end of the day, that had this been a real lesson for Ofsted, then I'd be failed. Jesus. And the reason? Because of the triangle group who decided to muck about with chalks in typical five year-old fashion and thus no learning was achieved. Words fail me. I begin to get very angry and defensive, and they try to soothe and placate my increasing temper, as they tell me how wonderful everything else is.

It takes me the rest of the week to stop going over it again and again in my mind. The whole process is a farce. If we hadn't been observed, and the pressure was off, I would have continued as normal, and the two groups left to work independently (which doesn't work so early on in the year) would have been allowed simply to choose, thus allowing us to teach the remaining groups more effectively and free of disruption, and then swap so that everybody would have completed the activity. I fight my corner, but I'm encouraged to just take it on the chin and let it go, the next one will be better. Meanwhile it's officially recorded as 'unsatisfactory' I'm sure.

Time. There's simply never enough of it, not with all of the expectations that have been foisted upon us. This thing called learning, and school life, is no longer a gentle wander through the years, taking delight in the small things and stopping, quite literally, to smell the proverbial roses.

There's no conkers on the nature table to be admired and fondled by tiny hands, no picture from home to be held up for all to congratulate the artist, and no time to talk about the new baby that's arrived at home, or the gymnastics lesson last night, nor the playdate with a friend in the class. No, we'll have none of that. There's LEARNING to be done, didn't you know? We would be penalised if they saw us in the morning. Thrown under a bus more like. If they saw. If they saw how we have the audacity to welcome tiny children to our collective home for the day. If they saw us deign to sit in chairs and talk to them about the weather, the funny thing that my dog did last night, or Mrs Wright's son's broken arm, rugby-related misdemeanour that rendered them both in A and E for hours last night.

If they saw us share a joke, talk about what we might like to do today, and how we are feeling. And heaven forbid that we start the day with some fun. A song, a bit of brain gym to get the brain moving. We join in with them, we dance, we laugh. How very dare we? For don't we know, THIS IS LEARNING TIME! What they want to see, what makes their pulses race and hearts skip a beat, their faces light up in great delight, is if we scratch the formalities, ditch the social graces and instead, as soon as they walk through the door, bark a command for them to retrieve their little whiteboard and magic marker from their drawer and begin to write their number bonds to ten or write a sentence. Before they've even had a moment to reacquaint themselves with us or their friends, or indeed this place called school. These are the next generation, your poor little children.

16

Doing time

Taken from an excerpt of one of our weekly newsletters. 'Each half-term as most of you know we issue a gold certificate to those pupils with 100% attendance. As you can see for the last five years there has been an improving figure for the same half-term.'

Uh, hold up. Just a moment. Let me see if I've understood this correctly- you're going to reward children for not getting sick and being unable to come to school with a half-termly piece of paper to take pride of place on the fridge at home for all to see? Woah, woah, woah! The Big Guns continues in her letter. 'The Government's expectation is that pupils will be at school 100% of the time.' Oh well then, if the government says that why then we must of course trust that they know best! What nonsense!

I do get it, I really do, that to do well at school and be pleasant and productive members of society, children must have attended school consistently throughout their school years. But where once the interpretation was reasonable, and a common-sense approach was adopted, now the pendulum has swung a hundred and eighty degrees in the opposite direction.

What complete rubbish. I have seen firsthand how ridiculously pedantic and unreasonable 'government targets' have pervaded our once happy, child-centred environment.

Attendance is rigorously monitored via the register system. There's a whole host of scrambled and irrelevant letters that are used to mark the box when a child is absent.

When we take the register we leave each box blank unless they aren't here, and fill in a capital letter A for absent. When the register is returned to us to call in the afternoon session, this letter is likely to have been changed by one of the office ladies after further and scrupulous investigation, i.e. cold calling the parents to find out just where child X is. The weekly newsletter makes our expectations of attendance very clear. 'Attendance of 95% is satisfactory and below 90% is deemed to be persistently absent. We know that there are times where some children have operations, have chicken pox etc. but this is all recorded clearly on our system. Please remember that it is highly likely that those booking holidays during term time will face a fine. Please speak directly to Mrs Big Guns if there is an exceptional reason why your child needs to be absent from school during term time.'

Now I happen to think that the Big Guns has actually put this as kindly as she could have, given her own pressure from the county to ensure our collective attendance remains well above the target. But when you stop and think about it, hasn't it just gotten utterly ridiculous? Let's take holidays for example. Twenty-five odd years ago, I never ever saw the end of any school year, as my parents always booked flights to our house in France around the 15th July, before the extortionate flight prices increased. Year after year I would be 'that' kid that nicked off early, transported to southern France where my sisters and I would spend the majority of the next six weeks. Back then, it's my understanding that you were entitled to fourteen days, i.e. two school weeks holiday at any time during the school year and nobody batted an eyelid.

And even now as a teacher, nothing winds me up more than reading in the media that almost every county fines parents who breach the new rules of no holidays at all during term time. Once again, it's a failure of the system, which as per usual, perceives academic success to be the be all and end all of life, when actually, it is extremely healthy for a happy life to spend time away from the constraints of work and school. Not to mention the benefits that will be reaped by exploring another city or country. It's not even that really. The joy that comes from just being somewhere new, without making it all about educational discovery.

Given the mental health crisis we're now facing, why haven't the rule makers taken heed of the ghastly figures, and made it mandatory for every child to have fourteen days off school per year, whether they choose to go on holiday or just stay at home? It's not like their career's going to suffer because of it, is it? As a teacher, I'm for it. Which I suppose is surprising, but I know that my family didn't encourage us to take days off at the drop of a hat, we simply took off a few days at the end of the year when I can tell you honestly that very little actually happens!

It's healthy to take a break and not get all caught up in work and school. We're all humans, not robots, and we're being encouraged to soldier on regardless of how we might be feeling, thus breeding a generation of unhappy, anxious and depressed adults. Mrs Wright had the balls to say what she was thinking to one extremely anxious parent we had a few years back, whose daughter was a bundle of nerves at age seven. She wanted to be first to do everything, but when she couldn't do the work she became almost hysterical. At breaking point, and needing to impress upon her mother how her own anxiety was projecting on to her daughter, Mrs Wright simply said cheerfully 'look, if you carry on like this, she'll be on Prozac by the time she's doing her GCSE's.' I held my breath, fearing a backlash, but she took it on board and really tried to work with us to decrease the little girl's anxiety and improve her self-esteem.

The other issue to do with rewarding attendance, particularly in the early years at school, is that they don't really understand what it means. Every term the children who have attended school every day receive a certificate to take home, that we as the class teachers are given to hand out. And it's hard not to do it in front of them all. While those who get one are delighted, the others are confused as to why they didn't get one. And it's simply because they had a day off sick, something which they have no control over, which is hard for the five year-old brain to make sense of.

One day when I gave them out, tiny Jacob came up to me in my chair, and very sombrely questioned why he hadn't received one. Immediately I agreed with him, and thought I was sure that he'd been here every single day too. Only then I remembered. 'Oh Jacob. Do you remember you went home sick after lunch that day? Well that's why you didn't get one poppet,' I explained. He couldn't help feeling spewy and vomiting in the lunch hall one day, meaning he missed the afternoon mark in the register. He had zero control over that, and I just think that it praises those children who are fortunate enough to remain well all year, and sends the wrong message to those who inevitably get sick once or twice.

17

Target schmarget

Every term it happens. It's the great decider of learning, the data. I hate it. We all collectively hate it. It's what makes us nervous, jittery, and deeply unsettled. Well at least for me anyway.

Over the years the powers that be, not just those at school but the so-called leaders at the county headquarters, have ramped up the importance of data with frightening gusto. When I first started, it was barely a conversation, something mumbled so meekly that it could easily be mistaken for a passing utterance. Something about checking they had met the expectations for the end of the school year, at this time known as the Early Learning Goals. (My first job was teaching in a reception class, which at the time was exactly where I had wanted and imagined myself to be. Never mind that I couldn't answer the question in my NQT (newly-qualified teacher) portfolio 'where do you see yourself in five years time?' Uh, married and having children and not going to work anymore? So much for that).

It wasn't a big deal. I knew them like the back of my hand, as by the time I started teaching in 2007, I'd already spent a few years getting to grips with the lingo both during my volunteering period pre-university, and also during my official training. But I also had another reason to know it so well back then; I was interested in it. It was something I cared about, something I found useful to know, and consequently it was something I felt that I could talk about with a reasonable amount of conviction and authority. Who around me could have given a toss about listening to me was another matter, but it was comforting to feel a sense of achievement, that I, at all of twenty-two years old, knew stuff. Like people older than I, adulting in the real world, they knew stuff. And now, so did I.

It was just so much easier back then. The most frightening part for me while recounting this tale, is that it was merely ten years ago, not thirty or even forty like some of my colleagues would remember. Everywhere you look now, in the media and in general, teaching is painted to be in dire straits. We are in the midst of a recruitment crisis, and have been for the last few years. That has been well documented in the media, but I suppose apart from the obvious downside such as lack of pay swiftly followed by a lack of respect from both pupils and parents alike, what has been less well understood is that we are in the throes of a retention crisis.

I am on track to be one of them, at least I thought I would be over the last few years. Teachers far and wide are leaving the profession in their droves. The number of trainees lasting more that two years in the job is pathetically and worryingly low. But they're the smart ones. They are the ones who've seen the light, realising that the hoops that they had to jump through just to get here simply weren't worth it. They likely went down the route believing like many of us did, and still do, that they can make a difference. And we can, in some ways. That they have the power to change children's lives, in a heady and exciting and entirely altruistic notion that would outweigh the less than desirable aspects of the job.

But while we all started with similarly idealistic views, the love of the children, our dedication to education and the desire to be in a job that you actually enjoy going to do every day, they quickly realised that the fantasy did not in many ways match the reality. I know people who quite honestly got through the three or sometimes four years of training, showed up for work and then within the first six weeks on the job, thought, sod this for a game of soldiers, I'm outta here. I can make about twice what I'm making here and I won't have to kill myself working sixty hours a week, I'm off to the bright lights of the city. And they've never looked back.

I was always clear and focused in my direction (once said direction had eventually been decided of course). I can't say that being a teacher was ever a lifelong dream of mine, far from it actually. I was always good with children, I'm very calm and responsible, and I suppose maybe it was inevitable that I'd find my way into a sort of semi-professional role that utilised these skills.

Growing up I wanted to be everything under the sun. I dreamed of being a whale trainer at SeaWorld after the film Free Willy, circa 1993 came out, when I was ten years old. At the time I loved to swim, I was a confident and strong swimmer whose love of gymnastics could be combined into a dazzling display of athleticism at the pool in France every summer, where my sisters and I would frolic for hours in the forty degree heat. I loved nothing better than to stand atop the curved shiny handles that held the pool steps, and back somersault myself into the water. How I never slipped and broke my neck I'll never know. So you can see how whale trainer was a natural choice. That combined with the fascination for an animal that both awed and terrified me in equal measure. Ah, the dreams of a mind not yet soured by the realities of life! Well, you probably worked out that I am not a whale trainer at SeaWorld, but I'll bet it would have been fun. I assume you've all seen the documentary, *Blackfish*?

But when I was around eleven years old, a golden window to the world opened to small children far and wide, in the form of US television shows. All of a sudden, with the introduction and increasing availability of Sky TV, there was a whole host of programmes that opened our eyes to a world beyond the small home counties town I called home. And my newly-awakened eyes honed in on *ER*, first transmitted at 10pm on Channel Four on a Thursday night. I fell head over heels with this particular series. It was iconic for its time, as Michael Crichton's previously rebuffed screenplay for a feature film was re-developed for television in the form of a one hour show every week, following the doctors and nursing folk in the emergency room of a hospital in a major American city.

It was exciting, fresh and totally unlike anything we had seen before. Until this point the best thing we had was BBC's *Casualty*, but it was embarrassingly tame in comparison to the gory sophistication and emotional rollercoaster of *ER*. Not to mention the likes of George Clooney in his early thirties as the maverick paediatrician that set pulses racing. I'd always been interested in medical things, but this took it to a new level. They used real medical terminology, hastily reeled off in the throes of a complex and bloody trauma scene, that now not only gave us a glimpse into the workings of a real emergency situation, but we, the viewers, had the medical terms that made us feel that if we were to be confronted with such misfortune as the characters, that it was almost certainly within our remit to cross clamp an aorta and swoop into save the patient, right?

So during my mid-teens, I was pretty sure that I wanted to be a doctor. Now this might seem a little ironic, given that if anybody even hints that they may need to throw up, I am at least a hundred feet away. Preferably with a pair of earmuffs covering my ears to muffle the unpleasant retching sounds and a hand firmly over my mouth. And to think I ended up working with small people who unfortunately are prone to vomiting unannounced on a fairly regular basis. This aversion to bodily fluids, although strangely enough not blood, threatened to call a halt to proceedings. It began to dawn on me that dealing with puke and other assorted orifice-type needs that are part and parcel of the job might not be an ideal fit for this delicate doily.

That, and at the same time, my friends and I were tasked with doing some research into the world of work, as part of the school's effort to prepare us to make informed choices when it came to selecting our GCSE options for the following year. We spent the required hours in the school library, poring over dusty textbooks and trawling the tool that was fast approaching the new dawn of information seeking; the internet, circa 1998.

Heck, the school probably still had a dial-up modem. I wonder if their internet cost a pound a minute, that my dad reeled off dictatorially as he was the sole user of the newly-established information superhighway that was deemed far to expensive for anyone but him to use. It used to link in with the main telephone wire in the house, so if he was using the internet, that meant that nobody could use the house phone and if you lifted the receiver, all you heard was the loud shh-ing sound and occasional dings of the bounce-back. We were like kids in a candy store the day he toddled off to work and left the family *Gateway 2000* computer still connected, only discovering this when he called to talk to my mum and found he couldn't get through. Cue frantic mobile phone calls and mum hurrying up the stairs having been ordered to disconnect the line lest BT get even more of our money for this seemingly overpriced privilege.

So it was through this period of intense research that it began to dawn on me that in addition to my aversion to most things bodily, my own math and science grades might not stack up to meet the course requirements. It marked the realisation that the dream just wasn't going to happen. At least not this dream. So with a wistful last look through the medical textbooks, I bade a sad farewell to my favoured career choice.

The GCSE and A-Level years were really a test of many things. Of patience, resilience, and eventually, for most of the sixth-form staff, their tolerance towards me. I was never there, I hated it. While school was still mandatory, there was no option but to deliver myself there dutifully every day and go through the motions. The motions, by the summer of 2000, yielded me a pretty decent array of GCSE grades, from an A* in Spanish, my favourite subject, as well as A's for English language and Literature (be reassured, dear readers) down to respectable C's in maths and science. Looking at those grades was enough to close firmly the door to medicine, lest I had been in any doubt as to my potential capabilities. So like most of my friends, who were also seemingly directionless as far as the world of work was concerned, we headed off to study the subjects we were best at, in the vain hope that they would lead us to the right path. Or maybe at least the on-ramp.

It was at this point, refreshed after what would always been known as the 'GCSE summer,' whereby apart from the nuisance of such things as 'exams,' we had all been effectively pissing about since the middle of May, I returned to the school-turned-sixth-form-college ready to try and follow the next expected route of getting my A-Levels. A few weeks in and I wasn't feeling it. I wished I had moved on, like many of my friends had, to the more adult sixth-form college in the next town. It had a good reputation, but I just couldn't seem to bring myself to strike out into the unfamiliar, a pattern that was only just beginning to make its move and render me stuck in the same position many years later. So I began to become disheartened and overwhelmed with college, and began to withdraw with increasing regularity. Where at first the free periods were a source of elation at not having to do very much, let alone go to the place, I began to transfer this to most of my other lessons. It reached a point before Christmas where I was hardly there at all, but my family were mercifully far too busy to take much notice.

It was a particularly stressful time, looking back, and actually, even as I write this, I am flooded with what Karen, my therapist likes to call 'uncomfortable feelings.' The kind of feelings that just tell you you don't want to be going here, that you don't want to remember this. My mum developed breast cancer in the summer of ninety-nine, aged forty-one, when I was fifteen, and my sisters were thirteen and eight. Looking back I wonder how we got through it, as in a way, life and school simply carried on as normal. Now, in my own classroom, there's no way that a child would be going through such difficulty at home without it being flagged to a bazillion different staff, teachers, home school link workers and emotional literacy specialists. Or even CAMHS (Child and Adolescent Mental Health Service) if need be. But this just wasn't the done thing at the time, and we weren't really the type of children that went looking for sympathy from others, preferring to confide now and again in each other and our close friends. We were largely left to cope alone, and to essentially just get on with it, which we did, although I know that it just wasn't a happy time for anybody.

So by the first winter of sixth-form, we were slowly beginning to move past this unfortunate phase in our family history, save for one thing. My poor mum, relieved that after a mastectomy, six gruelling rounds of chemo and six weeks of radiation she had been given the all-clear, had done her research and started to wonder if there was any more that she could do. After consultation with her specialist she decided she would have a preventative mastectomy and also have her ovaries removed at the same time (the type of cancer was found to be particularly receptive to oestrogen).

We all hated when my mum went into hospital. And who wouldn't? Our sole parent was then a dad that ended up either working late and leaving us to get on with it, or working from home and forgetting to feed us or keep the house running. All of this added to the uneasiness experienced by five people all struggling to cope with this in their own way. I learned pretty quickly around that time that knowledge is power, and if my mum wasn't going to be around to take care of the house and chores and keep everything running smoothly then I was going to step up. She showed me how to use the washing machine and the dishwasher, something my dad still doesn't know how to operate, so that we would have clean pj's and school uniforms and dishes. Seemingly these simple tasks have a big impact on whether your life is normal or not, and we desperately wanted to feel that ours was. Maybe it was about being in control, that while we had experienced huge emotional upheaval over which none of us had any control over, maybe having some over the little things might help us to feel less unanchored and dizzyingly out of kilter.

During that summer, three weeks before school broke up, I quickly became the one who stepped up to the plate to keep the house running. The washing machine was a piece of cake, and the comfort brought by that basket of lovely clean washing still reeking of detergent was enough to help us feel normal. Or at least it did for me anyway. My dad's reluctance to get involved in many of the things that my mum usually did was probably his way of coping, so while I tackled the laundry, my sister began to cook and also helped with looking after our little sister. We were very lucky to have our Gramps just down the road, so in a sense we weren't left totally alone to manage the chaos. He was an amazing and comforting presence for all of us, and we appreciated him even more so during this time.

So on the day my mum went to have her second surgery, one dark and rainy day in December, the bitch of a psychology tutor, no doubt exasperated by my months of sporadic attendance, had reached the end of her tether and chose that particular day to deliver her final blow. 'Can I let you have it?' she blazed. Well, she exploded in a fit of absolute fury, no doubt sick to the back teeth to my part-time approach to learning. Too upset to argue, I wept, tears rolling down my cheeks as I just sat there and took it all in. No energy left to explain, no fire in the belly to argue. In that moment, I was just a seventeen year-old girl whose mum was just about to have another major operation and nobody knew or cared. I went home and told nobody. I put on a brave face for my mum and waved her off to the hospital, yet as soon as the front door shut, I slumped to the floor and allowed myself to sob.

I suppose given all I've just recounted as per my own experience of school life, one might wonder why in God's name I ever wanted to become a bloody teacher in the first place! Nobody had imagined this path less than me. After my mum recovered post-surgery, and life began to return to some sort of normal, a little ray of hope appeared in the most unlikely form. All lower sixth-form students were handed a multitude of forms to complete, in readiness for organising some work experience. As I mentioned before, none of us had a bloody clue about what the hell we wanted to do for all of our working lives, so trying to find somewhere to go that would be of benefit to us proved somewhat tricky. As my eyes scanned the pages of suggestions and organisations that would be willing to do show-and-tell all week with sixth-form students, I saw the words 'volunteer in a primary school.'

Immediately I knew this was where I needed to be. At least I thought I might vaguely enjoy it, and hoped to be able to go to my own old infant school just around the corner. As I filled in the form, I realised that instead of a week's block of experience, this would in fact be one day per week for the rest of the academic year. Now the reason that any of us had to participate in this in the first place was simply to ensure that we had some extra-curricular activities to add to our UCAS form that needed to be submitted in preparation for entrance to university the following year.

When the administration had duly finished organising the opportunity, and that first Friday morning rolled around, I toddled off to the school not having a clue what to expect. Nervous but also excited as to what it might be like, I was welcomed by one of my old teacher's, now the headteacher, who greeted me warmly and remarked how lovely it was to have ex-pupils back in to help. I was placed in the reception classes, and now I'm a teacher myself, I know exactly why. As a reception teacher, it's a brave and foolish person who turns down the offer of free and unpaid help, even if it's just for one morning a week. Lord knows I never did.

As I made my way over to the brand new building, entitled 'The Lodge' in reference to its log cabin-esque design, I had no idea that I was inadvertently, for better or worse, sealing my fate at an as yet unchosen career path. As I crouched alongside tables, joining in conversations with a whole host of new little faces, I felt myself becoming more and more comfortable. I questioned them about what they were doing, helped them to do puzzles, helped put jumpers on and off and dispensed milk and fruit, all the while trying to take in all of this new information, this new world it seemed. Three hours passed quickly, and after thanking me for my help, I walked home to decompress and make sense of my morning there. When my mum asked me how I'd got on, I was pleased to report back that I'd really enjoyed it. And here's the defining moment.

Just like in that episode of *Friends*, where they're in a flashback scene and Monica's trying to impress a less than interested Chandler with her culinary prowess, and he says to her 'oh, you should be a chef' and she replies 'ok!' this is how I ended up as a primary school teacher. After hearing about how much I enjoyed it, and knowing already that I was good with small children, my mum simply said 'you should be a teacher' to which I replied 'ok!'

And that was that. For the rest of the year, that school and those children were my refuge and my saviour. Whenever I had free periods, I would lend an hour here and there, all the while gaining a better understanding of how to teach the small people. In fact, it's a wonder I passed my A-Levels at all, given that I was rarely in college, a fact that came back to bite me in the tush when it was time for my tutor to write my UCAS reference. Now a hundred percent sure that I wanted to be a primary teacher, I had researched where I wanted to go and was ready to apply just like everybody else, save for one small thing. The resident witch, the leader of the sixth-form college, staged a protest and point-blank refused.

In fact, she felt so strongly that I was so undeserving of even applying, that she wrote a long letter to my parents about why she stood by that decision. I'm pretty sure I was the only person that ever read it, having intercepted it the moment the postman laid it at our door. I was boiling with fury inside, but I played it cool, and simply looked for another referee. Luckily one of my old teachers at the infant school was happy to recommend me, and wrote a lovely reference which told of my commitment to the cause, and I was promptly offered a place at my chosen institution.

But that letter. That letter made my blood boil. It was full of harping and criticism of my non-attendance, and even held the phrase 'quite why Betsy would want to be a teacher is beyond me, given that she clearly has no regard for the profession.'

Words of a woman scorned, that's for sure. When I qualified, four long years later, and held that white and purple certificate in my hands, bearing the words 'Qualified Teacher Status- QTS' I was both happy and relieved in equal measure. Perhaps deep down even I hadn't really believed that I could make it, but I had, and not only that, I'd done really well. I got a 2:1 for my degree, with a brilliant dissertation on 'The Summer-Born Effect' and a excellent result for my PGCE the following year. Four years of essays, teaching practice and a whole lot of studying had finally paid off. But what I really wanted to do, what I had to stop myself from doing lest I hurt my future career prospects, was go right back to that teacher, shove that certificate under her nose and say 'put that in your pipe and smoke it.'

But I didn't. I did dig out that letter though from the depths of a box in my attic, read it once more, and then tear it into little pieces, erasing the horrible memories and closing that painful chapter of my life for good. I'd made it.

18

The trauma of testing

A huge problem with the whole learning process is that the joy is sucked out of it due to all of the testing and assessing the poor small people have to participate in. By and large, the lower down you are in the school, the less formal testing a child has to suffer, in theory.

But in reality, every school works on termly assessments, in whatever form, to decide how the children are progressing and whether they, and in turn we, are meeting our targets. For us, this involves the trauma of formal papers in reading and maths, as well as spelling, punctuation and grammar (SPAG) that is the new buzzword from the government. Down in the trenches in Year One, our poor small people, having just graduated from reception, are now faced with their first ever formal test papers which need to be sat in the last couple of weeks before Christmas. Yes, those would be the weeks when we are in the midst of the chaos of producing and performing a Christmas play and we're all grey with tiredness and desperate for a rest. No chance. So it falls to us to try to find the time to do them in between the torturous rehearsals and group singing practices. And then there's the next dilemma. There's no way in hell that they can sit them all at the same time, and they're simply too difficult.

Trying to get thirty small children all sat down formally at desks is a no-no, as first off, we only have enough tables for half the class, purposefully set up this way to allow for oodles of play and minimal formal instruction. So these papers will be done in their groups of six with either Mrs Wright or I working alongside them, while the others play in the same room. So you can see that it's not going to be particularly quiet either.

But we'll get through it somehow. I want to keep it low-key, and when I show them the little booklets as a class before we begin, I always refer to them as 'quizzes.' I believe that it's important to show and explain this new and unfamiliar way of working, and reassure them that it's just a chance for them to show us how clever they are, and for us to know what we need to teach them next. I doubt very much that they buy it, but at least I've tried to spin it and paint a test in its most positive light, if that's even possible.

We model how to fill in the little booklets, uttering phrases like 'this is the little box where you can write your answer' and 'don't worry if you make a mistake, just put a line through it and write it underneath.' Mrs Wright always sits quietly at the back in her wheely chair, and backs up whatever I've said, reminding them that it's no big deal. Then there's the joint part, the question we toss out that they know the answer to already. 'Why isn't it a good idea to look at the person next to you's work?' Hands fly up in readiness to answer, before Hugo shouts out, bypassing all the rules. 'Cos' they might have got it wrong' he declares loudly in his broad Scottish accent. 'That's right' I confirm, before I give them a little pep talk about trusting in their own abilities. 'You're all very clever. I know that you can do this, and if you need some help, Mrs Wright and I are here to help you, so don't worry.' Mrs Wright rises from her chair as she comes over to collect the papers ready to pass them out and put them on their tables.

'And children' she chirps cheerfully 'just remember, it won't affect your career, the world will still keep turning' she says with a smile, as they listen keenly. 'Just remember my little rhyme.' At this, they all break into smiles before Jonty and Eric begin to lead the rousing rendition of a little gem Mrs Wright passed down from her own schooling, the others joining in swiftly. 'Good, better, best. Never let it rest. Until your good is better and your better is your BEST!' The word best is nearly always shouted excitedly, as they take great delight in reciting what has become one of our favourite class mantras.

As we grab the first twelve to come and work with us, the others are delighted that it's not their turn, and race off to choose their activity. Mrs Wright takes her charges to one table, I to the other, as we instruct them to write their name in the little box on the front and not do anything else! As I look around the classroom, I can see the train track being assembled, the dressing-up clothes being put on, and the pencil cases and paper being collected ready for drawing. I'm hoping that after five minutes or so of 'fuffling' and locating a pencil that actually works, that they'll settle down enough for us to be able to help administer these tests.

In the autumn term, the first paper is the reading comprehension. It's basically a story, carefully separated into manageable chunks, one on each page, with one or two questions on each. Never underestimate the fact that they've never done anything at all like this before, as we have to show them how to tick a box or circle a word to show their answer. Easy right? Wrong. And don't even get me started on the other way of answering a question, this is possibly my favourite one. 'Draw a line to match each word to the correct answer.' No! They find this one so difficult! While a few manage it with ease, the majority struggle. We've had lines all over the page, swirling around the entire page, all over the questions etc. It's really quite difficult for them, and given that they'll have to tackle these with frightening regularity over the next eleven years, it's important not to put the fear of God in them. After all, it's only a pointless paper exercise.

The most interesting thing about the reading comprehension paper, is that they don't actually have to read the text themselves. I know, it's a bit of a strange one. I didn't realise this initially, as traditionally, the whole bloody point is to read the story and answer the questions. It seems reasonable to question how accurate the whole assessment would actually be if we read the whole thing to them, but after checking with the Big Guns, I realised it could work. So page by page, Mrs Wright or I read the story, then the question, and then it was up to them to find the correct answer and record it in whichever way they were asked.

We got off to a reasonable start, but honestly, it didn't take long for the train to derail. Within a few minutes and by only the second page of the quiz, tears began to fall, yet miraculously not my own. I looked up from my own group to notice Darla, her face red and streaked with tears, with Mrs Wright right next to her, her arm around her reassuringly. 'Now come on my little treasure, it's alright, let's not get upset about any of it' chirps Mrs Wright, as she rubs her hand gently over Darla's tiny one, as Darla dabs her eyes with the other. 'Come on, I'll help you, won't I Darla' she continues, before raising her head to look at me. 'Exhibit A, Miss Graham' she says dryly, as I take in the scene. Shit. This is exactly what I wanted to avoid, and now poor Darla's grief-stricken that she can't do it. She's a bright little cookie, and actually one of the most capable children in the class, despite being one of the youngest, but she's lost her confidence, which is to be expected when faced with something so extraordinarily difficult. At least in her eyes. It's December, and she only turned five at the end of July.

I need to try and turn this around before they all go down, after all, there's nothing so contagious than tears and lack of self-belief. Armed with the knowledge that we can in fact read for them, I resolve to try and salvage what I can of the traumatic experience, promising house points and praising their efforts thus far. Darla's feeling a little better now Mrs Wright's moved her peg up the ladder to pink, and she's approaching the quiz with renewed optimism. As our groups make it through most of the paper and return to their self-chosen play activities, Mrs Wright struggles to organise and mark all of the papers. Even just these few booklets threaten to swamp what's left of the space on my desk, as we grab a handful each and try to mark them while we hear somebody read.

Because they need such a lot of support, the process of getting thirty people to complete three sets of papers takes a hell of a long time. Days and days of tears and lost confidence is enough to dampen our spirits, but we have no choice but to press on if we're going to meet the data deadline that's looming at the end of term. It's always slightly frustrating when they don't complete every question, even though we've played down their importance and reminded them to move on if they can't do it.

On Friday afternoon, when I'm marking the last few, Mrs Wright seeing to the last few children who we somehow haven't managed to read with the whole entire week, I happen across Julian's paper. He's a bright boy, coming from a highly intellectual family with a strong work ethic, but like Darla, he often doubts his abilities and puts himself down. In fact, it's begun to form a pattern over the year, as whenever I ask them all to think of something that week that they're proud of, he smiles in embarrassment, and tells me he can't think of anything. Similarly, if he doesn't grasp something straight away, like when he found it hard to split numbers in to tens and ones, he was quick to get upset and worry about being told off at home. I call him over to me, and ask him if he can have another go at the question that he's missed. He smiles, keen to please me, but I know he's left it blank for a reason. He, like several others I call back, returns to the table while chaos reigns around us as Mrs Wright shepherds the rest of them in getting their things ready to go home.

As is life in an infant classroom, I'm distracted and forget about those still working, and begin to tend to George who predictably can't locate any of his belongings and Natalie who's attempting to pin me down to exactly when she can sing her song in front of an unsuspecting audience - us. As I scan the room for George's shoes and book bag, I look and see Mrs Wright with a rubber in her hand, leaning over Julian who's got his head in his hands, tears silently rolling down his cheeks. As I watch, Mrs Wright puts her arm around him, picks up the paper and sends him to get his things to go home. She hands the paper to back to me. 'I've sent him to get ready for home. We're not having tears and stress over this in Year One

Miss Graham, it's ridiculous. He's getting himself all worked up over it, it's not right' she says strongly, making her feelings on the subject known. She's one hundred percent right, and I know it. He's a worrier already at six, and by doing what I'm supposed to do as his teacher, i.e. executing these blasted tests, I'm unwillingly contributing to the mental health epidemic we're now facing among our children and young people.

It sucks. I want to grab all of those papers and burn the whole bloody lot of them. It's stressful (for all of us), it's largely unhelpful, and I just don't believe we should test our children so formally so young. But once again I'm stuck in the middle. Of caring about the children and trying to nurture them and go against the grain, yet having to do precisely the things that I don't think are good for them.

The cycle simply continues, because no one person can upset a system that is so entrenched. A few years back, I had the pleasure of teaching one of the most delightful of little girls, fostered by a lovely couple a few months previously. She was only six years old, but had already had a really terrible start to life, requiring her to be placed in foster care. As a 'Looked After Child' she was given higher priority to be accepted into our school, and the school received extra funding because of her status. She was diagnosed with some learning difficulties as a consequence, but had huge potential we felt. My teaching assistant at the time worked exceptionally hard with her, reading with her daily as well as doing lots of individual and small-group work with her to help her to make progress. She responded so well, and it was one of the highlights of the year for both of us to see her go from stumbling over almost every word to becoming a fluent reader with excellent comprehension skills and jumping quickly through the reading level bands. We were so proud of her and her delight in her achievements was key to rebuilding her self-esteem and self-worth.

Despite her brilliant progress, there was always going to be a point where even our best just wasn't going to be good enough, at least in the eyes of the Big Guns and the rest of the SLT. When we had the termly data meeting at the beginning of April after Easter, I was swiftly brought back down to earth with a bump. The big question that the Big Guns will ask us around this time, is 'who's going to go beyond what's expected and achieve the highest level?' which at the time, was level three. The level three readers, writers and mathematicians are those children who are deemed to be achieving far beyond the expected standard, and whose academic prowess will paint the school in its most positive light, both for prospective parents and Ofsted. The problem is, sometimes there just isn't anybody! And for the leadership team, that's just not ok.

The children's achievements are tracked on the computer system from reception, so their future academic success is based largely on what they achieved in their first year at school. As I mentioned before about the horror of *Performance Related Pay*, the results will purely be whatever their teachers thought that they could give them (as high a grade as possible) without arousing suspicion and thus heaping praise upon themselves from the higher-ups for teaching them so well! Only they didn't. They fiddle the data so that they look good, and then when we get them in Year One, it's too late to really question why Connor's been marked up to genius level when yet in reality he can barely read at all. So the point to this long-winded example, is that the data is screwed from the beginning, leaving the rest of us on the shop floor to try and work miracles by making sure that every child meets expected or above, regardless of whether there's a chance in hell of them making it or not or where they started from.

We were personally thrilled with all of the progress that Amelia was making, but it wasn't enough. Because she was a high priority, and already receiving lots of support in school, we assumed that this would continue. In part because it was highly necessary in ensuring that she caught up, and also because it had been explained and promised to her extremely supportive and grateful foster parents whom we met with regularly. Not to mention we received more funding for her specifically from the local authority. So it came as a nasty surprise for me when I was told to stop doing as much with her, and focus instead on those children in my class who were deemed to be at the weaker end of average. The reason being that she was never going to make the expected '2b' average-Joe standard, and there were others that would. And the only reason for this is purely to make our (the school's) end of Key Stage One data look good.

The more children in the cohort that meet the expected standard or above, the better we look on paper. I was stunned, and anger bubbled inside my chest yet one more time. Because it was wrong. How on earth could the boss sit there and tell me to leave one of the most vulnerable children behind, just to pretty up our numbers? How could I look her foster parents in the eye after we all, the Big Guns and the SENCo included, had sat in those meetings time and time again promising to do the utmost we could to help her? Livid didn't even begin to describe my TA and my feelings about it. We decided that we would simply try and continue as we had been which meant that Amelia would receive as much 1:1 support from my teaching assistant as she could, but I would have to work with the rest of the children alone much more often.

Later in the week I sat in my therapy session, reeling off this sorry tale to Karen. As a parent herself, I wondered what it might feel like to hear that this kind of thing happened on such a regular basis, probably in schools everywhere. As a parent, how would you feel if your child's teacher knew full well that they were bottom of the pile and struggled to keep up, and promised to do everything within their power to help them to catch up, knowing that never in a million years would anything happen? Well I'd be furious. Are we simply here only to look after the 'bright ones' and just let everybody else just drift through the year before tossing out a school report that shows they've achieved diddly squat? It's extremely frustrating, and my blood boils at the injustice and the unfairness of it.

It's down to money. We're running on a skeleton staff. We already know we've not got a glue stick or a pencil to our name, and we've got no time, money or people to actually deliver any of these wonderful intervention programs. Quite honestly, it's a joke, and a colossal failure of the system.

Last year, I found a similar issue when explaining our class's termly data to the Big Guns. When Megan got her second consecutive low score on her maths paper, it only confirmed what I'd suspected for a few months. That while she appeared on the carpet to have grasped the different maths concepts we'd been learning, when it came to individual or group work she was stuck.

But kids are clever, and she watched what others did and copied their work, which for a time went unnoticed. But once we've done the assessment papers quietly and under semi-exam style conditions, it only served to highlight where the difficulties lay. I wasn't concerned to the point that I worried that she had learning difficulties at all- her reading was good, as was her writing, but it was abundantly clear that she required some small group or individual work to go over the basics and identify problem areas.

The dilemma for me is what to put on the data program on the computer. If I put her down as expected, knowing she's at the very weaker end of it, then she won't trigger any concern and the Big Guns will assume that she's just ticking along nicely. Wrong. But if I put her as below average, then she might get the support she needs, but I'll be flagged up because the data won't look good and she'll drag it down. It sounds terrible to even write that, as it's all such a farce. But this is honestly the thought process.

Well, unless you're Bebe Duke or Stella Stuart and you just say that everyone's on track or en route to genius level, thus receiving kudos from the Big Guns and congratulating themselves on their supreme teaching abilities.

Not me. I decided that Megan needed maths support more than I needed to save face. I've always been of the opinion that honesty is the best policy, and to just say two fingers to the whole stupid and nonsensical process, so I filled in that little square with the below average label, and braced myself.

And sure enough, my termly data didn't look great, while Bebe Duke's of course looked like the FTSE 100 had trebled in value overnight. But I simply decided to weather the storm. After all, it wasn't like I hadn't weathered more storms than Florida during hurricane season, and I figured one more red flag couldn't hurt. But it worked, and Megan was soon included in the little maths program once a week with Mrs Wright and a few others in our class. Well, when she like every teaching assistant, tried their best to implement them whenever they weren't covering the class and putting out fires elsewhere.

With the best will in the world, the reality across the school is that 'interventions' rarely happen. There's not enough time, enough manpower, and not enough money to employ anybody else to actually deliver them. Whereas TA's used to be mostly class-based, now the expectation is that they support the teacher and work with the children for part of the day, and the afternoon is spent working with different groups across the school.

It's a little better higher up the school, but down in the trenches in Key Stage One, it's very hard to make it happen at all. With everything being done in-house, it's easy for the TA's to simply be too busy within the classroom to actually be able to leave in order to execute them. Put bluntly, we need them. We need them because we can't manage the child that's beating up his classmates, and we can't teach one group and leave anarchy to reign as we ignore the rest to work with six. Likewise when somebody wets themselves or has an accident, it's not really ideal to be all alone no matter how close to the office you are. It just doesn't work. So it's simply one more thing that unfortunately falls by the wayside. And it shouldn't.

We need to employ designated people that are additional to our fantastic support staff, in order to maximise productivity on all sides, and save teachers sanity in the process. What could be better? Except it'll never happen, there's no money. When we're already drowning in the red, it's a struggle to just stay afloat, let alone try and improve the outcomes for the pupils in our care.

Another huge factor in not being able to help the struggling children, is the slave labour being forced upon the teaching assistants. While a few over the years had somewhat willingly signed up to become what's known as a 'Higher Level Teaching Assistant,' or HLTA, many decided it was not for them, and that if they'd wanted to be afforded all the responsibilities of a teacher, they'd do it for more than a two pounds per hour raise. The HLTA's can legally be responsible for teaching classes whenever it's needed, and effectively assume the role of the teacher, sometimes minus the planning part of the teaching. But what it also means, is that they're the first port of call whenever a teacher is off sick, as let's be honest, they never call in a supply teacher as they couldn't afford to pay her. What could be better for a school in dire financial straits? Pull your support staff from class to cover teacher absence and we only have to pay them two quid more than we usually do? Where do we sign up!

As if that wasn't a huge strain, now that things have taken a further nosedive financially, it's the TA's themselves that are being pulled, leaving a whole hoard of quietly aggrieved TA's and a trail of pissed off and abandoned teachers in their wake. Mrs Wright is a prime candidate, being permanently cheerful and the possessor of a can-do attitude, and she's always being kidnapped to babysit a child that needs 1:1 support, or to help another TA to cover a class. In the school's view, two TA's maketh a teacher, although neither receive an penny extra at all for the donkey work. Poor Mrs Wright, there's no job that she's not been asked to oblige by the Big Guns, who's taken quite a shine to her. Well who wouldn't? She's covered for countless classes. She's the first port of call if I'm ever off sick, manned the office telephone in times of crisis, gone swimming every week with a class without complaint, and even schlepped a plant given as a gift for the reverend out to his car! There's no end to the woman's talents.

But enough is enough. The system is fractured and broken, and even though the loveliness of the children and the joy of teaching still largely outweighs the bad, surely we need to find some real, workable solutions that don't destroy the children's love of learning, and ones that don't contribute to the demise of morale and take advantage of the goodwill of the staff that will eventually run out? And one that doesn't involve the teachers having to endure the endless dilemma- fiddle the results so your ass isn't on the line, or tell the truth about their progress and risk the furore and threat to your continued employment that will inevitably follow. It's a tough one alright.

19

Conversations

'You'll have to be patient, I say gently, head down as I mark Ava's literacy book at my desk. I don't look up, but I just know the crowd has gathered as I begin to distinguish three different and yet familiar little voices. 'Oh, my mum says I have to be patient at home!' pipes up Jonty, more than happy to be included in our conversation. 'But what does patient mean?' asks Thibault, in his thick French accent that belies his dulcet tones. (This kid is the loudest in our class, and if you need someone to rally the troops and shout above everybody else, then he's your man).

Jonty loves to be in the know, and quickly starts to fill him in. I half-listen, pen in hand as I quickly highlight with a fuchsia highlighter pen the capital letters they have used correctly and the question marks they've remembered to use to finish their questions. It's bollocks, the lot of it, but I play the game. It's just this sort of ridiculously useless and tedious exercise that is like the proverbial ball and chain around my ankle, that takes a disproportionate amount of time relative to any of the actual teaching that goes on around here.

'Patient means that you have to wait for something. My mum says I've got to be patient when she's in the bathroom and she won't let me in' Jonty explains cheerfully. Thibault's brow unfurrows as he begins to make sense of Jonty's very clear explanation of this concept called patience. Meanwhile I ponder the suffering of poor Jonty's mum, not even granted thirty seconds of alone time in which to pee in private. 'Oh' he says, while Jonty jumps in again. 'My mum takes ages in the bathroom, does yours?' Thibault's vocal volume starts to rise as he becomes more animated, keen to engage and answer Jonty's question. 'My mum does that too! She spends a long time in there and she takes her phone in there with her.' 'She takes her phone in there?' enquires Jonty. 'My mum does that too!'

At this point I put down the green highlighter pen 'growing green' which marked off any of their spelling errors and lack of punctuation. They're five! Jesus Christ, life's too short for this. I look at the three of them, the two boys and Vanya, who's yet to contribute to their little discussion but listening intently and with interest. They're all clutching their yellow literacy books open to the double-page where their work is, against their chests, ready to fling them in my direction the minute I ask if they have finished. And I laugh a little.

Because I can well imagine poor Thibault's mum, desperate for some respite from her two little horrors, seeking the solitude that can only be provided from behind a locked door, no doubt the only one in the house. I wonder what she's up to on her phone? She's probably googling cocktail recipes and wishing it was happy hour, or maybe she's trawling Mumsnet, seeking sympathy from the other mothers who are equally exhausted and praying it's nearly bedtime. We'll never know.

Another dawn, another day. The bell has rung, and I've already braved the cold to make a thirty-second dash to the playground to greet my little line of small people and collect them in to start the day. I've become a bit lazy over the years, so I usually just gesticulate with my head to the child at the front of the line to follow me, while I, with arms firmly crossed against my chest, walk as fast as I can to the corner of the playground to oversee their delivery. They all want to talk to me at once, and I try so hard to listen, but I just want them to get inside!

Once I can be sure that the last person is moving in the right direction and that nobody has made a great escape, I send them to join the throngs of children from the other three classes in a sea of coats and hats, as they all try to fit through the one outside doorway. How we manage to get a hundred and twenty children processed through such a tiny space at the same time is beyond me. Particularly when you see the amount of garb every single child brings in with them on a daily basis. Sometimes you'd think they'd be going backpacking in the Himalayas for a month rather than spending six hours in a school in leafy suburbia. We're supposed to go through that door with them, but I don't. I always make sure they're heading through the doorway and then seize the opportunity to slip in through my own back door to avoid being rendered unconscious by walking past the boys toilets. Ugh. I gave up that long ago.

I make it to my cupboard on the opposite side of the classroom, the only real space in the room that's truly mine. Even my desk is a free-for-all, forever covered with things I didn't put there. My lukewarm cup of tea resides on the highest shelf next to my handbag, and while the first few little people breeze into the classroom, happily chatting away and go to put their water bottles away, Mrs Wright and I savour that precious fifteen to twenty seconds of time to speak before we are inevitably interrupted. If we're lucky we might get to talk about last night's telly, if not it'll just be the language of command, as I throw a mass of incoherent and vague instructions at her about what the plan is for the day and which is the most pressing of my misdemeanours to deal with first.

'Good morning my dear!' beams Mrs Wright as she sidles over to the cupboard, her face flushed with the freshness from the morning walk to work, hair billowing around her lovely face as she carries her sustenance to get her through the first hour- coffee. 'Morning, I can't put a good in front of that I'm afraid!' I chuckle. I can't even begin to tell her what's already kicked off in the thirty minutes that I arrived before her. I flick my eyes around the room, making a quick check that the children trickling in aren't killing each other on their way to the carpet, as I fumble in my handbag for my hairbrush. 'Hey, how was Fat Club last night?' I ask excitedly in anticipation. It's always a source of amusement on a Tuesday to hear the tales of how the ladies at Mrs Wright's local Slimming World group get on of a Monday night. She's done brilliantly, losing almost a stone since the start of the term. It must be because we've nixed the sherbet lemons, damn it.

We used to fall upon them around two-thirty in the afternoon, desperate to counteract the mountain of fatigue and desperation that threatened to overwhelm us. Now we're being good there's hardly a morsel of anything nice, just a few spotty bananas that are well past their sell-by date and some mouldy oranges that we stashed from the leftovers from the children's free fruit every day. Unsurprisingly uptake has been slow.

'Ooh, it was alright actually' breezes Mrs Wright with a grin. 'I lost two pounds. Clapped all the fatties who lost weight. I clapped so much I was waiting for someone to throw me a fish!' We both chuckle, only now out of the corner of my eye, I can see several children crowding around us, including Rebecca, who no doubt has some sort of ailment she wants to share with me. 'There were loads of new people last night. Well, it's January isn't it. I'm not kidding you, some of these women must be eighteen stone. One even gained eight pounds over Christmas!' 'Oh my goodness!' I squeak. 'How is that even possible? I mean, how can you gain eight pounds in two weeks?' I ask, rather dumbstruck at this unnerving prospect and equally terrified that it is actually possible. 'Oh' says Mrs Wright with a dismissive wave of her hand 'They've been on the Prosecco every night, they said so. A couple of bottles a night, then down to the kebab van next to the dump' explains Mrs Wright, as I listen, captivated and unable to suppress my laughter any longer. 'Jesus' I respond, utterly awestruck.

'Miss Graham' wails a little voice from below me. That's the end of our conversation then. I begin to tend to Rebecca, while Mrs Wright grabs another slurp of coffee and then wanders to the middle of the room before raising her hands in mid-air. 'Children, come and sit down on the carpet. The office will be open for business in a moment and we'll deal with all of your enquiries when we're ready!' 'Miss Graham, my leg hurts' Rebecca states with great seriousness, as she looks up at me intently. My face breaks out into a huge smile, as I know exactly where this is heading. 'Rebecca, yesterday we had everything! You said your cheek hurt when you poked it (to which Mrs Wright replied dryly, when reminded of this for the sixth time that day 'don't poke it then dear') your teeth hurt and then your leg hurt' I sigh in exasperation, as her face breaks into a sheepish smile at having been rumbled. I look down at her huge brown eyes, as she looks expectantly up at me, waiting for my response. 'Why don't you tell me which parts of you are well?' I suggest.

I think there's a cancer slowly seeping into and infiltrating the bodies here. We've lost the ability to care for each other. There's no longer a genuine desire to help anybody through the difficult periods of life that unfortunately come to us all, no willingness to help another person to rise up in the face of adversity. No, now all you get is an 'are you ok?' and a *Return to Work* form rammed in your box by the utterly useless and woefully inept business manager. She's the one in charge of the finances at school, and one look at her and you can see exactly why we're broke. Useless doesn't even cover it.

20

The snowball effect

Some days it's just relentless. The pressure seems all too much, and it all feels overwhelming. You see we've got a huge problem. Over the last few years, expectations - I truly loathe that very word- have just gotten absolutely ridiculous. It never used to be like this. Sometimes, when my little mind has some precious time to wander, I wonder if, had I known that it would be like this, would I still be here? I think the answer would be no. The government pressure has completely buggered up education in this country, and sadly we're not alone. Ofsted, the messiah of education, is a dirty word, and some sort of self-proclaimed God of education which we all seem to have no choice but to bow to.

They, the collective lump of rule-abiding, target-obsessed, progress rate-driven heads and their equally officious SLT (Senior Leadership Team) are like puppets, happily entrenched in this world after years of being indoctrinated by this melee of jargon-filled rubbish. They're like victims of Stockholm syndrome. They've spent so long on their beloved courses, network meetings and local authority shindigs that they actually identify and believe in the perceived power of knowledge that has been bestowed upon them. And worse, payback rolls downhill, as they want us too, to believe in it. To get excited about data, to be dazzled by rates of progress and value-added (eleven years in and I'm still none the wiser), and to be passionate to drive the school forwards. Uh, where are we going? I don't see a map?

And I'm not ashamed to say that after eleven years of teaching, I still know bugger all about what these things actually mean. I don't understand the pupil premium, or the data dashboard. I haven't got a Scooby Doo about what the governors actually do or who the head of the trust is. Does anybody really know? Do they really care? Maybe the cheese really does stand alone. But I don't. I don't believe it. And that's not just the belligerent non-conformist in me either. I don't believe that children are numbers on paper. They are so much more than that. I don't want to lump them all together as one, they're individuals. I don't want to call them a 1a, or a B1 as it's now called, simply because, well, they're not.

The problem is the pressure comes from the top and like a champagne fountain (sadly no champers is likely to ever be found in our neck of the woods, we're far too broke for that), trickles down to the little people at the bottom, us. And by the end, the bubbling, sparkling glory has seeped from the top and found itself a cosy new home on the ground, filling the glasses to the very tip until no more liquid can fit. Leaving the shiny glasses on top empty, and with just a tiny sliver of film as it ebbs away from the rim of the glass, down, down, down. I'm a bit crap at metaphors but you get the idea. All the fat cats at the top, with their brilliant and groundbreaking ideas that will transform the lives of pupils far and wide, now sit pretty, their pockets nicely lined with their six-figure salary. And they're no doubt satisfied, smug in the knowledge that they have made our working lives about a thousand times harder than necessary.

Those at the bottom of the pile, the teachers and children, are the ones that bear the brunt of these ill-advised and woefully misinformed visions of how education should be.

And here's a classic example, from the front line. Because they don't want to know about what it's really like on the front line, of course they have no interest in that. But let me tell you what it's really like for those of us that do walk these paths all day, every day in its relentless and increasingly stressful torture.

A prime example of this kind of educational, data-obsessed hysteria was one cold and bright Thursday afternoon in early February. We'd just battled through the morning's proceedings, bashing out maths and English in the usual timely fashion, interrupted by assembly and playtime, and now after a hour spent in wild abandon in the cold winter chill of the play-ground, we return to our regularly scheduled programming.

After that sodding bell has tolled twice signalling the end to the brief respite from the small people, and we've all grabbed enough liquids and snacks to see us through the long afternoon, I settle them into their handwriting session, marking out letters on the board for them to practise on their mini-whiteboards from the comfort of their carpet places. 'Mrs Wright, we've got so much to do this afternoon!' I squeak, my voice rising now the magnitude of what lies before me to achieve has finally dawned. 'Don't panic Captain Mainwaring!' she breezes, taking a quick swig of the tea I managed to make for us at 12.59, just before the bell rung at 13:00, rendering us unwilling and thirsty hostages in the classroom for the next two uninterrupted hours. There's nothing worse than being denied liquids, people. That and it's vital for Mrs Wright and her overactive bladder. When else can the poor woman escape for three minutes of solitude and serenity than when she has to make a dash to the ladies?

We're not really supposed to have tea or hot beverages in the classroom, for obvious reasons, but everyone does it. While we're all happy-ish to follow almost every rule by the book, this is perhaps the only one where we stand united in our defiance. I don't know who brought this one in, but really, denying teaching staff caffeine at any time of the day? It's a brave person that's going to challenge that rule. Good luck. There's never any danger of burning children (just in case you were wondering). By the time said tea is removed from its perch on the high shelf in the cupboard, far away from all the action and is finally at a drinkable temperature, we're in full swing with the learning, so it's largely a futile exercise bringing it to the classroom in the first place. It only adds to the general detritus and it's another half-filled cup that will have to be juggled along with all the others en route back to the dishwasher later. That's if I remember. No wonder I always go home with a banging headache, I never see the bottom of a cup between 8am and 5pm. I suppose that's why I've long been fantasising about an office job, one where I can languish over my morning cup of tea while swapping stories from the night out at the weekend with other humans who can appreciate my tales.

When they've finally shuffled their way to the carpet, and we've waded through the reams of playground fiascos that Mrs Wright has spent her time being harassed with all lunchtime, they settle into their handwriting session, broken and largely dry marker pens squeaking back and forth as they copy the cursive letters I've just shown them on the big whiteboard. It's supposed to be a silent and peaceful time, yet there's always somebody whispering on the job, and the quiet is broken by endless requests for toilet visits and drinks. Oh, and tissues.

'I'm really stressed.' I whisper in hushed tones, as we sit in the tiny wooden chairs at the pencil table. 'What's up my little treasure?' muses Mrs Wright, glue stick in one hand, tea in the other, as she begins the arduous yet all too familiar task of sticking in thirty bloody 'LO's' into whatever subject book is needed for my lesson that afternoon.

LO is short for learning objective. Apparently in 2019 children can't learn anything unless said little box clearly outlining what exactly we are intending to learn is dutifully stuck into every book before each lesson commences. 'Ello, ello, ello' is usually Mrs Wright's witty repartee when I thrust a bunch of white paper rectangles at her every couple of hours. Two fingers to this nonsense, but alas, we play the game, and the poor woman smiles as she goes off yet again in search of a glue stick that still works.

'It's crazy, they've got to do topic this afternoon, but there's so much stuff that they haven't finished that I actually don't know when we're going to get it done. I can't just keep throwing books at them, they'll clock off! But if we don't finish it, it looks like I haven't done anything with them, and they'll be on me about the books when they do the next book-look' I rant, trying to keep my irritation nicely under wraps, lest the little people are alerted to my displeasure. 'What?' scoffs Mrs Wright, her face etched in confusion, looking up from her post on glue stick mountain but still swiping that glue randomly across the beautifully cut pieces of paper I've left her. God, how many times have I shown her how to glue it around all the edges so the paper doesn't curl up once it's stuck in. It's like teaching the children 'around all the edges and then draw a big cross through the middle from corner to corner, then press all the edges down once you've stuck it in!'

'Ah, the snowball effect' she muses, sitting on the tiny wooden chair, knees wedged against the hard table. 'What?' I question, confused. 'The snowball effect, that's what it is' chirps Mrs Wright from behind a mountain of topic books newly adorned with the next learning activity for us to leave incomplete by 3pm. 'Every year it's the same. We start out nice and slowly, give them a chance to settle in, and then lo and behold, here we are at the beginning of February and already they're pushing to get more done than we can possibly achieve. Half of them are still five Betsy' she states with great seriousness, looking up at me from the latest wadge of gluey paper. 'I know' I sigh, shuffling through my planning folder to find the correct place to have a quick squiz at today's lesson plan. 'But this isn't us, is it?' 'No, it certainly isn't' she affirms quickly 'and don't you go kowtowing to them. We go at our own pace.' Mrs Wright is right in that respect. We are the mavericks of this patch, we pay lip service to so much and refuse to be beaten into submission by the powers that be. But every now and again it seems our hand may be forced.

And this is how it goes. After the dreaded afternoon ritual of whiteboards and pens, when I can stand the hubbub of noise no longer, I finally ask them to put the lids back on their markers and hold their whiteboards on their tummies so we can admire their work. They're all desperate to read what they've written, as their hands fly up and a few boards get waved around dangerously close to their neighbour's eyes. I choose a few, and a couple of excruciating minutes pass while we listen to their muffled reading, before I call time and ask them to put all their equipment back into their classroom drawers and NOT come to my desk to show me their writing again. The chatter hits full volume now, as the girls linger at the drawers as they gather to admire Mila's pen from Smiggle with the pink pom-pom on the top. They're pretty good at these little routines, and can usually be relied upon to make it snappy, and return to their carpet places within the time frame, so I tend to just leave them to it.

The boys? Not so much. They like nothing better than to try and ram the whiteboards into the drawers while they're still shut, expecting them to just fit in alongside the jumper that bulges out, already preventing the drawer above from shutting. It always resembles a rugby scrum, met with a serious amount of pushing and shoving, cries of outrage and usually if you're lucky, a drawer to the forehead or an eye. The culprit usually has no idea that he's even hurt anybody, as he treads firmly on Mrs Wright's size seven foot as they wander back towards the carpet.

'Ouch!' yelps Mrs Wright, still sitting alongside the table nearest to my desk, glue stick still firmly clutched in hand. 'Carlos you've just trodden on my foot, that hurt! Did you even know that you did that?' she asks, as a little group begin to form around her as they wait to see how this will pan out. 'I don't think he even noticed Mrs Wright, that's really sad isn't it?' I join in, talking across the children as the noise begins to quieten and more heads look up in interest. Note that 'sad' in teacher-speak refers to any type of delinquent-esque behaviour, that cannot be described by such words as 'angry,' 'furious' or 'what the hell did you do that for?' lest they be too detrimental to the child's wellbeing. Therefore any of the above, and other less than desirable situations throughout this book shall be referred to as 'sad.'

'That's a real shame, you haven't even noticed that you did that, did you?' she continues, her toes still smarting from such a vicious attack. Carlos chooses this moment to take a vow of silence, and refuses to answer any of her questions. 'That really hurt! All of you boys need to be much more careful and really look where you're going! You need to wait your turn rather than all trying to get to the drawers at the same time, you're lucky you haven't had somebody's eye out yet! Right, move your name down that ladder Carlos' says Mrs Wright firmly, as she looks at me with a pained expression.

This is just a teeny example of what happens probably a thousand times a day in classrooms far and wide. The egocentric child is well, just that, egocentric. With girls maturing faster than boys, it's no wonder that this lack of empathy manifests itself like this. They lack the awareness to see how their actions affect others, and it's a constant struggle for teachers to help boys catch up. If you hurt yourself in class, trust me, it's the girls who'll see you right. There are always exceptions to this rule nonetheless, namely in the form of Jonty, who is always quick to show concern for both Mrs Wright and I. Notably while I was standing at the front of the class, pen in hand as I modelled simple sentence writing on the whiteboard and then inadvertently stepped backwards onto somebody's whiteboard rubber, nearly taking myself out. 'Are you ok Miss Graham?' he hurriedly enquired, his voice filled with concern, no doubt realising I was one step away from total humiliation going ass over tit on the floor. Cheers buddy.

The solidarity of sisterhood seems to be formed within the

nursery and reception years, and the girls can be relied not only to support each other, but also the clueless and somewhat simple males around them. In our group they certainly have a good reason to stick together- there's only nine of them and twenty-one loutish, lads-on-tour, rugby-scrum-resembling boys for company. It's a good thing Mrs Wright has had two boys, isn't it? There is a chance I could be slightly biased towards the girls, being one of three and simultaneously adopting my mum's disdain for boyish activities. I actually had a good mix of both boy and girl friends growing up, and spent a great deal of time climbing lamp posts and header-ing footballs with the local cul-de-sac gang. But mum never understood how we could really be friends. After all, boys were the noisy, dirty, loud, football-loving miscreants that she was fortunate enough not to have produced. When I announced I wanted to have Jonathan Campbell over for tea after school when I was six, she was perplexed. 'But what will you play with him?' she enquired suspiciously, imagining that the sea of Barbies and the Fisher Price kitchen likely wouldn't really float his boat. 'Lego' I cheerfully replied, referring to the hours of fun the Lego pirate set had provided for my sister and I.

When they finally wend their way to their carpet places, and peace has been restored, I ask for Kieran to switch off the lights while I turn on the Smartboard and begin our afternoon lesson. Children far and wide are known for not being at their sharpest post-lunch (come to think of it, neither are we), so most of the important stuff, i.e. maths and English, is taught every morning, so that learning time isn't wasted with any of this airy-fairy rubbish, like history, topic and art, or basically anything that might actually float a few boats.

It's a shame really, but that's the way it's always been, and I suppose even I, a fierce critic, would have to agree that it's hard to teach the three R's in the afternoon while half of them have got their heads on the tables and Lola's having a nap in the book corner. In her defence, she had gotten back later than planned after a trip to the States over Christmas last year, and her poor little body clock was way out of kilter and unable to cope with the seven-hour time difference. After declaring her exhaustion, she snuggled up on the floor with a cushion while we ploughed on with our handwriting lesson, and I failed to notice that her wriggling in the distance had subsided as she fell into the deep land of nod right at the base of Mrs Wright's wheely chair, her head resting awkwardly on the cushion she had placed over the wheels.

There wasn't a lot we could do really, as we called for some helpful onlookers, namely from the office, to take a peek and then phone her mum to come and collect her. I made an executive decision not to wake her, and as the children moved off into free choice time and the room grew noisy, we covered her with a blanket as we all tiptoed around the sleeping beauty. And she stayed deeply asleep, even despite all the chaos whirling around her as they crawled around on the carpet with the Duplo bricks and squealed with the puppet theatre. Knowing Lola's fiery and tempestuous nature, I knew she wouldn't take kindly to being woken, so I delegated that to her mother when she arrived. And true to form, she was a grouch-bag, and didn't want to put her coat on as her mum picked her up and promised us that she would try to keep her up and get her back on schedule. Needless to say we were a bit more careful the rest of that week when she cried that she was tired, and did our best to keep her busy lest she should find her way to the book corner for another snooze. What a sweetie, I could have squished her that day! It wasn't the first time, and it surely won't be the last.

Childhood is so fleeting, and kids seem to lead such busy lives these days. When my sisters and I came home from school, we too liked nothing better than to veg out in front of the box for an hour or so, either at home or at nanny and gramps's, unable to even communicate how our days had been until this little ritual had been completed. And I am largely the same now, unable to talk or chat about my day until I've had some down time. There seems to just be so much pressure on children these days, with homework and extra curricular activities, that there aren't actually a lot of free hours between school being out and bedtime.

It may sound like I'm not a big believer in clubs and sports, but that's far from true. I believe that sports play a huge role in the development of the whole child, and I was lucky enough to pursue my passions of dance and gymnastics which I still continue into adulthood. It's just that we are in an age where some parents will do whatever it takes to ensure the success of their child at any cost, which makes me wonder whether children really have enough time to just be a child. After all, they'll only get one chance. I began to wonder if there were other people out there that felt the same way that I do, and did a little research. On my travels, I found this quote from The Danish Way of Parenting website.

Today almost everything is connected to learning, but what if we removed this educational element and just focused on having a good time? This is an important question for me to address – as

I, as a young mother, tried to understand my children's desire to play when growing up and the value it brought them to play freely.

To be honest, it was not always easy to understand their play but it gave them a way to digest their impressions after a long day in kindergarten or school. I gave them time and room to follow their needs and I knew instinctively that they just needed some time, where nobody demanded anything from them. I knew it gave them time to adjust and even though resilience was not what I was aiming at, that is exactly what it taught them along with the ability to be true to themselves! Resilience has been proven to be one of the most important factors in predicting success as an adult. Not only in terms of professional or private success but also, in terms of being a happy and whole person.

I couldn't agree more, but I highly doubt I'll manage to start a movement. On with the lesson. Today I'm teaching the next lesson in our science topic, seasons. This is one that quite interests me, but even more so, it's right up Mrs Outdoorsy's street. The careful and skilful questioning begins. 'What do you know about the seasons?' I enquire, tossing out my question to the thirty tired children before me. Little hands shoot up, and squeaks of 'ooh, ooh!' fill the room.

'Eric?' I choose, as he offers his answer, up right on his knees in his quest to be selected. 'It's when the weather changes' he explains confidently. 'Sort of' I say, 'you're on the right track' as I move on to the next question to steer them in my direction. 'How many seasons do we have?' I ask, as the same familiar hands rise up while the rest of them stare blankly at the Smartboard screen at the picture of the blossom tree and daffodils, and some tear up tissues into little pieces into a pile on the floor in front of them.

'Darla?' I ask, as she bravely responds to the question, spouting out the correct answers. 'spring, summer, autumn and winter.' 'Good girl!' I affirm as she smiles, pleased that her answer has been acknowledged.

I begin to flick my way through the downloaded powerpoint presentation carefully selected to fulfil the lesson objective. 'Have a look at some of the pictures on here' I instruct. 'Which season do you think this would be?' I ask, pointing to the colour photograph of baby lambs, crocuses and chicks hatching out. The chorus of 'ooh, ooh, ooh!' begins again, some desperate to share their understanding while others like Willie just sit there in a haze of disaffection, his eyes almost pointing in two different directions, likely wondering if now might be a good time to ask for a toilet break.

As we wend our way through the remainder of the powerpoint slides, chatting about the seasons and what happens in each, the clock hands creep round to 1:45pm. They've been sat down since they reappeared from lunch play at 1:00pm, so I'm conscious that they need to move about, and sure enough the restlessness on the carpet has become apparent.

Mila sits beautifully like the model pupil that she is, listening carefully and looking at the Smartboard for the duration, ready to tackle the task that is to be recorded in her book afterwards. And then we have the other end of the scale, the not-so-model pupil, today in the form of George, who has spent the last forty or so minutes rolling around in his carpet space, lopping onto the children either side of him and zipping and unzipping his velcro shoes throughout the entire lesson.

You're now entering the danger zone, I tell myself, as my

audience starts to glaze over. 'Right, ok, let me tell you what you're going to do today' I continue cheerfully, as the yawns begin to creep in and Willie puts his hand up to go to the toilet. 'No Willie, you're not going now, you should have gone at lunchtime. You can go in a minute when I've explained what we're doing, ok?' And from my right hand side, a green science book neatly emblazoned with our school logo appears in my peripheral vision, being proffered by Mrs Wright, in true Blue Peter 'here's-one-I-made-earlier' style. 'Here we are my dear' she smiles, handing the book to me, already open at the page ready for me to show the children what they need to do. She's worth her weight in gold this one.

Perched on the wooden handle of my brown recliner chair, I hold the book open, carefully drawing their attention to the sodding LO and then translating it into something meaningful that a child can actually understand, and then explain what they have to do. 'To recognise and understand the four seasons. To be able to explain what happens in each season'. Translation? In normal, human, children-are-not-thick speak, this means 'draw a picture in each box about the seasons and write something that you know that happens.'

And having run through it all, and just to make sure that nobody could be in any doubt as to the task that looms before them, I ask for a few suggestions for each one. 'What could you draw for autumn?' Brown leaves, wind, the nature table, conkers and pine cones are the responses that come back so I'm pretty sure they've got the concept.

Mrs Wright, finally having reached the summit of Mount Glue Stick, stands up and shuffles the piles of books neatly organised into their groups ready to hand to a child to give out.

'Could the triangles go and sit at the big table' I encourage, as the noise level begins to rise and the triangle group begin to charge at Mrs Wright in order to reach the books first. As they settle in at their tables, we pull up our chairs to work alongside each group in an attempt to ensure that they understand and complete their work correctly. As they chatter happily while working, it seems they've got it. I'm just hoping they can get it finished sometime before the end of the day, so that this doesn't become the latest set of books with work that's incomplete and saved for Friday afternoon finishing.

21

The candy man

'I didn't get any sweets' whispers a little voice below my feet. It's Christopher, in a mournful and despairing tone. How strange, I thought, as being sat in the front row, he was one of the first to be given the kind offering to celebrate Natalie's birthday. 'Put your hand up if you don't have any sweets from Natalie' I request, as Hannah and Mila raise theirs. 'Ok, don't worry. Natalie, look, Hannah and Mila need some' I motion, as Natalie begins to tread a little path towards them, clambering over the sea of coats and bags, her plastic bag of mini Skittles in her hand.

'And me,' cries Christopher, seeking my urgent attention. I'm partly sceptical, and I have a hunch I know where this is going. From the brown recliner on the opposite side of the carpet, Mrs Wright intervenes, likely having the same suspicions that I do. I am almost one hundred percent sure that Christopher was given sweets along with everybody else, and is trying to pull a fast one on us.

'Christopher, bring me your book bag so I can check and make sure you're not getting confused' directs Mrs Wright as we exchange a knowing glance. Christopher ambles towards her, his hands stuffed in the pockets of his hoodie, where he is also concealing his water bottle and stretching the fabric of his clothing. I'm sure we're going to find the loot right there.

He smirks as he extends his hand holding his book bag towards Mrs Wright. She's dealing with this one, so I return my attention to the melee that is home-time taking place before me. 'Well done Natalie, come and get the rest of your sweets now darling,' I say, as most of them talk excitedly about the sweets they've received and she collects the remainder to take home.

And then my ears are met with the sudden sound of wailing. The sound that would indeed be made by a little boy who did hide sweets in his book bag in the vain hope of receiving an additional packet. Mrs Wright's face is angry, her voice curt as she holds the skittles in her hands. 'That's disgraceful, just greedy. I'll have these now, naughty boys that tell lies don't get sweets Christopher. That was just ungrateful, now you won't be having any. There was no reason to do that, it's just pure greed' continues Mrs Wright, as the rest of the class look on, taking note of the apparent consequences.

The wailing increases in volume, as Christopher makes his way back to his carpet space at my feet, no doubt full of regret at his error in judgement. 'I'm really disappointed in you Christopher, that's such a shame. You'd had such a good week, I was thinking about letting you have Niblet, (the class toy bunny) for the weekend, but I don't think I can now. What a shame.' I repeat, as the rest of the class listen and look on, glad that they didn't decide to try to go for one extra like Christopher.

'Right, let's do the story' I chirp, immediately moving on as Christopher continues to howl amidst the silence. We listen to the story, Mrs Wright and I making the raised-eyebrow-of-judgement faces as we wordlessly express our displeasure and surprise. As the bell rings and I make my way across the classroom to dismiss them, I reassure myself that Christopher has indeed learned a valuable lesson, one which hopefully he won't need to repeat. It's blisteringly cold as we stand together in the doorway, calling the children in their overexcited, thank-God-it's-Friday delirium to head home to their parents for the weekend break. Once the last child is gone, we breathe a sigh of relief that yet another particularly stressful and unrelenting week has finally come to its exhausting end.

'I feel sorry for Christopher, I don't know why he did that!' I lament, as I pull up the blinds (so the parents can't see us in all of our dishevelled, hysterical, herding-cats chaos while we get them ready for home) and start to make sense of all of the detritus on my desk. 'Betsy, that was just greedy, he was just being belligerent. He had no need to do that, he was just being selfish, and it's backfired on him, big time' says Mrs Wright firmly, more than experienced at dealing with this sort of carry on. I know, you're right, but I sort of feel bad for him, even though he's learned a very valuable lesson' I say regretfully. 'I've never seen him cry before. Well, I suppose sweets are the ultimate prize really' I continue, as I put away the reading folder and tuck in a stray chair.

'Well, he has, and I expect he'll think twice before lying to us again' affirms Mrs Wright with a smile. 'He smirked at me, and as soon as he brought me that book bag I knew exactly where the sweets were' she repeats. 'Do you think we were too hard taking the sweets away though?' I waver, as I start to question whether the punishment had indeed fit the crime. 'Of course not!' cries Mrs Wright with a chuckle. 'I used to do exactly the same to my boys. They're mine, you're not having them!' she laughs, as I relax and laugh too. 'I know, you're absolutely right' I reply, 'he was a toad and he'll not do that again in a hurry' I rationalise, winding the windows open to air the room out. 'Exactly' chirps Mrs Wright, leaning over the table towards me extending her hand. 'Skittle?'

22

I'm an emotional girl

So says the song, courtesy of Mary Chapin Carpenter. Which leads me to believe that probably the hardest part of the job is your emotions. And by emotions, I mean your ability to suppress them no matter what chaos might have erupted at will in either your personal or professional life.

Broken up with your boyfriend? Nope, no tears in front of the children please. Text from husband asking for a divorce? No, no time for shock and/or tears, just plaster that fake smile on your face and carry on with the learning. About to be called in for a bollocking by the boss? No, sweetie, ignore the wobbling voice and the tears that threaten to fall, maintain that Mary Poppins-esque cheeriness to your voice and steady that quivering hand as you continue on in the unrelenting pursuit of learning.

The small people must never know what tragedy has or is about to befall you, you must carry on with the best of British, stiff upper lip and all that. I always think of it like that God-awful '*Toddlers and Tiaras*' programme, about child beauty queens, where on losing the most prestigious title, the girls are told by adoring mothers 'keep a smile on your face baby, no matter what.' And that is what we have to do.

One of our resident kooks, my co-teacher a couple of years back who was quite clearly the most inflexible adult I have ever met, is a classic example of the kind of machine-esque behaviour that I suppose the Big Guns rather likes. Somebody so devoid of experiencing human emotion that she was seemingly unable to relate to either her coworkers or her tiny charges, and allow no matters of a personal nature to interfere with the proceedings, i.e. 'the learning.'

It's quite an extraordinary feat to be able to do that really. I take my hat off to her. I can't do that. You see I have a heart, and when misfortune strikes, it unleashes emotions that I feel deeply. I'm not able to turn them off, turn away and ignore them. But if they happen to appear at inopportune moments, then I have to suppress them with the best of 'em. I'm the queen of that.

Mrs Wright had the misfortune of being her right-hand man that year, working next door to me but yet still so far away through that faintly chequered glass window that separated us. It was a very long year for all concerned. When she arrived late one morning, a bit of a wreck after some trouble at home, Sensible Sally, we'll call her, was oblivious. 'Honestly Betsy, she's a nutter' wailed Mrs Wright, recounting the tale to me. 'I could come in, and say 'my husband has just been diagnosed with leukaemia, my house burned down last night and I was hit by a car on the way in this morning, and she'd just thrust a handful of papers at me and say 'but can you laminate these?' without even a word!'

I'm not even kidding. It seems that a lot of people just don't have time for other people and their problems, but frighteningly they seem unable to cope with being around others who might be unhappy. There's a huge lack of empathy in this zoo. And if it's not just in this particular school, they by God, we're in trouble. Because the next generation are going to need all the guidance they can get, given these troubled times where mental health in children and young adults is on the rise.

I think it's good for the children to see you cry. To see you laugh, share a joke and most importantly, share a bit of yourself with them. It's not just good, it's invaluable. For they can see that while there is still the very clearly defined relationship of teacher and pupil, they can see that we are above all else, human, and that it's ok to express yourself in front of others. It's a very powerful message to send, and one that should be at the centre of our work.

It's ok to be disappointed. If a school trip gets cancelled, we talk about it, and instead of just brushing it under the carpet, it's good to verbalise and acknowledge our collective disappointment. (Well, maybe just theirs, see earlier chapter on the ill-fated zoo trip). If they fall over, we are trained to say with all the positivity of a children's TV presenter, dressed in kooky outfit complete with some equally insufferable animal sidekick, 'up you jump! You'll be fine!' while they shake, convulse sometimes, and wail as blood trickles from a gashed knee or a split lip.

I adopted this choice phrase, simply because everybody else did. I didn't want to be different from the bunch. I wanted to get it right and do the right thing. But had I stopped to look around, I would have realised much sooner that those words actually do little to comfort a crying child or ease their pain.

So after some thought, I decided to adopt a new approach. The approach that acknowledges the pain of another person, rather than just quickly trying to erase it without a trace. So when they come up to me in the classroom, faces streaked with tears having just slipped off their chair and banged their chin on the table, or been body-slammed by one of our rugby-scrum, heavy-handed boys on the way out of the room to get their snack first, I usually say 'oh, that must have really hurt, that's not nice is it?' or words to that effect.

Because when you think about it, who wants to go to somebody who just brushes your suffering under the carpet? When the shit hits the fan, I want people around me who will almost feel that pain along with me. They won't tell me it'll be alright, or deny my feelings, they'll give me a hug and tell me that whatever's happened, why, it really sucks. And that it's ok to feel like poop, because they are your feelings, and what's happened really is rubbish.

When the chips are down, I don't want someone to turn away, to not know what to say when I'm at my lowest ebb, and to tell me to come back when I'm happy again; aka the 'don't bring me your pain' approach. I want somebody to listen to me while I get all of those tumbling thoughts that have been filling my head out into the open, and to offer some perspective, rather than telling me they're a bit busy and to come back in a week. Because what they're really telling you is that your unhappiness is too much to bear. I want someone who acknowledges where I'm at and says, 'I hear you, I'm here with you, I am here for you' and will stand by you and go the distance. And I truly believe that's what the children need too. Who wants a teacher to tell you to jump up when you're sporting a war wound the size of Texas and dripping blood, or when your best friend's just ditched you for somebody else and you feel all alone in the world?

So the next time some bad news hits you- maybe your husband's left you for somebody else, your parent's been diagnosed with cancer or your house has just burned down, ask yourself if a cheery 'up you jump, you'll be fine!' from your nearest and dearest will really go very far towards soothing your distress. I imagine not.

We can all do better, and I think emotional intelligence is talked about too much, without an understanding of what it actually means in practice. It should be a huge part of teacher training, and at the forefront of what we do. After all, we are working with children, not machines, and they are impressionable little people who will that take their cue from us.

When I get emotionally upset, I find it extremely hard to hide it, although the paradox is that working with small children can actually be as much of a blessing as a curse in tricky times. There's something about their innocence, and their ability to live so completely in the present that gives you the strength to face another day. When you have no choice but to smile, to speak kindly and maintain a cheerful and jolly exterior no matter the internal turmoil, despite the effort it takes, it's also strangely healing.

And I swear that they know if you're having an off day. Of course you never hint at what's upsetting you, that would be wrong on so many levels. But perhaps they pick up that you need that extra hug, that funny phrase that'll make you laugh, or even just a friendly smile to lift you enough to make it through the day. Lola was always good at that. Her beaming smile and her sense of humour was always exactly the tonic I needed on a bad day, which luckily were few and far between. Mrs Wright is also my saving grace. I mean, you try not to crack a smile the second she enters the room and passes comment about the histrionics of the parents she's just been accosted by in the car park. Mrs Wright had me adopt her mantra for when things are bad, and was always quick to give me a squeeze and her wise words. 'Double lippy my dear, double lippy.'

Through my own troubles, I began to realise, that perhaps it wasn't always healthy to be 'ok' all the time. After all, on replying to anybody asking how one is, the response is almost always 'I'm fine,' or as I now think of it 'False Information Nicely Expressed.' I began to be more willing to show my feelings towards the children more easily, instead of pretending that everything was perfect.

When the children came to me with friendships issues, as Emily and Vanya did one day, I took the opportunity to put what I'd learned into practice. 'Vanya rolled her eyes at me and she was mean to me' grumbled Emily tearfully as she stood in front of me, Vanya remaining at the table trying to finish her maths work she'd been struggling with for the last half an hour.

Feeling a little worried now, and trying to ease her discomfort, Vanya looks up and quickly states her case. 'I'm not, I'm just grumpy and I feel moody.' I think Vanya expected that I would be quick to ensure that she apologised to her friend and would be reprimanded for being unkind, but I made a point of looking directly at her before I said a word. Calmly I spoke. 'Vanya, you don't have to be happy, you can be grumpy, it's absolutely fine. We don't have to be happy all of the time.' And she nodded her head at me in response, before continuing with her work, as I suggested Emily might like to leave Vanya and have a little break from each other temporarily.

We can't be happy all of the time.

23

Rugby scrum

'Ok guys, show me that you're ready' I request, as we're in the throes of rounding them up and getting them ready to send out the door one Tuesday night. God I'm exhausted and it's only the start of the week. At least it's only a three-and a-half-day week before term break. Thank goodness for small mercies, as by God, Mrs Wright and I are done.

As that clock's inching its way between ten past and quarter past three, suddenly feeling tantalisingly close to the finish line and yet still frustratingly far, I grope for anything interesting or pertinent to talk about as filler until we're rid of them (in the nicest possible way) for the day. 'Right, don't forget, it's rugby tomorrow morning' I smirk, a wry smile on my face as I watch Mrs Wright put her head in her hands in disbelief. Oh, how the poor woman has suffered this half-term.

You see rugby has been a new and recent addition to our weekly schedule, and it's taken its toll. Where a few weeks ago, Wednesdays for me were a doddle, having only to teach two lessons during the morning, and having planning time all afternoon, it's just gotten even better, in the form of some free and expert coaching from the local rugby club who volunteered themselves for a six-week program with all of the KS1 classes. And they just happen to take place on my easiest and possibly favourite day of the week, meaning that it takes up one of the two teaching slots. Plus, there's even the regular assembly thrown in too, it's a win-win situation! Except it's not, it's really not. Poor, poor Mrs Wright. She loathes Wednesdays with a passion, never more so now that rugby has been added to the mix.

And here's why. Number one, the clothing. Having not organised this directly ourselves, we were merely presented with the information and a timetable, plus a vague copy of the letter sent to the parents informing them of the new agenda every Wednesday, and left to go along with it. As it's no mean feat trying to process one hundred and eighty children through a tag rugby game each week, they were asked if they could please dress their children ready for the game before they came to school.

Most heeded this warning, some did not. And that is where the chaos began. Week after week, every Wednesday morning, a totally random assortment of outfits appeared -some dressed correctly in their outdoor clothes for rugby, others in their school PE kits, complete with pristine white t-shirts and sparkling white trainers, while the remaining few arrived in their school uniform. I think this is where Mrs Wright's blonde bob began to turn a feint shade of grey.

Every Wednesday became a race against the clock to bring them in, register them and then organise their clothing. Those that came correctly dressed are quids in, taking up their seats on the carpet as dear Mr Wild and his eighteen year-old accomplice, Mr Tanner began to explain the rules of the game, while in the background, Mrs Wright, Mrs Beale and I ran around trying to locate PE kits and swap clothing until everybody was reasonably attired to go and brave the mud and cold.

Number two was the time and the ensuing confusion. When they went to rugby, we were delighted to have extra time to prepare for the next lesson, and once that was done, enjoy a cuppa and a chat while we made an effort to plough through the marking backlog. But over the weeks, we began to dread their return. Imagine thirty small children all caked heavily from head to toe in thick, gooey mud, preparing to cross the threshold into your beautifully clean classroom and carpet. Not a pretty picture.

The first time, upon recognising the horror that flickered momentarily across my face, Mrs Wright took charge and insisted that from now on they must come in via the tiled floor of the cloakroom, removing their muddy shoes on the way. A smear of mud here, a trace there, Lord, they were covered! As Mrs Wright reminded me cheerfully, 'the world will still keep turning' and 'that's a sign of a happy day Miss Graham!' I resigned myself to rugby being yet another thorn in my side.

Then came the changing back. Into what? The problem was that rugby happened to fall on the same day of the week that they had their sessions with the sports coaches, thus requiring them to wear their school PE kit. And as if changing twice in the same day wasn't enough, Wednesdays were rife with after-school clubs, football and dance that required yet another change into football kit or tutu. The poor children were mightily confused, and on return from rugby, questioned what exactly they were supposed to wear. As we stood there, scratching our heads in collective despair while the room was a sea of dishevelled children sporting various bags of clothing, we realised we had to make an executive decision.

'Right' I begin, clapping in unison with Mrs Wright until

we've got everybody quiet and listening, before I endeavour to explain what's going to happen. 'If you have your PE kit, you need to change into that' I explain. It doesn't take long before I'm interrupted by Thibault's booming voice. 'But what if your PE kit's dirty?' he asks, as Mrs Wright and I exchange a look.

Mrs Wright lets out a sigh before she takes over. 'Thibault, if your PE kit's covered in mud then there's not a lot we can do really is there?' she offers, a hint of exasperation in her voice. 'That's why you were supposed to come in wearing your rugby clothes and change into your PE kit later so you'd have something clean to wear, wasn't it?' she continues, as Thibault stares blankly and then reluctantly nods his head in agreement.

I interject. 'Thibault, you'll have to stay as you are I'm afraid and put your school shoes back on, as your other ones are too muddy.' I carry on. 'If you only have your PE kit, you'll have to wear that with your school shoes just like Thibault is' I explain. 'What if we're doing football after school?' asks Teddy, sitting in the midst of all his clothing which looks like his PE bag has just exploded around him. I sigh again. 'Then you can change into your football kit after PE this afternoon, just like you normally do' I explain.

Then Rebecca pipes up, her voice full of concern. 'But what if you're doing dance after school?' she questions. 'It's just the same as normal darling. We'll get changed after school into your dance clothes ready for Miss Madeleine' I smile, as she smiles back at me, reassured that things will stay the same. 'Does everybody understand?' I throw out, waiting with bated breath for the response. A chorus of 'yes' assures me that they have, as they begin to organise themselves.

Mrs Wright collapses in a heap into her brown easy chair, as

I return to my perch on the edge of mine. It's a great viewing point and a prime hotspot for overseeing just what everybody's doing as they spread out far and wide across the classroom. 'My God, this is a form of torture!' she chuckles as we survey the detritus covering the entire floor. 'I feel like reporting Stella Stuart to Amnesty International for organising this!' she laughs, as we both stare wide-eyed at the chaos.

'How many more weeks of this have we got?' she asks me, exhaling a loud sigh. 'Another five' I reply, wondering how the hell we're going to get through it every week. 'Remind me to pull a sickie next Wednesday' mumbles Mrs Wright with a wry smile in my direction.

Week two arrives and it just doesn't get any better. Another rugby lesson means another classroom and cloakroom that look like we've been burgled. Another week of mud, another week of muddy rugby boots that nobody ever remembers to take home and then float about the cloakroom until the following week. I'm amazed we haven't had more complaints, given the amount of clothing and footwear that has gone astray.

Finally, by week three, Mrs Wright's patience with reuniting lost clothing with their owner snaps. 'That's it, I'm going to find a bloody box, any box, and when they've finished playing rugby, they can dump their dirty boots in there and take them home that night on the way out' she decides, as she slopes off to find an old plastic container large enough to hold sixty mud-encrusted shoes. It seems as good a solution as any, and I don't hesitate to agree.

The thing that some would find strange, particularly in the upper years of the school, is that a teaching assistant would be given so much leeway to make decisions without consulting that teacher. But I wouldn't give it a second thought. We are a team, and this is a joint effort. Yes there's the formal designation of roles, but every day, from 9am until 3pm, we're simply two adults in charge, running the class together. Part of what I love about her is her ability to use her initiative, and to know when and how to swiftly intervene and keep order or take control. Namely when Mrs Case from the office breezes in, armed with the register and some pertinent information about an absence to discuss with me.

I'd had them all lined up ready for lunch, the children all standing quietly, ready to say the lunchtime prayer. As she engages me in conversation, on the periphery I hear the noise level begin to rise, but I needn't worry. As the matter requires more of my attention than I expected, Mrs Wright doesn't take half a second to recognise this, before getting them quiet again, saying the prayer, and then leading them off to lunch. By the time we've sorted out the problem and Mrs Case departs, the classroom is empty. The ability to see what needs to be done and act upon it without waiting for approval or permission, is not to be underestimated. There's many a teacher in the school that wishes that they too had a TA like Mrs Wright.

24

The new age dawns

The first day of the third and final term of the year passes in a foggy, caffeine-necessitated haze, as the pair of us try to stifle the increasingly frequent yawns emanating from our poor, tired and still broken bodies. It turns out that two whole weeks off doing absolutely sod all has done little to repair the damage and stress of the previous twelve weeks.

Day one and I'm knackered. It's partly my own fault, having resisted turning the light out last night in some sort of twisted defiance that the new term dawns tomorrow. Truth be told, I've been feeling a little anxious, as it means it's time to exert energy and apply some serious effort like a horse on the final stretch of the Grand National. We're heading towards the data finishing line in June, and boy, it's got to be good. It's a shame my pay won't go up even if it is anything resembling good, but the Big Guns is still pushing, pushing, pushing.

Surprisingly, the children are the epitome of refreshed, the boys sporting freshly-razored cuts and the girls fringes neatly trimmed. A few have the glow of the mediterranean sun dancing on their golden brown skin, as they squeak and chatter their way to the meeting place that is the world map carpet. Some have been skiing, some to the beach. Holidays in India (to see family), Ireland, Switzerland and Madrid are just a few of the desirable locations that our little rabble have been exploring while we sat at home watching the rain fall down.

Our class toy bunnies who are handed out to the best-behaved child every weekend to take home, have been on more foreign holidays than both Mrs Wright and I knocked together. They've delighted in the sights of Dubai one October half-term and took in the view from the top of the Burj Khalifa. They've seen fall in Boston, had a mini-break in the Alps and over Christmas, they spent it on safari in South Africa. I'm not even kidding. This time they've had to surrender their passports in favour of a trip up north to spend it with Dylan and his family, visiting airplane museums and roughing it in the great outdoors, UK-style. When the child returns to school, the bunnies somewhat inevitably looking and smelling like they spent a week in the trunk of a car, they delight in sharing their addition to the class book, as they spend what feels like an eternity stumbling over the few sentences they've managed to write, while Mrs Wright and I take a squiz at the photos to see what they've gotten up to. And whether we should feel a teeny bit jealous or not.

'Morning everybody!' I call, as I feign enthusiasm as the chattering dies down and the room begins to quieten. Mrs Wright takes up residence in her easy chair, and I in mine. Mrs Beale walks in, a few minutes late, mumbling her good mornings as she struggles to chew and swallow the croissant she holds in one hand that she's picked up along the way, her thermos of coffee in the other. You can't keep a New Yorker from baked goods in the morning really. As she unpacks her stuff, which seems to be encroaching ever further from her table and into the main areas of the classroom, she plugs her phone charger into the wall socket and the iPhone dutifully powers up in readiness for the morning's texting. Yes, that would be the kind of texting when one's supposed to be working....

I pick up the register and begin to get involved in post-holiday chatter, partly as an ice-breaker as we've not seen each other for two whole weeks and even the adult me finds it a bit of a culture shock. When it gets to ten past nine and NO LEARNING HAS BEEN STARTED I apologise to the children that we don't have time to share any more news right now, and that we need to do roll call so that the lovely office ladies won't come chasing us for the register that is late, and they can order their lunches for them.

Register complete, the VIP's need to be changed. We have little laminated sheets on the wall with their names on, and each day we have one boy and one girl who are selected to return the register to its residence in the office, and general responsible duties throughout the day. Well it was supposed to be one girl and one boy each day, until I had a rugby team of boys and a pitiful amount of girls, so now it's just whoever they choose. When everybody's had a turn (providing no-one's fiddled with the names, i.e. moved theirs back to the board that says they're waiting for a turn) then we start over.

In the teacher's eyes, this little ritual is utterly pointless, and can often be a very painful and drawn-out process as those on the carpet pipe up about whose turn it is, usually complicating the process and confusing us all. But if you're five, it's extremely important, and a sort of rite of passage. The prestige that comes with having been chosen to be a VIP is not to be sniffed at, and a source of great pride among them. As the VIP's are finally chosen, and they carry the little blue velcro bag that contains the register toward the office, I look at the sea of faces before me.

And then I notice George. Dear George, or Jorge as Mrs Beale calls him, has a sort of mystical glow about him. Something is different, but what? Has he been replaced with another child? Have we somehow acquired a newbie without our knowledge or consent since spring break? Gone is the pale and pastiness of the previous seven months of winter, his green eyes now alive and sparkling having replaced the cold and vacant stare that offered no words, no communication, and certainly not much in the way of learning since September.

'George?' I whisper, in a haze of disbelief, 'is that you?' He flashes me a beaming smile, and crosses his legs as he wriggles backwards into his own carpet place, sitting up straight in front of Mrs Wright's chair. Normally George is a prime carpet-roller, who spends more time with his legs outstretched before him as he rolls around or turns to whisper to Matthew who sits behind him, a disgusting piece of detritus being rolled around between his thumb and forefinger. He rarely participates, and generally takes a vow of silence if he is called upon to answer a question as he's usually clueless as to what's been going on the whole lesson. 'George, you look simply gorgeous!' squeaks Mrs Wright, her face beaming as we exchange a smile. 'Where did you go on holiday? Did you have a lovely break?' she asks. One thing about George is that he relishes the praise and individual attention that is so often bestowed upon him for all the wrong reasons, and he clearly can't wait to answer Mrs Wright's question.

'I goed to Madrith' he explains, and being half-Spanish, his pronunciation of the Spanish capital is spot on, emphasising the 'th' rather than the 'd' at then end of the word. 'And, I went to Tenerif-e' he coos, his huge eyes lighting up his cherubic little face. 'Wow, that sounds amazing George!' I continue, 'what did you do there?' George begins to regale us with his tales of how he visited the space museum, and how he played with his brothers on the beach. 'Well, George, was it sunny? Was it nice and warm?' asks Mrs Wright, as the rest of the children listen earnestly to this interaction. 'It was really sunny, and, and, me and Enrique and Juan had ice-creams!' he explains, smiling as he talks about his brothers. Mrs Wright smiles at me, and we both marvel silently at the profound effect that two weeks in sunnier climes seems to have had on George.

'Well, George, you look like you've had a good rest, and you've had all that lovely sunshine. It looks like it's done you a world of good,' affirms Mrs Wright, as George turns around to offer a wicked grin to the rest of his classmates and Mrs Wright and I chuckle. The rest of the day, it's like George has had an epiphany. It's like the light switch has been flipped, and the one that's been firmly fixed in the OFF position since September, has suddenly done an about turn, and powered up.

Having been on a go-slow for the past seven months, he's like a different child. Now dear George might be one of the youngest in the class, but we've always known he's got a good brain on him. He's a whizz at maths and anything to do with how things work etc, but getting it down on paper has proved to be a bit of a challenge, as has his concentration span.

It's also a prime example of why this traditional sort of Year One setup really isn't suited to him or his peers. If he were in his native Spain, George likely wouldn't start school until he was nearly seven, and I really think that if he did, then he wouldn't be rolling around on the carpet all day, his eyes almost pointing in two different directions. He wouldn't be forced to listen, to sit up straight, to concentrate and apply himself, because he'd be allowed to learn through (more) play, with no expectation of him sitting down with a pencil and recording it all in a book just to satisfy the Ofsted 'evidence of learning' criteria. He's just not willing and/or ready for that. And he's not the only one.

It really makes you think though, doesn't it? Why have we learned nothing from our European counterparts over the years? Most don't begin formal schooling until six, or often seven, when children who have participated in a relaxed, playful, child-centred environment that is pre-school education, take much more readily to acquiring arithmetical concepts and the beginnings of reading and writing. The broken British system ignores all the research, all the think-tanks and blindly carries on doing what's been done a hundred times before, and all with the same disappointing and demoralising outcome. You do what you've always done, you get what you've always got.

The remainder of the week, George is like a new man. He's got a new lease of life, a spring in his step. Maybe all of that Spanish sun has seeped into his brain and altered the chemicals that no doubt have been scrambled by the unrelenting dark and dank of the British winter. Or maybe, just maybe, George relished his freedom, his escape from the confines of his day to day life. One where he was expected to trundle into school day after day and absorb knowledge like a sponge without much regard for his needs and interests. Maybe he ran free, followed his own ideas, played until he was ready to stop, rather than being held hostage to an appropriately timed ringing bell. I know exactly how he feels, because it was exactly the way I felt when I booked a Christmas vacation to the Bahamas a few months back. There's nothing like a warm breeze in your face, the sand, the ocean, and twenty-five degree weather in the dead of winter to lift your spirits. The ocean is good for the soul, as is family time, play, the pursuit of hobbies and such necessities as a good night's sleep that are essential for good heath and wellbeing. I know it did wonders for me.

And George's newfound enthusiasm translates to our phonics lessons, where his voice is the loudest as we all stare at the animation that helps us to rote learn the 'tricky words' every day. He's raised his hand to answer questions, and tried hard to improve his handwriting, in the hope that he can please us. And he has. He beamed as his peg was moved up the ladder, and smiled as we've told him how well he's learning. And it's lovely to see.

At the end of the day, he's one of the last out the door as we touch base with his mum. 'How was your holiday?' I ask, as she regales me with how lovely the weather was and the delightful family time they spent together. She remarks how the winter seemed interminably long here, and Mrs Wright tells her that George looks a picture of health. She's smiling as she's really pleased to see that, having been worried about his pallor and lack of energy these last few months.

We say goodbye, and Mrs Wright pulls the door firmly shut. 'Ah, it's so nice. I'm glad they had a good holiday, he's like a different boy!' I say to Mrs Wright, as she pulls up the blinds. Always an advocate for fresh air and a good dose of vitamin D, she chuckles 'I think all George needed was a holiday!'

And who could argue with that?

25

To the beat of our own drum

One evening that week, we were ordered to suffer for an hour at the hands of Liz Dawson, who this time chose to lead the weekly staff meeting on a new music program she'd discovered. Being the music coordinator, this is right up her street, but she might have her work cut out trying to convince the rest of us.

After the children are duly dismissed, the rest of us trudged down that hallway to her classroom, and took up residence on the tiny wooden chairs carefully arranged in a semi-circle in front of the Smartboard. This had better be good.

'Right everyone!' she exclaims loudly, trying in vain to quieten down the room and get twelve adults to stop nattering and give her the full attention she demands. Two of our crew have managed to get out of it, either by illness or an 'appointment' so they are MIA. Lucky buggers. The Big Guns is mysteriously absent as well, but that's a perk of the job, and no doubt there's something far more urgent to attend to than this drivel. How I long to be able to pick and choose. Liz Dawson quickly starts jabbering away, her condescension almost presidential now, as she makes it clear that the rest of us know jack shit about anything musical and she is the self-appointed professor.

Over the next hour, she takes us through the new interactive program, carefully broken down into year groups, a series of lessons already available for use with the small people. In fairness, I can see how the program may actually prove to be a useful tool for many of us, given that music, just like the arts and anything remotely creative is way down on the totem pole and most of us never have the time to teach it anyway.

Having a designated website, with all of the interactive resources and songs at our fingertips should ensure that even the most reluctant or ignorant among us should have a pretty good chance of getting it right and imparting some knowledge to the children. Unfortunately, as is nearly always the case with these type of displays, there is the need for audience participation. Cue twelve adults being handed triangles, xylophones and claves to play at the appropriate time dictated by the on-screen instructor. Dear Lord. It makes for embarrassing viewing that's for sure. I can't make myself join in. I'll watch, and suffer through, that's a given, but I can't make myself ting the little triangle on cue or bash the claves to correspond to the pulse. If I wasn't seated so far away from Bebe Duke, it'd take all my willpower not to beat her to death with one of the bloody claves.

After the meeting finally ended, and I escaped home to once again question the meaning of life, I resolved to do my best and try it one afternoon with my class. I'm always better when I can be in control, and having acquired the necessary knowledge, I was pretty sure that I could do a reasonable job. So the following afternoon, after handwriting and quiet time, I explained to my class that we were going to do music. 'What?' they exclaimed, surprised as it was now April and the only music we'd done was when we sang and played instruments for the Christmas Play four months ago. 'Mrs Wright, would you like some special helpers to help you collect some instruments?' I ask out loud, as backs begin to straighten and fingers are pressed to lips in the hope of being selected. 'Hmm, who can I choose?' I question, as I pretend to consider very carefully who will be released to go on a jolly to the music cupboard with Mrs Wright.

I try to choose children who I know will be a help and not a hinderance to poor Mrs Wright. After all, they do say that many hands make light work, and I'm not expecting her for a moment to schlep all that gear from the hall to our room and back again on her own. 'Willie, Hannah, Vanya, Faris, would you like to go and help Mrs Wright?' I ask, as they jump up excitedly to help. The disappointment of the other twenty-six is palpable, but nevertheless, we're almost on the road, at least the road to achieving some sense of musicality, if that's possible. 'Righty Ho! Come on then, my little band of merry men!' chirps Mrs Wright, as she makes her way out of the classroom, the excited little helpers following eagerly behind.

In the few minutes that she's gone, I give the others a brief run-down of what we're going to do. As they get themselves comfy and I fire up the Smartboard, Mrs Wright and her helpers return with the large collection of instruments this thing says we're going to need. As they set it all down on one of the tables at the back, Mrs Wright pulls up her wheely chair alongside the table nearest to me, invites dear George to come and join her at the table, and braces herself for the cacophony that will inevitably ensue.

We're supposed to use the songs set down for Year One, but I had a look at them already and they're really boring. Always one to be open to improvisation, I decide we'll do the Year Six program which offers much bouncier and familiar songs, namely a pop song that ninety-nine percent of them will likely know. As the background music begins to play, the children begin to join in spontaneously and sing the tune they all know. Then we have a bash at clapping the rhythm.

It's quite interesting to step back and watch them for a moment, to see who finds it surprisingly difficult. As the teacher, you don't always have the time to look around and see who is excelling or struggling with a concept, which as I write this, sounds appalling coming from a teacher. But it's true. There just isn't enough time, and that's where Mrs Wright comes in, as she wheels her chair around the room like Lightening McQueen, alerting me to those who have not understood or who are streets ahead of everyone else.

We like to be participants ourselves, and join in together with the children to clap the different rhythms. They know the song, they can clap, therefore you know what's coming next. I cannot put off the instruments any longer. 'Mrs Wright, can you get the shakers out please?' I begin, as she gets up and moves to the table in readiness. 'Right, when I call your name, go and collect an egg shaker or a pair of chiquitas and then come back to the carpet' I instruct as I begin to call a few names. NB; although it takes forever, name-calling, group-calling and whatever-category-you-can-think-of-calling is inherently necessary. When thirty people are in a confined space, it's downright dangerous to allow them to all rush forth to do anything at the same time, for obvious reasons. Can you imagine if everybody got up to grab a shaker at the same time?

We'd have tears, bruises, and quite likely a drop of blood

here and there too. Some days we still have that happen despite carefully reducing the number of people moving around at the same time.

Now that everybody has their shaker or chiquitas, and most are settled on the carpet ready to begin, I load the next page with the backing track and the animated parrot that's going to tell us what to do. I am armed with my own egg shaker, ready to join in and model what they have to do. The parrot counts us in and then the backing track begins to play. And then, rising slowly and then becoming louder and louder, the cacophony of egg shakers and chiquitas playing reasonably in time fills the room.

As the noise reaches deafening volume, and we can stand it no longer, I raise my hand and put it out straight in front of me, in the international sign of 'stop.' Slowly, the noise level decreases, and one by one they fall silent. After issuing a few more instructions, reminding them to copy what the blasted parrot on screen is showing them, we go again, the egg shakers and chiquitas uniting in an off-time, slightly off-key, glorious din. As I watch the sheer delight in their faces, shaking their instruments now completely out of time with the music, I look to my right at Mrs Wright and smile. As she looks back at me, a wry smile on her face, she pipes up dryly, a lone chiquita in each hand. 'Even Elton John had to start somewhere Miss Graham.'

26

Monkey puzzle

As we slowly but surely get into the swing of things, there's another hurdle to cross, albeit a rather enjoyable one.

We're off to the gym, my favourite trip of the year. After the debacle last year of that bloody zoo, the same trip that we'd vowed never to do again as long as we lived, it's nice to have sailed into calmer waters with this little crew, and we feel optimistic that history won't repeat itself. Two other factors are in our favour.

Firstly, this is April and not September, and we've got a pretty good hold of them now that we've been in close company for the last seven months. And secondly, we're staying local, very local. Local being the operative word, because as we both know from experience, there is little benefit or enjoyment to be had trekking all the way into the city on a coach laden with sixty small children for anything but a jolly up.

So now we're executing a tried and trusted formula, a trip we in fact did make last year with our lovable rogues, that after that rocky start, went off absolutely swimmingly and without a hitch. It's a trip to the local gymnastics club, a comfortable and familiar second home to me where both the coaches and facilities are excellent, making it a very enjoyable experience for all in question. The only slightly concerning thing that needs to be remedied before we can go next week, is to find another two parent helpers. Having received back all of the permission slips allowing the children to take part, a quick glance at the forms has shown that many aren't willing or available to help.

Now as it stands with legal ratios, which are 1:6 when the children are under eight years old, I need one adult per group of six children. Mrs Wright shall take one, her lovely sister (dutifully cleared by the DBS check already) shall take another, while Mrs Beale will accompany one child with special needs, therefore unable to take a group. The teacher is always the leader, and for good reason. We never have a group ourselves to look after, as really the best thing is for us to oversee the entire event. That means I'm three adults short. Jonty's mum kindly volunteers, but as for the remaining two, I'm stuck.

I accept that shepherding small children on any educational visit is not everyone's cup of tea, but you'd be surprised how it actually causes great competitiveness and upset among those parents who clearly make it their mission to be chosen. I've witnessed arguments, and sometimes outright brawls because parents haven't been selected, it's absurd. 'But you promised!' they shout as they angrily accost us at the end of the day, before storming off to inform the headteacher that they've purposely been snubbed. All in front of the children who are hanging on their every word after they've just been dismissed at the end of the day. I just don't get it. Every year we have it, the fighting, the conversations at the end of the day asking if we've decided who's going yet, the stress, and it's so tragic it's laughable. I sometimes joke that if they're so keen that they can go instead of me.

This time round the parents are genuinely delightful, and we really haven't had any issues to write home about. One morning, when the children have gone to assembly, gifting us with a maximum twenty-five minutes in which to get things done, I remember we still need to sort this out. 'I'll go grab the list from the office' I explain to Mrs Wright, as I run and collect the class list to see who we might be able to ask. As the three of us sit down, Mrs Beale included, we scan down the list of names one by one. Now there's certainly a method to this. In fact, I borrowed a line from a TV show that I thought fit the bill and describes accurately how I feel about it. 'It's like a deposition. They're (the parents) looking to gain information to use against us in court. We're looking to limit that information.' And that is truly how I feel about it. Because we don't want to be sat next to them on the coach while they try to elicit personal information from us that we do not wish to share.

They always start slowly, with mundane yet probing questions such as 'do you live locally then?' but then end up enquiring as to the state of your marriage or in my case, if I plan to get married and/or have children. All before 10am. Nice. I think some are genuinely interested in figuring you out more as a person, a person who spends all day every day in the company of their child, and it'd be quite nice to be able to just relax and share a little. But from experience, others will purely seek to try and catch you off guard, when you're in a state of heightened awareness-it being a school trip and all, and then try to gauge how their child is doing in more detail, or trying to get you to dish the dirt on other teachers. In this instance, even I would remain tight-lipped about how much I despise Bebe Duke, such is the oath of office 'thou shalt not throw another teacher under the (proverbial) bus.'

There are quite a few people who despite the fact that they've volunteered, there's not a snowball's chance in hell we would take. As lovely as they are day to day, they are the helicopter parents. The ones that worry constantly, fuss over their child and tie up all our time at the end of the day as to whether we've changed their library book this week and whether they have eaten their snack today. Unfortunately these are the kind of parents that will have their own agenda, and that agenda will be to smother and only look out for their own precious child. In the unlikely event of disaster, I need parent helpers who will step up and take responsibility for their entire group and be of great assistance to a frazzled teacher in a time of crisis, not someone whose only concern is to make sure Sophie's pulled to safety and to hell with the rest of 'em.

Then there's the nightmare parents. They are the ones that have no qualms about writing the most appalling and downright rude letters over minor issues such as reading books, or PE kits, or dance festivals that they feel are a waste of curriculum time (no joke, I had a huge letter from Christopher's mum after I decided the class would participate in the local authority dance festival alongside other schools earlier this year) that render us speechless. But just for posterity, we keep them quite safely as evidence, a paper trail of sorts, in a little box on my desk. Not before sharing them with our colleagues for both amusement and sympathy. And then they have the gaul the expect the furore to have died down enough that they feel they're in with a chance, and that their company would be welcomed!

Does an aneurism hurt? Like hell I'd take them. In what lifetime would I wish them to accompany us on what is already a reasonably stressful event, knowing that the sole purpose of their offer is to simply catch a firsthand glimpse of how Mrs Wright and I handle the children so that they can report back. Nuh uh, over my dead body.

The last and lovely group is made up of perfectly delightful parents who either have additional small people to look after or work themselves, thus making volunteering impossible. As we reach the end of the list of names, we realise that it's this core group that we shall have to draw upon, and that with some advance warning, they might be able to shuffle their workdays around or arrange some childcare. As the three of us toss a few suggestions around, there are a few obvious choices; Dylan's mum, Jordan's mum and Damien's mum. As well as some definite no's.

It'll be the job of Mrs Wright to start the cold-calling, as she heads over to the office to find the necessary numbers. 'No problem my dear' she muses as she collects the list from me. 'I've got the gift of the gab. I used to go the whole distance of the Harrow road to fill my quota of toothbrush sales when I worked for Palmolive, then I'd knock off early for the day.' If there's ever a woman who can sell to the masses, and make the worst idea in the world seem an attractive proposition then it's her. And after a ten minute spell in the office on the phone, Mrs Wright duly returns with the good news that all three can make it. Crisis resolved.

By midweek, the weather has turned from shivery and ten degrees to unbelievably hot and pushing twenty-six degrees. It's April, and the first week back. We knew the blue skies were coming, of course they would be. After an utterly shite two-week 'spring' break, naturally the weather Gods would smile upon all those children heading back to school, robbed of any sunshine in their glorious hiatus from all things education.

It sucks. I love the sun, but not at school, and not when in very close proximity to thirty small children. It's pretty grim for all involved really. All of us, squashed into our tiny cramped classroom, them sat knee to knee in their carpet places and us resting in our wheely chairs, all gasping for the precious and pitiful stream of cool air that the one dusty desktop fan can circulate. Normally I like the windows firmly shut, and Mrs Wright frequently walks in to the airless room declaring 'morning girls, I think you've used up all the oxygen in here!' but today, I'm cranking those windows myself, at 8am.

Every hour feels like torture as those hands on the clock almost feel as if they're moving in the opposite direction. At the start of the day, the children all saunter in, blinking in the brightness of the sun, already scorching down on the playground as I lead the line in. The girls are decked out in their white and red print-dresses, each with the little coordinating belt around their middles carefully buckled. Most of the boys are decked out in knee-length grey shorts and their white polo shirts, hair smartly brushed and ready to go. Well, apart from George, who still has yesterday's dinner speckling his shirt and a general look of grubbiness. I guess last night was no-bath night in his household.

Mrs Wright is a fierce champion of boys in shorts. 'I'd have my boys in shorts, the first day back after Easter.' She's exclaimed in delight each day this week as one by one, the heat has won them over and the boys have pulled out their shorts. 'Wow! Hugo! Move your name up the ladder! And you Samuel, great stuff!' she squeals, as their little faces beam with pride at having been picked out from their peers and bestowed the prestige of moving their tiny named wooden peg from green to pink on the behaviour ladder, aka, *the ladder of judgement* (we'll come to that later).

We all feel fresh, alert and ready to board the learning train, and I, full of good intentions, try to feel positive that we can make it a good and reasonably productive day. But as the mercury rises and the day wears on, it starts to unravel. After playtime, I look around at the sea of increasingly dishevelled children wandering into class, talking over each other as the endless requests for water bottles and toilet breaks begin, and I have to try and get excited to teach their phonics lesson. I'm hot, and feeling more irritable, as I send them to collect their whiteboards and pens and then squash themselves back into their spaces on the carpet as I fire up the Smartboard.

A few moments later, Mrs Wright returns from her coffee break, heaves a sigh as she picks up the reading folder and thumbs down the list. 'Shall I take a dally (daily) reader?' she asks, as she settles herself into her green wheely chair near to my desk. 'God bless you' is all I can muster, my eyes fixed on the screen in front of me as I surf YouTube, trying to find good old Mr Thorn and Geraldine the Giraffe to teach the next digraph. 'Willie, nip and get your books' requests Mrs Wright, as Willie gives up the futile search for a marker pen that actually works, and trudges off to the cloakroom to locate them. Good luck. By playtime, the cloakroom, or at least our part of it, usually looks like we've been burgled.

Geraldine, she must be the richest giraffe in the world, I reckon, and come to think of it, so must Mr Thorn. By all accounts, he's a clever sort of bloke. A teacher whom no doubt realised that unless he was willing to climb the greasy pole of management, he'd likely have to find creative ways to supplement his meagre income, namely in the format of puppeteering in order to teach small people their letters. The self-produced videos on YouTube (Mr Thorn Does Phonics) make a Key Stage One teacher's job a little bit easier, as let's be honest, it's much easier to have someone else make a tit of themselves than you having to do it. And you know what, since I've used his videos through which to teach phonics, it's gone down a storm, largely because children are far more likely to learn if they feel that that are being entertained rather than endlessly talked at.

Geraldine is dubbed the 'phoneme queen' by Mr Thorne, who in each five minute clip, tries, sometimes with great difficulty, to get his herbivorous companion to learn each of her letter sounds, including the ridiculously difficult for this age group 'digraphs' and 'split digraphs.' Do you know what a digraph is, let alone a split one? (What the dickens are those? I hear you say. They're basically a posh word for 'two letters that make one sound.' Like five year-olds really need to know this. I didn't know this until I was twenty-two). He usually sends her on a bit of a goose chase around his typically overpriced not-a-lot-for-your-money London pad to find whatever articles might be lying around that start with that sound, before she proffers them at the camera while we at home pause and count the sounds in each word before trying to write them on our whiteboards. It's actually pretty good, as it's mildly amusing for the adults and therefore wildly entertaining if you are five, as Mr Thorn praises Geraldine's good efforts as she either refuses to say the sound and/or bites him on the hand to their great roars of laughter.

It's all about keeping things interesting, and if this is what works for them, then that's what we do. Above all, learning should be fun and engaging, and I'm not just going to do death by powerpoint lessons that the curriculum content seems to demand. As long as they are learning, then who can argue? The current Ofsted thinking being spouted to us by the boss is that they (Ofsted) can criticise what you do (ie; if the learning has been achieved) but NOT how it's done. Somewhat of a relief but not enough to make the entire process less stressful by any means.

So every day, straight after playtime, it's phonics with Geraldine in all her long-necked, Indian chief, feather-wearing glory. I'm secretly quite jealous of Mr Thorn, as it seems he's managed to become a sort of self-made icon, at least in the teaching world, with twenty-nine thousand subscribers on YouTube. He can often be found hocking his wares as he shamelessly self-promotes his books and merchandise through Geraldine in the odd episode. Well, there's no such thing like self-promotion is there? I wish I'd been a bit more entrepreneurial really.

As the next Monday rolls around, we're ready and excited about our first field trip this year, to the gym. I'm genuinely looking forward to it, even though there's still a whisper of unease just in case any tragedy should befall us. If there's an accident or a problem, it shall fall to me to take the blame. And on a trip just as this, I suppose there's a slightly higher potential for harm given that we're going to be physically active and not just parading around a museum or zoo on foot. Not forgetting last year when Sophie's leg mysteriously went from under her on a vaulting exercise on the floor, which rendered her unable to walk and me having to carry her six year-old frame across the car park back to the coach to go home. I was so worried that night, expecting her to have ended up in A & E that evening, but alas she returned the next day and was running around the playground with her friends. I've never been so relieved to see anyone run.

The children are excited, that's for sure. I mean, who wouldn't be? Only a half-day of lessons and then they will be transported to somewhere that has all the elements set up for a good kids party. As we gather on the carpet that morning, I remind them of what's going to happen and what we'll be doing later on. 'Have you remembered to dig out your leotard Mrs Wright?' I question in front of them, as they turn to grin at her, seated in her familiar brown recliner.

Mrs Wright's face breaks into a huge smile as she ad-libs with gusto. 'Oh yes, Miss Graham! Don't you worry petals! I got it out last night. I've washed it so it's all ready, and I'll be putting it on later ready to whizz around those bars and give you all a demonstration!' she coos, as the children gaze on in amazement. There are a few cries of 'no you won't!' from the few, but I can tell just by looking at them that despite her protestations to the contrary, they don't know whether or not to believe her.

As we return from lunch, expecting to leave in about half an hour's time, there's a problem. Apparently the coach driver has read the time wrong, and having been parked outside for the last forty minutes waiting, he's frantically trying to get us all on board before he has to abandon us to go to his next job. No amount of negotiating changes his mind, and after the quickest possible turnaround that we could muster- getting the children in from the playground, registering and then toilet-ing them before the journey (of critical importance as you can imagine) - as we finally emerge and make our way towards the gate, we catch sight of the large beige vehicle pulling away from the vicinity. Great.

One of the office ladies comes out to inform us that she made a mistake when she booked it, and gave him the wrong time, hence why he arrived so early. What can we do? We can't let the children down, although I think even they've realised that this isn't going to happen, given that our transportation has just done a runner. I can't lie to them. 'Ok everybody,' I say as I look at all the little faces in the line. 'Let's turn around and go back to our classroom and we'll have a chat when we get back there.' Murmurs of 'what?' and 'why are we going back to school?' fill the air, as we reluctantly lead them back to our place of safety, where I quickly explain what's happened, much to the bemusement of the parent helpers who've accompanied us.

Tasking Mrs Beale with the job of entertaining in them in my absence, Mrs Wright and I head to the office to apply some damage control. Surely there must be something that can be done? This has never happened to us before, and I knew that they'd be more than a little disappointed to have to miss such an exciting event. Well, at least in their eyes. As we congregate in the office, we try desperately to call around to see if any other companies have a driver free, and, oh, say a fifty-seater spare coach at the drop of a hat? At first it's not looking good, but then one of the coach companies gives the green light, and can be with us in ten minutes! Hurrah! The original coach will pick us up from the gym as planned, and in ten minutes we'll be on our way.

I return to class where Mrs Beale has been singing French

songs with them courtesy of YouTube, and give them the good news. There's cheering and whooping as they rush to line up and we go forth to the playground to await the miracle vehicle. As we climb aboard the swanky and clearly much more expensive coach, seat belts buckled and excited chatter filling the cabin, Mrs Wright and I breathe a sigh of relief. 'Can you step on it?' I ask the driver, who promises to do his upmost to get us there in time, without speeding or doing anything dangerous. It's highly unlikely we'd even be able to travel at more than thirty miles an hour given the weight of the bloody thing, but hey, it was worth a try.

Somehow, by the grace of God, we arrived unscathed and ready to go, only five minutes late for the session. And relax. Now that the small people have been carefully shepherded across the stony car park and into the safety of the gym, the fun can begin. And begin it does. Twenty minutes of warming up, clambering through the foam pit for good measure and some stretching and we're all ready to try out the equipment. Over the next hour or so, they're jumping off of the tumble track, swinging on the bars, bouncing on the trampoline and practising forward rolls. As the children roam about, sheer excitement and delight shining on their faces, I watch nervously through gritted teeth, praying that nobody injures themselves.

It'll be more than my life's worth to have a serious gymnastic-related injury happen on my watch. Actually that's not specifically true. Before we are permitted to go anywhere with the small people in tow, three thousand pages of paper (the risk assessment) must be filled out and then passed on to the powers that be so that it can be approved. This tedium has only worsened over the years, as fears of being held liable or even sued are at the forefront of every headteacher's mind. So now there's a whole rigmarole to go through before we even set one foot out the front door, by way of a pre-visit by whoever's leading the trip.

An hour and a half later, breathless with exertion and enthusiasm, we lead thirty red-faced small people back down the gravel driveway and back to wait for the coach to collect us. They're happily exhausted, and we're blissfully injury-free. It's a win-win for all of us. The only slight downer is that the coach hasn't arrived yet, and we're standing at the edge of the narrow pavement while cars drive past ready to drop off kids for the after-school classes at the gym. Good old Mrs Wright wanders off to try and keep a look out, and eventually flags down the slightly befuddled driver who wasn't exactly sure where to park. He turns the huge vehicle into the car park, now blocking it for anybody else.

I'm momentarily panic-stricken, worrying about rendering the gym unusable while we board. Sod it. Nothing else has exactly gone to plan today, so I give in to the lovely parent helpers who encourage me to just make everyone else wait. A rallying cry, and do you know what, I'm caving. As we clamber aboard and buckle them all in, traffic mounts up behind us but mercifully there's no impatient beeping. Relief suddenly fills me as we begin to trundle home, that we pulled it off successfully despite the circumstances. Meanwhile Mrs Wright, seated behind the elderly driver, leans forward as she directs him as to which road to take next. Turns out he was new to the company and had no real idea of how to get us home.

Well, what's one more obstacle hey?

27

Un-constructive advice

As I flick my eyes up and down over the page at the columns of original and ridiculous targets that once again I've failed to meet (apparently I've 'ninety-percent' met them) my insides burn with irritation. I'm seething with a sort of pent-up rage that's been bubbling under the surface for the past ten months.

You see, what I've kept from you until now, is that despite all of the fun, the kindness, the care and good teaching of the children, I've actually spent ten months batting metaphorical balls back and forth across the tennis court of 'disciplinary action' with the powers that be as my opponent. The whole upsetting process has been made all the more irritating and enraging, because it's not anything to do with the teaching, nothing to do with safeguarding or not treating children the way that is expected, it's the thing that you go for when you've got nothing else on a person; their timekeeping.

That's right, after a few months of 'informal monitoring' I was slapped with the first white envelope inviting me to come to a meeting to discuss the error of my ways, in their eyes at least. Upon closer inspection, said envelope contained a lovely excel chart, kindly filled with the alleged times that I'd arrived late each morning. Now this might be a good time to explain about a teacher's working hours. Teachers do not actually sign a contract that sets down any contracted hours, the main reason being that one will inevitably spend more than the suggested thirty-five hour week that many other professions work, given the nature of the job. The headteacher can therefore make a reasonable expectation on his or her staff as to when they must arrive by, but by the grace of God in my school, we are trusted as adults to be able to manage our time efficiently and are free to go within a respectable time frame after the children have departed. The set time of 8:30am every morning was therefore perfectly reasonable, given that the school day does not officially begin until 9am. Arriving by 8:30am therefore gives us enough time to get prepped for the day, and if you're lucky, a cup of tea and a natter with your nearest and dearest before you're on stage for the next seven hours.

Now I did my best over the years (having worked there for the last eleven) to meet that expectation, but arriving on time in general has been something that has eluded me for my entire life. But as long as I arrived 'around' 8:30am, I never had any problems. Until this year. Lateness is a theme that has pervaded my entire life. Christ, I was late for school myself endlessly during secondary school because my five year-old sister threw a fit every morning about getting dressed, yet somehow I never managed to get the three consecutive 'lates' that would have meant the ultimate punishment- the after-school detention. Another example of my invincibility or so I thought.

I'm the last to arrive in any of my friendship groups, the continual butt of the jokes about the time that I left the house or caught the train. One of my best friends actually used to tell me the wrong time we needed to leave on purpose, and move it forward half an hour so as to ensure that we could make the drive from suburbia to London on a Saturday night before the pub closed.

I took it on the chin, laughed it off among my friends, yet always felt slightly guilty that people had to wait for me. But the real reason, the reason I was so embarrassed about and felt I could never tell anybody, was that since my early teens, I've suffered from a lot of anxiety. And from that anxiety, came the need to ensure everything on my to-do list had been completed so that I could leave the house. Unfortunately with anxiety, the more you feed it, the more it takes.

While I hated it, I needed it to feel safe and it enabled me to be able to face the chaos of the day, resting easier in the knowledge that I had done exactly what I needed to do. The only problem was that it was utterly exhausting. What you feel you need to do means that you start the day with the weight of the world on your shoulders, dragging yourself up every morning at 6:30am just like everybody else, but trying to fit in ten times as many things.

Such was the embarrassment I felt that I couldn't explain why I was late, so had to take the role that I'm sure my boss cast me in, as a lazy toad who just couldn't be arsed to get out of bed until 8am and then had to scurry to get herself to work in the nick of time. Only that wasn't me. The only person I eventually confided in was Mrs Wright, who being the wonderfully supportive friend that she is, actually warmed my heart when she told me 'I'm not thinking any less of you, or judging you. I'm actually really pleased you felt you could trust me enough to tell me.'

And now the chips were most definitely down, and I had no way of defending myself. I think when the Big Guns actually handed me the dreaded white envelope, I didn't even have to ask what was in it, and muttered something like 'oh, I've been expecting this!' Poor Mrs Wright, my long suffering co-captain has steadied the ship and helped me sail through these choppy waters, and propped me up when I've wobbled. I've got an alarmingly high stack of white A4 envelopes marked 'Miss Graham, Private and Confidential' that have been hastily rammed into the depths of our junk cupboard, treated with the contempt they deserve.

When the ball started rolling, I gingerly slid my thumb under the flat ridge of the envelope, mildly curious to see just exactly what my crimes were, and also how much damage control might need to be taken. But after several more arrived in quick succession, usually within a few days of each meeting, the avoidant in me quickly froze, and delegated the task of sifting through the next wrap sheet to Mrs Wright.

She quickly assumed the role of my PA, thumbing through the pages of documentation and 'evidence' and summarising the main points and informing me of what I needed to do. There's something about hearing the black and white, no-nonsense but also less hysterical version of the charges that made them somehow seem less overwhelming. And slowly, after the necessary information was imparted, I would find myself wandering across the classroom towards Mrs Wright and the envelope, and then somehow find the courage to pick up that envelope and read it for myself. 'Shall we set fire to them at the end of the year? What do you think?' suggests Mrs Wright cheerily after the latest post-meeting wrap up.

The most ironic part of this sad tale, in that among the original charges, the funniest thing was that the timings at which I had been logged to arrive at work had been recorded as '*Monday*

11th June, 8:32am'- two minutes after the deadline! Talk about pedantic, and if it hadn't been so ridiculous, it would have been tragic. Oh and guess who else was a key player in all of this? Why the one who also had to crane her neck to peer through the cloudy glass of the uncleaned-in-a-whole-year windows to record my arrival time- why Bebe Duke, that's who.

'Right, hang on a minute, let me get this straight' chuckles Mrs Wright as she thumbs through the papers with me after school that day. 'The person that hates you most, that tried to get you fired once before, the one that's got it in for you- she's doing the timekeeping!' she exclaims in disbelief. We both dissolve into laughter despite the fairly sombre occasion. Because it's downright ludicrous. If I were the boss and trying to use this small grain of leverage that I'd inadvertently given them by being one or two minutes late every day, then wouldn't I want to ensure that should things escalate, that my evidence was from a credible and impartial source?

***

'My mum's friends aren't being very nice to her at work' pipes up Toby, as he removes his hands from around my waist after rushing forth at me for a hug as I cross the playground on my return from lunch. 'Oh, that's not very nice, poor mummy' I respond, wondering just where this conversation is going. Toby continues 'yeah, they don't want her to be at work anymore so she's going to have to find another job.' Before I can respond, he scampers off to join in with a game of chase with Jonty and Damien. Poor Toby's mum. The woman has likely found herself in a similar situation as I do. However, it's oddly reassuring to know that arbitrary disciplinary nonsense does also pervade other workplaces, even if you're a high-flying London marketing executive. If only Toby's mum knew the sad reality of her own son's teacher. If only I could talk.

***

'I'm decompressing' is all I can muster, as I bury myself in our cupboard and flick through my phone, trying to soothe my angry form at the end of the latest review meeting. I've just had another meeting with the Big Guns to discuss whether I've met my ridiculous targets for the half-term. And I had. In their eyes however, it's another story. 'You've met them ninety percent, I just can't tick them off quite yet.' It's nonsense. Purely because 'get here on time every day for God's sake!' couldn't really stand alone as a target. Three more had to be created to make the monitoring plan look a bit more credible, as if there were more serious problems beyond the only crime, the inability to make it there on time every day. The Big Guns needed to add some more, so I have been observed teaching my class every week for four weeks. Now that it's been extended, I'll have to go through the whole rigmarole for another four weeks. Terrific.

When it began, I braced myself for the stress that it causes, being watched by your (woefully inept) line manager that ultimately has the power to decide whether you meet the target or not. It was undoubtedly enormously stressful, not least because everything had to be planned for to the nth degree. What will they do if they find it too easy? Have I made it easy enough for the lower ability ones to gain something from it? Have I got all of the things I need to actually teach the lesson? Now anybody can plan a good lesson, but ultimately it's the execution that will be the decider. (I hasten and also feel the need to add that every single observation I had over the year, including these, which I think amounted to ten, was deemed to be 'good' with some outstanding features.)

As is the case over my entire career thus far; I am a good teacher. I consistently achieve good, I've had a few outstanding observations, and I'm happy with that. Call it my lack of competitive spirit, but I simply don't feel that need to be outstanding, as a lot of my colleagues aspire to be. And that's not because I'm lazy or I don't want to give children the very best teaching that they could possibly have, it's just that I'm content with being 'good.' Teacher observations are graded, (sometimes officially-don't get me started) as being one of four categories; Outstanding, Good, Requires Improvement, Unsatisfactory).

In truth, I think the reason that consistently good is all I aspire to be, is that it feels as though the goalposts have shifted for us in the same way that the levels and grades have conspired to make the children's experience of learning less enjoyable. It feels as though where once my best was good enough, now it simply isn't. And this is what really grates on me. I don't want to try and hit three outstanding observations this year, or any year come to think of it. You've made it too hard. I don't want to feel that I'm slowly and subtly being pushed and squeezed in the direction of what the county feel is right for me, and that my consistently good teaching is no longer good enough. Like it or not, this is where we are at. Is it any wonder why plenty of teachers feel like jacking it in?

Of course not, when the pressure is constantly increasing. The pressure to be better, and to compete against each other. But what for? It only serves to create the same bad feeling and disaffection that the children feel, when their best efforts are no longer praised and they are told that their best does not meet the required standard. Have we ever stopped to think for a moment as to how demoralising and damaging that is? I still remember to this day, on one of my favourite US TV shows as a kid, when a girl of about twelve got herself a 'D' in Spanish, and brought her report card home to show her dad.

Now part of the reason I loved this particular show was because there was always a touchy-feely moment near the end, when the twinkly music would play and a good life lesson or moral would be learned. It might sound sappy but it stuck with me all of these years, as she asked her dad 'but what if I work as hard as I can and I still can't get an A?' And he responded 'then I'll be proud of you for working as hard as you can.' So why aren't we proud of today's school children for doing their best and working as hard as they can? For the same reason that us teachers aren't granted the same privilege- we want more out of you.

It's mid-April when I have the next review meeting to be told I need to repeat another four-week monitoring period. I would never normally defy the rules so vehemently, but today, quite frankly, I've had a gutful. I had to abandon poor Mrs Wright just to go and have the bloody meeting in the Big Gun's office, so she was just expected to get on with it and hold the fort until I returned. Mrs Wright calmly carries on, bible in hand and candle in the centre of the room lit, as she reads the Easter Story to the weary children quietly gathered in a circle around her. I told you she was a saint.

I feel horrible. For not taking over immediately and relieving her of some of the strain, after all, I'm the teacher. But the shred of self-esteem I've been clinging on to is vastly disappearing, and having to endure yet more ridiculous meetings like this is enough to bring anybody down. And I don't want my bad feeling to seep over into how I behave with the children. Mrs Wright knows that, she knows me better than anybody else here. So like a trouper, she carries on, seemingly without a care in the world, and leaving me to gather my strength to face the world once more, or at least, our little world, where it counts the most.

Remember my earlier chapter about emotions? Well, teachers often have to attend meetings during the school day. Those would be the kind where the poor unsuspecting TA's are basically just informed (occasionally) that they're running the show, with thirty children as their cast, and no crew on deck, and told to just get on with it for an hour, with no extra pay I might add. It's only when the shit hits the fan that you don't want to walk back into your room again, but you have no choice. To turn on that pageant smile (thanks to my dentist, and the tooth-whitening program, I'm pretty much there. God bless that peroxide) and carry on like the puppet that you are, regardless of any feelings you might have. And that feels like the worst thing for me. It would be nice to have that space to process the event, especially if you've just had to fight tooth and nail or had a big barney with your boss, to regroup, but alas, it never happens. There's not even a water cooler, where you might be able to spend a few minutes idly pouring icy water into a paper cup as you stare longingly out of the office window, dreaming of a world which does not involve such tedium.

I got my latest grades back too and I only passed every observation. Every bloody one. I'll bet that was a bit of a disappointment for them. God damn it, I'm a huge pain in their ass. I'm not a bad teacher so I can't be fired on the spot, which makes the process a sight more tricky for them. So they've had to get creative if they're going to find alternative ways to solve this particular problem, i.e. me, and if it wasn't so tragic it would be laughable. In the seemingly endless array of meetings I've been obliged to attend, I've actually had to suppress a few titters and try hard to compose myself in the face of such farcical proceedings. Nobody has a bloody clue what's going on, and every question I ask is met with a round-the-houses sort of rambling conversation that leaves me more in the dark than before, if that's even possible. If schools had to be part of the real business world, they'd crumple like cheap tin foil under the slightest pressure.

28

Death knell

'Hold on just a moment, what school do you work for? I need to just check that we don't represent them.' Fat chance, like they could afford you. Oh wait, neither can I, come to think of it.

I'm on the phone with my lawyer. Given what's been going on for the last ten months, and given that I'm in the process of repeating another four-week period of monitoring, it seemed prudent to at least get some advice. I can't actually believe I'm in this position, but nevertheless, the fire has ignited in me and now I'm like a dog with a bone trying to reach a satisfactory conclusion to the matter. She was supposed to call me at 12:30pm, bang in the middle of my lunch hour one Wednesday, but she said she needed an extra fifteen minutes. I unloaded the dishwasher, watching the clock creep into the danger zone, knowing full well I was not going to have the time and space needed to deal with this properly. The whole bloody point of squeezing this in during lunch was so that I didn't have to do it at work. After all, if you're trying to find out if you can get one over on your employer, it's probably a good idea to play your cards close to your chest and not defame them while they've got their ear and a glass to the door.

She finally calls me, a very pleasant woman probably not much older than me. I'll bet she's taking home about quadruple what I do. It takes me about ten minutes to relay the whole mess in bits, well, at least the parts that I can remember, while she interjects with lawyer questions, no doubt trying to extract the important bits from amidst the rambling incoherence that comes from me.

I can't think straight, it's all come out in a jumble. As it would anyone really, when asked to retell ten months worth of misery. Ten months of pointless meetings, warnings, threats of warnings, improvement plans. It's a bloody wonder I can remember, self-preservation having filtered much of it out. We finally arrive at the part about my options. I'm all ears, as she reminds me that she won't charge me for this call, but that anything afterwards will incur her hourly rate of an eye-watering two hundred and seventy-five pounds. Yikes. I think I get about fifty quid a day, Mrs Wright about nine pounds an hour. Talk about no justice.

I've had enough. Enough is enough, and I want to put an end to this nonsense, not keep going round and round in circles with them. So I cut to the chase. 'Can I sue them?' is what I'm really going for, but as expected, the answer is far from clear. 'Well, my feeling is that they've probably done just enough to tick the right boxes and cover themselves' she muses, 'but you could raise a grievance. I think that would be the best thing to do. Start by looking through their equal opportunities policy, and we can go from there.'

I hang up the phone, looking in dread at the numbers on the clock, which show just how seriously late I'm going to be. Talk about irony. I frantically shove the rest of the piece of toast I made into my mouth, ram the lock on the patio door shut, as I throw my shoes on and mumble some flustered goodbyes to the dog while he barks me all the way out of the front door. As I speed away, I silently say a prayer in my head: Oh God, please let Mrs Wright have gotten back before I did. Poor Mrs Wright had a rare lunchtime appointment herself, and although she should be back in time to save my bacon, there's no guarantee.

She did. But that doesn't mean I haven't been clocked coming back in at 13:15pm, ten to fifteen minutes late, depending on how you look at it. It honestly never happens, and I feel guilty, yet I know in my absence the children will be supervised. Mrs Wright hasn't eaten her lunch either, but she made it back to the prison by the skin of her teeth, and thankfully by the grace of God, she's done the register and started the handwriting. We barely manage a quick conference as they settle, so regretfully we put it all to one side to recommence the learning. She takes a reader (and her sandwich) into the group room, while I try to get my pulse rate down from ninety and send for Toby to fetch his reading books.

Later on I send for Mrs Wright to go to the photocopy room and fetch the giant binder that contains the paper copies of all the school policies. It seemed a wise thing to do following my lawyer's advice. A few moments later she returns empty-handed, and I immediately suspect foul play. 'I'm so sorry my dear' she begins, smiling 'I got Brenda-ed.' Enough said. Brenda, the woefully inept bursar speaks more slowly than the small children, and if you get caught by her, you won't get away in a hurry. What transpired, is that dear, elderly Brenda happened to wander into the room just as Mrs Wright held the heavy folder in her hands, before asking twenty questions about who it was for and why it was being removed, finally exploding 'if Betsy wants it, she can come and get it herself! She shouldn't be sending you to do it!' One might question why such a strong reaction was warranted. Maybe she had an inkling that the disciplinary procedures were anything but watertight.

The now slightly bemused Mrs Wright remains calm, with a hint of a smile on her face as she tries to make sense of this nonsense, before reluctantly returning the folder to its home on the high shelf above the laminator. Now most people, when they explode in fury at you, are generally able to read subtle signals in body language and facial expression that suggest the person you've just bawled at might be just a tad miffed with you. Not dear Brenda, who recovers herself immediately, before breaking into a huge grin and carrying on a conversation as if nothing had happened. 'Did you see *I'm a Celebrity* on TV last night?' she grins, leaving Mrs Wright two shakes away from clobbering her.

Most people would probably choose to give in, but we decide to use our trump card, in the form of Mrs Beale who loves confrontation and rises to the challenge. Knowing that adults aren't really ever allowed to leave the classroom at all, she takes a piece of maths work that she'll pretend she's copying for the child she supports. 'I don't care!' she says defiantly, 'I'm 'onna go get it!' And off she goes, duly returning a few minutes later with the heavy orange folder and some fake and highly unnecessary photocopying that promptly hits the bin. True Bronx spirit that is. I suppose I'll have to find some time to extract and actually read the policy, likely taking it home. I wonder if anyone will miss the folder while I borrow it, so hastily I ram it into the depths of our overflowing cupboard until we're ready to return it.

That night, I realise I forgot to take the bloody thing home, so instead I decide to have a look on the website, where all the school policies are stored for parents to peruse. My mum and I scroll down the page, while I scan to find the correct one. The mouse hovers over the icon marked 'Nut Awareness Policy.' 'What's that?' questions my mum. 'Is that for reporting nutters in your school?' I wish. Of course it tells of the school's stance on children with nut allergies in school, but I can certainly see how it could be misconstrued given our conversation. Christ, my school's full of them. Now where's that form?

As we skim down the page, I finally find what I'm looking for, in the form of their 'Grievance Policy.' However on closer inspection, I find the words that tell me I'm stuffed. 'A grievance cannot be raised when it is in relation to any disciplinary procedures.' Bollocks, now what? I decide to email my lawyer again. After all, it's not like I can call her again without ending up two hundred and seventy-five quid down, so this might be my only option.

Despite my cheerful day-to-day persona, it has gotten me down. I do love my job and I don't like being in trouble. It feels doubly unfair given I'd eventually had to embarrass myself and disclose the very thing that I'd fought the hardest to keep hidden, anxiety, only to find out that it achieved nothing at all except to amuse the Big Guns no doubt. And now I've got a black mark on my unblemished record, a *First Written Warning*, for timekeeping. (I did note that the policy says it remains live for six months, and given that it was issued at the start of the year and it is now June, that it's now null and void). 'Is it? Ooh, I don't know! Is that what it says?' exclaims the Big Guns when I remind her of this. 'I'll go back to Lesley and ask her' referring to lovely Lesley, the HR lady and her partner in crime.

The problem is, that even after they've issued the warning, they still want to make a plan of action to try to remedy the whole mess. Whereas I'm quite happy to just take the warning and call it a slap on the wrists, the aim is to engage me in a process to improve my timekeeping, hence why this hasn't gone away. I asked a good friend who works in HR at a multinational company for a bit of info, hoping he might be able to make heads or tails of this, yet still with a hint of embarrassment. I was a little relieved to hear that while he couldn't be sure of the legalities himself, he had had a similar thing happen to him early on in his career, and told me not to sweat it, which went some way to removing a little of the stigma for me.

Having already embarrassed myself and suffering the indignity of having to explain just why I'm always late to work without actually using the word anxiety, in front of several members of the governing body no less, it made not a jot of difference and the warning was issued. They suggested I go and pay a visit to occupational health, and I was surprised to find that I went quite willingly. There, one bleak and cold, miserable Friday in February, I met with a lovely doctor who asked me to describe what had been going on. He assured me that he had no knowledge other than a simple referral sheet bearing my name and who I worked for, and I began to fill him in. As he asked me some difficult questions, namely what kind of impact this was having on my life in general, I did get a bit upset.

He was very kind, and arranged for me to have some NHS funded CBT, assuring me that it really was in my best interests to disclose this to my employer, however reluctant I might be. I sadly agreed, heading home where I spent the rest of the day feeling extremely low and wondering just how on earth I had gotten to this point. Thankfully it was half-term the following week, and I didn't have to face anybody as I waited anxiously for the occupational health report to arrive. When I read it, although it made for uncomfortable reading, I was hopeful that it might explain all of this mess and that there would be some understanding. The doctor even asked if they would kindly consider revoking the warning given the nature of the disclosure. With trepidation, I responded to allow them to release it to the Big Guns only, having little faith that it would remain private beyond this.

Then nothing. No acknowledgment, nothing. I eventually, after the break, had to ask her directly if she had read the part about revoking the warning. 'Oh, I don't know, I'll have to ask the HR lady and get back to you' was the response. 'Good grief' exclaimed Mrs Wright when I filled her in moments later. 'They couldn't organise a piss-up in a brewery.' And so they couldn't.

When eventually I was summoned in to the office, good old Lesley, now practically on first name terms after so many meetings, declared that no they couldn't, as if I had wanted to make a disclosure, then it should have been at the appeal meeting in January. And that was that. And that's when I knew I needed my lawyer friend. I rationalise that it's just a bump in the road, albeit a very rocky one, and decide the only thing I can do is to keep on truckin' and make one last push to get the silly targets ticked off once and for all. Just knowing that I've had some legal advice, albeit an expensive move, gives me the courage to go on, knowing that I'll only use it as a last resort. As Mrs Wright reminds me, with great seriousness, that enough really is enough, and this needs to stop one way or another very soon. I can't argue with that.

Sometimes I wondered how I managed to carry on seemingly without a care in the world, pretending to the children, the parents and my colleagues that everything was fine and dandy, but I did. Mrs Wright and I carried on injecting fun and good humour into the very fabric of our school lives, and continued to teach the children well, as well as providing the emotional care and stability that they needed.

I'm reminded that lots of people, when faced with constructive dismissal or disciplinary woes, eventually crack under the pressure and either resign or go on long-term sick leave. I did neither. I came in every single day, put a smile on my face, and decided that I would get through this, if it was the last thing I did. As you know, 'double lippy' is Mrs Wright's mantra for the tough times, but it really helped. Simple power play. You either let them win, or you don't. And I didn't.

The weekly observations were undoubtedly a stressful experience for all of us, but after I demanded an extra observer, having realised that my line manger designated the task was anything but impartial, I was on fire. As a naturally shy and fairly reserved individual, I don't tend to perform well when I'm centre stage. Strangely a lot of teachers feel the same way, as while we feel one hundred percent comfortable hamming it up for the children, add adults to the mix and it's a very different kettle of fish.

The children, who usually feel the pressure as well, really rose to the challenge, and although initially slightly perplexed at the intrusion of two familiar teachers once a week, they simply became used to it, and we began to return to business as usual. The only tricky part was explaining why in fact they were there, as it might seem rather strange for them week on week to have two extra bodies in our collective personal space. After all, it's not like I could say to my lovely bunch of five and six year-olds, 'hey, the management think your teacher's kind of rubbish. We're hoping we can stress the hell out of her by judging her lessons every week so that's why we've pulled up our chairs at the back of your class with clipboards in our hands, but don't you worry petals, you just crack on,' could I?

So every week when they arrived, clipboards duly in hands as they settled themselves in the tiny chairs at the back of the room out of my direct line of sight, I settled them on to the carpet and put on my actress voice and lied through my teeth to them all. 'Right everybody, Mrs Bates loves coming to see you learn, so she asked me if she could come and see your English work this morning, because you're all so clever!' I explained, trying to believe the words myself. And this was all that was needed. No questions asked. They happily carried on, and as they relaxed, I did the same and tried to pretend we hadn't acquired the unwelcome visitors.

The best parts were when they saw us as we truly are; excited, enthused, kind and fun. Mrs Wright taking on the role of Jack from Jack and the Beanstalk, sat up straight in her easy chair as the children took turns to read out some of their questions they had written on their mini-whiteboards was a definite high point. The woman loves a chance to ad-lib, and I marvelled at her ability to be so in tune with them.

They were positively eating out of her hand, as she made up answers on the spot to their great guffaws of laughter, while I steered the questions beyond 'what colour hair do you have?' and 'why were you cross with Jack?' It was utterly perfect when Nina was selected to ask Mrs Wright, aka Jack, a question and fired off 'but how did the beans become magic?' and both observers joined in with our collective laughter. 'I thought this was supposed to be a question to ask Jack?' I asked Nina as we all giggled. It definitely showed us in our true light, and the result was another resounding 'good' with no points for development given.

By the time I reached the finishing line at the beginning of June, I was ready to collapse with nervous exhaustion. There was to be a review meeting the first week back after half-term, to hopefully sign off all the targets and put this thing to bed. I couldn't think of a single ball that I had dropped, an observation that had gone badly, yet I worried it could never be enough. After all, if they want you out, they want you out.

The meeting date came and went, which only served to highlight just how ridiculous and ill-advised the whole process was. Eventually a yellow post-it was shoved under my nose with a new date for us to meet, the Big Guns, I and dear Lesley from HR, in another month's time at the beginning of July! While I was sort of relieved that we could just relax a bit and enjoy the last few weeks free from the strain, Mrs Wright was spitting feathers on my behalf. 'You mean you've done everything they've asked and now you have to wait three weeks to get it all finished up?' she ranted angrily. And I got it. I just couldn't feel anything by this point.

But it was interesting, and anger-inducing in equal measure, to know that this had all been so high-priority back in the autumn and spring terms, when frankly nothing much else was on the agenda. But now that it's almost the end of the year and there's data to be analysed, staffing to be sorted, and the whirling dervish that is Scott the Sheep has just arrived, that this all falls by the wayside. A minor inconvenience now that there's more exciting stuff to play with. Not if you're the poor teacher they did this to though. Having already had verbal confirmation that it was all done and dusted, I knew I could never trust it until I held it in writing in my own two hands.

As I sat in Karen's little cabin that week, listening to the occasional whooshing of cars going past the busy country road, I relayed the latest update and voiced my concern at having still received nothing in writing. 'Maybe they ran out of paper' she suggested dryly, making the corners of my mouth turn upwards into a smile. The poor woman knows just how many white envelopes I've been the unfortunate recipient of this last now thirteen months, and she's had to listen to all of my feelings about it.

The end finally comes on the penultimate Monday in July, during a half-hour meeting. There were still parts of the conversation where I wanted to argue, to suggest how bloody unfair the whole damn process was in the first place, but I had to remind myself that this was the end, and it really was in my best interests to button it. As I returned to class afterwards, where Mrs Wright had held the fort once more, I felt distinctly lighter. We didn't really have a proper chance to discuss it until later in the day when the children had gone home, when the two of us, hunched uncomfortably in the tiny wooden chairs, began to dissect it all.

'It was fine, I'm just glad it's over' I breathe, feeling a sense of calmness pervade my being. 'You'll never guess what she said at the end though' I venture, as Mrs Wright takes a sip of her tea, the only one we've managed to drink the entire day. 'Good old Lesley (from HR) said 'I hope it's been a positive experience for you' I relay, waiting for her reply. 'I hope it's been a positive experience for you!' shrieks Mrs Wright, as she almost spits her tea out. 'Oh, brilliant! I loved it! Why don't we do it again next week!' she laughs incredulously, as we shake our heads in disbelief.

It's over.

29

Summer fun

'Your toenails look like mine when I've painted them' observes Nina dryly, as my pink painted toes semi-encased in bright green Birkenstock sandals hover near her eye line as she sits on the carpet. Suffice to say I painted them yesterday in a hurry, and I've clearly managed the similar ability of a five year-old.

We're into the final half-term of the school year, and it's all I can do to stop myself from blasting out Madonna's *Holiday* song at full volume. We actually did do that last year, when our little topic project was to sort pictures into two groups, work time and holiday time and then stick them into their books. It actually made for a very cheerful and busy afternoon as they beavered away cutting and sticking, the tables a sea of paper as I alternated between playing *Holiday* or Dolly Parton's *9 to 5*. Well, nobody said I couldn't.

An impromptu meeting with the Big Guns later in the week brings me swiftly back to earth from fantasising about the summer holidays. 'If Ofsted came in, they'd be all over Year One like a rash' smiles the Big Guns. 'I'm sorry, what?' I reply, as my frazzled brain struggles to keep up. It's the phonics data apparently. It was worrying low (in the boss, and the county's eyes) at around sixty-six percent in 2015, so we've spent the last several years executing 'interventions' in a timely fashion, i.e.

before June, so that it got us out of the red and into the black, with a far more wholesome eighty-three percent. But each year they just move the goalposts. If we got eighty-three percent last year, well let's try to get ninety percent this year, never mind which children we've got. This means that ninety percent of our children have to achieve the pass mark that may or not be changed after the entire country has finished the test, in order for us to give ourselves a pat on the back that we've managed to keep Ofsted away for another year.

Now that it's looming ever closer, Mrs Wright will be trapped in that little room day after day to practice the 'alien words' with the poor souls who realistically have little chance of ever passing it. It's also SATs week, which mercifully has nothing whatsoever to do with us, but which has resulted in Mrs Wright being kidnapped and held hostage to invigilate in some of the Year Six classes. 'You won't see me until after break my dear' chirps Mrs Wright on the first day of SATs week, swapping her trainers for pumps at five to nine that morning. I can feel my irritation prickling, I don't want to be without her, because it'll be bloody hard work without my co-captain.I sigh, and I resign myself to a miserable morning left to sail the ship alone, and go to collect the children in. Every year the TA's are 'borrowed' to be used as invigilators for the Year Six children doing their tests.

We've got ourselves settled on the carpet, when back she comes with a piece of paper in hand, full of the joys of spring as she realises she's not needed for another ten minutes. As I wearily begin to take the register, I cast my eyes across the room. There's not a whole host of happy faces today. I look at Vanya, asking her if she's ok. 'I'm feeling grumpy today, and I don't know why' she frowns as she skulks around my chair one morning. Then Christopher starts sobbing. All I did was say good morning? I guess not everyone's a morning person.

Somehow the show will have to go on, so after calling the register, I decided to go off track and start the day with a song. 'Shall we do a song to try and cheer Vanya and Christopher up?' I suggest, as they all happily agree. 'Christopher, would you like to choose?' I ask him, as I scroll down the page on the computer to show him the section before he chooses an old favourite. As a class we love our music and songs, and it's a really good way of breaking the ice in the morning, as well as getting us all in a positive mindset to begin the day. Mrs Wright and I are like the Captain and Tennille. Well, after all, 'love will keep us together' as the song says. They love a bit of chit-chat every morning, and to be honest, so do we. It's our ritual, and having successfully improved the mood of both Christopher and Vanya, there's a much better chance that they'll be receptive now to the learning we'll have to start.

In the meantime, Raphael's waving his hand madly, trying to get my attention. He's desperate to tell his news, so I encourage him to share it with us all. 'I'm having a barbecue tonight' he beams, informing us how dad is going to fire it up when he gets home ready for an evening of al-fresco dining and sopho-moric hijinks in the garden. Mrs Beale pipes up in her New York drawl. 'What should I bring?' Raphael and many others chuckle, as we exclaim 'but why haven't we been invited?' It's mindless trivia, but it gives us all a much needed lift in the morning before we put the chains around our ankles once more in the pursuit of learning.

By Thursday, we're all feeling weary, as the June gloom is upon us bearing a cloudy, sunless sky. It's PE, and after almost nine months of training, the whole thing is far less excruciatingly painful than it was in the beginning. Nevertheless, while for most children doing anything sport-related is the highlight of their week, others aren't nearly so enthused. A little trick they've picked up is to mysteriously 'lose' their PE kit, which let's face it, isn't really that hard to do in that tardis of a cloakroom. Usually after they return, declaring it missing, they're offered the helpful words from both Mrs Wright and I 'if I come out there, am I going to find it?' which usually makes them hesitate for a moment before deciding it is in fact worth another look, returning moments later with the bag swung around their shoulder. Voila!

But every now and then, even Mrs Wright must admit defeat and declare the bloody thing MIA. Now the small people are very clever. If they don't want to take part, it's a brilliant trick to hide your PE bag. But every now and again it backfires on them, to find that it's not the dance lesson they hated but in fact gymnastics with a whole room of exciting equipment to try out! Only they have to sit and watch, being that they're sans the proper attire. Bummer. Then there are the long-term offenders, children whose PE kits we haven't seen for yonks, and somehow slip under the radar, as is the case with Hugo today.

'Can you phone Hugo's mum, that's two weeks he hasn't had his PE kit' I sigh wearily that morning. Mrs Wright dutifully scuttles off in search of the contact number hidden deep within the grey folders in the main office. The children begin to get changed (those that do come bearing a PE kit that is), and pretty soon the noise level is rising and there's a sea of what would appear to be abandoned clothing occupying the floor. A few minutes later, Mrs Wright returns, beaming cheerfully as she makes her way over to her brown recliner.

'Children, listen,' she begins, and the noise begins to lower, as she looks at Mrs Beale and I, before she continues what I know will be a humorous tale. 'Children, I went to the office to phone Hugo's mummy, and I accidentally dialled the wrong number in the folder. Mrs Benzie the office lady had to come and help me' she continues, as the children scattered in various parts of the classroom and in various states of undress, look on earnestly to hear what she has to tell them.

'Well' she carries on, beginning to chuckle. 'I've just had a very nice chat with a lovely lady up in Manchester!' she laughs, looking at Mrs Beale and I as we start to chuckle. 'And do you know, it's gorgeously sunny up there today!' she laughs, as we dissolve into giggles. It could only happen to her.

After a return trip and a voicemail message to Hugo's mum via the correct number this time, she apologises profusely that he's lost it, and promises to deliver a replacement the following day which she dutifully does. There'll only be a few more sessions left as far as PE goes this year, but at least he can take part from now on, whether he wants to or not!

30

A Royal castle trip

Another year, another trip I didn't book. Bebe Duke was the self-appointed coordinator of this one, and granted it's one we do year after year so it shouldn't come as a surprise. School trips always have to be booked well in advance, and it's not uncommon to book it for the following year immediately after you've just come back.

As the day dawned, the weather was cloudy and very cool, although not as cold as last year when we nearly froze to death in the middle of May. Last year was reasonably eventful for other reasons. In addition to it being twelve degrees, I'd woken up with a pounding headache and a temperature, certain I was coming down with something. There really was absolutely no suggestion of calling in sick, so I had to just dose myself up and pray that the day passed quickly. There is just no way you can call in sick on a school trip day, the feeling being that if you can walk, you can work.

I really felt that on a regular day I'd have done exactly that, but in addition to all the kerfuffle and procuring of another adult to lead the trip, there's always the fear of judgement from your colleagues that you might just be faking, looking for a get-out clause. Not to mention I would have felt awful abandoning Mrs Wright on one of the most stressful days of the year, plus as sick as I felt, the thought that it might be the

Big Guns who stepped up to the plate was enough make me a whole lot sicker. You've got to get on with it.

Once we were underway, and we had survived the reasonably short journey to the castle unscathed, as well as suffered our way through all of the security check and x-ray machine debacle, the next logical step was a toilet break. Having done this all before we left school, we're now an hour on and the only solution on trips is to go en masse on arrival so that we can get on with the itinerary without having to keep stopping for one or two overactive bladders. Not including Mrs Wright's of course.

It was at this point, as we all congregated on the concrete steps while queueing for the loos, boys on one side, girls on the other, and the parent helpers deliberately posted inside, that both Mrs Wright and I noticed Matteo. And by noticed Matteo, I mean that we noticed how grey and pale he was, sitting slumped on the cold stone steps, his head in his hands. He'd been off sick at the tail end of the week before, and in the chaos of trying to get out of the door this morning, neither of us had registered just how ghastly he looked. It was a simple error on our part, as while we had checked off all the important stuff, i.e. registering, toileting and ensuring the children all had a coat to wear and a lunch to bring, we hadn't actually managed between us to look at the fine print.

If I had had the time to look at him carefully at school that morning, I would have realised immediately that he was not well enough to attend, and gently had to explain to him that I thought it would be best if he went home. The problem is children are always very disappointed when this happens, and for good reason, but there is a reason we can't take them any less than one hundred percent fit, and today is a case in point.

Poor, poor Matteo. I sat down next to him and put my arm around him and asked him how he felt. 'Do you feel sick? Does your tummy hurt or is it just your head?' I questioned, feeling his forehead with the palm of my hand. He answered quietly 'It's just my head.' I felt so bad for him, yet even his response didn't reassure me that he might not spew at any time, so I told him to just sit right where he was, while I zipped his coat up to keep him warm.

'Is daddy at home today Matteo?' I asked, already trying to locate my phone from one of the inside pockets of my jacket. 'I'm going to see if I can get daddy to come and pick you up, ok?' I explain, as he nodded quietly. 'I'm going to ring school and see if they can get his dad to come and pick him up', I informed Mrs Wright, who agreed that he was so unwell there was really no other solution. After checking with her that she was ok to man the group and get everybody together after they'd finally finished in the toilets, I wandered a little further away where it was quieter and began to make the call.

When I had finished explaining our predicament to the office ladies, they assured me that they would get in contact with his parents and ask them to come and pick him up and then call me back to let me know what was happening. In the meantime, we had no choice but to continue. It's sort of any teacher's worst nightmare on a school trip, and I had fortunately never experienced this before. But now here we were, in the middle of a castle, freezing our tush's off on the coldest day in May, surrounded by throes of excited Japanese tourists all pointing and smiling at us, while we had a child so sick he could barely stand up. But as with all catastrophes school-related, the show simply must go on. So off we hiked, up the hill and round past the room where we would have our activity with one of the guides later, and then back down near the chapel as we waited for the changing of the guard.

And it's no easy feat keeping everybody together. As each parent helper kept their little group of six together, I still had the job of making sure that all thirty are on the path, not running and keeping an eye out for the vehicles that frequent the place. We had no choice but to wait for this part, as the children all desperately wanted to see the changing of the guard that we had learned about already back at school, but it was also a good point of exit, as we waited for Matteo's dad to come and get him. By the time the guard had been changed, and the crowd began to disperse, we were still waiting. By this point poor Matteo, quiet as a mouse and not his usual impish self, could barely hold himself up. Mrs Wright picked him up and carried him, and I took over the remainder of her group.

Now you'd think that if you were an aide at a public place such as this, then if an adult teaching assistant approached you, carrying a sickly small child, explained the predicament and asked for some aid in exiting the castle, then surely you'd be more than willing to help? Not so. As we were already positioned near to a natural exit, we had hoped that when the moment came, Mrs Wright would be aided in beating the crowds and allowed to slip out and hand Matteo safely to his dad, without then having to rejoin the hordes of people queuing to go through security again. But they were very reluctant. It was difficult because we knew that if Mrs Wright went out, then we might well be an adult down for a significant period of time while she visited security before finding her way back to us.

After some negotiation, it seemed to dawn on them that Mrs Wright was indeed part of a large group and this wasn't normal practice. The caped crusaders were then in fact very helpful once they understood the problem, and after what seemed like forever with both of us squinting at the wrought iron gates to catch a glimpse of Matteo's dad, they were more than happy to accompany Mrs Wright through to a very apologetic and grateful father, and then permitted her to come right back through the same gates.

The rest of the day passed uneventfully, as we toured the exhibits and the rest of the castle. I did end up hopping straight into a boiling hot bath myself at the end of that day, and then spent the rest of the evening shivering underneath a duvet, feeling as rubbish as I'm sure poor Matteo did. But we made it, and it was over, at least for another year.

A year on, and we're off again, praying the mercury is kinder to us this time. The morning's proceedings of getting everybody equipped and ready for the day have been largely successful thus far, save for Holly's mum nipping into the classroom to accost Mrs Wright in the very moment I stepped out to go to the toilet before we left. Even the teacher's got to go, you know.

Mrs Wright is performing a miracle, and simultaneously managing to coral excited children onto the carpet so that we can depart swiftly. Between us we've sent every group to the toilet, swapped full-on rucksacks for office plastic bags, provided extra snacks and water for those who've forgotten to bring their own, namely poor old Timothy who's in floods of tears and embarrassed to be the only one. It's Mrs Wright who swoops in to give up her own water bottle for him, and rounded up a banana and a satsuma from the free fruit supply in school for him, and now it's just a case of making sure that every-one's bladder needs have been met and everyone accounted for so that we can actually leave the building sometime before ten-thirty.

As I head to the toilet, I stop by the foyer to talk to my parent helpers (carefully selected of course) to thank them for their offer of help and to let them know of the order of the day and also which group of children they have. School policy is that we never give any parents a group with their own child in it, for obvious reasons, but the mums are cool with this, and just happy to be here.

Meanwhile, back in the classroom, Mrs Cox rocks up with Holly, who's a few minutes later than everybody else, and gestic-ulates towards Mrs Wright's own group list in her hand. 'I need one of those.' Mrs Wright looks up from soothing Timothy, mystified at her strange request. 'I'm sorry, what do you mean?' she replies, her brow furrowed in confusion. 'I need to know which group of children I'm with' Mrs Cox continues, smiling brightly and obviously expecting to be gifted with a group list like the other mums she passed on her way in. 'I'm sorry' Mrs Wright begins to explain, realising just what's happened here. Mrs Cox, being the over-anxious helicopter parent she is, seems to mistakenly think that when she'd submitted her offer of help weeks ago by filling in the form, that she was a shoe-in to go. Jesus Christ. 'I'm afraid we've already sorted parent helpers for today, I'm sure Miss Graham would have notified you in advance if we were going to take you too?' she continues, trying in vain to get rid of the woman and see to all the children now fooling around in excitement on the carpet.

By the grace of God, Mrs Cox realises she's got the wrong

end of the stick, kisses Holly goodbye and then departs before I return. Mrs Wright tries to fill me in while we line them up, but I'm confused, my brain on overload trying to remember the medicines, the vomit bucket and spare clothes along with my phone and my own lunch.

'I don't understand it!' I exclaim, as above the hubbub of chatter, Mrs Wright affirms that Mrs Cox indeed thought that she was due to accompany us. 'I never said she could come! She filled the form in, asked me about it at the door one day but never in a million years did I agree! What I said was that we hadn't decided yet, and that we'd let her know. How she took that to mean she was in, I don't know!' I chuckle, as Mrs Wright grabs her backpack and thermos and raises her eyebrows at me. 'It's because she's absolutely barking, a complete loon' she affirms, as we begin to count the children. 'I mean, really? Why would you just assume that you were going when neither of us had asked her?' squeals Mrs Wright as we go along the line. 'It just beggars belief!'

We continue to muddle along in the confusion, counting heads until I am certain I have the magic number, which today is twenty-nine, as poor Millie is too sick to attend. 'Let's just get them on the coach' I reply, already feeling exhausted and it's only 09:10am. 'Have a look and tell me, has Bebe Duke gone already?' I ask Mrs Wright, as she bobs her head to look through the dirty glass window to peer into her classroom. 'All clear' she replies, as she gives the green light to get moving, and begin the parade across the playground and out through the gate towards the coach.

Lucky for us, Bebe Duke has gone first, which should allow communication to be kept to the bare minimum between the two of us. It's no mean feat given that we're going to be sharing transportation and in seriously close proximity all day. In typical BD fashion, instead of heading upstairs and filling all the spaces on the top floor of the coach as is customary on being the first group out, she's decided she wants to go on the bottom, so we have to trek all the way up the narrow stairs past where her bunch are already sitting, to navigate the way to our seats.

Having successfully assigned most children to a seat, directing them into each row of two, with a friend or foe, there's no time to faff about, as the next obstacle is to make sure that everybody's buckled in tight. As I wander along the aisle, helping here and there to fasten a buckle or check that they've managed it, my eyes are drawn to George. Dear George is sat bang in the middle of the very back row, his tiny index finger poised over the large red STOP button. 'What's this?' he muses, tiny finger now hovering alarmingly close and tantalisingly within pressing distance. 'Um, should George be there?' enquires one of the parents already seated near him, to Mrs Wright. 'Good Lord no, I wouldn't have him there, not in a month of Sundays!' she chirps cheerfully, squeezing past me in the tiny aisle as she swoops in to solve this particular problem.

'Undo your seatbelt George' she instructs, turning quickly behind to look at me, as I stand over Holly, happily sat in her own seat in the row in front, next to one of the few female companions in our class. 'Holly' I sigh, 'can you switch seats darling, I need George over here nearer the mummies.' She gives me her beaming smile, as she unbuckles her seatbelt and stands up. Mrs Wright takes her hand 'Holly, hop in here dear, I need you to be a rose between two thorns' she gestures, referring to George and Matthew who will now be either side of her. Holly settles into her seat, delighted at having been selected to preside over the boys. 'Now Holly, if you're going to be a wife one day, you need to learn how to get your husband to behave and mind himself' muses Mrs Wright, as all three children look up at her smiling.

After a final headcount and a quick nod to Bebe Duke downstairs that we're ready to go, we make it down to the relative safety of the front of the coach. There are really no perks at all on a school trip, but if you're groping for one, then sitting at the very front furthest away from the children is a tiny triumph. The delight of sitting among the children is duly delegated to the parent helpers. After all, it seems only right that they should bear the brunt of the cacophony of noise and chatter that will be constant until we reach our destination.

We're barely down the school driveway and I'm still hoping my headcount was correct, as we begin to rake over the shenanigans involved in just getting all seventy of us (including all accompanying adults) to this point. It's 9:25am. Mrs Wright reaches down between her feet and reappears with a brown thermos, which she begins to unscrew. She pours an inch of what appears to be coffee into the small lid and tries in vain to bring it to her lips, as the ten-tonne-Tessie of a double-decker coach bumps violently over the multitude of speed humps that line our route. The coffee sways alarmingly, lapping heavily at the edges of the cup, as Mrs Wright manages a grateful slurp. Now that everybody's settled and we're moving, we begin to try to unpick the debacle with Holly's mum earlier. 'I don't get it! How do you just rock up on a trip without being invited? Having already booked the day off specially?' laughs Mrs Wright. 'Doesn't she know we pull names out of a fictitious hat?' she chuckles, in reference to our deceit as to how we select just who's in and who's out.

The rest of the day goes off without a hitch, as we tour the same exhibits as last year. By 2pm, the chill in the air and the need for another toilet visit quickly became too much, and I suspected it was all over. As we made our final march right from the top of the castle and back to the coach area, I was overjoyed to see the large blue double-decker parked outside, ready to deliver us all safely home. Another ten minutes of shuffling everybody into and out of the toilets and back on to the coach, and we can finally relax a little. It's almost always quieter on the journey home, as little heads begin to droop and eyes begin to close, lulled into a sleep by the gentle rhythm of the coach.

As we pull up beside the school, we pile off and lead them back in past all of their parents as they make their way to the door to collect them. They're all in good spirits although rather weary, as are we. Finally, once the last child has been collected, Mrs Wright and I deliver the medicines and the vomit bucket that mercifully we haven't had to use, back to the office. Then we're both out the door, too exhausted to talk and desperate to get home and switch off. 'I'd call you later' begins Mrs Wright as we reach our cars 'but I'm too exhausted to talk' she explains, as we both go our separate ways.

I'm just relieved that it's all over and hey, I didn't lose anybody, so I'm happy. All I can do as my mum answers the door is smile and say the words 'don't talk to me. (Please) Just make me a cup of tea.'

31

Happy half-term

'There's a reason we have half-term you know,' Mrs Wright muses, her eyes fixed firmly on me with not even a hint of a smile on her lips after the last child has walked out the door on Friday afternoon. 'It's so we don't bloody kill 'em.'

The reward of a week off has finally been given, and the anticipation builds through the week. The problem is, once you are gifted those nine glorious days of freedom, where the world could literally be your oyster, what exactly do you do with them? When it finally arrives, my mum was always quick to remark 'is it half-term again?' How strange that two people can have entirely different recollections of the same time period.

I can't believe how exhausted I am. Has it really only been six weeks? It doesn't sound like a lot, but boy it feels like a life-time. The last week was particularly brutal, for many reasons, but the overwhelming one was the fact that we were all ill and literally dropping like flies. There's definitely something doing the rounds, and it's come as a bit of a shock. I don't get sick! Surprising really, considering that we work in one of the most germ-infested environments one could place themselves in. I'm pretty hardy, and I genuinely can count on one hand the number of times I've been infected by my charges. The odd bout of tonsillitis, the odd sniffle here and there (the kind that renders you grouchy, fed up and generally under the weather, but not nearly as sick as your spleen sitting next to you on the couch and needing to skip work) but it's a rare occurrence that I might be home and I'm actually sick.

But we feel it this week. Headache-y and alternately nauseous, it's hard to keep calm and steer that learning train on regardless but it's got to be done. There's been spontaneous sobbing that one's tummy hurts (not from me actually), white faces and quiet children, whispers of 'my head is hurting,' and sometimes flushed faces with eyes that threaten to spill tears fairly imminently. I've spent a lot of time holding hands and walking them to the office to sit quietly and see how they feel, before usually we decide to send them home. That's all pretty normal day to day, but now that I feel a bit peaky, I'm ninety-nine per cent sure that we've a big problem that could be a stomach-flu apocalypse.

The ill-feeling is not enough to dampen our spirits though, as it's midway through the warm afternoon. 'Mrs Wright, if you should feel an overwhelming urge to pick up a book and mark it, I'll love you forever' I chuckle. It's Monday afternoon and I feel really ropey, but the show must go on. Mrs Wright picks up Ryan's English book and leans back in her wheely chair, pink and green highlighter pens ready in hand. 'I can't read any of this, I think he's written it in Swahili' she laughs, as she calls Ryan over to her. When he arrives she questions him. 'Ryan, I can't read any of this, what's going on? Have you written this in Afrikaans? I think we've got a few languages on the go here Miss Graham!' Ryan giggles and delights in the attention. He is indeed learning Afrikaans, as his mum comes from South Africa, but nevertheless, he has in fact written in English, however hard it is to decipher.

Mrs Pegg wanders in, armed with her little charge's book, as we begin to have a conversation while chaos reigns around us. There's about fifteen of them outside, little pails in hand as they shovel the sand into plastic pots and try to squish each other from the prime spots around the sandpit. In the builders tray, Willie and Adrian are building a tower with the little Jenga bricks. Well, Willie built a pyramid but since Adrian's arrived on the scene, the pyramid seems to be missing more than a few bricks, as Adrian decides he'll nab a few of those for his own creation. Meanwhile Julian follows his own agenda and scoops sand from the sandpit into the brick tray, to the shrieks of 'Julian! Don't!'

My attention turns to Mrs Pegg, who proffers a green science book she holds open at the correct page. 'Look Miss Graham, he's done that all by himself, I didn't need to do anything at all!' she marvels, as my eyes scan across the page at Kazim's work on how to grow a plant. He's had to fill in a little weekly diary to record how his sunflower had changed over the last few weeks. As I glance at his writing, letters now near-neatly formed, and little drawings carefully coloured in, I thumb back to the beginning of the book to make a comparison. Mrs Pegg's face lights up with pride, delighting in her charge's progress over the last eight months. 'I don't know whether to praise him or myself!' she grins, referring to Kazim's apparent triumph to near-genius level.

Finally on Wednesday morning, ironically the first day this week that I did not feel like death and began to feel human once more, the peaceful harmony is broken abruptly by a rather loud booming voice. 'Miss Graham, Gabriel's been sick,' Damien relays to me in his usual dulcet tones across the classroom.

He's just uttered the words every teacher dreads hearing. I feel my stomach lurch as fear rises within me and I fight the urge to take ten steps backwards. Never mind the fact I'm already thirty feet away from him on the opposite side of the classroom. 'Uh, Mrs Wright…' I manage, but Mrs Wright is already catapulted from her wheely chair next to me as she dashes off to get help, while Mrs Beale is on the way out of the back door, her hand over her mouth, her emetophobia apparently ten times worse than mine.

I won't go anywhere near him, I can't. The sensible and caring thing to do, would be to rush straight over, help him out of his chair, then swiftly turn him around by his shoulders and rush him as quickly as I can to the safety of the office and the wipeable floor of the medical room, praying that he doesn't take out some unsuspecting wanderer on the way. But no, I'm rooted to the spot, sat tight in my chair, as I will the fumes not to reach us and tell the others on his table to move away. A few painful minutes pass, where time has seemingly stood still. Christ, Mrs Wright has been gone for a bloody long time, I thought she was coming right back. Without her, I'm screwed, as God knows what I'm meant to do. I haven't had children yet, and certainly never cleared up vomit before. And no, there's not a first time for everything.

As the entire room stands still, twenty-nine pairs of eyes also fixed firmly on Gabriel, my worst fears are duly realised, as the poor guy barfs up a whole load more of his breakfast on to the table in front of him. And onto his English book. Finally, like a paramedic, Mrs Wright appears in the doorway, suitably attired in the trademark plastic disposable gloves and a trusty bucket conveniently lined with a Sainsbury's carrier bag inside, and saves the day as she helps the poor chap up and escorts him to the medical room. The room is subsequently filled with cries of 'eew!' and 'that's disgusting!' and the highly exaggerated nose pinching and coughing that only five year-olds can do so well.

As I force myself to glance at the innocent victim in all this, the table (and my £25 brightly decorated wipe-clean table-cloth), I decide the only sensible thing to do is to jump ship. It's gorgeously sunny and warm, and the back door is already wide open (for obvious reasons) as the gentle breeze spills in. 'Right! Everybody listen!' I say, raising my voice a little above the ruckus. 'Everybody pick up your book, pick up your pencil and go and sit down on the floor outside.' Lord, I think that's the only sensible suggestion I've had all day. Excited at the prospect of a change in our familiar routine, they clamber over each other in their haste to get outside.

Safely outside in the abundance of fresh, odour-de-vomit free air, they settle themselves onto the asphalt and the grass with very little fuss. It's very commendable actually, as they seem to sense that this is not the time to muck about. Or perhaps they can just see their teacher's hanging on by a knife edge and is a little off her game. I pop back into to survey (from a great distance) the clean-up operation, thankfully being led by the caretaker, who mercifully is still around and hasn't finished the first part of his split shift today. You see, he's the first port of call in any situation involving bodily fluids, with a wealth of God-knows-what chemicals hidden in the depths of his little store room. But unfortunately, as is nearly always the case with these things, ninety-nine percent happens when he's not here. And who does it fall to? Why the poor office ladies of course.

Why they would ever want to work in a school I'll never know, as you can bet your life that such attractive tasks as 'puke or poop clean-up' don't feature in the job description. I tell a lie, they are in fact included in the job description, heavily disguised by such wording as 'tending to sick children who are awaiting parents to collect them.' Any idiot can read between the lines on that one. But God love them, they step up to the plate and pitch in, time, and time, and time again. There's three of them, so I suppose if you play rock, paper, scissors often enough, the chances of it having to be you are reasonably slim. Thankfully they are all mums, so this sort of thing that while unpleasant, is still fairly familiar and not too far consigned to the history boxes in their brain. Usually all of these incidents are a two-man job, with one to participate and the other to be a witness. To make sure that nobody can accuse you of doing something horrible while small children stand starkers with the door wide open in full view of any visitors heading towards the boss's office or anybody using the photocopier. Welcome to our school!

They don't physically clean up children, it's never been that way (well, unless it's shower-worthy, which is quite rare). They don the plastic gloves, grab the box of wipes, clean undies and a plastic bag, and talk the child through what they need to do to sort themselves out. If it's super bad, then they'll call a parent to collect them, but nine times out of ten it's an unpleasant but reasonably rectifiable situation, pardon the pun.

Anyway, back to today. Today it's Gabriel's turn to be 'that child,' except this time he's not had an accident, he's sick, and in need of comfort until his mum can come and pick him up. He's a trouper, sitting calmly on the little bed in the medical room, having been offered some water to sip in a little paper cup. Mrs Wright kindly goes in and sits with him, perching on the edge of the sideboard and asking him how he's feeling now. I walk past to see how he's doing, and quietly wonder if the germs are airborne and if we're breathing them in as we speak. And it's so close to half-term.

I return to class, reassured that he's ok and mum's on her way. Breathing a quiet sigh of relief, I don once again my calm and cheerful persona, as we settle back into completing the word endings sheet and trying to make it to playtime. Mrs Wright returns, freshly washed and now rubber glove-less, and fiddles with the bracelet on her wrist. 'Urgh' she moans, giving it a little sniff. 'I think this needs another rinse. If they hadn't insisted I put gloves on in the first place I'd never have got it covered' she smarts, resigning herself to having to buy another.

'I'm so sorry' I chuckle, but I also feel more than a little guilty. 'I just can't do sick, I should have gotten up but I was just glued to my chair! You know what I'm like when it comes to bodily fluids!' I laugh, as she sits down beside me on the bench. 'I know, I'm sorry, I just couldn't' pipes up Mrs Beale in her Bronx drawl, likely feeling the same mix of guilt and relief that I do at not having had to participate directly in the clear-up operation. Mrs Wright laughs loudly, as she recounts the event. 'I was up, out of my chair in about two seconds flat! Bloody lot of use you two were, standing there like Gumby!' she gesticulates, as I laugh so hard the tears start to trail down my cheeks. As I reach for a tissue to blot the tears, I apologise again. The woman is a legend, there's a reason we're so good together. And while I may not be brilliant when it comes to vomit, she steps up, knowing my limitations. I'll have to buy her a bottle of wine for this.

The bell finally rings, as we bring all the books in and send them off to collect their fruit and milk. Not before I've lined them all up and insisted they hold out their hands as I go along the line squirting a large blob of the foaming alcohol rub into their cupped palms. Let's hope we don't all go down with it, who knows who else might already have it? 'Anyway' breathes Mrs Wright, as she picks up her handbag and reaches for her compact and her lippy. 'I binned his book by the way' she muses, as she guides the bright pink lipstick around her lips. 'Ew, thanks, I forgot about that' I chuckle, reaching for the two strawberries I removed earlier for myself. No way am I taking them from the pack now the children's hands have been all over them. Normally I don't give germs a second thought, but today I'd be a fool to be blase. 'Well, my dear, at least that's one less book to mark!' grins Mrs Wright broadly, as she saunters off with Mrs Beale to the staffroom for a coffee.

32

All aboard the learning train

The learning train is supposed to leave promptly at 1:15pm every day, whether we're ready or not. Unfortunately for it, I've gone a little off track and popped *Riverdance* on the Smartboard screen. As the beautiful orchestral Irish music booms out from the two speakers, the children stare at the screen, transfixed. It's like nothing they've seen before, which is exactly the way I felt when I first saw it myself at age twelve.

Now I didn't just pop it on to entertain myself this afternoon, in favour of abandoning the learning, but truth be told, it feels wonderful to be able to share something new and different with them. Not to mention seeing it through their eyes. Every day for the last year or so, whenever I've taught handwriting and they're left to practice alone, I put on some peaceful music for them to listen to while they work. At first I wasn't sure if they'd like it, but after I saw how much it made them relax and work calmly, I was more than happy to pop it on in earnest every day. I change it up every day, thinking about what musical styles I'd like them to experience. So one day it's the homespun warbling of James Taylor, another day the hauntingly beautiful voice of Eva Cassidy, then the classical pianist Yiruma.

Whatever I put on, they seem to enjoy, and I always feel any edge of prickliness in myself begin to dissipate. There's also been some research that suggests that listening to classical music as one works can actually help children's brains. One thing's for sure though, if ever I forget, then I can be sure that some will remember. Vanya often puts her hand up, just as I've got everybody quiet, we've performed the modern day miracle that is ensuring that everybody has a marker pen that actually works, and the requests for water and/or toilet breaks have been met. 'What is it Vanya?' I ask, expecting another problem that needs my attention before we begin. 'Can you please put the quiet music on?' she asks softly with a smile. And so I do.

It serves us well in many ways really, as straight after lunch is usually when the Big Guns does what we call a 'parent show-around' and drops in on every class without warning. It's the source of a lot of stress among staff, as instead of such things being marked on the big board in the office, or alternatively in the school diary, she tells no-one these are happening. I'm sure it's on purpose, just to catch us out. The thing is, I think that prospective parents should just see us as we are, and so the boss leading them round without our prior knowledge or consent should be no issue at all. The problem is her. She's not quite savvy enough to realise when it's a good time to just come on in and see us in action in all our dishevelled glory, or when somebody's just been sick or we're in the midst of serious behaviour issues and she should just keep on walking.

Luckily, Mrs Wright and I decided we didn't want to be caught out as much as we had been, so as I mentioned at the beginning of this book, we've devised our own codeword-mistletoe. There's absolutely no hidden meaning, no clever thought process that led us to it, and it's not an original idea. I borrowed it from my brother-in-law. When Christmas, or should I say the ten minutes of the day that he and sister number two feel they can manage having spent the day with his parents, gets a bit too much, they have a codeword. A codeword to use instead of having to say out loud 'for the love of God, get me out of here! A la Chandler Bing, he simply whispered under his breath the word 'mistletoe' while repeatedly screaming at her with his eyes. Mrs Wright is always happy to go along with most of my ideas, and this was no different. So now, every time we catch sight of the top of the Big Guns curly mop of dark brown bobbed hair, the word 'mistletoe' will duly be uttered across the classroom by either of us, giving us vital and ample warning of the impending attack.

I hasten to add that it's not because we're not teaching, or doing something we shouldn't, it's because generally when the Big Guns rocks up, it's right at that inopportune moment that Mrs Wright has just sent Dylan to change his reading books and for all of two and a half minutes she will be sat alone at the table, looking as if she's been doing jack shit! Similarly for me, it's a case of being caught out in between calling children to read, or when I've momentarily ducked my head around the group room door to check if Mrs Pegg's survived the morning with Bebe Duke. Or if I've got my face in my cupboard at the well-known two o'clock slump in an attempt to take a quick swig of my stone cold tea.

Ninety-nine times out of a hundred this cunning codeword has saved our bacon. And we're good, we're very good at ad-libbing. But for those rare times when there's no time to get the word out, Mrs Wright is a master of creating a conversation related to all things education so as not to arouse any suspicions that we might be slacking from the Big Guns, e.g. 'so Miss Graham, I was just saying that Meghan is reading all of her high-frequency words, shall I move her up to the next reading level? What do you think? Oh hello Big Guns! I was just saying how well my intervention program is working, Meghan has come on in leaps and bounds!' You get the idea. When you've got the gift of the gab, you've got, well, everything it seems.

I've digressed a little from the *Riverdance* tale I originally started to tell you. Sorry. That's what happens when your brain is scrambled, trying to remember and juggle a million ideas all at the same time, which is much like a typical school day. Anyway, I happened to listen to the music one day while in my car, and decided to try it out during handwriting the next day. They listened while they wrote, but when they had finished, I decided that since they were curious, I would put the video on the Smartboard and let them watch the dance as well. They were in awe, their bodies jerking rhythmically as they moved, unaware of their motion in response to the video clip.

'I can do that,' piped up Mrs Wright proudly from her pew in her green wheely chair. Is there nothing the woman can't do. She carried on, 'well, after a couple of bottles of Sauvignon blanc' she mused, smirking at me. I seem to have totally misunderstood the point of the wine. 'What, one in each hand?' I chuckle, picturing the inebriated and somewhat lapsed Catholic diddly-dee-ing merrily with a bottle of the best in each hand firmly clamped down beside her thighs. Just an image I had.

My seventh-grade form tutor was a jolly, middle-aged Irishman, who delighted in explaining to me why Irish dancers had to have their arms down by their sides. He told me they weren't allowed to dance ('it was blasphemous to be having fun in those days' agreed Mrs Wright) so they kept their hands beside them so they couldn't be seen dancing through the windows outside. It could be utter bollocks for all I know, but I remembered it all these years later.

'Come down Killorglin high street with me on a Friday night and they'll all be doing that!' advises Mrs Wright knowledgeably. She leans towards me and whispers quietly with a wry smile. 'I think the learning train has derailed Miss Graham.' It certainly bloody has. It's not even 2pm and we've meditated, handwritten, and then watched 'Reel around the Sun' from *Riverdance* on the Smartboard, but I don't feel any learning's been lost, to the contrary actually.

Darn inspiring it's been. I've never seen so many small children filled with the spirit of the jig and reel, as I watch them jump, hop and in some cases stamp as they try to replicate what they've just enjoyed. I think we've got a few Michael Flatley's in the making, certainly if Henry is anything to go by, as he cavorts about with great concentration, trying hard to get the rhythm just right, a huge grin on his face as we watch him.

On a serious note, this is what the 'curriculum' used to be about. Back in the day it was about inspiring children and tailoring their learning to suit their interests. It seemed a sensible school of thought, one that felt that children indeed learned best if their curiosity and interest had been piqued. We were tasked with trying to ignite the fire and let them lead us, the feeling being that real and deeper learning comes from meaningful and real experiences.

It's not rocket science though is it? Why do any of us pursue particular interests and hobbies? Because the fundamental principle is that we are highly motivated and curious, excited by the prospect of improving our skills and developing our talents, through a medium which excites us, be it dance, music, art, sport, whatever. I see it in class every day, that when children are interested, they naturally become more open to learning and acquiring new skills.

But what happens when it's not on the program? When this dish has unwittingly been removed from the menu? Over the years, the one-size-fits-all approach has killed the curiosity, as well as the flexibility and freedom to explore and think creatively. Instead, we carry on, terrified pawns in a game that's all gone very wrong. We live in a constant fear of recrimination, that if we don't put the right levels in boxes, then our name will be mud, and Ofsted will come knocking at our door. But who stops to look at how the current ideals affect the children? Nobody. Because nobody cares what their experiences are, the only concern is their ability to meet ridiculously difficult targets that they should know nothing about.

One school I trained at was a real inspiration for me, back during my final year of teacher training in 2006. Twelve years ago there was far less of this nonsense, at least that's how it felt. The second of my teaching practices was in a beautiful country school in a small town in a rural county. I loved it from the get-go, and enjoyed the idyllic setting as much as the values and approach of the school itself. I was placed into a mixed reception/Year One class, which was a thoroughly interesting and worthwhile experience as it's quite a feat having to teach two different age groups simultaneously, especially if you're a newbie.

The team of three classes each with the same mixed-age split due to pupil numbers, was a warm and friendly environment, and had there been a job being offered there for the following year, I surely would have taken it. The teacher in charge, and my mentor, was fairly young, and extremely passionate about early years education. In contrast to many other schools, they weren't at all risk averse, in fact quite the opposite. They were eager to try new approaches and trial new ideas, and it was very refreshing. It took me what felt like forever to get my head around the myriad of rooms, children of mixed ages everywhere ('are you a Year One or a Year R?') and new collection of teaching assistants that roamed here, there and everywhere. But in spite of what at first seemed like utter chaos and confusion, after a couple of weeks, I began to see that this not only worked, but it was far from the airy-fairiness I had imagined it would be.

The classes had adopted the Reggio Emilia approach, something I knew absolutely nothing about at the time and which left me frantically googling by night after my first few days there. After copious information gathering it became much clearer, and I had a far greater understanding of what the intended benefits might be. Here's how it worked. Ordinarily, in my teaching experience since, the topics, although having been chosen carefully in the hope of inspiring children's curiosity and interest, the learning is already decided on a half-termly basis, whereby we already have a week by week plan to follow to the letter. And there's not really much scope for development or leading from their own interests.

So if we were to do the Year One topic of Space, we'd be looking at the history and development of flight, and then ordering the different modes of transport on a timeline, via an age-appropriate cutting and sticking activity. Not very inspiring really is it? There's undoubtedly learning to be gained, skills to be acquired, and knowledge to be passed on, but it's very much scripted, in the sense that 'I have the knowledge, I will pass it to you the learner.'

The Reggio approach doesn't work like that. For their topic, the mixed reception and Year One children's topic was simply 'Water.' The three teachers and I met beforehand, and thought about how we wanted to present the initial topic. Then we asked each child to generate a question, something that they themselves wanted to find out about. It could be absolutely anything related to such a broad heading, and with them in their classes, we asked and then recorded their answers.

Once we had this information, it was back to the drawing board as we looked through all of the sixty children's responses. Armed with this information, we grouped them into whose questions and desires were most similar, and took groups of about twenty children each. The idea was that we adults would simply be the facilitators for aiding the children in whichever way we could, in finding satisfactory answers to their questions. For example, Cassidy wanted to know 'where does water come from?' while Maeve wanted to find out 'are mermaids real?' Now any fool can see that when you've got questions as diverse and at completely different ends of the spectrum that these two were, it would be tricky to try to tailor your learning time to catering for both.

So we didn't. And it worked so well. During the first week we each took our group off to the library to borrow some books to try to answer their questions. The next week we helped them to set up their own experiments related to water, and the week after we worked together for the whole day while we beavered away with scissors and construction paper to create an aquarium to play in. We spent hours cutting out blue paper waves and taping them to the walls, drawing fish and decorating them, using whatever we could find to replicate seaweed etc.

They were utterly engaged, and totally in their element. The older ones were able to help lead the play and aid the younger reception children to achieve what they wanted, especially when it came to the fiddliness of cutting out and sellotaping!

It was unlike anything I had experienced before, but rather than cower in fear of the boss happening upon this free-flow play supposedly masquerading as learning, they didn't, knowing full well that their headteacher recognised the value in this and knew that this is what children in their earliest years of school should be doing. It took me a while to get my head around it, but I was very much included in all of the planning and delivery and being on my final teaching practice there for four months, it provided me ample time to really get stuck in. It really exemplified all of the feelings I have about early education twelve years down the line.

Why are many of today's children so disengaged and dying of boredom in stuffy classrooms far and wide? Because we, the teachers, have simply become puppets, teaching merely to get children to pass tests that are of absolutely no value to them at all. And that is something that even Bebe Duke and I are united on, as well as most of my other colleagues. Many of us do try our best to go beyond what the National Curriculum tells us is necessary, and make it our mission to spark curiosity and interest in some of the dullest and mind-numbingly boring concepts that we have no choice but to teach. Why was I so impressed by the Reggio approach all those years ago? Because it epitomised everything that I love about teaching; starting from the children's ideas, going off on tangents, following their interests, and not feeling like I've been boxed into a corner with nowhere to go. Giving children ownership and choice in what they learn is empowering, and it is a huge factor in motivating small children. After all, we are born with a natural joy of learning, it's only school and the target-driven culture that sucks the fun out of it, and ultimately disengages them.

So much of what happens today is merely a paperwork exercise. One of the phrases that popped up in recent years is 'evidence of learning,' and every time I hear it I can't help but want to strangle the person that says it. It is absolutely the most ridiculous three words I've ever heard in education, and nothing riles me faster than they do. Because to me, and to probably every person out there that isn't a teacher, the word evidence is something that is required to prove or disprove a case in a court of law, and not something related to the work in a child's English book.

But now, every time the Big Guns or Liz Dawson come to check up on us or do a 'book look' (whereby they collect a top, middle and lower achieving child's English, maths and science books and review them in one of their leadership meetings), the focal point, the jewel in the crown, is their ability to scour the books as they pore over weeks and weeks of work, looking to find 'evidence of learning.'

And by that, it means that if they can't find much in poor Nathan's maths book, then your head will be on a plate as they conclude you either haven't done enough teaching or taught whatever you did well enough. The whole focus is undoubtedly not to find out if the children indeed learned something from your science lesson last week, but if they managed to get it down on paper. Which begs the question, what evidence of what can actually be found? That they were present? That they can copy the date and the title? That they can glue in a sheet correctly or label a picture of a plant by copying the person sitting next to them? Whatever the so-called 'evidence of learning' that they feel confident that they can glean from these books, it doesn't tell you at all if the child is a genius or as low as the Mensa score can go.

So it's another useless exercise that only serves to create extra stress on the teacher, who has to ensure that even the youngest, and often least able children are able to record something in their books to show what they've learned (or haven't, as the case may be), and also for the children, who no doubt feel the pressure to get everything perfect which frankly for their age, is a ridiculous and unreasonable expectation. They're not stupid, and I'm sure they can sense themselves how silly it all is.

When I look back at my own school years, I thank God that I got through school before it became a hysterical, farcical process, full of useless jargon that we are filling children's heads with, and that when I wrote sentences and coloured my pictures in, I enjoyed the process and wasn't aware of any pressure to try and always go one better and achieve the unachievable. I was blissfully unaware of any targets my teacher had for me, any expectations she held that my work could be better, and simply enjoyed the learning and the opportunities that we were given.

Looking back now it seems reminiscent of a bygone era, which is a real shame. One thing's for sure, when I have my own children, I don't want them coming home to tell me 'I got a level three for my SAT's, and Mrs X says I now need to read with more expression' or 'I met my target in maths today mummy, now Mrs X says I need to try and meet the next one before Easter, and then I can have three house points.'

Because I know I won't give these statements the time of day.

I know what I'll be asking, and I know what'll be important to me; did you have fun today? Who did you play with? Were you kind to other children today? I think the idea that learning is a chore is fast becoming the feeling among primary school children, yet if you removed them from the environment, then the genuine desire to find out more and to experience new things can be ignited in true passion.

I read online a little while back a thread on a discussion forum that made me feel extremely sad about the state of things. A mother had written for some advice to help her to know how to help her five year-old daughter, who was in Year One at the time. The little girl had come home and said to her 'there's something wrong with my learning mummy.' It transpired that this was the little girl's feeling after conversations with her peers, and comments from her class teacher. This tiny girl already had the feeling of failure before her school years had really begun, and it made me want to weep. In my classroom, this is precisely the type of issue I will try at all costs to avoid. That a small child of barely five years old already has serious doubts about their own capabilities, and is already comparing themselves to their peers.

It makes for sad reading that's for sure. But what can we do? I suppose all I can do in my own classroom is try to ensure that the educational jargon isn't trotted out to them and to protect them from as much as I can. Mrs Wright and I try to build self-esteem, confidence and really nurture all thirty of them, in the hope that whatever the storm they have to weather, enough good has been done to see them right. It's my wish anyway.

33

Swim team

It's Monday afternoon again, and this time I have a new challenge to face: swimming. Of course I don't have to swim, but the Year Fours do. Apparently after a short survey, thirty-six of the sixty do not swim.

So desperate to do what the government have said, the Big Guns was practically begging me to arrange the lessons through the local swim club, and if she'd have had the time to do it herself she surely would have. So after a swimming survey littered with detailed questions such as 'can your child swim twenty-five metres without armbands?' and 'can your child use a range of different strokes confidently?' the results yielded a surprisingly firm and resounding no from over half of the year group. Jesus. I imagined I'd be phoning the company up and enquiring about the possibility of six lessons for a mere handful of below par non-swimmers, not the whole bloody job lot of them.

Unfortunately as is often the case with the prospect of anything being 'free,' the parents have clocked this quickly, and filled in the forms in earnest. Where once our reasonably wealthy little county was filled with children all consistently clambering up the ladder of the swimming stages, it would seem that suddenly there seems to have been a sharp drop in those reaching the goals. At least once they realised that paying through the nose for weekly lessons could be ditched temporarily in favour of school-funded swimming.

They have us over a barrel really, as the National Curriculum demands that every school offer swimming to its pupils as and when they see fit, thus ensuring that the long-term goal of leaving primary school being reasonably proficient in the water has been met. I think it's a very sensible idea, as of course the ability to swim is without question, a life skill.

But the post-game wrap-up seems to suggest we may have been duped. Good old Mrs Wright, she suspected all along, as did the ladies in the office. But we like to give them the benefit of the doubt, and so arrangements were duly made for all of those who felt they could not meet the required standards.

There's never enough of anything in a school, especially in the form of manpower. Knowing full well we'd never in a million years find enough adults to shepherd the two groups there and back to the pool, and also babysit the poor souls too proficient to attend, I knew there and then I'd have to fall on my sword, and as the one organising it, volunteer the services of poor Mrs Wright. In typical fashion, she rose to the occasion and gave the green light, which meant one less victim to have to try and cajole into taking on a very unattractive role, with absolutely zero extra pay or perks: i.e. what is essentially standing around for forty-five minutes in a stiflingly hot, chlorinated greenhouse while they swim, thus missing your lunch and then enduring the delights of coach travel with thirty-six nine year-olds.

Most people/parent helpers/honoured volunteers with any sense would tell you to jog on, but alas the unachievable has been achieved and we managed to scrape together enough manpower to make it possible. I've spent weeks sorting this one. Weeks of enquiring phone calls to the swim club 'yes, but how many children can you actually fit in the pool?', 'when can you actually do the lessons?,' weeks of emails to coach companies trying to marry up their availability to the dates for the lessons that we have been allocated. Finally once it was all confirmed (all two thousand pounds of it) I began the administration part of the deal, i.e. coordinating permission requests and doing a risk assessment.

The endless PPA sessions that have been hijacked by this bloody swimming has been criminal. Last week I spent forty minutes trying to chase up the permission slips I hadn't received, sending out new letters and instructing the teaching assistants in those classes to chase them up daily. They were absolutely brilliant, skilfully accosting children and chivvying them until the slips had been safely returned. Then it was collaborating the whole host of pertinent medical information requested by the swimming club and passing that on to them. By the day before, I was pretty confident I had all my bases covered. People, lunches, coaches, transport.

But then Monday came. A first glance in the office this morning told me the ice was thin, and had I dared to enquire further, I might have managed to put out the subsequent fire. Unfortunately my mind was also on my own class, you know, being primarily a class teacher and not an events organiser, like an ex-boyfriend of mine. Plus in a nightmarish roll of the educational dice, it dawned on me while brushing my teeth that morning that it was the National Phonics Screening week so I would be out of class being tortured slowly as the children come out to me one by one to read forty words that make sod all sense to anybody, and not in fact re-enacting a scene from Cinderella as per our English plan.

Focused on the task in hand, cup of tea by my side as I relied on the caffeine to keep me awake as they stumble over 'p-o-d-e' and 'qu-or-g' - you get the idea, swimming drifted to the back of my mind. After all, I had just made all the arrangements, and save for going with them and holding the two teacher's hands myself, I reminded myself that my part of the task had been done, and there was nothing else I need do.

As the bell went for lunch and the first group had departed, I suddenly had a thought, and wondered if the class teachers leading their classes had remembered to pick up the smorgasbord of medications that we have no choice but to bring. Why didn't I just keep my mouth shut? There seems to have been a major breakdown in communication. As I raise that very important question, Mrs Wright stands with her little blonde head peering through the office-side of the hatch, as Mrs Brain, looks up at me sternly from behind her wire-rimmed glasses, bundle of papers in hand and a pen tucked behind one ear and utters a very strong and assertive 'no'. 'But, but they needed them' a little voice in my head whispers. How the hell can they have gone off without them? 'Ok,' I say calmly, as there's not much point in stating the obvious. Mrs Brain glares at me as she reluctantly removes a list of names from their little plastic sleeve, as she identifies who did indeed need to take something with them.

As I rifle through the plastic drawers in the medical room, frantically trying to identify which children's stuff is housed in each box, I begin to pull out a wealth of plastic tupperware, a myriad of boxes and cartons filled with tablets, lotions, potions and inhalers. Not forgetting the crowning touch, the Epi-Pens. I swear, I could shove an Epi-Pen into the thigh of any grey-trousered child with my eyes closed by now. 'Good grief!' exclaims Mrs Wright as we pore over the multitude of medicines that seem to be required. 'Are we going by coach or by ambulance?' she asks, our eyes finally meeting across the air of apprehension in the medical room.

'I'm sorry, but this is not my job' grumbles Mrs Brain rather rudely. Now I'm feeling under pressure. It's not my bloody fault either, all I did was organise the trip, it's not my responsibility to make sure they take what's needed. But I can see it from both sides. On the one hand, I'll bet that they were rushing to get out the door on time, and it was easily forgotten given that this is something they've never done before. But on the other, it is one hundred percent the class teacher's responsibility to make sure that the medication that's needed for any time outside of school is duly taken along with you.

Now as it happens, Victoria has severe asthma and needs her inhaler, which is now at school and not at the pool with her. Jesus. How did they forget to take this? Luckily, the most allergic little boy who carries a box of tricks including the dreaded Epi-Pen, hasn't gone yet, and Mrs Wright can now take this with her just in case, but whichever way you look at it, we're still stuffed as far as the other two go.

I cut my losses and leave them to sort it out, although I'm pretty sure I'm not popular. After lunch I put it behind me and carry on in better spirits, as I eagerly await the return of Mrs Wright with the second group of swimmers. At two-thirty, she arrives, sauntering into the hive of activity of the classroom like Dorothy Lamour, a strong cup of tea in her left hand. 'I am here, my dear' she muses, as she steps around the boys building Duplo and finds her way to her easy chair. I'm eager to hear the debrief, and slightly afraid of what other dramas might have befallen the swimming crew after medicine-gate.

As I look at her more closely, I realise that her usual coiffured blonde barnet has increased in volume just a tad since her departure. Mrs Wright reaches up and runs both hands through her hair. 'God, it was like a bloody sauna in there!' she chuckles. 'The helpers and I had to take turns sticking our heads outside to get a bit of oxygen' she remarks, referring to the tightly enclosed, humid tent that housed the 'indoor' swimming pool.

'If I get bloody Mrs Walters asking me about my boys, my marriage or where I'm going on holiday I'm going to knock her into next Christmas' she continues dryly. Unfortunately the last member of the adults on her team was the least desirable choice, pipped only at the post by Mrs Cox, Holly's nutcase of a mum. Trust me, I'm sure that would have been far worse.

'But did it go ok though, was everything else ok?' I ask, concerned that more problems may have arisen. 'No, no, it was fine!' she affirms, taking another slurp of her tea. 'I tell you what though' she muses, looking directly at me across my desk. 'Non-swimmers my ass. I've never seen so much backstroke in my life. They can backstroke better than me' she declares knowingly as she raises an eyebrow. 'Mark my words, future Olympians, the lot of them' she says coldly.

Bloody liars, the lot of them.

34

Potty talk

Jacob gallops his way to my desk, and stops before it, his two pointer fingers directed towards me. 'Miss Graham, can I go to the toilet?' he asks, as I look up from the mountain of RE books on my desk.

'Jacob, I think you need to do your work' I answer, a hint of irritation in my voice having spent the last thirty minutes or so watching him play imaginary games with his pencils and slither around on his little wooden chair never once with his bottom on it. He gives me a little 'oh' as he takes in my response, clearly somewhat disappointed by the outcome.

'Anyway' I continue, 'haven't you already been once this afternoon already?' I'm trying not to let them go five times an afternoon to get out of doing their work, but by this point I genuinely can't remember if he has already had a hall pass or not. He looks at me squarely, as he begins to talk with his hands and explain. 'Uh, it's just that I have a problem with my willy' he confidently states, without the slightest hint of embarrassment or discomfort. Well, he is only five. I cut him off mid-sentence, 'just go!' I sigh, as I wave him away with my hand and he scampers across the classroom on his merry way. Boys.

I return to the classroom having escorted the majority to the lunch hall one morning, to come across three stragglers on my return. I didn't even know I'd missed them, but when I give them all the opportunity to go to the toilet before we go, the boys immediately disregard this as unimportant, while the girls relish the chance to go together as a little group. As they stand in the doorway, massaging the Magic Soap (alcohol-foam rub) into their paws, I shoo them along to go and have their lunch.

Just as I thought I'd gotten everybody to where they're supposed to be, I catch sight of Tirza, Vanya and Charlotte walking towards me back to the classroom. On closer inspection I can see that Charlotte and Tirza are deep in conversation, although Tirza looks a tad upset, her little brow furrowed into a frown as she looks at Charlotte. 'Oh, girls! Where have you been?' I ask. 'Everybody else has gone!' Charlotte looks a little sheepish, as she explains and states the obvious.

As we move to the doorway and the Magic Soap to go through the motions, I notice Tirza's face looks pink, and I can see a few tears prickling in her eyes. 'What's the matter?' I ask her, my own face full of concern.

I hate it when they cry. You only have to think of what it represents to you as an adult; i.e. all trace of dignity has disappeared, the walls have come down. It's a last resort. Tirza looks up at me, her little hands cupped together as she massages the Magic Soap, Vanya close beside her for moral support. 'Charlotte was going to tell of me' she whimpers, as a few more tears fall. Charlotte immediately looks uneasy, as she gives her side of the story. 'I wasn't' she says, somewhat apologetically by this point. She doesn't like to be in trouble.

'Well look' I begin, turning to the three of them as I speak. 'I haven't heard anything, Charlotte hasn't come to tell me anything, so don't worry about it.' Charlotte is keen to get away and takes the safest approach and heads to the lunch hall. I reach over to rub Tirza's back, as I question her. 'Why did you think Charlotte was going to tell of you?' As Vanya takes her turn with the Magic Soap, Tirza turns to me to explain once more. 'Me and Vanya went in the same toilet 'cos we were having a chat about something' she says tearfully. Maybe Mrs Wright and I should try that, then we might get to catch up sometime before Friday at 4pm.

And now I understand. It doesn't happen very often, but every now and again, we have the chat about how only one person goes into the cubicle at a time. There's always shenanigans going on in the bathroom, namely because they aren't directly next to the classroom where they can be closely supervised. Sometimes we'll have multiple toilet cubicle occupants, another time we'll have somebody climbing atop the sink unit for a bit of a giggle, just to see if they can. Then there's somebody that likes nothing better than to wet their tiny hands, soap up, and then massage the mirror until there's a big, cloudy mist covering the frame in its entirety. Then there's my personal favourite, fruit in the toilet.

They delight in discovering this one, rushing back to the classroom to report back to us all with a foghorn voice 'there's a banana in the boys toilets!' they exclaim. My response is usually one of two things; either a) I don't want to know, or b) go and tell the ladies in the office. And they're off like a rocket, rushing forth to stand on their tiptoes at the office window, their tiny clenched fists repeatedly knocking until the office ladies can ignore them no longer, and give up trying to balance the accounts or see to the sick and injured. The poor unsuspecting member of the office team that has the misfortune to be the first responder, usually resigns themselves to donning a white plastic glove and heading into the cesspool. Ugh, the ick.

35

Positive touch

It's Friday and I've been asked to go on a course. Well, it was 'suggested' yesterday by the boss, after she informed me that I'd be having what many would consider to be the class from hell next year.

Not rocket science really, she wasn't exactly going to give me the easy lot, saving them instead for the poor newbie who'll be starting with us come September. She's only been on the job for a year, so it's hardly fair to give her a bunch of reprobates in return for signing on the dotted line. But I'm fine with it, I agree, and Mrs Wright and I clocked this weeks ago, somewhat resigned to what I hope will once again be 'our' fate.

Instead of feeling disheartened, I'm actually feeling quite inspired. Because investing in the children is what Mrs Wright and I do best, our perfect mix of fun mingled with a 'firm but fair' approach. Not to mention calm, loving, nurturing. They'll only be five, this is exactly what it should be like in every KS1 class, but we both know the reality is far from true.

It's all about building genuine relationships with children, showing that we really care about them, and taking the time to listen to their ideas, their news but also their worries. And this is what enables us to teach them well and bring them along. So when it was confirmed, I had been one step away from going to her and saying 'bring it on.'

Now that we've successfully hoofed Bebe Duke from her post (I promise you, she actually went willingly. She couldn't stand the idea of working together for another year either) things are feeling infinitely more optimistic, save for one thing. The boss is still keeping it under wraps as to where the TA's are next year. We're down a SENCO for a few weeks, so the task has fallen to her to have them in one by one and give them some airtime and let them state their preferences for the coming year.

Mrs Wright and I want to stay together, and put it this way, I'm not doing it without her. No way Jose. No way am I taking on the most difficult mix of children yet, and running the show with somebody new. I doubt I can actually remember how to work with someone else we're so in sync. It's another battle I hope I won't have to face. It's best for me, best for Mrs Wright, and without a doubt best for the children. We can one hundred percent turn this around, but only if we can carry on with our more gentle, child-centred, sod-the-institutionalised-learning approach. But until it's confirmed, I worry. Mrs Wright less so, she's quite confident. But I rarely get what I want, it's hard to believe that I could. Sod the fingers and toes, I'm keeping everything crossed.

So off I toddle dutifully one Friday morning in late June, with Lena, the lunchtime supervisor lady that has been called in to be the 'challenging' child's 1:1 every afternoon this term. The day doesn't start well, as parking at the office it's being held at is horrendous. And by that, I mean that there's a huge giant car park outside, but here's the snag; no one outside the bloody employees can park there, and since this place is a voucher parking zone, I'm at a loss as to how I'm going to safely park and not have to walk five miles back to the office.

On my third whizz around the same block, hoping in vain that I'll find a street to park on that won't get me a whopping fine, I spot Lena. She volunteers to go in and explain I'll be a bit late, while I admit defeat and head for the 'stacker' and the ten minute walk back.

I'm approaching half an hour late when I finally arrive, and follow the maze of hallways to find the right room. Taking a deep breath, I open the door, bracing myself for the embarrassment and unwanted attention that arriving late always brings. But I needn't have worried. Twelve ladies sit in comfy chairs inside the small room, six on each side, as I spot the blonde, motherly-type middle aged lady, standing at the projector screen. As I quietly close the door behind me, she greets me. 'Oh hello darling, isn't the parking awful out there? Come and sit down.' I certainly wasn't cruising for a fight, but I had prepared my defence, always used to having to bob and weave in the face of trouble. But her words completely knock the wind out of my sails.

Instead of criticising or admonishing my lateness, she completely diffuses any hostility I might have carried by acknowledging my struggle, and welcoming me into the group. I'm thirty-four years old, but in that moment, I felt accepted and wanted, and immediately she had me. And this set the tone of the whole day.

While I had been expecting a crash course on restraining socially deviant under-elevens, surprisingly it gave me so much more than that. I can honestly say that it is the only course I've ever attended in twelve years of teaching that hadn't kept me clock-watching all day, fidgeting continuously in my chair and questioning why I ever decided to become a teacher in the first place.

The lady, it turned out, was herself a mother of three, and an ex-headteacher who had spent a huge proportion of her time solving behaviour problems in children and teens. Far from the death by powerpoint courses we're all used to suffering, it was interactive, real, useful and peppered with anecdotal scenarios that she herself had been involved with. The more I watched her, the more I grew to like her, and given our less than ideal situation for the coming year, I was interested to hear how she would approach this. Think *Supernanny*, but for older kids. She was brilliant. I asked a lot of questions, when normally in every staff meeting I take a vow of silence, knowing full well I'll be shouted down by some of my loud mouth colleagues. But if you had been my boss, and seen my contributions, you'd have believed there had been an imposter.

This lady was brilliant, and it was interesting to hear her perspective on many serious issues, and also challenged us to think about why we make children behave in particular ways. She reminded me of the sad reality for many children today, learning for and by compliance, and not for the joy of learning. That really resonated with me, namely because it reflects how I feel every day with my class. Why do we have to do what we've always done? Because we did it? Because our parents were taught in the same way? Food for thought most definitely, but what's the point unless you are going to try and affect change?

What did reaffirm my belief system, and perhaps almost give me the permission I feel I needed to continue on with my slightly less hysterically academic approach to school life, is the need to have fun and to laugh. Laughing releases endorphins, and the lady felt that if you can make them laugh, and then laugh with you, then you're sorted. And I was already sold on that back when I first started. She's never spent an hour with Mrs Wright, our resident comedian!

Because what I've said before and firmly believed from the beginning, is just this. All that nonsense about getting children to solve a learning problem the second they walk through the door every morning. Would you want to? Or would you want to spend a few minutes with your friends, settling in once again with the adults that you as a five or six year-old are going to have no choice but to rely on for your every need for the next six hours? It beggars belief that this is not the mandate for a positive and engaging start to the day, but thanks to the government, and thus school leaders, the belief that any deviation from the prescribed is incorrectly deemed to be 'lost learning time.' Unfortunately as a teacher, this latest fashionable phrase will be trotted out to you time and again, both in day to day conversations, staff meetings and during official lesson observations. Learning should take place from 9:01 until 3:15pm. Any deviation from that and you'll be throwing up red flags left, right and centre and drawing unwanted attention and criticism from the powers that be.

Throughout the day in question, I was reminded of the fact that I am lucky to work in a school that isn't rife with children labelled as 'problem children,' whose behaviour is the stuff of legend, quite literally. (Don't get me started on labelling, I'm very much opposed to it).

Peppered throughout the ongoing discussion that day were the cries of 'my Mark done that. Yeah, he don't like that. He used to hurl a chair at me when I asked him to get off the table and sit down' and ' yeah, he's a runner, legged it round the playground and over the school gate. We had a whole load of people tryin' to catch 'im.' I must admit I found it quite alarming that the stories that they told were so commonplace, and it got me thinking about my own experiences, both as a student and later on as a teacher.

When I went to school, I really can't remember extreme behaviour from anybody in my class, save for one child who I remember sitting cross-legged on the floor outside the head teacher's office during infant school. But the stuff I'd heard all day; rioting, climbing on top of tables and jumping from one to the other (and leaping on to the TA who was terrified he would hurt himself, thus making herself a prime target for jumping on), making a great escape because you don't like what the teacher has said, being violent towards other children and adults, made me realise that this is fast becoming the norm, and this concerns me greatly.

It beggars belief that courses such as these even exist, but it seems that they do so for good reason. After all, it's usually not the teachers that have to deal directly with such extreme behaviour, the sad reality is that it falls to the unwitting teaching assistants who no doubt never imagined in their wildest dreams that they'd wind up spending their working days akin to a prison warden rather than a supporter of learning.

As the course leader so beautifully put it to the ladies sat alongside me, 'we'll pay you minimum wage, you'll have a fifteen minute break but you won't actually get it, you'll be sworn at, scratched, bitten and kicked, your lunchtime will be half an hour but you won't get it, you'll spend it putting out fires instead- would you want to sign up for this?' I scanned their faces and saw their heads nod in a sad sort of acknowledgement that this was indeed their reality. Every day, for thirty-nine weeks of the year.

Now one could argue that I felt more confident, being really one of the only teachers in the room as most were teaching assistants working directly with so-called 'difficult' children. But the reason was that understanding behaviour, in particular the emotions and the anxiety that usually precede less that compliant behaviour, was literally right up my street. I delighted in the fact that I already knew a lot of the answers, and smiled in my head at the realisation. Just like the children, I learn best when I am interested and excited by something, and this was the complete opposite of any other course I've ever attended. No one was brandishing powerpoint slides about bloody phonics, no one was banging on about how to improve problem solving skills in maths, no one was trying to excite me with the latest SATs data from the county versus the rest of the schools in the country. Really, it was about what we seem to have forgotten about in this educational setting called school, the person doing the learning, the child.

In truth, there was a bit of role play thrown in, and yes, by the end of the day I had indeed learned how to safely restrain a violent child lest they should endanger themselves, other children or adults, but it gave me so much more than that. I walked out of there feeling a sense of calm and peace, and not just because it was Friday.

Granted, the fact that I had spent the majority of the day solely in adult company, and not had the stress, noise and chaos that is a warm June day in the classroom with thirty five and six year-olds helped a lot, but my spirits were buoyed by the positivity and genuine enjoyment of the experience. I cruised home feeling hugely excited to return on Monday and recount all of this to Mrs Wright, and anyone else who might ask. Whatever happens, I know we'll be able to cope.

Before I left I asked the lady for her contact details, and organised for her to pay us and our little charge a visit in September. I figured it couldn't hurt to be prepared.

36

Sports day

All is not well in the Olympic village. As I mentioned earlier, I'm the reluctant PE coordinator, and for the second year in a row, it will fall to me to organise the whole bloody event.

It absolutely terrified me last year, as to put it bluntly, the majority of my colleagues expected me to either fail or call in sick. I'm pleased to report that despite a very bumpy ride, not only did I pull it off, but it went brilliantly, with several emails via the school office from parents affirming how much they and their children enjoyed it. The main reason for my terror is that I don't like to stand out, to draw attention to myself, and much prefer to remain behind the camera so to speak. But this particular event requires one to be at the very forefront of proceedings, and emcee the whole day.

Now, ask me to organise the equipment, send out the invites, organise the TA's who have to score each race, and I'm all good, but ask me to stand and shriek into a microphone in front of four hundred children and their assorted relatives for six hours? Jog on. No way was I doing that. Luckily I managed to rope in one of our resident sports coaches and a good friend known for her vivacity and genuine enjoyment of public speaking, so my bacon was saved. This time round I wasn't so sure.

Last year, despite actually having an argument with one of the SLT members in my classroom that morning after he had kindly come to check that I had everything ready to go, he inadvertently let it slip that the boss did indeed want me out. I'd long suspected it, although she always feigned innocence whenever I had the gaul to bring it up during one of our 'chats', but hearing it from one of her right-hand men was not exactly what I needed to hear. I really lost the plot with him, and even though I felt a little bad that I'd been so cross, I did appreciate his help, although I'm sure he had to deal with the fallout that comes from being the broken link in the chain.

Exhausted, harassed by the beginning of the disciplinary proceedings and overwhelmed with having to put on something akin to the scale of a bloody *Live Aid* concert the next day, it was hardly a surprise that emotions were running high. But from adversity often comes a spark of fire in the belly, and something within me made me dig deeper than ever before in readiness to fight back. Mrs Wright, always on hand to back me up, was a fantastic support, as together we sat down and wearily began to turn our attention to preparing for the event and away from the disciplinary scaremongering.

'Right my dear' she chirped, clipboard at the ready. 'Let's think about what we need to do. Clipboards we've got. I think we need to go and get all the equipment and check that it's all there first, what do you think?' she asks. I run my hand through my hair as we face each other in the quiet classroom. 'Ok,' I begin, gathering my strength and focusing my scrambled mind onto what we can do, and what needs to be done.

The four billion items that we actually need for the day aren't kept in the main school building, and instead are held hostage in the attic above the performing arts space. Another waste of precious funds. Years ago somebody gave the green light for this monstrosity to be erected bang in the middle of the playground, where it now sits, oddly positioned as it obscures the main building and is now both an eyesore and a completely useless addition to the premises. The original idea was that the room would be used to do art, music and dance, and after a thirteen-month build and an official opening, they realised the floor was uneven and the walls not soundproofed. Lack of funding and the realisation that it hadn't turned out as they hoped rendered the building largely empty, save for the huge storage room that lay above it.

Now this room is the size of a football pitch, and when it was new, could have easily been converted into a beautiful apartment. Instead, it became the local 'Lock 'n' Store' where the PTA and the caretaker took turns to dump a complete load of useless shite up there, thus filling it to the eaves and rendering it a challenge like climbing Mount Everest just to get in there. It's June, it's thirty degrees, and we're all knackered. I know all that stuff is up there, but do I really want to be the one that brings it down? Not really. It's not like my colleagues will all rock up and lend a hand, far from it.

My logical brain kicks in, and I realise I have the solution. A solution that isn't going to mean Mrs Wright and I are going to have to stay super late after school as we make a hundred trips back and forth to lug bean bags, hoops and space hoppers down the steep stairs, sweat pouring from every orifice. 'I know' I venture, my face breaking into a wry smile. 'We'll get the children to do it.' Mrs Wright looks up at me from her perch on top of the table and smiles. 'Perfect!' she replies cheerfully. 'There's always more than one way to skin a cat.'

Before you worry about how much learning time was lost,

or if any part of this exercise put the small people at any risk, fear not. So as not to draw too much attention to ourselves and our crew, we waited until just before playtime, once the English lesson had been taught, the work done and the books marked, before Mrs Wright made her move and sneaked away to the office to collect the key under the guise of refilling her glass of water.

As I look at the sea of happy faces before me on the carpet, I wait until they're quiet before I start to speak. Mrs Wright returns, glass of water in one hand, key in the other, as she returns her glass to our cupboard and takes up residence in her easy chair. 'Right guys, we've got a little job to do, and I really need your help with this. You know how it's my job to set up for sports day?' I begin, as they start to nod in agreement and call out 'yes', 'well we need to go to the other building and go and get all the bits and bring them back to our classroom so that they're ready for Friday. Everyone can carry something, after all, they do say that many hands make light work!' I continue, trying to make it seem exciting.

Mrs Wright pipes up, her enthusiasm bubbling over as she gathers them. 'So, children, your mission, should you choose to accept it, is to come to the store room and grab all the gear and bring it back here as quick as we can! Do we accept the mission?' she cries, as shrieks of 'yes, yes!' begin to fill the air around us. 'Right then, quick, go and line up at the door' she instructs, as they race to see who can be first, the room filled with excited chatter.

I can always rely on Mrs Wright to fire them up, and right now I really need that. After all, it's not really an enticing prospect, ferrying and gathering, but because of her positivity, we've just duped them into thinking we're on a mission to the moon. By God, the woman could have said we're about to go on a nature walk and they'd be walking on air. I do love the innocence of childhood.

Praying we don't get spotted, I lead the line across the playground towards the towering building. I've no idea if we'll be able to find what we need, but we'll certainly try. Now I'm not actually letting them upstairs into the loft space. Instead they'll have to wait patiently below in the foyer while I hoof it up and down and pass them each something to hold. And it works a treat. They delight in the responsibility that's been placed upon them, and apart from a few tussles over space hoppers and the occasional sneaky bounce, our little army march defiantly back to our room, where we stash the loot in the middle area of the unit until Friday. Job done.

Mission accomplished, equipment checked off piece by piece, we congratulated ourselves on our preparedness and toddled off home. The day of the event, I arrived super early, circa 7:30am in readiness for setting up. I was fully prepared to have to set up the whole bloody field on my own, but I was pleased to discover my colleagues outside and ready to help. I guess they were so shocked I turned up in the first place and didn't do a sick-out.

The day went swimmingly, and I went home satisfied that I had exceeded the low expectations of myself set by others, and took it as a small victory of sorts. One of the parents in my class even popped her head round the door after school to say her own mother had thought it was the best sports day she'd ever attended. I just smiled politely, a strange mixture of happiness and relief, while Mrs Wright merrily called through the doorway 'do you want to put it in an email?' (to the boss).

Bless her, the lady actually did, and it was forwarded to me from the Big Guns. But despite the contentment that I'd done a good job, I couldn't help but feel sad that if only they (the parents) who heaped praise upon me really knew what kind of horrible and malicious persecution I had no choice but to contend with. If only I could tell them. If only they knew. But I couldn't, so I had no choice but to accept their praise and thanks while behind closed doors I felt a fraud, undeserving of any good wishes. After the event I breathed a sigh of relief that it was over for another year, and resolved that I would make it my mission to ensure that PE wasn't going to be my subject next year.

Fast forward to September. The Big Guns knows I hate PE, therefore I'm stuck with it again. As June loomed ever closer, the fear and apprehension began to bubble, and before I knew it, we were back for a repeat. This time I feel slightly more in control, and have a clearer idea of what needs to be done. In the days before, we took the children back to the store room to collect the equipment, to the same enthusiasm as last year. With all the other things going on that week (the data dead-line), it was hardly surprising that time got away from us, so we earmarked the Thursday afternoon while the children were in full flow with choosing, to continue the preparations.

In the noisy classroom, where children lay colouring on the floor, Duplo farms were being created and medieval battles being enacted outside complete with pretend swords and shields, we began our task. 'Can you please come in a bit earlier on Friday, you know, to help set up?' I ask, as we check off bean bags, coloured hoops and plastic eggs and spoons. 'Yes, of course I will' smiles Mrs Wright, as she sets the air horn she's just tested back on the table. 'Five to nine instead of nine? How'll that do for you?' she smirks, as we both dissolve into laughter. We all know how hard it is for the woman to leave *Lorraine* (Kelly) of a morning.

'Have we got the parachute?' I question, as she peers into a large bag to check. 'Here it is. God, look at it, it's filthy. We never replace anything do we here?' she muses, shoving the grimy article back into its bag. 'What about the trophies?' she asks, remembering the debacle last year when I forgot to collect them from the previous winners and had to go and hunt them down minutes before the official prize giving. 'Oh, whoops, no, I forgot about that' I respond, quickly scanning the room for a responsible and eager messenger. I spot Lyla happily crafting at one of the tables, her little friends settled either side of her, a sea of coloured pens and scissors atop the table. 'Lyla' I call, raising my voice so that she can hear me over the din. 'Can you do a job for me?'

Lyla's face lights up, as she rushes over to me, eager to accept her mission. 'Can you go to Mrs Stuart and Mrs Pepper and collect the trophies? We need them for tomorrow?' I ask. 'Yes' she replies keenly, excited at being trusted to leave the classroom and venture further afield upstairs. 'Do you know where to go?' I continue, as she nods her head confidently. I'll have to trust that she does. 'Why don't you take Nina with you?' I suggest, as Nina immediately links hands with Lyla and they exchange a little smile. The girls, excited by the prospect of a little freedom, step carefully over the toys as they make their way out of the door. I suddenly doubt that they'll know where to find the upstairs classroom, so ask my student helper to go along. 'Go and get the trophy back from Stella Stuart. Prize it out of her hands if you have to.'

The day finally dawns. Jesus, I've been woken from my sleep on a few occasions this week, worrying about it all. Have I got enough bean bags? Did I remember to print out the score sheets? Have I got enough helpers? You'd think I'd been asked to lead the next shuttle to the moon. I decided to go in early, knowing I really need to be in around 7:30am, a whole hour earlier than my usual arrival time. It's a beautiful day, as the sun shines brightly, ready to fry us all from 9am. Perfect. I prayed all week that we'd have some sudden cataclysmic thunderstorm that would rain it all off, but given that we haven't had any rain for nearly two months, even I realised it wasn't likely.

The solidarity between Mrs Wright and I has been my greatest joy, and I can count on her one thousand percent to be in my corner. And I don't mean that she showers me with praise left, right and centre for the sake of it, like some sort of feel-good candy-striper. The good friend that she is means that sometimes I hear things that I might not want to, because she cares too much to lie to me. That's what friends do. But it's a rare moment of unity when Mrs Beale joins the pack and pulls towards instead of against us. Namely by texting both of us (she has an MA in texting) from 6am this morning and insisting on supplying refreshments for us. She's been a champ, offering to bring bagels, juice and coffee for breakfast after we've set up. I'm in! I've been up since 5:30am, and that sounds right up my street.

The thing about sports day is that it isn't just the kids who get competitive. You seriously would not believe the kind of build up and hype that there is preceding a day like this, and that's just from the staff. Stella Stuart keeps on wandering into my classroom randomly, trying to start a conversation with me in order to gauge just how much we've been practising, while simultaneously scanning the room for any traces of beanbags or hoops that might indicate foul play. She's on a mission to win. Well, she's won the bloody trophy every year thanks to her brazen cheating and own interpretation of the scoring system. But not this year, and not if I'm organising it. Last year, in the aftermath of disappointment, one of our aggrieved teachers and Emma the PE leader took it upon themselves to go through the finer details, and over a Nando's, found the unmistakeable proof that she was cheating.

While the teacher's only job is to start the race, it falls to the TA's to score using the scoring sheets. However Stella Stuart began calling out the points for the TA's to record, under the guise of helping them, hence the hugely inflated scores. Having gone though the scoring sheets it became immediately obvious to them that it simply wasn't possible to achieve more than the maximum number of points for the bean bag in the hoop race! But nobody ever confronted her, and instead we just let her and her class bask in the knowledge that they came out on top, while the rest of them quietly seethed. This year, I'll be adjudicating myself, if I have to swelter courtside in the thirty-degree heat to make sure the other five classes have more than a snowball's chance in hell of trouncing her.

I'm pleasantly surprised to discover many of my colleagues are here and ready to help set up, particularly my male coun-terparts, who performed the majority of the donkey work, such as erecting gazebo's to keep us all from frying out there all day. Well, save for Bebe Duke, notable in her absence, yet sitting four feet away in her classroom in full view of the field, eating a bowl of cereal. Whatever.

As the event gets underway, I'm relieved that thus far, things seem to be going without a hitch. Granted the children are slowly dying of the exertion, but kudos to them, they're giving it their all and overflowing with competitive spirit. The races are really eight different events that each class rotates around until all have been completed. After all the score sheets have been collated, there is a winning class as well as a winning school colour house.

Now we've invited the parents of course, but we can't possibly have them wandering all over the field and getting in our way, so the caretaker has kindly cordoned off a little pen to contain them so that they can be right in the middle of all the action. There they can cheer, whoop and scream at their little darlings to run faster, hop better and kick a ball with more gusto till their heart's content, but never cross the barrier between spectator and participant.

This wasn't my idea, it was inherited from the previous organiser, but it's actually quite a winner, given that they can't obstruct the teachers and the hopefully smooth running of the whole event. Having now been in charge of the delivery these past two years, it's a nice surprise for me not to have to lead my class around all of their events in the blazing heat. It's a rather delightful bonus to be able to stand underneath the shady canopy right outside my own classroom, preside over the running, and not have to do a lot beyond setting up the equipment in the morning. Maybe the power's gone to my head. Either that or sunstroke is beginning to set in.

Anyway, despite the weather being phenomenally hot, the

day went off without a hitch. The slightly sad part for me is that I don't really have any contact with my own class all day, while Mrs Wright runs the show alone in my absence. The only snippet of contact I managed was just before they went out to begin, where instead of the usual 'it's not the winning, it's the taking part that counts' speech, Mrs Wright was busily leading a rousing rendition of 'we're gonna win! We're gonna win!' as thirty children dressed in brightly-coloured red, blue, yellow and green t-shirts, shrieked and pumped their fists in the air as they lined up ready to go. After a play outside at lunch, the little faces are already flushed, sweaty hairlines slightly glistening and water bottles recently filled are tightly clutched in their hands as their excitement builds.

As I stand in the doorway for a moment just to check that everyone's ok and Mrs Wright knows which race to start at, Willie's mum rocks up behind me, a bottle of Piriton in her left hand. 'Hiya, can I just give him some medicine for his eyes?' she enquires, as I scan the line to look for Willie. What's happened to him? I'm all in the dark. One look at Willie tells me that this is one hundred percent necessary, as I take in his red, puffy eyes that appear to have come into contact with an allergen over lunch. He's not worried though, not a jot, as he flashes his mum a big smile. 'Oh Willie' I respond, before offering his mum our group room where she can privately administer the miracle Piriton. 'What happened to him?' I question Mrs Wright once Willie's mum's out of earshot. 'I don't know really' begins Mrs Wright, searching her scrambled brain to try to remember all of the lunchtime incidents. 'I think the office phoned his mum, he's got a touch of hay fever. It's rife with the stuff out there' she continues. Ah well, the poor guy. At least his mum's got the antidote and he won't have to miss the races.

As Mrs Wright fumbles around in our cupboard for her sunhat and her water bottle, I take a moment to gain their attention and wish them luck. Just as I begin, Logan's mum appears from behind me, brandishing a bright blue pair of trainers. 'Can I just give these to Logan?' she asks, as I quickly try to locate him. He's right in front of me, as he waves a foot in the general direction of his mum, the foot clearly contained within a new-looking green sports shoe. 'Oh' I venture, all confused. 'Logan these are your trainers aren't they?' I question, wondering just why we are playing swapsie-shoes just minutes before we're due to start.

Logan's mum jumps in, as she rustles the plastic bag in readiness. 'He's been saying this morning that he didn't want to wear his PE trainers, so I brought these ones instead' she explains, as I look on. 'Do you want to wear these Logan?' she asks him, as he looks at her likes she's got two heads. 'No, mum, I want these ones' he repeats, his arms stretched out either side of him as he stands in the doorway like a starfish.

Mrs Wright heads out off to their first event, as I return to the canopy and prepare to start the races. Or rather, instruct my co-captain today, Mr Hughes, to get the ball rolling. I'm pleased to see that it appears to be going to plan, despite the searing heat and that the children are more than invested in doing well. The bigger children we've corralled into helping do a fantastic job of running back and forth to deliver the score sheets to the adjudicators, as one by one the events are completed.

By half-past two, we're nearly finished. The only race any of us under the judges station got to actually watch, was the one set out right in front of us, the running race. And one of the reception classes were up. It's hysterical watching them, after all this is the first time they've done anything like this before and they always interpret the rules in their own way.

As the horn sounds to begin, some run as fast as they can, somebody's shoe comes off, another one at the start line forgets to go, and so on and so on. One little girl completely lost her confidence among the noise and cheering from the parents at the sidelines, and stops mid-way. The Big Guns did what I like to hope any one of us would do. In her skirt and heels, completely the wrong attire for anything sport-related, she rushed forth across the lanes to take the little girl's hand and run with her to the end, to the enormous cheers from all of the reception parents. A nice thing to do rather than leave the distressed little thing just standing there. As the final horn sounded, we rounded them all up to sit together underneath the beating sun, as the atmosphere built while the final results were decided.

I'm not competitive at all, but I'd be lying if I didn't say that I'd be over the moon if Stella Stuart didn't win for the first time in several years. As the tension builds, the ladies doing the scoring continue to punch the numbers into their calculators as we wait with bated breath to find out the winning house and winning class.

The Big Guns takes the microphone and begins to thank the parents for their support and the children for their brilliant participation during what's likely the hottest day of the year thus far. As I'm handed the piece of paper, I smile, before handing it along to her to announce. She reveals that Bebe

Duke's class have come in third and there is an abundance of cheering and whooping from her children. The second placed class is revealed to be my own, which means we've beaten Bebe Duke. That's enough of a victory for me. And finally, by some miracle, Stella Stuart's been pipped at the post by the other Year Two class, led by Mrs Pepper. The class enjoy the triumph, not least because her children have completely trumped Stella Stuart, and even they're surprised to hear it!

I glance at the children all sitting on the dusty, African-savannah of a field, and catch sight of Bebe Duke placing her arms around Stella Stuart in commiseration. As we all disband, and the hoards of children are led in to get ready to go home, I breathe a sigh of relief that it's over. And as for Mrs Pepper's class winning? Well, justice has been done.

37

Vive la France

It's a sad day when you've got no TA's on the penultimate Monday of the school year and you've no choice but to go it alone all day. Mrs Wright and Mrs Beale are on the course that I've just been on, and I want to call in sick.

Mrs Wright, when presented with the idea, replied cheerfully 'I don't want to go on any course, I don't want to go to the swimming course, hell, I don't even want intercourse!' as she squeals down the phone to me. 'Hold on!' I answer. Now she's going too far. But it proved to be as useful to her as it was to me.

It's actually quite rare to ever have the class completely by myself. I'm very lucky to have two extra bodies every day which means three adults versus thirty kids. But it's bloody hot, pushing thirty degrees and we're all tired, strung out and incredibly ratty. Not to mention wondering how on earth we managed to make it through the previous thirty-seven weeks seemingly harmoniously compared to the last push before summer break. Things are starting to fall apart, and it's a daily battle to keep tempers from flaring and ensure that everybody's hydrated and not dying of heat exhaustion.

Did I forget to mention that the last few weeks of the year are NOT for winding down? Oh no, just when you though we could hit cruise control, the powers that be begin to request more demands. There's the data that needs to be on the system by the final week in June, so that the SLT can spend hours after school 'analysing' who hasn't met the grade, and yet never asking the most important question: why? Because they aren't interested in the fine print. No, we've just got the work them harder.

Then there's the reports. Every teacher is required to report to parents how each child is performing in every subject that we teach, and sometimes those we actually don't, like outdoor PE that's taught by specialist coaches from an outside company. Do you know how long it takes to write a school report? Hours, that's how long. Each double-sided document takes over an hour to write, that is once you've torn yourself away from the TV series you've got playing simultaneously, settled yourself in a reasonably quiet place, and gathered a multitude of refreshments that might make the task a little less arduous. But even once you've got into a rhythm, it's no easy feat. You've got to essentially find an extra thirty hours from your life in which to complete these in time for the boss to read and approve them. It's like climbing a bloody mountain. So when does one write them?

Well, just as the weather turns, and the summer weekends become a smorgasbord of exciting social invitations that you inevitably have to turn down. In truth, I don't turn them down, but then I'm left racked with guilt that the free time I did have each weekend has been so frivolously spent not doing what I know needs to get done. I resolve to do one or two each weekday evening, but honestly, I'm so knackered by the time I can sit down and turn my attention to them, and my brain is so fried after a whole day of teaching that my eyes become glazed and I make a promise to myself to clear some time to start earlier the following night. Well, that was the plan. At least until *Love Island* began, then forget it, I was screwed.

The only way to do it, I've decided, is to fall into one of two categories. Either you become a smart-ass, completing thirty reports during the week off in May half-term, or you do what Stella Stuart does, which is to overwrite the ones from last year. Actually I think overwrite is a tad generous, as all she does is change the names. With option A, you have the smug satisfaction of returning for the last half-term having completed the task that no one wishes to undertake, the only downside being that you've worked your entire vacation. On the flip side, if you choose Stella Stuart's approach, you get both a half-term and the sense of freedom that comes with not really having to apply much effort, i.e. just hitting copy and replace with whichever child comes to mind next. Decisions, decisions.

Whichever path you choose, the outcome still needs to be achieved, and that is the biggest thorn in our sides in the run up to summer vacation. Having breathed a collective sigh of relief, you'd think that most of the bigger jobs were done, and that you could enjoy the last few weeks of term having gotten your class to where you want them. Nope.

We're supposed to be having a 'fun' week, a chance to go off topic and have a whole week designated to pretty much whatever the heck we want. Sounds like a great idea right? Wrong. For those of us, i.e. me, that have spent the previous thirty-odd weeks going off on a tangent in a bid to bring some excitement and enthusiasm back into the word 'learning,' it's another imposed program that's been foisted upon us. Now we're supposed to pick a country, any country in the entire world, and study it in detail over the course of a whole week.

The first problem is that we're supposed to agree together with our year partner as to what we want to do, but given that Bebe Duke and I are not even on looking-at-each-other-face-on terms, let alone those that involves words being uttered from mouths that each other would have to hear, it's going to be tricky. So in the end, the Big Guns, having already suggested in her usual way that we might 'have a chat' and discuss it, realised that this was never in a million years going to happen, and instead chose for us; France. A country that I know little about beyond the primary school basics, and had little to really bring to the table.

So this week we are supposed to be immersing ourselves in all things French, and the only vaguely exciting activity activity I've managed to conjure up is colouring the French flag. Fair dues, I did try to make it exciting, and we had had a good chat about all things France and looked at a brightly-coloured powerpoint to get us started. But this tired teacher, in the penultimate week before summer break was certainly feeling the struggle.

'I haven't finished my flag!' bemoans Vanya as we're on our way out to play. We've only been colouring for around an hour, the majority of the first session of the day. Everyone else has finished, shoved them all crumpled into their drawers and dived for the fruit before they hit the playground. But poor Vanya has one speed, and it's slow. With no Mrs Wright, I'm having a bit of a sense of humour failure, and it takes every fibre of my being to refrain from uttering the words 'there's a shocker.' It's not important, it doesn't matter, and I need a cup of tea, so I adopt my Mary Poppins demeanour and respond with a cheerful 'never mind, pop it in your tray and you can finish it

301

later, off you go out to play' and send her on her way, as she smiles and skips out to the playground.

When, oh when will Mrs Wright be back? After muddling through Monday, on Tuesday when the dear ladies return spirits are infinitely brighter. A quick catch up before they come in reveals Mrs Wright had just as brilliant a time as I did on the same course last week. 'God, wasn't it good?' she affirms with great seriousness. 'I felt so different at the end of the day, so calm, not like when I've spent the day cooped up in here listening to this' she continues, as she gesticulates to the classroom with one hand, the other reaching down to swap her trainers for her work shoes. I'm really glad she enjoyed it, I knew for a fact that it would be right up her street just as it was mine.

I take one look at Mrs Beale though, and realise the same cannot be said for her. The words of the character Roz from the TV show *Frasier* 'you look like you've been ridden hard and put away wet!' spring to mind, as she sits atop one of the tables, looking like she was at an all-night rave and slept a couple of hours in the trunk of a car. Such is Mrs Beale's apathy and inability to pay attention to what's going on, that come Thursday when we managed to rope Benoit's mum, a native French speaker into giving a talk on France for the children, the whole thing ended on a bad note, namely in almost killing Hugo.

Benoit's mum, when asked if she would be happy to regale the class with all things French, offered very kindly to provide a buffet of French delicacies for the children to try. It was such a lovely thing to do, and one which she refused to be reimbursed for the purchase of the food items, that we went ahead, despite the trepidation about allergies that food sampling naturally brings. As soon as she arrived and began to present the power-point she'd thoughtfully prepared, with Benoit as her helper, Mrs Wright sat alongside for crowd control while I nipped to the office where the medical information is kept, to make sure that I knew exactly who could and could not try particular foods.

There are four children, Hugo included, with a various assortment of milk/wheat/gluten/egg allergies, who would unfortunately be unable to try the cheese, French bread, pain au chocolat and other French pastries that had been provided. I checked, I triple-checked and then I headed back to class to fill both of the ladies in. While some could have something, poor Finley could have nothing at all, so after explaining to a rather disappointed but amazingly accepting little boy, he took it on the chin and Mrs Wright went off in search of a piece of fruit so that he didn't feel left out. With Finley sorted, I knew that the three remaining children could have one thing or the other.

As they sat in the circle, Benoit passing around the food on paper plates that his mum has cut up into child-friendly pieces, I kept my eyes on the three boys, having reminded them that the bread was fine, but that they wouldn't be able to taste the cheese or cakes. And somehow, Mrs Beale got involved in passing out plates of French delights- chocolate cookies, pain au chocolat and all those lovely chocolatey things that small children fall all over in their haste to tuck into. Unfortunately she passed the plates around to everybody, and Hugo, utterly absorbed in the excitement of the whole event and entirely trusting of Mrs Beale, happily helped himself to all the sugary treats. Yes, those would be the treats that contain the allergens milk and egg. And now begins my panic.

As I look around the circle to see him happily scoffing, my face darkens and my pulse begins to rise as I look at Mrs Wright. 'She's just let Hugo eat a chocolate cake.' As she looks at Hugo, and then back to me, we've now got a major problem on our hands. We've stupidly put ourselves in exactly the place I didn't want to be in. Is he going to throw up, pass out? Will he go swiftly into anaphylactic shock and need to be resuscitated? It doesn't bear thinking about.

As I begin to panic, Mrs Wright, always the fountain of calm, quietly calls Hugo over to her, and begins to ask him a few questions. 'Now Hugo, you've just had that chocolate cake darling. Do you eat those at home? How are you feeling right now?' Meanwhile I exit the scene and head to the office to ask for some advice, and work out how much damage control is going to need to be done.

The ladies in the office kindly dig out Hugo's medical files from the vault, where it reaffirms my fears about what he's just ingested. Jesus, we're screwed. I'm really cross, because I know that if I were Hugo's mum, I'd be furious that staff had given him something he's not supposed to have, and essentially gone against her wishes. Just as I'm catastrophising, Mrs Wright returns. 'Look Betsy, he's eaten it now. Let me just phone his mum and see what she wants to do' she suggests, as I nod my head in agreement. 'Please let her know how sorry we are, and that it's our fault' I advise her. 'Now, now, it won't come to that. Just leave it to me' she says confidently, as I return to help Mrs Beale with the others.

There's a coolness to my demeanour, as I'm pretty annoyed that she wasn't as concerned as we were about protecting those children with allergies. But with hindsight, she probably forgot, getting swept away with the occasion. Plus I suppose I bear that ultimate responsibility for them so it falls to me to ensure that we're all singing from the same hymn sheet. Meanwhile, while I'm fearing that at best, Hugo might have vomiting or the runs, he's completely oblivious and now running himself silly outside on the field with all the other children high on sugar. Mrs Wright reappears, a bright smile on her face and a piece of paper in her hand, as she sits down on the edge of the table. 'Crisis resolved Miss Graham, he's fine. Apparently the allergies are mild, and he does have milk and eggs in cooked foods at home, it's just on their own that's the problem.' Thank God.

And when Hugo's mum arrived to collect him as normal at the end of the day, I apologised profusely and she kindly told me not to worry about it. It gave us the chance to update his official records, and the matter came happily to its end. Mrs Beale wasn't particularly popular however, being three steps behind with what's going on, but I rationalise it's simply another storm in a teacup, and tomorrow is another day.

38

Home and school

I think the problem is, in this particular workplace, and possibly in teaching as a whole, you are encouraged to be 'the star.' In a world where everyone can be a leader, there is little place for those of us that don't really want to take centre stage.

What if you don't want to 'lead from the middle' (a course for developing school leaders at a middling level in their career, and also one I politely declined to be a part of on more than one occasion), or aspire to assistant headteacher or the big kahuna, headship?

What if that was never, ever on your radar, despite the fact that you know exactly what stupid ideas and initiatives you'd bin the second you'd got one hoof through the door? I think that sometimes there just isn't really a place for you, you who appears to lack any ambition to be anything other than what you initially signed up to be in the first place: a classroom teacher. What if you just want to come into work every day and enjoy teaching small children? What if you just want to ensure that some of the mistakes that the previous generation made with us aren't repeated, and that the next little bunch will be a little more emotionally equipped to cope with the learning that is being delivered at an inhuman pace?

Some of us put in a huge, even colossal effort, that goes largely unnoticed. Some of us prefer to do things quietly, without drawing attention to ourselves. This is me. I think I'm quite creative, not particularly in the traditional artistic sense, but possibly more in the creative thinker sense.

I like to be excited by new ideas, and things that inspire me I try to bring into the classroom in some way, as my own personal contribution to making our lives that bit richer. When I think of all the ideas that I've managed to move from the confines of my brain and transfer into real life happenings, I'm rather proud. Because I've done them quietly, discretely, and without campaigning for recognition.

How sad that we don't put the mental health and emotional wellbeing of children at the forefront of education. In the modern world, there's less time for everything, not least parenting which is what is largely going to be the biggest factor in facilitating good outcomes for children.

Homeschooling is a topic I hadn't really thought much about until I started to write this book. I happened to stumble into a video on YouTube of a popular celebrity who had decided to home educate her two daughters after they became unhappy at their (private) school. For all of the academic suffering, social difficulties and challenges that most children inevitably face somewhere down the line in their school years, I have always believed that despite all of their flaws, school does do a lot for the development of the whole child. It teaches you how to get along with other people, some you like and others that you don't. It teaches collaboration and teamwork and how to treat others around you, but the main one is that it teaches you to conform. But through watching this video, granted it's only one person's perspective, I found it quite thought-provoking and it challenged many of my beliefs.

As a teacher, much as I love being able to change some of the aspects of education that are so constraining, there are plenty of things that I can't and that I have no choice but to deliver. And I've often wondered over the years, as my frustration grew, what decision I myself would make if I were a parent with a child about to enter education. Would I actually want to inflict this broken and inflexible system on my own child?

Perhaps it's because I only have my own experiences to draw upon, that a part of me wants to believe that some of the horrors that I've described would simply not exist elsewhere. And it might be partly true. At least I'd very much like to hope that there are schools who wholeheartedly embrace a more child-centred approach and make it a priority to hire nicer and more empathetic and caring teachers. I'd imagine there must be no worse a feeling for a parent than having to drop your tiny four year-old off every morning and relinquish them into the hands of a complete stranger who doesn't find them as remotely precious and lovely as you do. And if I were a parent having to drop my child off to the two loons who run the reception classes in my school, well, I wouldn't.

But even if such a school does exist - one where the teachers are happy, married/unmarried, have their own children/ are happily childless, gay/straight, back or white, it doesn't matter to me - as long as they are happy and are committed to educating and caring for children, that's all that really matters. In my school, a workplace rife with unhappiness in the form of failed marriages, divorces, lack of relationships, barely controlled mental illness and just plain crazy and odd in a few cases, it concerns me greatly that they are put in charge of children where nobody really knows what's going on behind their closed classroom doors. When you look at half of the workforce who are quite frankly barking, and wonder how they've narrowly missed being sectioned, it really makes you think twice about how they've been allowed to be placed in sole charge of some of our most vulnerable beings in society. Mrs Wright always reaffirms my belief when she says 'have you seen that film, *One Flew Over the Cuckoo's Nest?*

39

Discipline

It's a given we were going to have to talk about it. I've always tried to find my own way, in the sense that I could only do what felt right for me. Now every school has the appropriately titled 'Behaviour Policy' which is trotted out to the newbies when they start, kindly informing them of how we do things here. The feeling is that the best thing as a school is to have a consistent approach to dealing with and managing children's behaviour on a day to day basis that ensures that we are all singing from the same collective hymn sheet. Easier said than done.

I believe that it's a legal requirement for all schools to make their policies available to parents either on the school website or in paper form at the office, so that every one of the key players involved (the headteacher, the teachers and the parents) are all clear and comfortable about how children will be treated. It's a brilliant idea, but in practice, let's just say that the reality of this is very different. While we have a school system in place, how each teacher works within this is quite obviously open to interpretation, and given the nature of the beast, it's not unusual that the over four hundred children throughout the school will likely have very different experiences.

We are all human beings, and our own childhood experiences as well as our training will no doubt give way to some contrasting approaches. As I've talked about already, during my childhood I was over-disciplined, and consequently I always made a conscious decision that when I became a mother, or indeed a teacher, that I would go out of my way to deal with situations in exactly the opposite way than I experienced myself. Throughout my training and my years in the class-room, I learned quickly that there was never going to be a 'one-size-fits-all' solution or approach to managing difficult situations. By far one of the most useful pieces of information I ever received has stuck with me and really resonates; criticise the behaviour, never the child.

Earlier this year I witnessed one of the TA's who was covering for me one afternoon during my planning time, humiliating a little boy in my class with special needs. It was a sobering reminder of how not everybody on the team understands how detrimental such treatment can be for a child, particularly one who has some special needs.

Owen found it very tricky to get himself dressed and undressed independently, and needed pretty much 1:1 help at the start of the year from Mrs Beale, his designated helper. Quite honestly, when we first did PE and the room was rife with clothing scattered in every direction as the twenty-nine others were excitedly getting changed into their sports clothes, Owen simply sat there on the floor with his unopened bag next to him, watching in confusion. As Mrs Beale removed the necessary items one by one from his PE bag and handed them to him, he honestly looked like he'd never seen a t-shirt or a sports shoe in his life. It was very frustrating for the short-tempered Mrs Beale, who was instructing him while she looked away every so often to roll her eyes and exhale loudly. He required a huge amount of modelling, but by the end of the year, he could pretty much do it himself.

One time back in October, I remember looking over to see him sitting in the middle of the floor, fully dressed in his PE kit, legs stretched out in front of him while Lauren and Tirza took charge. They were like mini-mothers as they each had hold of one of his ankles as they tried to ram each foot and push them into his sneakers while he sat back on his hands, his face absolutely devoid of any emotion.

As I listened to them, I smiled as I realised that they had adopted the same encouraging tone of Mrs Wright and I, in an attempt to help Owen to dress himself. 'Now Owen, can you do your shoes up?' chirped Tirza cheerfully, as Lauren rammed his school clothes into his PE bag and pulled the drawstring closed. 'And then you can hang your bag up Owen' she instructed, offering him the red bag. They totally relished the responsibility, and in one sense, it was really a delight to see how they spotted a problem and chose to help to solve it. Moments like those really mean something to me.

But one Tuesday afternoon when I wasn't teaching and the aforementioned teaching assistant was semi-in-charge, I happened along to grab something from my classroom and saw just what I feared might happen in my absence. Owen was unlucky in the fact that his EHCP only granted him a specific number of hours of support, less than the thirty hours of the school week, which meant there were several afternoons every week that he simply had to go it alone and just fit in with the rest of us.

In the typical 'we're-strapped-for-cash' style of problem-solving, it was suggested that on these afternoons Mrs Wright might have to step up to the plate and be his 1:1, leaving me on my own with the rest. Only this never worked, because Mrs Wright was one of the three TA's designated to teach both classes for alternate hours during our release time every week, despite the fact they get paid no extra for assuming the responsibility.

As I popped in that afternoon, I noticed that most of the children, having already changed back into their school uniform after their games lesson outside, were now sat on the carpet as we waited for the TA's and the sports coaches to swap over. But Owen was standing at the back of the classroom, Mrs Gladbourne towering over him as she surveyed how far he'd got with the getting dressed. The poor guy had gotten dressed, but as is often the case among the small people, he had clearly been unable to turn his clothes the correct way out. And so he stood, his trousers inside out with the large white pocket flaps sticking out, his t-shirt back to front so that the high collar rested backwards up against his chin.

And then she laughed. At him. In front of the others. 'Laugh Owen!' she cried, 'it's funny. Children come on, laugh, it's funny isn't it!' she encouraged, as a few nervous titters began from the others, namely from Christopher who as we know doesn't need much encouragement to make fun of others. 'You look like an elephant Owen!' laughed Mrs Gladbourne. I froze, simultaneously horror-struck and angry. I couldn't believe that anybody could be that thick to not realise that it is teasing, and as for encouraging the other children to join in the abuse was just ludicrous. I couldn't believe the lack of empathy, and the complete lack of understanding. The woman had two daughters herself, and I wonder how she would have felt if that was her child being ridiculed for something he had little control of. It made my blood boil, as I looked at Mrs Wright, both of us so surprised that this would even happen and too stunned to react. I looked at Owen, his face blank but his eyes looking into mine.

And immediately I was furious. Furious with Mrs Gladbourne, who exerted her power as an adult to humiliate a child, and equally as cross with myself for being unable to put a stop to it. I'm his teacher, I set the tone, and he knew that we don't behave like that when I'm in charge. I felt unable to call her out, and looking back, I wish I had made my feelings very clear on the subject, right in front of my entire class, who were as confused and awkward at being caught in the middle, receiving a very different message than they were used to.

I felt like Owen's eyes implored me to step up, and I wish with every fibre of my being that I had felt able to. After all, I knew that if I had been a fly on the wall in that moment as his parent, my heart would break into a thousand tiny pieces just to witness the embarrassment and humiliation of your precious child by the very people you trusted to prevent this sort of thing from ever happening.

I did have a talk to them all (the children) afterwards, and I took Owen aside later on to explain. And I explained to all the children that Mrs Gladbourne should not have behaved like that, and that it was wrong. In that moment, I felt so passionately that I couldn't give two fingers as to whether it was the right thing to say or not. I guess you're supposed to present a united front, with all of the staff singing from the same hymn sheet, but I clearly undermined her authority and I couldn't have given a toss. My only regret is that I wish I had confronted her directly and made my displeasure known, but having already had the difficulty with Bebe Duke to contend with, I wasn't looking to add to the hostilities by losing another, albeit indirect team member. God, it's like the bloody Gaza strip here some days already.

Another real gem was the idea that you should never scold a child when you can see that they are genuinely remorseful, and I always make sure that I put that into practice. We were lining up one day, the usual chattering and shuffling around as we got ready to go to assembly, and a couple of children were having a bit of a barney at the back of line about whose turn it was to go at the very back (a much-coveted place). While I stepped in to sort this out, Mrs Wright was simultaneously manoeuvring the few girls we had from their little groups and splitting them up so they'd slot nicely in between some of the boys who might choose to muck about and chat. By the time we'd got everybody settled, I returned to the front of the line in readiness to lead them to the hall.

As I turned to clap and gain their attention, I caught sight of Jonty, stood silently just behind me. One look at his face told me something had happened, guilt and unease written all over it. I immediately knew, before I realised what had happened, that he was genuinely upset. I was also slightly mystified as to what could have happened in the thirty seconds between my moving from the front of the line and back again to the front! On closer inspection, Jonty held two small, long, wooden and clearly fractured pieces, one in each tiny hand, having inadvertently been fondling a pencil while chatting, and then snapping the object clean in half.

Now some of my colleagues, think Bebe Duke for starters, would have immediately raised her voice to deafening volume for all to hear, and started bellowing about him having damaged school property, and that tired old line that frustrated teachers far and wide use to humiliate children 'would you do this to your things at home?' What bollocks. It's such a waste of time, completely illogical and ultimately the only thing to be gained from any situation like this is that you've asserted and reminded the children of your authority, and humiliated them in front of their friends in the process. Round of applause for you, what a great teacher you are.

Investing in the children you are charged with caring for for the year is the biggest factor in academic success, and knowing any child for several months (that is, if you've bothered to show an interest in them or learn anything about them beyond their name) should help you to decide whether the situation requires more formal sanctions or just a gentle discussion. The look on Jonty's face immediately told me which of the two he needed, not to mention that in all honesty, I can't really get excited about a broken pencil. It takes more than that to get my heart pumping. Similarly when one of the TA's used to gasp in horror loudly at break time in the staffroom that made me jump out of my skin and shriek 'there's no biscuits!' I knew there and then I'd have to make alternative arrangements.

The first words out of my mouth to Jonty? 'Oh dear' I venture, as my face changes into one that it might had I been mildly disappointed at having spilt my tea or dropped a plate on the floor. Giving the child a chance to talk is key, there's no need for me to say much more than that.

'It was a accident' Jonty begins, nervously nodding his head up and down as he scans my face for reassurance. 'Ok' I calmly tell him, mindful that the room has grown awfully quiet and that this is now a very public event with twenty-nine pairs of eyes all focused on him. 'Pop it in the bin, we can't fix it' I instruct. He turns and drops the sharp pieces into the bin, then returns to his place in the line. 'I'm sorry' Jonty offers, clearly quite downcast at his error in judgement. Then all I do is offer some reassurance that I'm not angry, that accidents happen and it's not the end of the world at all. 'I know you won't do that again' I smile, as he nods his head in agreement, and smiles as his face is flooded with relief. And then off we go to assembly. Done and dusted.

You see, there was no need to turn the classroom into a war zone over a bloody broken pencil. Sadly I can assure you that this is not the case in my school, with one teacher famously refusing to let anybody in her class out to play after a pencil was broken, holding them all hostage over their playtime until somebody 'fessed up. Pick your battles people.

Growing up, my house was always filled with shrieking and shouting, my dad turning the air blue if we ever made a childish error in judgement that resulted in a drink being knocked over or a curtain rail being pulled down. Ok, so that was kind of a big deal, but it really got to the point that we were terrified to drop, spill, break or make a mess and left us all literally treading on eggshells around him. So during my teaching years, I've made it my mission to react in completely the opposite way, and not to react in the way that my dad did which left me feeling anxious and unloved.

I always tell the parents at parents evening about our approach, happily delighting in admitting that Mrs Wright and I regularly fall over, drop things, break stuff and pay no attention to it, for the sole purpose of teaching the children that there's no need to blow a fuse or sweat the small stuff.

Because in any classroom of thirty children, whatever their age, the reality is that things inevitably will get broken, accidents will happen, liquids will be spilled and damage will be done. The trick is not to react in a negative way that admonishes the child and damages their self-esteem and confidence, while teaching them that we can fix things and it doesn't have to be a national crisis.

A few years ago, while I was teaching in Year Two (six and seven year-olds), we were teaching them about weighing and measuring in maths. We had a set of little plastic scales on each table, and gave them some glass jars filled to the brim with hundreds of tiny lentils, the perfect staple for this sort of thing. I was working with one group, my back to the rest of them in that moment, when I was alerted by some squeals and cries of 'uh oh!' as more and more heads looked up.

As I turned around in my chair, I saw poor Anna, her hands still holding the heavy jar which had inadvertently tipped over as she attempted to pour the lentils into the little bucket on the scales, a sea of them now adorning the floor next to her chair. I still remember her worried little face behind her purple square glasses as she awaited my reaction, her peers looking on clearly enjoying her misfortune. My reply was automatic. 'Oh dear! Never mind, pick them up then. Perhaps some of you on Anna's table could help her? Thank you Erin, thank you Jacob' I praised, as they left their seats to help, as I turned my chair back around to face my group. No fuss, no scolding, no humiliation. Move on.

You have to be very careful about what you say, particularly in times of trouble, as the last thing you want is to damage their self-esteem or negate their perception of themselves. Children buy into all the things they are told about themselves. If those things are negative—that they are worthless, lazy, stupid, ugly, a failure, or will never measure up to a sibling—it can leave them feeling both unworthy of a better life and powerless to change.

David Sack, MD, Psychology Today, May 12, 2015.

Our school-wide system used in every class, is the behaviour ladder. A long strip of laminated cards hang vertically at a focal point in the classroom, with a named clothes peg for every child clipped to it. If I remember correctly, there was little explanation or discussion as we were just handed the colourful plastic hanging, and instructed to display it somewhere prominent where the children could see it easily.

I'm not sure whether actually that's the right thing to do, as it makes any kind of misadventure a very public rather than private affair, but then sometimes it's the peer pressure that keeps us all in check. It helps us regulate our behaviour and conform to what's expected of us. With little or no clue how really we were supposed to use it, I instructed Mrs Wright to hang it up on the edge of the whiteboard in front of the world map carpet and held my breath.

Here's how it works. In the middle of the three foot long vision, there's a bright green A4 space bearing the title 'expected learning/behaviour.' At the beginning of every day, every child's peg starts on the green. Above it is the pink card 'above expected learning/behaviour' where their name can be moved if they are essentially going above and beyond in terms of behaving well or completing a piece of work to the best of their ability. The ultimate accolade, and the proverbial icing on the cake for the children, is the card above pink, a white background over which a large gold star is displayed, bearing the words 'excellent learning/behaviour.'

To them, being allowed to move their peg to the star is akin to winning an Academy Award or an Emmy. The pride and delight that positively beams from their face when they are on the star, is wonderful to see, for two reasons. One is that as a teacher it is genuinely lovely to see how proud they are of themselves, and two, it sends a very powerful message to the other children, that they too could choose to up their game and receive the same kind of accolade that being on the star brings.

Now from the Big Guns, the instruction was that if a child has done something well, then alongside the child's little award, their parents should also be informed so that they can 'ooh' and 'aah' over their little poppet's triumph. With this in mind, I now hand anybody on the star the prestigious 'star certificate' written and signed by me to take home to show mum and dad. Sometimes, as is the chaos that is trying to herd cats and get them ready to go out of the door at the end of the day, the task of completing that precious certificate often eludes me. But don't you worry, they won't forget! I'd be rich if I had a pound for every time somebody said to me at precisely 3:14pm 'but you haven't given me my star certificate!' mournfully.

Going up the ladder always works well, but just as payback always rolls downhill, the same can be said of the pegs on the behaviour ladder. The next one down after green I think is yellow, titled 'first warning-make the right choice.' Moving on to yellow is pretty much an hourly event, as it's highly likely that a few of your 'key players' are going to misbehave or fail to tow the line at some point during each lesson.

Likewise there's always a rogue one or two who might just be having a bad day, when after repeated requests from me to stop calling out and interrupting while I'm teaching, over-enthusiasm or lack of filter get the better of them, and their peg swiftly descends down the chart. Usually it's coupled with 'that's a bit sad, isn't it' from me, as I pinch the peg to clip it into its new position. If I'm feeling particularly irritated, a very effective way is to just stand up, move over to the chart in complete silence, select the appropriate name and silently move it down to yellow, as they sit and stare eagerly to see who it's going to be, while I return to my chair and make a point of making direct eye contact with the perpetrator.

After yellow it's orange- 'second warning- make the right choice quickly' which quite often has a handful of pegs on. The final blow, the ultimate no-no is the red card- 'final warning-time out'.' Now going down to red is a very big deal, especially if you are five. When your little wooden peg follows that path and hits the big red card, two very unwelcome things are going to happen. Number one, you're going to have time out, likely by visiting the headteacher's office, and the following day miss some of your playtime, and number two, the crowning touch, is that your nearest and dearest will be informed, either by telephone or at the door at the end of the day. Terrific.

Reds don't tend to happen that often, but we'd be lying if we said we didn't have a couple a week. The most frustrating thing for us, is that the red is nearly always a result of really minor things, such as repeatedly talking over a teacher, not listening, hurting somebody, which are all pretty low-level, escalating quickly over a small period of time. But when they're in quick succession, a one-way ticket to red is the only conclusion. And it's almost worse for me, because I feel like a complete tit having to follow the behaviour policy to the letter and dutifully inform parents via the phone in the office (where everyone can hear) that Tom is on red, but not for heinous crimes like flattening somebody at playtime or throwing his chair across the classroom, and instead for interrupting, making fart noises and scribbling over his neighbour's whiteboard work.

Having to justify why he or she ended up there is the thing I find the most difficult. At least if something serious happens, I can be fairly confident that when the parent answers the call, like a lawyer representing a client in trial, I have prepared a good case. Nine times out of ten they are so shocked/appalled/horrified that their usually lovely child could behave so badly, and happily offer to reinforce the consequences at home. It goes a long way to have parents that back you up, and take the time to talk to their child later that evening and express our collective disappointment in their home environment. It's often the case that in the safety of their own home that they will feel more comfortable explaining why they did what they did, and sometimes that dialogue with parents is the best way to move forwards. For the child, it sends a clear message that school and home are interlinked and that it is a partnership of sorts.

Missing playtime is where it hurts for children, so this is often the consequence for the small people. I don't doubt that they have quite a nice time, sitting on the comfy chairs by the office, reading books or having a natter, but at the end of the day, I know that they are usually remorseful and will try as hard as they can not to end up on red again. In this day and age, even after the parent phone call, the higher-ups still have to fill in paperwork documenting the misdemeanour and then sending it home just to be sure that parents are clued up. Is it really necessary? Another paperwork exercise and some more fodder to add to the class behaviour file that lies stuffed into the darkest depths of my cupboard that none of us will ever look at again.

Early last year, after a week or so, a lovely parent asked me at the end of the day how her son was getting on in class. It's fair to say that the road had been fairly bumpy thus far, and I knew she knew that he was a bit of a handful, talking over me and being quietly disruptive on the carpet. I'm not Bebe Duke or Stella Stuart and I can't be blunt, abrasive and brutal, it's not me. I think there's a way of explaining without ruffling people's feathers, especially when they are the very people who you need most to be on your side for the next thirty-eight weeks as you teach their child. Plus Oliver is standing right there, nuzzling into his mum as he grins, knowing full well that I'm about to dish the dirt.

Smiling, I explain what's been happening, but I also keep reaffirming that he's lovely, that it's early days, and that ultimately, we'll get there. And I wholeheartedly believe that this is simply teething troubles. He's a dot in the ocean compared to any serious problems we might encounter, and compared to some horror stories I've heard of other children, delightfully easy and workable. We had a very positive conversation, and like I said before, his mum knew exactly what he was like and what the issues might be.

I was quite surprised though the next day when he came to me at register time and proffered a small homemade card, lovingly decorated with a beautifully coloured flower pot and flowers on the front. As I opened it to read it, I could see he had copied his mother's writing, and in his own shaky handwriting, had written 'I'm sorry I talked over you. I will make you happy again. Love Oliver.'

I was quite touched by this, and gave him a hug to thank him, while he grinned from ear to ear behind his glasses. I made a big deal about it in front of the rest of the children too, and both Mrs Wright and I praised him for his efforts in wanting to make amends and for his thoughtfulness. I actually kept that card for ages as I felt it was such a lovely thing for a parent to get their child to do. Sometimes people really do listen and it was so refreshing to feel supported as this is not always the case.

The nice thing about Mrs Wright and I is that we are never too proud to admit that we've made a mistake or got something wrong. I wondered slightly whether we might end up undermining ourselves as the adults and leaders of the class when she found two spare pegs and wrote our names on them before adding them to the green card alongside the children's. However, I decided that she was right, and that they do need to see that we are fallible, and willingly went along with her idea. So every time Mrs Wright would inadvertently trip over a child or accidentally squish their little fingers with her size sevens, she was quick to laugh and call for a keen assistant to do the deed. 'Megan, go and move my peg down the ladder!' she would chuckle, as Megan beamed and giggled in delight at wielding such power over Mrs Wright's little peg and excitedly moving it on to the yellow 'first warning' card.

Likewise, when Sophie was laid out on her tummy on the carpet drawing with friends one day, I accidentally trod on the back of her calf as she moved after I'd already lifted my foot to take my next step. Bugger. I tried so hard not to tread on her, but it must have really hurt, and I felt awful. I gave her a cuddle and sent her to the office with Julia for the magic cotton wool, telling Julia to tell the dear ladies that Sophie's horrible teacher had squished her. She was quite teary, and I really felt a bit rubbish.

After about ten minutes, I sent a grinning Julia back to the office to collect her, and told her to say 'Miss Graham's really sorry, will you come back so you can move my peg down the ladder?' A few moments later, amidst the children dotted in every corner, toys littering the floor, a smiling Sophie returned, bent almost double as she hobbled through the doorway holding one of Julia's hands, the other still dabbing the miracle cure of the wet cotton wool to her injured leg. Oh the joy that moving my peg down that ladder brought!

Sometimes injustice will really play on a young mind, at least in the case of Marco this year. Having been quite unkind to Aubrey along with Damien, they earned themselves a yellow warning and a time-out by my chair. After five minutes or so had passed, Marco called to me from his place on the floor beside my brown chair. 'I'm really angry about this' he said calmly, to which I replied, somewhat surprised that he was able to verbalise so clearly how he felt. 'Come over here and talk to me then. Why are you angry?' I asked him, as he began to explain how he had been cross with Aubrey when a game had gone awry.

'Do you know why I asked you to sit by my chair?' I continued calmly. 'It's because you were not very nice to Aubrey. You were teasing him and called him names and he was really sad wasn't he? He was really crying because that hurt his feelings and that's why he came to tell me about it. Now you know that that's not a nice thing to do is it? We've said that Aubrey shouldn't have done what he did, but that you and Damien shouldn't have teased him when it had all been sorted out, should you? Now I think you need to go and say sorry to Aubrey for being unkind, and then go and move your name down the ladder.'

Marco did indeed go and apologise, and later on his peg, along with Damien's returned to green on the behaviour ladder. But it's the talking rationally and explaining and also allowing him his turn to express how he felt that led to it all being sorted out without World War Three beginning.

There have of course over the years been a few deviations from this approach. When I was in reception, probably only in my third year of teaching, the children were regularly allowed the freedom to play outside in our little playground while the adults rotated round to supervise them. Myself and my TA at the time, Mrs Pegg, were sat inside the classroom, working with groups while others pottered around playing, when our ears pricked up to the sound of wailing. This wailing increased in volume quite markedly as whoever it was approached the open back door.

It was one of those cries that told me instinctively that this was going to be bad, and there would likely be blood. Just like with a baby, the cries of pain, anger and fear are all very different, and I felt sure that my ears had detected cries of serious pain and shock rather than the result of just a tiff with a friend. I looked towards the door, my breath held in expectation of what I was about to be confronted with. I was picturing blood streaming from a head or maybe a leg, and braced myself in readiness for a run to the office or worse still, an ambulance call.

As Sara walked through the door, still howling and shrieking, I immediately looked at her for any clues to fill in the missing pieces as to what had caused such screams. 'What have you done?' I asked, as she took a breath and began to speak.

'Erin wouldn't give me the sand toy I wanted, she said she's having it forever!' she wailed, as I felt my adrenaline beginning to pump for all the wrong reasons. I looked at Mrs Pegg, and she looked back at me, her face beginning to display some of the fury that was quickly building inside me. 'Sara' I began, struggling to contain myself as my blood pressure began to rise.

'I am so cross with you, how dare you come in making all that noise!' I said through gritted teeth, although not shouting. 'Mrs Pegg and I thought something terrible had happened to you outside. I thought that we'd have to take you to hospital with all the noise that you were making' I seethed, my voice beginning to rise a couple of decibels.

Mrs Pegg joined in to back me up, eyebrows raised as she looked the little girl in the eyes. 'You do not need to make all that noise young lady! Miss Graham is very cross, and so am I! Go and sit down on the floor by the board for five minutes and have time out' continued Mrs Pegg, as we exchanged another look of disbelief.

I didn't lose the plot with her, I didn't lose touch with the rest of the planet either, but it's fair to say that I was really cross! Granted it wasn't my finest hour, but I really had to explain why even at five, we don't just act like the world has ended just because we're upset. In truth, it was the classic parent overreaction when because of your fear and subsequent relief that no harm has been done, you explode and release all of your emotions onto the child, mostly out of how bloody terrified you were.

After a five minute cool-down period for all three of us, my feelings on the subject were communicated calmly but very clearly. A slightly tearful apology later, she skipped off to choose a different activity, this time within view of the classroom, and reminded of the usual instruction to them all; if you can't work it out by talking to your friend, then come and ask a grown up for help. And not give the teachers a heart attack in the process.

See, I did tell you I wasn't perfect either.

40

Scott the sheep

As I mentioned earlier, something happened to the school in the summer term that made the end of my disciplinary issues fade into the background. The school accepted a child into one of our reception classes as we had an empty place. Quite literally, the more children you have in school, the more money that comes in, so it is quite literally a case of bums on seats.

The Big Guns will never turn down an opportunity to fill an empty space, and rightly so. In the primary years, there are clear rules as to how many pupils can be allocated to one teacher, and for Key Stage One the limit is thirty. As the children become older and move into Key Stage Two (years 3-6), the number of pupils rises, each class having a maximum of thirty-two children. So naturally the Big Guns was happy to fill this place in reception and have two complete classes. The only thing was, proper preparations were overlooked and I don't think anybody really knew what we were collectively letting ourselves in for.

You see the little boy had not long arrived in the UK from Russia, his family being very well-educated and offered jobs here in the pharmaceutical industry. While he did understand and speak English, his experience of nursery and school thus far was therefore extremely different to life in a British school. Oh, and one more thing. Did I forget to mention that the poor little boy had serious medical issues that nobody really knew how to manage? All these factors combined made for a very eventful last term of the school year this year, and then the good news, that Mrs Wright and I will be having his class from September. Brilliant. Except everything I've witnessed from afar has made this situation sound a whole lot worse than it actually might be.

Little snippets began to trickle down from Mrs Wright, who spent quite a bit of time in the general vicinity of him every lunchtime, as he 'played' on the field with everybody else. I use the term 'played' loosely, as any outdoor playtime offered a whole wealth of opportunity to beat other children up, even the Year One's and Two's. Day after day, Scott kicked, pushed, punched and scratched his way through the lunch playtime, leaving a trail of upset and maimed children in his wake, left for the poor TA's to try and console. Here's where it got seriously ugly. Scott never took too well to the word 'no' and consequently he took out his frustration on whatever was closest to him- usually the staff. Because of all the children's stampeding out of the lunch hall in their quest to reach the field first, Mrs Wright unfortunately coined the nickname 'Scott the Sheep' in reference to his release from the metaphorical pen of the dining room. And it's stuck.

In the typical fashion of most schools I'd imagine, upon recognising that he would indeed require 1:1 support immediately, and without any time to advertise the position or interview, the Big Guns and Liz Dawson did what they all do- redeploy somebody else. And that meant Mrs Gladbourne was now charged with being his minder every morning until the end of term. I'd like to say that if we'd had any bloody money and we weren't so far in the red that we'd have hired a specialised person who was both qualified and willing to take on the challenge, but the truth is if we did have the money, it simply wouldn't have been spent on him. The only way to be able to get him any help, is to get the funding from the local education authority by submitting a dossier of information as to why this is imperative, and wait on their decision. But the wheels of justice turn very slowly, and as I write this, those wheels have only moved a fraction.

So Mrs Gladbourne began her service by being prized from the clutches of Bebe Duke every morning and moving in with Liz Dawson and her crew. We tended to keep well out of it, but little by little, information would trickle down the grapevine as to how each morning had panned out. Not well, as it turned out. Mrs Gladbourne, a law unto herself and on a mission to turn this so-called 'bad boy' good, only served to exacerbate an already inflamed situation. One day she was kicked, another day she was pushed, until finally by mid-week, when she'd been scratched and punched repeatedly, eventually admitted defeat and was sent home in a tearful mess.

Incident reports were filled in, meetings in hushed tones in the photocopy room with the Big Guns where we could all hear, and occasional phone calls to his unhelpful parents to inform them. What a palaver. In one incident that week, Mrs Wright happened to be on a walk and talk with the Big Guns who had a free moment, to fill her in on a concern we had over a child in our class, when she was interrupted and the whole thing put on hold. As they both paused mid-flow, they heard the screaming, and then saw the poor child being frogmarched by not one, but four adults all trying to bundle him down to her office, all holding an extremity. Even the caretaker pushed from behind as they tried to manoeuvre the writhing wildebeest from A to B. 'Ooh, Mrs Wright, I'll have to catch up with you later' hurries the Big Guns, as she wearily heads towards the scene, as Mrs Wright watches on in disbelief, before replying 'oh yes, I can see you've got a lot on your plate!'

By this time, poor Mrs Wright's fear had begun to build. Not only had it begun to build, it had begun to be a huge topic of conversation both for us and across the school. Once the Big Guns finally confirmed that we were to have him next year, that's when Mrs Wright and I knew that proper plans needed to be put in place. Now it was a quiet comfort to know that we had been chosen especially to take him on, precisely because of our calmness and caring nature, not to mention our positive and humorous approach to school life. And I know we'll be able to turn it around. But before we can do that, there will likely be a period of adjustment, when I know that we'll need support and back up from our superiors. But how likely are we to get it?

Granted, the Positive Touch course went a long way to empowering us should we be confronted with such extreme behaviour, but what will happen if he kicks off when we say no and he wants to do his own thing? We began to question the specifics and express our desire for a consistent approach.

One thing that we did decide to do, which hasn't happened before, is that we were invited by Liz Dawson to spend a bit of time down there getting to know him. Seeing him in action more like. Now the brilliant thing about the small people, is that any situation, no matter how odd/strange/unfamiliar etc, can be explained away to them quite easily, and passed off as the norm. So our presence there was merely bigged up by explaining that as their new teachers, we had simply popped down to their class to get to know them all and to see what they were learning. Sold. Meanwhile we were on a mission to get to the enemy, and pick up the trade secrets from the people who were currently in the thick of the battle.

We started slowly. First I popped down for half a morning leaving Mrs Wright and Mrs Beale in charge, and then we switched. With three adults, it was easy enough in those last few pointless weeks before the summer break, where we do sod all anyway, to rotate around and free up one person at a time to go and gather insider information. Not just on Scott the Sheep, but on all of them! To begin with, it was all calm at sea. It was quite nice to be a fly on the wall, not least because I was the observer while Liz Dawson did her teaching. Having put me through so much nonsense already this year, it was nice to have the shoe on the other foot.

She has a knack for treating them as if they are Year Six and not reception, and shouting loudly, so it wasn't a surprise to see what needed to be undone next year once they were with us. But Scott was happy as a clam. He sat nicely on the carpet with the other children, joined in with the little phonics game they did, and then came to the table with his group to do some handwriting. He was strangely compliant, and I found myself wondering about all of the bad press the poor guy had been given thus far. I certainly hadn't seen him smack, shout, hit or hurt anybody, child or adult. So far, so good.

I reported back to Mrs Wright and Mrs Beale, and began to wonder if this had all been a fabrication, an exaggeration, a pack of lies. Then Mrs Wright went down. After my morning of essentially just dossing about and watching the way the children played and interacted with each other and the staff, I expected that Mrs Wright would have had a fairly similar experience, but it proved not to be the case. When she returned, just after the lunch bell rang and the children had been safely delivered to the lunch hall, it was clear things had not gone to plan and that she'd borne witness to Scott's quick temper.

The poor woman looked ashen as she sat on the table across from me, as she proceeded to explain what had happened. 'I am just so shocked by what I've just witnessed' whispers Mrs Wright, as we speak in hushed tones so that Bebe Duke can't listen through the interconnecting door. 'What?' I ask, confused, as I came away thinking the whole situation might have been grossly overstated and not nearly as terrible as we'd been led to believe.

'Well' she begins. 'It started off ok. Scott was playing outside, and Liz Dawson suggested I read with him as I wasn't really doing anything. And here's where it all went wrong. As soon as I called him over to me, he refused to come. So I said, 'come on Scott, you show me where your book bag is,' and reluctantly he came inside, but not before shouting at me repeatedly 'I hate you Mrs Biff, I hate you!' as he kicked the book bag around the cloakroom.' Scott has somehow taken to addressing Mrs Wright as 'Mrs Biff,' after taking a shine to the *Biff, Chip and Kipper* books from the Oxford Reading Tree that dominates our reading scheme.

'It all kind of went downhill from there really' continues Mrs Wright sadly. 'Liz Dawson came to investigate- well, only after I told her he refused to cooperate with me, and she just looked at him and walked away, telling me it's best just to leave it. What kind of message is that sending here?' she asks, her face full of concern, as is mine. 'Then, to top it all off, Frank decided he wanted a piece of the pie, what with all the attention now on Scott, and I watched them literally punch, hit and scratch themselves in battle before eventually Frank had to walk away and said 'I hate you Scott.' Liz Dawson just said we should step back and watch and let them get on with it!' she explains, absolutely incredulous. And so am I. I can't believe Liz Dawson didn't intervene, given that it sounds like the two boys have come to some serious blows, and that are likely going to injure both themselves and each other.

'I'm just speechless Betsy' offers Mrs Wright. Crikey. It takes a lot to render Mrs Wright speechless. Dear Lord, what's happened down there? 'I'm telling you, this is unlike anything we've ever seen before. When he sees red, he just goes. I'm fifty-six years old, that's too old to come to work to be a punching bag for a five year-old boy' she says with great seriousness. I knew she was worried, but I had no idea just how much. After all, it's much easier to be optimistic when you haven't seen *Mortal Kombat* played out between two pre-schoolers with your very own eyes.

As we congregated before I left at lunchtime, Mrs Wright and I grabbed a few more seconds to mull over the events of the morning. As the reception children were evacuated from the lunch hall, ready to be let loose on the field, Mrs Interfering, the lunchtime coordinator couldn't resist her moment to swoop in, her ridiculous walkie-talkie in her hand, as she interrupts and directs Mrs Wright to the field. 'Yes, I'm on the way!' Mrs Wright smiles brightly as she turns to reply, before turning back to me, annoyed at having our conversation once again cut short. 'Why don't I just put a broom up my arse?' she jokes, before heading over to the field for her half an hour of '*George, Don't Do That*' a la Joyce Grenfell.

Mornings with Scott continued to play on Mrs Wright's mind, as we considered whether we should just leave well alone until September where we could all have a fresh start, but Liz Dawson was adamant that our presence was valuable and welcomed. We agreed that given yesterday's events, that perhaps we would come together next time, in order to get the same picture on things. Liz Dawson was highly in favour, so we engineered for us to pop down again the following morning, leaving Mrs Beale with our lovely bunch.

Take two, and we're braced and ready. However, on arrival, it seems that Liz Dawson has neglected to mention that she's off to visit the next lot of children coming to school in September at their nurseries, so we're in charge. Brilliant! Despite the initial hesitation, we're coming round to the idea. The idea that we get to pretend to be their teachers, just for the morning, is quite exciting really. It was sort of like a dry run and a glimpse of what life might be like in September. We had a blast. A very adrenaline-like blast, but it was good just the same. And after three hours we simply handed them back, our heads swimming with useful information- who doesn't get on with who, what triggers so-and-so's bad behaviour etc.

We left there strangely exhilarated, and personally I felt a lot less anxious. September could be a totally different story though, we'll have no choice but to wait and see. 'I think I'll come in dressed in my sumo suit just in case' smiles Mrs Wright as she winks at me. 'You know, to prevent death-in-service and all that.' You never know, we might be glad of that in September.

41

Winding down

As the last week is finally upon us, and the weather fluctuates with clouds gathering above, the countdown is on for the last day. It's been a tiring last few weeks, and the children, like ourselves, are done. Day after day, that sun burns fiercely outside as they run themselves silly at playtime, returning sweaty, dishevelled and exhausted. We've had tears and heartache over the small things, they're fed up with each other and fall-out's with friends are rife.

And day after day, Mrs Wright and I drag ourselves in, which frankly feels equivalent to climbing a bloody mountain every day. The last two consecutive Fridays I've overslept. I'm convinced even my iPhone just doesn't do Fridays either and is staging a protest. Despite our collective tiredness, there's been a lot going on, as we've cleared the classroom around them and torn down the board displays before re-backing them. All while the children played both inside and outside the classroom. There's always that lovely quality in small children, that they never realise when it's just not a great time to interrupt, or when we're in the throes of something complicated. Not least when we're trying to re-cover a display board with a huge roll of brightly-coloured paper, a two to three-man job every time.

Later that day we sat together while they watched a movie of their choice as an end of term treat, to write their goodbye cards. Once we began, I writing the main part before passing them on to Mrs Wright and Mrs Beale to sign, half-wished that I hadn't decided to write a personal message in each one. But I knew I wanted to give each child their own individual card rather than writing something generic and insincere. We had made a little poem as well, laminating it and giving it a ribbon handle for them to be able to hold it, as well as a little charity bracelet bearing our class motto about kindness, which Mrs Wright and I wore every day.

As we spent the best part of the first hour of the movie writing the cards, talk turned to the summer vacation coming up at 3pm tomorrow. Mrs Wright is already feeling a touch sniffly, and fearing a holiday spent in isolation fighting off a mystery virus. 'I'll have six weeks of dysentery and rickets, and then just as I'm recovered it'll be back here to the cries of 'oh, did you have a nice summer?' she chuckles in mock seriousness.

I try to stifle my giggles as the movie continues playing as Mrs Beale, also amused, pipes up helpfully 'Well at least you'll be skinny!' As we fall about laughing, I throw my two cents in. 'And you won't have to go to your club any more either!' referring to Mrs Wright's Slimming World membership. We're a great team, and we'll be reunited once more after the summer break for more fun and frolic.

***

You might think or feel from reading this, that given my perception of all things education, that the most obvious solution would be for me to fold up my tent and move on, and never look back. But I didn't. I'm still here. And I know why. And maybe you do too. Because despite all of my criticism, my frustration, and my internal conflicts about my abilities, I know that I'm a good teacher, and deep down, I do love what I do. It took me so long to realise it, but I already knew the answer to why I hadn't handed in my notice and taken a different path.

I love working with children. I love seeing their fresh faces each morning, full of optimism about the day ahead. I love seeing their faces light up each time they discover something that we already know and take for granted that we can do with ease. Each time they care for each other, pick each other up when they fall, and seek to repair their broken friendships, my heart fills up as I marvel at how simple life is at five.

When Mrs Wright and I begin to see the fog of the first few months of each school year lifting, and our influence begins to show itself in their behaviour and their thinking, it's extremely rewarding to know that all our investment is paying off. As one of many influences in their lives, I hope that we and the time we shared together, play a small part in shaping the people that they are to become in the future. Connection is the key, and it's what Mrs Wright and I try our hardest to do every day, no matter the busyness of the classroom and the pressure to tick some silly box on an assessment sheet. After all, what I fundamentally believe is that for children to be successful in life, they need to have emotional security from the people who raise them.

The myth that what it takes to be a good parent is to live in a huge house, take foreign holidays several times a year, and have the typical two-parent family is in my view outdated and untrue. As an anxious adult myself, I believe that the best thing that any parent can do for their child in order to set them up for a happy life, is to love them unconditionally, support them, cheer for them and commiserate with them, talk openly, spend time together, and be emotionally connected to them.

Those of us who experience chaotic childhoods are often not emotionally equipped for handling all the curveballs that life can unfortunately throw at us, which makes for an unhappy existence. I haven't had children myself yet, but when I do, I know that all I will want is for them to be happy. To be nice, kind, empathetic people with lots of friends, and frankly I won't care about whether they're making expected or above expected progress in school. Because the chances are they'll find their way, as we all do, and when they do, I want them to be happy.

I knew when Lola sat on my lap that day, her little chest heaving as she gasped for breath between sobs, that I was part of a system I no longer believed in. I realised that whatever my feelings, I was and continue to be a pawn in the game and am guilty of perpetuating this cycle, however hard I try not to.

What would I want from a school, though? The truth is, I don't know. I suppose having vented my spleen endlessly through this book, you'd rather expect that I had an abundant amount of workable solutions that would make the lives of teachers and children better, but I don't.

Because I don't think we're ever going to have any govern-ment that abolishes all testing in the primary years, and that prioritises the mental and emotional health of pupils beyond hitting pointless targets that only serve to increase the prob-lem. SAT's results, phonics screening results, none of it really matters. The process ultimately serves no-one, and is only used as the stick to beat the school with if they don't fiddle the results in order to look good. Do you remember (if you did them) your SAT's results? And did they have a resounding impact on your success in life or future employment? I'm going to wager not.

What I would like is a system that looks at individuals as individuals, and not just numbers. I wouldn't want any future child of mine to just be seen as a number on a piece of paper, their ability and self-concept already pre-decided by teachers who treat them as just one of many.

I want him or her to have a teacher that genuinely cares for them, who wants to get to know them and understand how they tick, and create a nurturing environment and a climate of self-acceptance, where they feel valued and special. And for it to be a reality, not just printed text in the glossy school brochures sent out to parents. Ultimately I would like every teacher to have more concern for children's emotional wellbeing and mental health rather than just their grades.

Teachers do a bloody important job, and you know what, it's time that we told them that. It's not easy being responsible for the development of young minds, especially given the turbulent times we're living in, and the children before us are the future doctors, nurses, accountants, lawyers, artists, performers and the like. Not to mention that they'll be the ones looking after us when we're in the nursing home, so if that isn't a reason to get it right, I don't know what is!

Now if we can just convince the government to bump us up the pay scale (I think something similar and akin to 'Prime Minister/ Head of MI5/ Hedge Fund Manager' should do it) it might go some way to boosting morale. Well, that and getting rid of all testing during the primary school years. After all, whereupon our official job title is simply *'classroom teacher'*, in reality we are a multi-tasker unlike any other. A counsellor, a parent, a UN peace keeper, a mediator, a facilitator, a wiper of tears, wiper of noses, a snack provider, a conflict resolution specialist, an expert negotiator, an entertainer, an example and so much more.

Epilogue

As the morning wraps up and the clock hands inch their way towards lunchtime, we settle ourselves onto the world map carpet. A sea of new faces gaze up at us, waiting for us to speak. I ease myself onto the curved handles of my easy chair and take up my perch, as Mrs Wright gets comfy in hers as she crosses her legs, her size sevens hovering alarmingly close to Nathan's face. We've just met our new class for next year, and they've spent the morning exploring their new classroom and familiarising themselves with the Duplo train, the princess dresses and the sandpit outside. Thirty small faces, so beautiful, so expectant, and so keen to please.

I ask them 'have you all had a nice morning?' and await their response. As they respond in a cheerful chorus of 'yes!' Mrs Wright and I smile at each other. It'll be hard work, but nothing good ever comes without effort, and I'm looking forward to putting it in. Thirty new characters to learn about, thirty new people to get to know, and a whole host of fun, laughter and learning to be enjoyed. Whatever happens, despite all the craziness that goes on behind the scenes, I know they'll have a ball, and with any luck, we will too.

As the morning draws to a close, and after accompanying them all to the hall, waiting around until they're all seated with their little tray of pasta shells in front of them, I head back to my classroom and release the breath I've just held for the last three hours. Mrs Wright is fumbling around in the cupboard trying to locate her belongings that we had to hide from Scott the Sheep, lest they be used as potential weapons. 'Well?' I ask her. 'What did you make of that?' Mrs Wright reaches into her knock-off handbag for her trademark bright pink lippy, opens her compact and begins to spread the lipstick across her lips as she paints her mask back on. 'It'll be alright' she muses with a wry smile. 'We've just got to think outside the (sheep) pen'.

Praise for *Do You Love Me or What?*

'Has Sue Woolfe revived the short story in Australia?
You would believe so if you read this range of stories,
elegant and satisfying, and so percipient of human yearning
and loss – that is, with the eternal concerns of human
existence. An innovative and charming novelist,
Woolfe brings the same qualities to these tales.'

Tom Keneally AO
*Internationally acclaimed author, historian and
playwright, Booker Prize winner and two times winner
of the Miles Franklin Award.*

'These stories are so achingly intimate, so immediately
known, so emotionally satisfying and moving, and written
in such luminously simple prose that it's impossible not
to be enthralled at once and lost for hours in the joy of
reading. What a gift to the hungry reader!'

Alex Miller
*Bestselling author, two times winner of the Miles Franklin Award
and the New South Wales Premier's Literary Award, and winner
of the Commonwealth Writers Prize.*

'A beautifully crafted journey through the complex
chambers of the human heart, each story with its own
revelation of what love might mean. There is rare
insight and compassion in these stories, especially
for those who don't "fit in".'

Patti Miller
Bestselling author, essayist, academic and life writing mentor.

Also by Sue Woolfe

Painted Woman (1989)

Making Stories: How Ten Australian Novels Were Written,
with Kate Grenville (1993)

*Leaning Towards Infinity: How My Mother's Apron Unfolds
Into My Life* (1996)

Wild Minds: Stories Of Outsiders And Dreamers (1999)

The Secret Cure (2003)

*The Mystery of the Cleaning Lady: A Writer Looks at Creativity
and Neuroscience* (2007)

The Oldest Song in the World (2012)

Do You Love Me Or What?

SUE WOOLFE

**SIMON &
SCHUSTER**

London · New York · Sydney · Toronto · New Delhi

A CBS COMPANY

DO YOU LOVE ME OR WHAT?
First published in Australia in 2017 by
Simon & Schuster (Australia) Pty Limited
Suite 19A, Level 1, Building C, 450 Miller Street, Cammeray, NSW 2062

10 9 8 7 6 5 4 3 2 1

A CBS Company
Sydney New York London Toronto New Delhi
Visit our website at www.simonandschuster.com.au

National Library of Australia Cataloguing-in-Publication entry
Creator: Woolfe, Sue, author.
Title: Do you love me or what?/Sue Woolfe.
ISBN: 9781925533286 (hardback)
            9781925533293 (ebook)
Subjects: Short stories, Australian.
Dewey Number: A823.3

Cover design: Alissa Dinallo
Cover image: Steven J Gelberg/Trevillion Images
Typeset by Midland Typesetters, Australia
Printed and bound in Australia by Griffin Press

Contents

Do
You
Love
Me
Or
What?

*Do You Love Me
or What?*

I've never been really sure what friendship is about, and at what point it melts into love. Other people seem to know, as if knowing it is something you're born with, as solid as a part of the body, your arm perhaps, or your leg. Sometimes I've managed to ask, 'What is friendship?' but it marches out of my mouth in a grand uniform, as if I've trumpeted, 'What is truth?'

So now I'm on the boat with the achingly pretty her, the last boat ride we'll have, and the river that used to unite us is rushing by too fast and all the things we haven't said are rushing away as well. When I look around, that swoop of trees recedes where we had our secret adventures, our wash breaks on that sunny stretch of sand as it has always done, all as if nothing heart-wrenching is happening – there, it's all gone into the distance. What's falling away are the claims that the things we've shared will have on her life; the person leaving easily forgets them, but for the one who stays, memories are like a city of clouds weighing down the sky, a city of black stones where you put down your suitcase on a dark footpath and know you're going to be desolate from now on; there's a storm that will refuse to break, but refuse to drift away. You'll just be left waiting, waiting, waiting.

We're not on the boat she wrecked, of course, but on another boat she found washed up in the reeds, and helped me fix, in penitence, and I was grateful for that, though it was no substitute.

Some things are solid, there's no dispute about that. Years ago, I'd flown from Brisbane to a memorial service in Tennant Creek for a man I once loved and shouldn't have, sitting through eulogies from people who thought they knew him but didn't. I was babbling in pain and fury for anyone who cared to hear, and everyone heard but didn't care. It was she who took my hand. 'I know how you feel,' she said. I'd never laid eyes on her before, this young, pale, pretty blonde stranger who took my hand. She nodded at each fresh outburst of mine, she kept nodding all day. *I know how you feel.* Grief had not singled out me alone to torment; her kindness gave me belonging, made me one with the heaving, grief-swollen world. Later she introduced me to two Aboriginal women, who both echoed, 'I know, I know. I know how you feel.' Both of us – she and me – had lived with their people out in the desert, me for one year as his tormented lover, her for ten years as a community nurse.

I know how you feel. I'd already met Aboriginal women like that – something about the way they looked at things, something about the way they were brought up. They understood how you felt.

It was a memorial because the man I shouldn't have loved had been missing in the ocean for three breathless weeks. It wasn't his funeral, no one was admitting to that yet; we were just remembering him. In my dreams I had watched his body as pale as a fish, a human body undulating as helplessly as weed, his small compact body with its magnificent chest that once sat so proudly on his narrow hips. I'd blamed his chest for a lot. In the life he'd led in the desert, being a leader in desert communities, he was always missing, always turning up in some unexpected place, he and his chest had been too busy to ring to tell me where they were, they'd been out doing something more important than remembering to ring me, they'd been rescuing. When I'd told his best friend he'd gone missing, the friend had just laughed: 'He's always missing. He always turns up.' But he had dived, this desert man, into a boiling ocean to rescue a stranger.

At the memorial some of us kept saying he'd drowned, and some, like me, kept saying he'd turn up. Both of us were right. He was washed up on a beach three weeks later.

You don't forget people who hold your hand and say, 'I know.'

At some moment in my babbling, she interrupted me to say:

3

'Where do you live in Brisbane?'

I was cross at being interrupted, but I managed:

'On an island.'

'What island?'

I didn't want to think about my island.

'You won't know it.'

'What's its name?'

Some people persist in asking questions. *What's the street address?* they say. *How can you live without a street?*

She waited.

'I've lived there since I inherited my mother's house. She bought it when I was grown up, in her old age, looking for peace.'

Her hold on my hand was slackening. She didn't ask about my mother and whether peace is findable, she just asked again: 'What's its name?'

She was persistent, this one, but I wanted my hand held, so I told her.

She didn't let go of my hand.

'It's my island too,' she said. 'When I was a kid, we lived there.'

She named a valley on the island. I knew it, though I hadn't been there for a while. A well-watered creek flows into it.

We were two and a half thousand kilometres away.

When I could make my mouth speak, for coincidences always startle, I said:

'Must've been a while back.'

'A while back,' she said. 'A great place for a kid.'

I was jealous of her straightaway. I wished my mother had brought me up on the island, away from my father. I knew there'd been only one house in that valley.

'It'd be fallen down now,' I said. 'Your house.'

'I went to see if there's anything left, and we didn't have much luck,' she said.

'When?'

'A few years back. Now my parents live in' – and she named the nearest town, thirty kilometres to the mainland – 'and we hired a boat to have a look.'

'Must be something left,' I said, a plan already forming, not quite a plan, more like a glow. 'A well, a fireplace or something.'

I didn't think there was.

Some months later, on my island, when the dreams of the man tossing like a fish were starting to fade, I traced her and invited her to come and stay in summer. After all, I'd been in the desert, I knew that whites like to leave when the temperature climbs above forty – those who can. I remembered the mention of her parents. I offered everything I could think of, that she could stay with me and come and go to them in my boat. And we'd have adventures in my boat, we'd go and look for her old house and see if anything was still standing.

It took three years of invitations before she accepted. Perhaps, looking back, she wasn't all that keen. Maybe, as my mother always said, I push people too far.

I seemed to have weathered the years well; I married the man everyone said I should've loved all the time, a kind, dependable man who painted pictures and came with an inheritance. I felt lucky to get him. We'd known each other at school in Brisbane, though I'd never spoken to him, being too ashamed. He'd come from what my mother would've called 'a good home'. My mother had been brought up in an orphanage herself, abandoned there by her mother who didn't want a daughter with a withered arm. My mother would've been delighted with my new married life, its regularity and a plan for every day and meals on time – except that she'd died long ago. I wish that all her sadness was buried in the ground, but it wasn't, not quite.

The only thing wrong with my marriage was that there was something missing. The way things that can't be named persist.

The thing was, it was good in bed at first. He was accommodating and generous as a lover. But then, after some months, the old problem came up. My mind is always such a nuisance. I feel I could get by well enough, if it wasn't for my mind. To be excited in bed I started acting as if I was glamorous and taunting, eager to abandon all modesty to sex. I tried to tell him, I even tried dressing that way, going to a sleazy shop when we were in town and buying scarlet tassels for my nipples and a black corset that looked good on the mannequin, though not good on me. But he said:

'What's come over you?'

'Just trying out stuff,' I said. 'Different selves, you know.'

'I like us the way we were,' he said.

So after that, I kept quiet.

But he was dependable and we loved each other and I was glad to have his boat because we needed something to get safely to the mainland, and my mother's boat had fallen to pieces by then. Often the waters are troubled. You could be swept out to sea. He had children in their twenties on the mainland and we'd ride over the waves to be their parents, trying to be a family, trying, all of us, to come from good homes.

I should've known she'd be trouble when I met her at the airport, but when I hope things will work, I keep on hoping. Pushing people too far. She stepped off the plane reeling drunk. The man I love had no sympathy for drunks.

'Where's she going to stay?' he'd asked, uncertain from the start.

'The cabin,' I'd said.

I'd spent weeks painting it and hanging curtains. It was looking like a little home, a good home.

'I thought you were going to start writing your novel there,' he'd said.

'Soon,' I'd said.

I earned a modest income writing online advertisements for real estate companies. I'd become good at '3 bedders' and 'district views'. Writing like that can give people grander schemes for you. You don't like to disillusion them, in case.

'You ought to give a novel a try,' he'd said.

I knew he'd like that, because then we'd both be struggling with the muse, a flighty creature and often a lonely struggle for him. But I had, at the moment, more important fish to fry. What he wanted had to wait.

I got her to our boat moored on the mainland, and I was relieved that by then she'd sobered up. I didn't want him to get cold feet. I'd pretended all the trip that I hadn't noticed her state, the way you can do, you can look away when drunks hiccup and even when they laugh at nothing like galahs. I drove the boat while she stood beside me, obviously itching to drive herself, but it was his boat and I didn't think he'd like that. When we got to the island, I was proud to show her around the cabin. We put her bags inside. It felt a very large act, the tiny movement of putting her bags inside. She seemed delighted.

She and I spent that summer boating and laughing and getting stuck in the shallows and lost in the mangroves. We yahooed like kids, searching for the remains of her childhood. She remembered a dam but the lantana was impenetrable, even when we went there with axes. I secretly didn't care.

The sky was a limitless blue that you hoped would go on forever, never a whisper of clouds. The sun was always the luscious colour of bananas, apricots, peaches. We'd take sandwiches I'd slopped together, a thermos made to her liking with strong, sweet black tea. I learned to like it too. Looking back, I think I was trying to borrow her former self, to steal it somehow.

I couldn't tell her, couldn't tell anyone about my handsome, charismatic father who brought glamorous mistresses home, while my mother with her withered arm pretended she didn't care. I pretended it as well, while inside I was ready to murder one of them or both of them or all of us out of shame and pity and jealousy too. The first time I heard one of his women in orgasm, I started to run up the hall to her, thinking that Dad was attacking her. My mother grabbed me, digging her nails into me, her face stretched taut. 'No, no,' she kept saying, though I knew she wasn't saying it just to me.

In those long listening nights, we lived intensely – she in plummeting despair, me – I must say it – me in a crimson bewilderment of excitement and hate. Afterwards, in the school playground, I walked away from games of hide-and-seek and chasings and snakes and ladders, like an alcoholic offered a mere sip of lemonade.

Now, too late, I was insisting on playing. Not even the man I love wanted to play with me, not even in bed. I reasoned that she was my guest and should be a good guest. On our adventures, she'd take a bottle or two of wine, but that was all right, it helped her horse around, though I didn't ask why she needed its help. Perhaps I should have. Perhaps they hadn't been such great days, before the lantana tangled up everything. I didn't join her in drinking the wine. I've never been able to develop a taste for it, its tartness makes me shudder. I'm more a prim water drinker. It's no virtue, it's just my taste buds.

And, I admit, there was something else at the bottom of my hopes. It turned out that she'd been friends with the man I shouldn't have loved. In the way of whites in the desert, their lives had brushed several times over the years, they'd lived with the same desert people. Oh, they'd never slept together, she assured me before I even thought to ask, but she carried somehow a whiff of him before he'd become a fish, almost as if he hadn't died.

'When's she going home?' the man I love asked.

'End of summer,' I said.

He asked the same at the end of summer.

'Still hot over there,' I said. 'Maybe at the end of this month.'

By then it was March.

'When's she going home?' he asked at the end of March.

By then her mother had fallen sick. It would've been cruel to ask her to leave.

'When her mum's better,' I said.

He asked the same in mid-autumn.

'She's no trouble to us, is she?' I said. 'Up the back, tucked away in the cabin.'

Often she joined us for meals, because she'd run out of supplies – there's only one shop on our island and all it sells is fuel. It's for men at sea, the shop owner says – you have to get him to open his doors by sending him an email – and when I asked if he'd stock emergency supplies, just dried goods such as rice and lentils, he said no, he'd be always battling cupboard moth and weevils, and besides, real seamen don't eat lentils. So on our island you need to keep an eye on your supplies.

But if you're cooking for two, it's no more trouble to cook for three. She ate like a bird.

'In the desert they called me the name of a bird they loved,' she laughed. 'They loved me.'

She had a pretty way of throwing back her head. It made her laughter infectious. Except that the man I love didn't laugh. I think he didn't like being reminded of the desert, of my life when I'd loved someone else.

She'd begun to sculpt our bush block into a garden. She was good at gardening, and we talked endlessly about it, even at dinner. She believed everything depended on fertiliser.

'Chook manure makes the best fertiliser,' she'd say. She was most captivating when she knew she was being mildly unseemly, talking about manure at the dinner table. The man I love didn't come from a home like that. She liked teasing and he would shift his legs in annoyance, and get up to check what the tide was doing. I took her side, I thought that since we lived on the land, he was being precious.

'Finished yet?' he'd ask, gazing out the window.

'Chook manure?' I'd echo. 'Hen's or rooster's?'

That started a long discussion that left him out.

As I washed up that night, I stopped, the dish mop in my hand like a wand. It came to me, as a sudden thump in my stomach, that perhaps she teased the man I love because she knew she was captivating, and she was exasperated she couldn't captivate him. Then he walked in, and I dismissed the thought. It was more a feeling than a proper thought, at that stage.

He was thinking about her too.

'She's rough on the boat,' he said, finding a fresh, folded tea towel from the drawer. Sometimes I secretly opened and shut my drawer of folded, clean tea towels because to me the squares of tea towels showed how good our home is. There's something very endearing about a man you feel you've alienated opening the drawer and standing with your freshly folded tea towel in his hand.

He lavished endless attention on his boat. It was an old runabout from the 1950s. He'd just then put in new floatation under the floor, and painted a new name on the side – *The Carefree*. It was my idea, that name.

'Give her rules about the boat,' I said. 'I'm sure she'll follow them.'

'She thinks she knows everything about a boat,' he said.

'Doesn't she?' I asked in surprise.

'At that old house, she'd have just had a beaten-up old tinny,' he said. 'Not a boat you have to nurse.'

Maybe it was my fault, the way it all turned out. I wanted those adventures so much, nosing amongst the low-lying tangle of muddy mangroves and laughingly leading the boat like the dog I'd never had, and tying it up to rocks where it'd slip its mooring and we'd have to swim to catch it and give each other leg-ups to clamber back on board – the boat was our passport. My passport. Once, in a mere breeze, it swung around from the rock it was tethered to, and hit another rock. It was only a knock, no more than a thud. But we'd ignored one of the boat rules he'd given her, to always tether it at both ends. So from then on, I'd insist that we find two overhanging branches, to tie up at both the bow and the stern. Sometimes the search for two branches the right distance apart, as well as the right shape, made it impossible to go where we wanted, but I said we had no choice: I loved him, and he loved his boat.

When you're having the fun that life owes you, and you're holding your sides with gusts of laughter, you could believe that what you were doing was heaven. In heaven, you don't bother about old boats. Besides, it was his fault – he wouldn't come on adventures with me.

Winter was settling in.

'The desert is getting cold,' she said. 'They said it on the news. The nights, they're below freezing.'

'She hates the cold,' I said to him.

I asked him to put a pot belly stove into the cabin, like the one in our house.

'I'll do it for you,' he said. 'Not for her. For our future. Your novel.'

He was anxious to be proud of me.

It was difficult work, the cutting of the hole in the roof, and the tiling of the podium. We did it while she was visiting her parents. It was a surprise to her. She was delighted.

Over that winter it became her cabin. 'My cabin,' she'd say.

Sometimes she'd invite people to stay in her cabin. There were parties that we weren't invited to, though there were guests of our acquaintance amongst them, people from the mainland. I was embarrassed by that. They'd moor on our jetty, invite us to come and have a drink but the party was in her cabin and we felt out of place.

There's no laughter now. Even though her cabin is behind the main house, and a distance from the water, somehow the reflections from the bay ripple white light across the ceiling, white light across my sad hands. The furniture here in her cabin is mine, but the spirit is still hers. Now she's gone, my furniture continues to be ruled by her; it looks bereft but it's still the way she left it, the unexpected way she left it: the bedside table is perfectly square on to the bed, and the bedside table on the other side is also square on – not at an angle with the drawers open and piled with a tumble of clothes, like they were when she was here. The chairs at the old wooden table are now lined up like the unblinking soldiers you see in pictures of Buckingham Palace, the table is as clear and flat as the windswept desert. The sofa holds my cushions but the two blue velvet ones aren't lolling on it like discarded toys; they're proudly puffed up and standing on their corners like diamonds.

When I was in the desert with the man I shouldn't have loved, an Aboriginal woman came to our house when I'd been away, hiding, and without my knowledge, she'd cleaned my house. I only knew it when I dared to come home. She lived, like all her people did, outside her government-built house, and inside was only where you put things, and you only slept there on freezing nights or in thunderstorms. A house to them wasn't a place to dwell in, to inhabit, not even a place where your possessions lived – because you had so few. You inhabited the earth. I found out later that she'd cleaned my house in shame, for her husband had gone crazy in my house and that was why I'd gone into hiding, and that was her shame. She did it like I'd never done. The carpet was swept, the nap revealing the careful, firm strokes of a stiff broom – no easy vacuuming for her; the windows were washed of fingerprints and red dust; the lampshades that hung from the ceiling were now white when I'd always thought them pink; red dust no longer made rosy the white window sills; the little wasp nests that festooned the walls up high were gone, the muddle of pens and pencils and rubbers and rubber bands were all tidied away in drawers or put into pots, the green-grey verdigris on the bathroom taps had vanished. Even the teapot had been scrubbed, inside and out. The man who

I shouldn't have loved, who always knew everything, said that her generation of girls was trained as housemaids in the houses of white mistresses.

'They know what white women want,' he said.

'All of them? Know what all of us want?' I asked stupidly. He often hated me.

I suppose my friend had sat in the desert with the grandmothers over winter fires, tracing shapes with her white finger in the red sand as everyone recounted the demands of their mistresses of old who'd had so many possessions – all unnecessary. 'I had to peg out the socks with plastic pegs and the pants with wooden pegs!' 'I had to iron their underwear!' 'I had to spend hours ironing sheets that would wrinkle as soon as they lay in them!'

And as I gaze now in the silence at the perfect alignment of chairs in the cabin no longer hers, I ask: Had I in my fussiness about his boat become to her like those absurd mistresses?

When we were at home alone, the man I love and me, I'd taken to sneaking a look at the cabin, her cabin. There were cigarette holes in the mattress. I knew that she didn't smoke. That must mean, I realised, that she had a friend she hadn't mentioned, probably a lover. It wasn't surprising, for she was as pretty a woman as I'd ever seen. I collected half a dozen or so empty gin bottles and buried them in a big hole I'd dug out in the bush. I didn't say a word to him, nor to her. And I assumed she wouldn't notice empty bottles missing.

After I did that, things started going wrong. Once, when we came back from a few days in the city and she came back from a few days with her parents, I noticed our fireplace was still warm, as if the fire had just been put out. Another time, again when we were all coming back, us from the city and her from her parents, she wasn't at the mooring place at the public wharf to meet us as we'd planned. The people at the mooring were puzzled: they told me she'd been in such a tearing hurry to get home, she'd talked someone into giving her a lift. The man I love didn't hear this conversation, and I didn't pass it on.

I didn't know how to say to her casually, 'You've had a visitor!' Of course, I could've said 'visitors', which would be easier on us both – but nothing was easy by then.

The next time we all returned together, all but one of the water tanks were emptied. We have no town water, we rely on those tanks. The man I love asked if I'd left the cistern on when we left. It's a crime to leave the cistern on, for fear of leaks. I've known that since my mother's time. I'm careful not to commit crimes, meticulous at turning off the cistern, it's one of the things I do before I leave, I keep coming back to check, the way some people in the city can't rest until they've gone back half a dozen times to check if they've turned off the iron.

'I must've left it on,' I agreed.

She said nothing, she just gazed at the garden sadly.

They must've really had a falling out, she and her visitor, a bad falling out. Perhaps she'd captivated him and then, when he wanted sex, she'd turned and said: 'What's all this fussing? This is out of the blue.' I could imagine her saying that. There was something nun-like, strangely pure and shining-faced and sexless about her beauty.

One deception was leading to another. Deceptions grow, accumulate, spread like a cancer. Cancers are silent. And deceiving severs the thin, shiny ribbon between you, I know that now.

But I couldn't ask her to go. I still hadn't got what I'd wanted, there was something missing, there always is for me.

The last time, we were in the city in bed when a huge thunderstorm broke. We both woke, and held each other.

The man I love said: 'Lucky she's there. To look after the boat.'

'Of course,' I said happily.

But at seven in the morning when the storm had died, we were woken again, this time by a phone call from her. The wind had swung the boat, his boat, under the ramp that leads to the pontoon. The pontoon rides up on the high tide, and as the tide ebbed out that dawn, the pontoon had returned with all its weight to settle on the mud, crushing his boat.

He began weeping. I didn't know how to comfort him. I didn't need him to explain, though he explained again and again. It could only have happened if she hadn't tied the boat at both ends.

We raced to our island, getting a lift there from the mooring people.

He tried to bring it back to life, his boat, with its crushed hull and its engine coated in mud. He cried all day and night.

She somehow found us a derelict boat, abandoned, she said, amongst the mangroves. The man I still love looked up as she roared towards us in it, looked up from trying to bring his boat to life. He didn't help her tie it to our jetty, but at least he looked it over.

'No wonder it was abandoned,' he said.

'But it'll go,' she said. 'That's the main thing.'

'It'll ship water,' he said, pointing to a hole in the side.

'Not if you're careful,' she said.

His laughter was high.

'Either she goes, or I do,' he said later.

'Can I give her a month?' I asked.

'She must go this minute,' he said. 'No, that's ungenerous. Tomorrow.'

'Three weeks?'

We settled on seven days.

I kept deliberating how to tell her, what words to use, but I couldn't find them. You'd think it was easy.

'Might be time to push off,' I could say. Or, 'We'll be needing the cabin for his painting.'

No words were right. I tried to find them every morning in bed next to his warmth, but she and I would start pottering in the garden together, and the day would go. He and she would glare at each other over the table as we ate. She took to coming up to the house in the middle of the night for food.

He took to glaring at me.

After six days, when I still hadn't said anything, as I stooped to weed the young spinach, she burst out of her cabin.

She'd just been invited to a new desert community to work again as a nurse.

'Did you apply for it?' I asked, knowing my resentment was unreasonable.

'Of course,' she said. 'But word gets around. They know I'm good at nursing.'

I wanted to ask why she hadn't helped me nurse the boat, but I couldn't.

'When do you start?'

'I'll have to leave in a fortnight,' she said. 'Fourteen days.'

'I'll help you pack,' I said.

I pretended to him that I'd told her to go.

He laughed. Somehow he knew I hadn't.

I helped them both pack. The two people I loved, I helped them both leave me.

Just as he'd threatened, right on cue, out of the kitchen window I heard his boat shudder into life. I was drying the dishes. Not any folded tea towels in any drawer, not any promise of fun and laughter, nothing, nothing but that particular man and his particular ways could comfort me. I ran down to the jetty. There was no knowing how far he'd get with the ruined motor, how far with the crushed hull, whether he'd even make it to the mainland. I think he'd have been happy to die in his boat.

I carried his bags and boxes onto the boat and his canvases, painted and unpainted. I helped him stow away. I wanted to get into the boat myself, sit there as if it was my place, to say, 'I'm coming with you.'

'Will you ring?' I said. 'When she's gone, only thirteen days away now?' He never carried a mobile.

'Depends,' he said.

'On what?' I asked.

'Where I am. How I feel,' he said. 'You've taken no notice of my feelings. Someone's got to.'

He asked me to untie him. I'd always tied the boat up, I'm good at knots. But this time, untying him, I fumbled. My fingers seemed thicker. I couldn't see the knot for sudden tears.

The engine startled into life. I pushed him off. I pushed away the boat of the man I love. I watched his crippled boat go over the roundness of our body of water, the roundness that makes you realise that the planet is a circle. He didn't turn back to wave.

I listened to the news night after night. There were no accounts of a boat lost at sea, no account of blank canvases washed ashore. So I suppose he made it.

He didn't ring.

Thirteen days later, we packed her things into the boat she'd found. We were silent. We'd been silent since he'd left. Anything I said seemed like small talk: 'Sure you got everything?' She was. 'You'll have to tell me how to contact you.' She didn't.

She hadn't even wanted me to go back in the boat with her, in case, she said, our combined weight took it below the hole, and then we'd ship water. She wanted to send someone from the mooring wharf with it, towing it back to me.

But I insisted. I was the reckless one now. I wanted the excuse to go to the Brisbane wharf where he'd have landed. Somehow I talked myself into thinking he'd be there still, hesitating, on the verge of coming back to me, just needing a prompt. I imagined him standing there, his long, lanky body outlined by light, the edges of his shirt feathery with sun, one hand shading his eyes. He'd lift up his hand, holding it high and upwards, the wry way he always signalled when I was heading towards him in the boat. In a few minutes we'd swing around the corner and head towards the public wharf and he'd lift his dear hand in his special way, and as we slid near, he'd bend to catch the boat. I'd see his long arm reach out for me, his long-fingered elegant hand. His hands were always inquisitive and insistent as a dog's nose, feeling for me, nuzzling me, making me touch him, his long arms enfolding me.

But on that last trip I wanted to ask her the questions I hadn't asked, I wanted to ask her whether she'd wanted to come to us or if I'd just made her feel obliged. I wanted to ask who her visitor was, and if they had fallen out. I wanted to ask whether she'd stayed for my friendship, or had it been to captivate the man I love? I wanted to ask whether she'd loved me – or what.

But all through the journey, the silver river and our last time together rushed past, silent and unheeding.

We turned the corner to the public wharf. I stumbled with the ropes and almost fell over when he wasn't on the wharf, there were only the grey, weathered pylons. A gap in the air where I'd been sure he'd be. And then I knew the question I wanted to ask: Had I ever really loved anyone? Or had I just made them up: had I just loved thin columns of air?

But there was no one to ask. I tried to act as if nothing was wrong, here in front of this stranger, once my friend. I stepped out and held the boat steady while she put out her bags. I've had a long training in deception. I was expecting a hug from her but she'd already picked up her bags and all we did was lean towards each other, her slim body suddenly bony, her hands full, the bags clanging between us. She straightened, turned, and didn't wave, suddenly not at all waif-like, striding towards her own life.

I drove the boat home slowly because my eyes were blurred.

I took several goes to moor at our jetty, my jetty, because I couldn't see exactly where the end plank was, for the tears. Sobs were even rocking the boat. Eventually a breeze took mercy on me and blew me into place with a soft thud. I tied up with both ropes, bow and stern.

I opened her cabin door and sat on the sofa looking out at the river. A bird was calling out for its mate, its long echoes unravelling throughout the sky and into the room, into the furniture, the bed, the upright cushions, the neat table, the cupboard. Everything seemed to hold those echoes for ages. I waited till they faded. Then I stood and opened the cupboard, I don't know why, in case there was something left of her, a last remnant. There was only a tinny clink of disappointed coat hangers and, on the floor, an empty gin bottle on its side I left the door open and went back to the sofa. I didn't know what to do next, didn't know how to fill in the time, how to fill in my life. It seemed pointless even to make a meal. I just sat and watched a grey evening crowd around the bay, until greyness filled the cabin like smoke.

Her Laughter Like a
Song of Freedom

Gerard was a man who'd learned early to eke things out. When he was a child, his mother had come unexpectedly to his primary school one lunchtime and hugged him across the fence. Gerard had tried not to turn and check which children were looking. But that afternoon, when he let himself into his house with the key under the dead azalea, he found a note from his mother pinned by a knife to the doorframe. He thought he could make out the word 'gold'. His father, coming home some hours later, said it merely read 'gone to get dinner'. However, neither dinner nor his mother turned up and Gerard learned how to make the memory of a hug last. His mother on her eventual return seemed to be always frowning over a cigarette, as if cigarettes were her only hope, but even they betrayed her, he could tell that by the indignant way she stubbed them out in fierce circles on dishes, the sink, once even in the cat's plate. Family dinners were so silent you could hear everyone swallowing. Gerard tried to time his swallows to fit in with his parents' to be companionable, but no one noticed.

Then, when Gerard was fifteen, his father, a laboratory attendant who stole laboratory bottles for no purpose that Gerard could see, was asked by his Laboratory Head one rainy afternoon to be driven to the bus stop. Gerard's father was a procrastinator and hadn't emptied the station wagon of his latest haul. It was difficult to converse, what with guilt, the rain and the jangling of so many bottles. The Head became suspicious and silent. The Department had been asking questions about the disappearance of laboratory equipment, including bottles. When the Head got out and before he put up his umbrella, he broke the rules of politeness and peered into the gloom of the station wagon. Shortly afterwards, Gerard's father lost his job. Shortly after that, he left home, striding to the corner, his pocket ringing with all the coins he saved. At the corner, he turned to wave. He'd smiled a total of five times in Gerard's childhood, from the time when Gerard began counting, which was when he was in kindergarten. So a wave seemed to belie the threat of imminent aban-donment and gave the boy courage, and he jumped the gate (it was girlish to open gates, and he didn't want his father to loathe him for being girlish) and he sped after his father.

'Where are you going?' he asked.

'Nowhere,' said his father. Over a silent dinner that night, he asked his mother if his father had loved him.

'Who knows?' she said.

Some years later, when his mother died, Gerard decided to find a woman. By this stage, he lived alone in a small and grimy semi-detached house of cranky-looking red brick. He'd become a laboratory attendant like his father, but unlike his father, he collected nothing. Making things endure had become a lonely passion. After dinner, he didn't just go to bed as his mother and father had done; he'd think of how to do some eking out. When he'd sneezed his way through a box of tissues, he'd sort them and dry the most innocent-looking ones with a hairdryer. He split toothpaste tubes and bottles of cleaning fluid into two so he could use every last drop, and if the bottles had moulded handles, he'd take to their insides with a pipe cleaner. He spent many engrossing evenings unravelling the outer and inner tissues of toilet paper, then rewinding them onto two tubes saved from the insides of previous rolls. In fact, toilet rolls were the pinnacle of his night-time successes, he believed. The discovery of how to eke something out brought him an innocent and gentle glow, a feeling as if someone had just given him a hug.

One night, after cleaning his house carefully so it would be pleasant to come home to, he put on his best clothes and went down to the town, to a bar. It was early, about dinner time. There were puddles on the footpath from recent rain. The bar was dim and deserted. But, as if she were meant for him, a woman was sitting alone on a stool, drinking whisky. He stood at the other end of the bar, waiting. He knew how to wait, he had a firm belief in waiting. Anyway, it was interesting to wait for her. The light was tangling in her red hair. Her clothes were crumpled, as if she'd slept in them. She had dark circles under her eyes because she'd recently cried so much that mascara had slipped down her face. Gerard didn't mind; in fact, he thought that it all made her into someone who might like him. He was moved by the way she drank quickly, needily, like a wild homeless cat that had stopped cleaning itself, that had stopped wanting humans. This thought gave him courage to move closer to her, and speak.

'Would you like to come to my place?' he asked. He considered the possible attractions of his house, beyond himself. He'd left it spotless, especially the bathroom. He always scrubbed it with vinegar, as his mother had taught him. Today he'd done it especially well. His mother would have paused between cigarettes, so great would her admiration have been. He wished he could tell the woman that.

'You'd like my bath,' was all he said.

The barman paused midway through pouring her another whisky. His lips twitched, as if he was repeating the line to himself for future use, thought Gerard, feeling urbane. The woman said nothing, but tendrils of her red hair fell into the slop of whisky in her glass. Gerard wanted to take her hair and dry it on the soft lapels of his coat. He didn't have a chance to speak further, because she raised her pale face to him, almost as if she'd allow him to kiss her. It was all he could do not to stroke it. The longing to stroke her drew the right words out of him.

'Come home,' he said.

This time he didn't check the barman's reaction.

She drank the new whisky in two swallows. Gerard loved her pale throat, the way it distended.

She slipped off her stool. 'The bill,' said the barman. 'Of course,' said Gerard, who wasn't in the least miserly, just someone who eked moments out. He touched the notes tenderly as he handed them over, because he could do this small thing for her. Then he drew her little hand into the crook of his arm, and led her to the door. She was much smaller than him, so all he could see was the hair on her rounded head.

'You must have a beautiful name,' he said when they were out in the street, with the barman shut behind them.

'Beate,' she said. 'Of course,' he said. He was a little discomforted by her voice. It wasn't the fluffy, compliant murmur he'd expected, but deep and gravelly. He couldn't think of anything to say as they walked to his house. Neither, it seemed, could she. But as they dodged a particularly large puddle outside his gate, he thought of taking off his coat for her to step on. He didn't do it, didn't even offer to do it, but the gallantry of the thought made him feel a very nice person.

On his doorstep she raised her face to him. He could scarcely breathe for her beauty.

'What do you want from me?' she asked.

'You,' he said. He opened his door.

'What the hell's this?' she cried.

He'd pinned up two long strings from the ceiling and down the length of his hall, to which he'd pegged used envelopes with messages to himself. The messages, he saw with sudden alarm, said dull things like:

eggs
mop head
jam
pins
butter

He'd taken to popping used shopping lists back on the string when he came home from the shops in case he could use them another time, to save himself writing out a new list. He wanted to explain to her the economy of this strategy, but she interrupted him.

'Where's the bathroom?' she said. Her voice suggested she didn't require an explanation.

He led her to the bathroom. He had a vision of running a bath for her and sitting on the edge, perhaps on his best towel, but he tactfully withdrew and made himself go into his kitchen to prepare warm cocoa for them both. In the distance, as he moved between his shelves and his stove, he could hear her tinkling, and the whirr of his toilet roll on the holder. All the sweetness he'd felt for her came rushing back, and he handled the little pot of milk over the heat with great gentleness.

'What's your name?' she suddenly shouted from behind the bathroom door.

'Gerard,' he said, hoping it was a good name.

'Some loony's been mucking around with your toilet roll,' she shouted.

'I'm sorry,' he said, startled. He sank back into the kitchen.

'Have you got anything else?' she called. 'Any other rolls?'

'They're all like that,' he said.

Then he remembered the pile of recently dried tissues in his bedroom. They were wrinkled, he now saw with alarm and he tried to flatten them as he carried them to the bathroom door. He knocked, placed the tissues into her delicate hand and tactfully withdrew and sat on his bed. He heard a snort of laughter from the bathroom, but he tried not to listen. Suddenly, in the familiarity of his room, with his foot bent against the old wardrobe from his childhood, he seemed to be no longer alone. Beside him in a pool of grey light, he saw a being, transparent but denting the mattress, there but not there, dressed in elegant new clothes, with Gerard's hair falling no longer lankily onto Gerard's forehead, but stylishly. Before his very eyes, the ghostly Gerard got up, assured and poised, and walked into a bar, the very bar Gerard had been in this evening, but the ghostly Gerard was dignified, though humble, unremarkable but respectable. In that moment, Gerard felt a rush of joy. He believed that one day he could be that man, if the world was kind.

Right now, with Beate, the world had become bewildering. When he heard the shower tap turning on, Gerard felt bereft, more bereft than he'd ever been in his life. He saw with new eyes, as if through the bathroom wall, the bath soap Beate would be using right now. Last week he'd boiled down old bits of leftover soap to make new cakes, except that they hadn't come out as cakes but as clumps. Then he remembered that yesterday he'd almost run out of shampoo, so to get the last drops out of the bottle, he'd filled it with water all ready for his next hair washing. He was sure that she was laughing at him as she showered. He tried instead to concentrate on an image of her emerging pink and damp and rosy and approving, wrapped up like a Christmas present in his towel, but it didn't work. So he set the light low and got into his pyjamas. He was glad to remove his shoes before she came into the room, because he'd been making his shoe-laces last by not using them. (Lately he'd thought that he should make his mattress last longer by not using it, but he hadn't put that plan into operation yet, which he saw now was taking things to extremes.) He wanted to disown his thoughts, as if they weren't part of him.

She came into the room, arms folded.

'Are you the obsessive loony?' she asked.

It took all his courage to answer.

'Yes,' he said.

'Jesus!' she said again. She roared with laughter.

After a while, she picked up her cocoa.

'What are you drinking out of?' she asked.

So he had to explain how he saved up old jam jars. He'd given her his only cup.

She sighed.

'I put up with a lot,' she said. 'I've learned to.'

He was relieved, though sad, at the resignation in her voice.

'I'm nice,' he said, hopefully.

'I wanted more than nice,' she said.

'I'm sorry,' he said.

However, she got into bed beside him.

She was naked and warm, though damp. Her eyes were brown between thick lashes, and her nipples, high on her freckled breasts, were shaped like stars.

A puff of love returned to Gerard.

'At least my bathtub was clean, just like I promised,' he told her.

Love didn't last more than two weeks, to Gerard's relief. Beate seemed quite eager to leave, to stay with her sister, she said. Gerard hadn't heard about this sister; in fact, he hadn't heard much about Beate, although she talked a lot on his mobile, which he seldom used because there was no one to ring. What he'd learned was that she'd laugh at him in her gravelly way whenever he came into a room. When she

wasn't looking, he practised different styles of entrances —
thoughtful, urgent, passionate, absent-minded — to see if he
could enter in a way that wasn't absurd. But she continued
to laugh.

He made sure she had enough money to see her through
for several weeks, and he insisted on packing her a suitcase
with a week's supply of his favourite food, cereal. After
seeing her off, he went to bed straight after dinner for a
long time, tossing and turning as he tried to feel good about
himself. But as he shuffled his feet in the dark, the way he
lived seemed more and more shameful.

After some months, old habits returned, and with them a
new tenderness, if not for Beate, then for the memory of that
first night at the bar, when she had seemed like a lost, wild
cat. He eked this memory out through the next five years.

But one Saturday night, his neighbours had a party. They
didn't invite him. Gerard comforted himself that this was
probably because they didn't know he existed. Not many
people did. Anyway, so much noise came through his wall
it was almost like being at the party. He dragged his bed
to the wall, and listened to the music and chatter and a
woman's voice, a laugh that almost became a song. It wasn't
at all like Beate's laugh. It was a song about summer and
happy homes and love, and no one criticising anyone else.
A song of freedom. He went to his kitchen and got down

one of his drinking glasses (the old jam jars) and cupped it to the wall, not to spy but to delight in her. That's when he concocted the plan that changed his life. He knew how to change things. He would hold his own party.

He thought about it all night, long after next-door's party had shouted goodbyes and slammed car doors and driven off. He thought about the best time for a party, about the right date, about the wine. He was quite good at wines, because he'd used wine occasionally as a solace on cold winter evenings. He was rather fond of sweet, red, dusty, meditative wine. He thought it suggested poetry and a walk along a dark, brooding country road. He wasn't sure what people ate at parties, but he'd put out his favourite food which was still cereal. He might even buy little boxes of different cereals, he thought, so people could choose whichever one they wanted. He worried about bowls for people who wanted to eat their cereal wet, but there were always his jam jars. He tried to imagine people standing in his dining room enthusiastically eating cereal from his jam jars, but their faces were in the shadows, whereas his brimming table glowed under the bright lights of his imagination. His favourite daydream was about the music at his party. It would be the music of a woman's laughter, and that laughter would set him free.

He became so sleepless with excitement that he decided not to put the party off a moment longer.

✺

In Molly Dyson's thirty-ninth year of being a virgin, she unexpectedly found herself at a party. Later, she had trouble explaining the evening to herself, although later, much later at a happier time, she could tell her daughter about it and smile. Perhaps it had all happened because it already was a short-sleeved Sydney summer evening promising parties in perfumed gardens, even though all she was doing was coming home from work. The front door of the house round the corner from hers was open, and behind it was darkness, like a cave. Caves were connected with music for Molly Dyson because the first piece of classical music she'd listened to as a child, really listened to, delighting in the echoes and ripples and storms, was *Fingal's Cave*. The first paintings she noticed were Rembrandt's, where men glowed like wrapped Christmas presents amongst brown shadows. Later, she hid her love of lushness so well that anyone looking at her plain, embarrassed face would assume she was plain all the way through.

The music that erupted from the house was heavy metal, not lush at all, but at the centre of it, on this particular summer evening, there was a plaintive quality, like a child calling. She should have seen that as a sign of what was to come. But Molly Dyson had had a little brother who'd died in early childhood, and suddenly there in the road all she could think of was how the child's tiny hand had held hers, almost protectively. Her steps faltered. Just then, a man with flapping shirtsleeves, who was holding a jam jar of red wine, came to the door and glanced at the evening sky, glum on the steely roofs of buildings, and then at her.

'Are you looking for something?' he asked.

She laughed because she often filled silences that way. And also because someone had noticed her, and assumed she had a purpose. She tried to look purposeful. The man was smiling, his whole face glowing, she later remembered. His mouth was open, drinking in her laughter.

'The party's here,' he said.

Molly Dyson had always been convinced that the whole city was partying without her on those endless days when merely to go to bed was a relief from loneliness. And now, at last, she was included.

'Good,' she said. She turned a right angle on her sensible heel.

'I'm so glad you found it,' he said as she walked past him. He had an uncertain voice, as uncertain as her own, so she felt unusually sure of herself.

'So am I,' she said.

She went down the hall of the house, where messages, clearly important and urgent, hung from a string. She wasn't impolite enough to read them. However, she made a mental note to hang her messages up in the same way – not that there were many urgencies in her life. The house smelled of vinegar. Perhaps the man, her host, was a keen cook, and he was pickling something marvellous, lamb, with cucumbers, black pepper, exotic spices. She'd read in the newspapers about people who did things like that.

She looked around the room, admiring everything. The dining table was heavy with rows of empty jam jars. There were also lines of little packets of cereals. Perhaps they were for a party game! She'd been good at party games, she'd looked forward to parties when she was a child, to show off how good she was at carrying wobbly eggs on spoons. She laughed aloud to think how like those wobbly eggs she'd become. And the cereal boxes – no doubt for an apparently childish game, profound in its simplicity. She cast her mind around the possibilities, to be ready. Maybe you had to see how many cornflakes you could fit into a jar without squashing them – that might be it! And then you had to say what this was a metaphor of – what would she say? She was seeing the wide world at last, here in this unexpected moment she was suddenly sophisticated and cosmopolitan. All the petty and inconsequential things in her life were like a previously secret procession, heading towards the light of this party. She sat down on the sofa, which creaked, but to choose to have such an old sofa seemed nonchalant and whimsical. She wondered if everyone had gone upstairs. That must be what one did at parties these days. She thought how right she'd been not to give in to an impulse to run away and hide in a country town that might be friendly, when this could happen to her in the city. And just around the corner from her! Goodness, this might be the start of a new life! So she tapped her feet to the heavy metal, and tried not to lose the beat.

When the music stopped, the house was so quiet she could hear the roof twitching in the evening. Had everyone gone to sleep upstairs? A whole party full?

After a while, it seemed imperative to do something, so she went to the front door. The man was still there, finishing the last drops of wine in his jar.

'Where is everyone?' she asked.

She was used to people's eyes flickering towards her and away, disappointed that it was only her they were looking at. He was the first man whose gaze she had held.

'I didn't get around to inviting them,' he said.

He had a sideways, self-effacing smile. A strange but pleasant nudging seemed to happen in her stomach, at least somewhere in the region of her stomach. It made her dizzy. She thought of something to say.

'May I have a drink?'

He looked down at his glass.

'I've only got milk left,' he said.

He came back to the porch with a milk carton, two jars and an ice tray. She helped him dislodge the ice blocks under the garden tap. Their hands knocked together.

'I'm sorry,' he said.

'I'm sorry,' she said.

'For this,' he said, indicating the empty house.

'But it's so chic,' she said. 'To hold a party like this! It's so full of—' Her hands took in the air, the street, their lives. 'Possibilities.'

She tossed back her head and laughed. They went back to the porch.

'There's lots to eat,' he said.

'It takes me back,' she said.

After a silence, she added: 'Drinking milk, I mean.' And after another silence, she said:

'I always think ice blocks make things festive.'

After several refills of milk, he looked at his watch, which allowed her to look at hers. 'Nearly midnight,' she said brightly. She still believed in his party.

'What's for your dinner tonight?' he said, because of her bright laugh.

She was torn between honesty and the desire to make her fridge seem glamorous. She decided on honesty, which she always did.

'Old spaghetti,' she said.

'I have some cereal,' he said.

'I know,' she said.

There was a pause.

'To eat?' she asked.

They ate cereal in his kitchen. He owned two bowls, so they ate from bowls. There wasn't any sugar, and she didn't offer to run to her house for some, because she suspected her packet in the cupboard was limp with emptiness and perhaps black with ants. Besides, there was something brewing in the atmosphere, the way he dabbed his finger in the milk at the bottom of his bowl, touching the china as if – she thought with another blush – as if it was her.

The thought wouldn't stop. As if it were her breasts. What if he guessed her thoughts! He might laugh. On the other hand, he might declare love. She wouldn't know where to look. But when his plate was dabbed clean, she felt the thought fade.

She began to move her legs under his laminex table as if she was about to leave. She was at his front gate before he spoke.

'Would you stay tonight?' he asked.

She thought of her bed, narrow and forlorn in her silent house.

She stayed.

In the dark he seemed less shy. To her surprise, little was asked of her. Only that she hold him, which she was glad to do, damply and clumsily. She was also glad that the bedding operation happened at the far end of her body and she didn't have to look, just murmur encouragement.

By morning, she felt a certain fondness, especially because he'd ended with such gentleness her thirty-nine year wait. She boldly kissed his chin, though it was prickly already. She wanted to thank him, though that might not be appropriate.

'Why have you been a virgin so long?' he asked. She laughed, to fill the space of the room.

'I know!' he said. 'It was because you wanted to make things last.'

He touched her curly dark hair, as if he was marvelling that she was there beside him. It was very pleasurable to her to fill a room with an acknowledgement of happiness. It was almost like happiness.

'I might hold another party soon,' he said. 'If a party can bring you to me.'

'I'll come,' she said quickly.

'When?' she asked after a while.

'Maybe next year,' he said.

'That's not so soon,' she said, gently, so he wouldn't feel criticised.

She laughed again, to show how soon she wanted his party, and him.

'When would you come to another party I held?' he asked.

She wanted to say tomorrow, but that might seem greedy. She so wanted to be perfect.

'In six weeks,' she said.

He set the exact date, even to the hour.

He wanted to be prepared. He wanted to be sure she'd come, and he thought that exactitude might provide a guarantee.

She didn't like to tell him that in her happiness, she hadn't taken precautions. He would've assumed she had. She didn't know how to explain. She left the city immediately. And by the last day of winter, in a rented house in a country town that didn't prove friendly, she gave birth to a child.

She still didn't know what words to say to such an urbane man who was surrounded by urgent messages. In fact, she didn't contact him for three years.

But one day, because her child expected it of her, she wrote him a letter.

She counted the hours before he'd receive it. She thought he might read it when he got home from work.

After twenty-four hours, she allowed herself to think He'll be reading it now. Right now. She could imagine his face so clearly, reading her modest words in his kitchen.

She recited her letter to herself, sure she could even tell which word he was up to.

She waited for his reply.

But there was no reply, and as the days and weeks passed, she felt abashed. Perhaps this sophisticated man didn't even remember her.

She hadn't guessed that when she left the morning after the party, Gerard didn't clean or rearrange anything in his house. He didn't move the jars or touch the boxes of cereals. He wanted his things to be like they were when she'd gazed on them. He kissed the bed sheets every night, the very spot where she had lain. It was the most difficult waiting of his life, that six weeks waiting for their next party. All year lay in those six weeks, the heat of summer, the chilly fear of autumn, the dreariness of winter, the hope of spring. And then the joyful evening, which became the dreadful evening when she didn't come walking up the street into his arms, not at dusk, not mid-evening, that dreadful moment at three in the morning when he had to agree with the snickering voice inside him that she wasn't going to turn up. He'd wept then. He felt he'd never wept before, not when his mother left, not when his father left, if this was weeping. Grey-faced with exhaustion and despair, he couldn't go to work the next day, or for many days, until despair became resentment, and he could kick things, like the walls of his house, or himself.

When her letter arrived in the post three years too late, with her name on the back of the envelope, his heart had left his chest, and only crept back in terror if he promised not to open it, not yet, not yet. Because there has to be an end to pain. He didn't put her letter in his garbage bin, but on his mantelshelf, where he'd allow himself to glance at it, still unopened, his timid heart saying Not yet. It might be there still on his mantelshelf to this very day but he ran out of paper one day for a new shopping list, and his heart allowed him to take her envelope down, of course only so he could use the envelope for a message to be hung on his string in his hall. Once he'd torn the envelope, it seemed wasteful not to read her words, her wonderful, wonderful words. He shouted until his neighbours cupped glasses onto their walls to listen to the noisy man next door who'd always been so quiet.

He left the city that evening for her country town.

'That'd be Craig Johnson's old house,' said a taxi driver at the station.' Craig had some tenants, but they left a week or two ago. And Craig's passed on now.'

In the dark, he could make out a small house in a garden of weeds with a big yellow sign saying 'For Sale'.

'Where have the tenants gone?' he asked the driver.

'Don't know,' the driver said. 'She kept to herself. You can probably get in, we leave back doors unlocked here. We're not like you city people, we're all friendly.'

'How long have they been gone?'

'It'd be just a matter of days.'

He followed Gerard into the house. He heard her voice. He smelled her. Every door he opened, he was sure she was there behind the next one and the next one. The house was full of her laughter and of something else, the gurgling of a child. In a dark cupboard Gerard found a stuffed toy, a smiling shark with threadbare fur.

'Funny what kids take to,' said the taxi driver.

He saw Gerard's face move and feared he'd overstepped the mark and that he might lose his tip.

'She'd be missing it,' he added. 'It's been loved. Got kids myself. They always pester you to go back for something they've lost. And you always end up giving in.'

Gerard was holding up the toy. He could see dangling from its tail, and illuminated by street light, one single curly childish blonde hair. He turned to the taxi driver.

'What's the kid like?' he asked.

He was surprised to find that as he asked the simple question, his voice trembled. He cleared his throat, to cover the tremble.

'Smart,' said the taxi driver, who didn't remember at all.

'Smart!' repeated Gerard proudly. He put the toy on the mantelshelf, because a mantelshelf had brought her back before, or at least it had held her wonderful letter.

'A bit of a dump,' the taxi driver said, looking around.

'I'll buy it,' said Gerard. 'Can you take me to the owner right now, Craig Johnson, did you say — his relative?'

'Sure,' said the taxi driver, brightening up because this fare was turning out to be a good one.

'Once you put some paint on this place, you won't know it,' he said.

'I'll wait and see', said Gerard. 'You never know.'

Passport

He was my first love, and unrequited. The first of many, as if I must teach myself again and again that though you pull at invisible cobwebs in the dark, they cling, they hide you from what's possible.

We were one of those sad, violent families living noisily at the edges of a dusty Australian bush town. The trouble with such families is they only have each other, for relatives dare not come near, and each family member is too crestfallen to make friends in the great beckoning outside. It would've required smiles we couldn't muster, I couldn't muster. In that era, we had few media distractions – a crackling radio, a grey and white TV with American game shows, and a wall-hung phone that never rang.

But my father illuminated my life, partly because of his paintings, and partly because of his mystery. I didn't know how to love my mother.

I was the youngest child, the only girl. I was the one who tore home along the bush track from the school bus to watch my father paint. Most afternoons of my childhood till dinner time, I spent silent, motionless, not even slapping flies, listening to the quiet brush on the weave of the canvas, the quiet scrape of the palette knife, the dipping of his brush into the squeezed-out coils of colours, lazy despite their immanence, and my father's voice almost whispering:

'Out of the way,' if I was in the path of his hand. There seemed to be eyes on the ends of his fingers as he, gazing at the canvas, dipped the brush always into the right coil: cadmium yellow, cerulean blue, alizarin crimson, viridian green, vermilion, burnt sienna, lying in the ritual order that, even as a woman, I can still recite, an order that seemed intrinsic to the world, like the order of the planets.

There was a further delight: I found as I grew older that if I breathed with him – now in, now out, now in, now out – after a while he'd forget I was separate to him and murmur his thoughts: 'If I lighten that post with chrome white it will leap to the foreground' – and it leapt! – how can a person predict that? – 'What matters is not the shape of the leaves but the shape they cut out of the sky' – yes, now I saw that cut-out sky – 'It's not the flower itself, it's the feeling of the flower: see the petals without looking, enter them' – and slowly the hot room, sticky with sadness, dipped and fell away and I entered the fleshy petal.

Those afternoons were rainbows in my childhood.

They're my justification for the adoration: who wouldn't fall in love with such a parent?

We children could recite the romantic story of how our parents met. At a dance, my father met the local beauty, a girl with an exotic past, her olive Spanish complexion dramatic amongst the pale Anglo-Saxon girls, her long cascades of black wavy hair, her eyes as unfathomably dark as a country sky at night. He took from his pocket a piece of paper and a carpenter's pencil, and drew a house. We all knew what followed by heart:

'What's that for?' she asked.

'I'll build it for you if you marry me.'

'What are the little dots at the windows?'

'Our children.'

My father told me that when my mother introduced him to her mother at Central Station, the old woman punched him on the nose.

'What did you do?' I asked.

'Fell over,' he said. 'On my back. There on the platform.'

'Why did she punch you?' I asked.

'She thought I was putting off marrying your mother,' he said. 'She hated men. A man had just stolen her fortune.'

'Fortune!' I gasped. It sounded like something out of a fairy tale.

'But I longed to marry her – I was only waiting for the fuss to die down before I put my name on the papers. I was proud of winning your mother, the most beautiful creature ever.'

He paused, thinking, I was sure, of my mother's eyes, so sweet that when she fixed them on you, however thin and prickly you were with indignation, you'd become like water and swim into her. I longed to belong to her beauty, so some of it would somehow rub off on me.

'Beauty is a woman's passport,' she'd say. I knew she was implying that I had no passport, being plain-faced, red-headed and blue-eyed like no one else in my family. So I'd never have a passport.

I didn't ask, 'What fuss?'

Instead I asked the question that intrigued me more.

'What fortune?'

Apparently my widowed grandmother, descended from a Spanish family of great wealth and eminence, had entrusted her fortune to a doctor who then put her in an asylum, and disappeared.

My father's life before I and my brothers were born, a life in faraway London, was a closely held secret, tantalisingly hinted at, but whenever he'd begin to push the curtain aside, my mother, helpless in much else, had unexpected power: she could silence him.

Despite my mother's best efforts, my father's past in faraway London spilled out and we children delighted in glimpses of what seemed a scandalous life. For example, he'd gone without shoes, a glorious liberty we were only allowed on odd visits to the beach. Once, when I complained about soggy salad sandwiches for lunch, he said he'd have been lucky to get bread wrapped in a bit of newspaper.

'Newspaper,' I'd echoed enviously, and longed for school sandwiches wrapped in newspaper, which I'd be able to smooth out and read at school, rustling it like an adult. When I complained about having to eat an apple every day, my father said that he and his brothers considered themselves lucky that they lived near the markets, because markets have big rubbish heaps of fruit, if you got in early for the best bits.

'So eat your nicely washed apple and be grateful.'

Once he told a story of how he'd glimpsed ripe pears hanging from a tree and he'd climbed across a roof for them. I can see them still, the golden pendulous pears glowing against the dark leaves like light globes. But the roof turned out to be a glass house and he'd fallen through—

'Don't make out you were a thief,' cried my mother.

He was always hushed so easily.

'Did you get away?' one of my brothers whispered when my mother had left the room.

'I was always lucky,' he said.

When my brothers got jobs to deliver newspapers before school, my father said that, as a child, he'd got up at four in the morning and worked two jobs. Unlike my brothers who didn't want to go to school, he'd been in the scholarship class, the top class – and hoped to become an architect but he'd had to leave at twelve years old, as my mother had.

'Why?' I asked in quick sympathy, because I was the bookworm of the family and hoped to somehow be allowed to remain at school even though I was only a girl, and a girl's place was to become a housewife.

'To support my family,' he answered.

In my imagination he would've been like my brothers, bicycling around the neighbourhood, accurately hurling rolled newspapers over trimmed hedges and into neat front gardens, except it would have been colder in England, and he would've been wearing a thick coat.

There were no photographs of his parents, or Florence or John or Frederick or George or him – I could recite their names, these children of such liberty who were allowed to go shoeless and rummage in rubbish heaps. Only a postcard showing a suspension bridge – in Pitlochry, Scotland, said the quaint, old-fashioned print.

'I'd walk that bridge wearing a kilt,' he said. 'The wind would blow ice up my legs.' He added that he and his brothers and sister sometimes went for holidays to his mother's people in Pitlochry, but suddenly that all ceased.

Instead of becoming an architect, he went to work in a munitions factory with his older brother. By now the First World War had broken out. He walked miles there with George every morning, and miles back again at night. There were often explosions, and the workers were stationed in small huts to prevent any explosions taking the entire place out. Their hut exploded.

'Were you all right?' I asked.

'We were only singed,' he said. 'I was always lucky.'

Then he ran away to sea instead, to be a mess boy to escape his mother—

'Don't!' shouted my mother.

And so we never heard more about that.

By a peculiar quirk of fate, my parents shared the same birthday, the tenth of May, though they were born years apart. There seemed to be a decade between them – 'seemed' because I grew up thinking he'd been born in 1901, but my brothers thought 1903 or 1905. Again, we weren't suspicious. We were all firm in the knowledge, however, that he'd been born into the world's cultural centre, the most civilised, the most powerful, the only sophisticated city in the world, a land where all along the streets there were art galleries and paintings gleaming with oils – why, you could pop into any gallery and gaze at a Rembrandt whenever your mother sent you to the local shop for bones for the dog. Like his handyman work, he was entirely untutored in painting, but I assumed that anyone from such a land would be good at painting.

He'd joined the navy – we children never knew to ask if it was the navy or the merchant navy – and his ship had been torpedoed but had sailed on, eventually coming to this cultural desert, Australia. They'd moored in Adelaide, and then he'd fallen in love with the light. So he'd jumped ship. To my childish mind, this was of no more moment than his other exploits, say, with the golden pears. He'd gone bush and, to survive, had become a rabbito, and soon he was painting bush schools. My childhood picture of him leaving the ship was of a boy in a white and blue sailor suit – sailor-suit blouses were fashionable in my childhood, so I was on home ground there – stumbling down a gangplank like the one at Circular Quay, tripping over the raised boards meant to steady people's disembarking for he was too dazed by light, his astounded eyes not on the unfamiliar city before him, but on the transparent blue heights above. Or, as I got older, did 'jump ship' mean he dived off it? This, too, I was sure, was done in a heroic dive, my father in his sailor suit flashing past the ship's hull into the murky harbour.

With the immersion of children in the present, it was enough to know he'd come to Australia and met our mother, the important events to us. He was probably banking on that self-absorption. And he was glad to get onto a more comfortable subject.

'The smell of Australia,' he said. A man who crept up shyly on words, he struggled for more accuracy. 'The perfume,' he managed. He'd been up the mast, and for hours before he sighted land, he'd smelled the spicy eucalypts.

'I had to see those trees,' he said.

'What's a rabbito?' I asked.

'I was good at it – lucky, I was always lucky. Rabbits were everywhere in the bush, food for the taking. I'd catch them, skin them and sell them to housewives in the towns, they'd be at their doors, ready with the money. "Rabbito!" I'd call' – his voice high, remembering, laughing.

'Stop it,' warned my mother.

He yielded, as always, to my mother.

At school I was a late reader and when I finally learned to make out his signature on the lower right-hand corner of his paintings, I discovered that it wasn't the name we knew him by.

'You left out "Arthur",' I objected.

'I don't like "Arthur",' he said. He could often turn a difficult moment into a joke. He was always joking. 'If you had a name like Arthur, wouldn't you leave it out?'

It didn't occur to me until much later that it had been a difficult moment.

As I look back, I ask myself: was there a warning in her voice of what she might divulge to us if he disobeyed her? I knew, it seems for always, that she was desperate for us to be an upper-class family, like the one she'd originally come from. But at twelve the orphanage had disgorged her and she became not an heiress, but a servant.

Fate continued to lash. My oldest brother, their adored first-born, died suddenly from meningitis and then the next child while still a toddler was deemed unmanageable by the authorities, and taken away to die. In today's terms, he was autistic. In the fashion of the times, my mother was blamed. My parents hid their grief from us, though once I walked into a room and found my father sitting at his work-desk, head on his arms, weeping. I crept away.

In our bush townships, fires raged every summer. There were always ghostly, abandoned houses in the district, only a stone chimney and sometimes a shell of a structure still left. Anyone could buy them for next to nothing. My father would move our family into one of the blackened shells, put up a roof, and soon there'd be walls, floorboards, and when it looked like any ordinary house, he'd sell it and we'd move to the next shell. Later, the family could remember what year anything happened by what house we lived in. All around, less lucky families lived in Nissen huts. The family in a street nearby, the Ormes, cooked with open fires, so that in my childish eyes it seemed they were always on jolly holidays, camping like The Famous Five. Mum wouldn't allow us to play with the Ormes. They constantly appeared in her reprimands: 'You're behaving like an Orme kid.'

However, my parents behaved far worse than the Ormes. My mother's sadness turned into rages that to my child's eye could be triggered unwittingly by any of us. In these rages, she seemed to be in a trance. Once, I saw her jump through the glass front door and, crouching on the porch, she gazed in bewilderment at the glass fountain falling around her. Often at night, no doubt sleepless and fretting for her dead children, she'd begin to batter my sleeping father or my brothers. They'd wake up shouting and fighting off the nightmare. Many times the alarmed neighbours would call the police, who'd bang on the front door as if to break it down. They'd rush in, two or three burly men, much larger than my father, who I slowly began to realise was not much taller than us. Rescuers had such heavy feet. But they'd tramp out the front door as soon as they'd spoken to my incoherent mother in her nightie – I'd hear, with sinking heart, that ours was 'just a domestic'.

My father said my mother's nerves had been damaged. It was a time when men were responsible for household order, and against her nerves, he didn't know what to do. He believed that a dash of metho or turps, sometimes both together, would fix any wound. But where was Mum's wound? In those impoverished, pre-Medicare days, families like ours called a doctor only if death threatened. At the most he consulted the chemist, and about my mother's nerves the chemist had nothing to say.

⚘

Sometimes when I was alone with my mother, her rage would be triggered by something invisible to me, and she'd pin me to a wall and in an odd voice shout continually: 'Slut!' and 'Cretin!' When she finally sank to the floor exhausted, I never thought to cover her with a blanket, but crept away to hide, dazed by her rage, grateful she hadn't hit me. Only much later did I wonder if she'd confused us both and was raging at what she feared about herself. I longed for an ordinary mother but was too narcissistic and pitiless to love the one I had. In comparison, my father seemed solid and dependable. I gave him the love they both deserved.

So it was a shock that I still feel, the terrible day that he came into my solitary bedroom, with its old raffia pram of dolls that I was too old to play with but still too much a child to throw away. He'd never been in my room since he painted it pink with a blue ceiling, to remind me of the sky, he said. He seemed to be always in my brothers' room, laughing and horsing around, and I'd listen with envy to chairs toppling. He preferred my brothers, it seemed, even though I could list my advantages on my fingers: I was the one he asked about his new paintings – 'It's finished, don't you think?'; I was the one who did well at school, which is what he longed for with my brothers, to no avail; I was the one who watched him paint.

By this time we were living in the city. He stood looking out with a peculiar fixity through the dusty venetian blinds into the street, not at me as I sat on my bed, the book I'd been reading open on my lap. Black cockatoos were raucous outside on the telegraph wires. He had to raise his voice against them. He was leaving, he said, and taking my brothers.

I imagined, in the din, their new home with the smell of hot sweet cakes baking, along with linseed oil and metho and turps. All the walls would gleam with his paintings. There'd be a yellow ochre cat on the hearth, coiled up in peace, with shadows of Prussian blue at its folded limbs. There'd be no darkness in the house and even the nights would glow.

'And me – can I come?' I said. There'd be curtains floating at the windows, and I'd iron everyone's clothes, but at last leaving no creases.

Deep down, I half-knew the answer.

'No,' he said, watching the cockatoos fly off as if he'd never seen them before. Suddenly the room was very quiet. His voice dropped, confidingly. I was to stay behind, to look after my mother, that was what a girl must do, a girl must look after her mother, he needed me to do that. What would happen if everyone deserted her? And if he and the boys didn't leave, someone would end up in jail. I didn't want that, did I?

From somewhere, from a place I didn't know existed, I heard my voice, suddenly very grown up. My new voice agreed that I would do it. For him, for them, for him. I was fourteen years old.

'Do you love me?' I asked.

'Of course.'

'And you'll come back for me?'

'Of course.'

They left the very next day. That hurt me particularly, that while they'd toppled chairs in the boys' bedroom, they'd been planning their escape. Didn't one of them say, 'Shouldn't we take her?'

I let myself in fearfully that first afternoon but the house was silent. My mother was face-down in her rumpled bed, still in her defeated nightie. I went into the kitchen, till then her private domain, and she didn't shout. I opened the fridge door and found chops, and still she didn't shout. I cooked the first meal of my life, the first meal of our shared life. She accepted hers meekly, and ate her chops in bed, and I ate mine bent over a book.

When her rages began again, I'd breathe with her as I'd done as a child with my father. Eventually she'd stop, and I'd slip away and pick up a book, and pretend to read until my heart stopped hammering and I heard the door latch click behind her.

I began to wonder if books had the power to make her leave. In those days I'd finish one book and pick up another.

I methodically read around the shelves in the public library, encountering world literature alphabetically. Once, she came with me to the library and fingered the spines of encyclopedias, especially the children's ones with bright covers, but she didn't take them down. Perhaps by then she felt she had no passport, after all.

I escaped daily to school, though there were walls between me and my classmates that I couldn't begin to scale. I was no one's friend. Sometimes I'd write a note. 'My daughter has had a stomach ache for a fortnight.' My mother always agreed to put her signature to the notes, perhaps hoping I'd be company. But I was waiting for my father to return, to say 'You've done enough', and take me home.

Slowly, subtly, pity for my mother began to filter into me. It took a long time – how deeply vengeful a daughter can be – but slowly, subtly, I became aware that my mother was not a monster, only grief-sodden. Not powerful, only grief-sodden. I didn't know how to give her love, or how to ask for it. I wanted to tell her I loved her because she needed that comfort, but 'love' stuck in my throat every time I tried to say it. Such a tiny word, but sometimes to utter it feels as if you've lost something precious forever. I took to going into newsagents' and reading the verses on cards for mothers, as if they could advise me. But my pity was too late, for by now my mother was shouting at strangers in the street, at neighbours across the back fence, at astounded deacons in the hush of the church.

'Your father hates women,' my mother would say to me. 'He hated his mother and that makes him hate us.' I didn't search her eyes because there I'd find only unwavering conviction. All I could do was question the womanly figures in his paintings. I searched for an ugliness of expression, a spitefulness of the body, a threatening lift of the arms. But the women innocently strolled through the landscape and out the frames. I decided that my mother was wrong. The reason for his rejection of me must be far more complex, far more subtle.

At least I got my wish and stayed at school, because my mother's thoughts on anything were confused, and my father's thoughts we no longer knew.

Three long years passed. Then suddenly, out of the blue and probably because of my endless reading, I won what was then called a Commonwealth Scholarship to study at a university.

'Can I go?' I asked my mother.

She left the room. I didn't dare pursue her. I opened a book. But three days later, she told me that my father was coming to talk to me. Till that moment, I had no idea she could contact him.

Now, I dreaded his arrival. *Your place is with your mother. It's no use educating a girl. A girl can only be a housewife.*

He let himself in the front door. I ran to him, and stopped. He seemed smaller, bowed, abashed. There was a space between us, even when we embraced.

I thought I'd cry. I didn't cry. I was too shrivelled with waiting.

'The Commonwealth means the Queen, and if the Queen wants you to go to university, who am I to disagree?' he said.

Though he painted the Australian landscape as intimately as if he belonged to it, he still belonged to England.

To keep books around me, I became a writer. When I wrote my first book in my early twenties, a textbook that unexpectedly earned money, I bought my father a ticket to fly back to London, to home. His brother was unwell and my father had never been back; I assumed that was because we'd been too poor.

'To see George,' I said.

The ticket bore his full name. He wouldn't take it out of my hand.

'I mightn't get back,' he said.

I thought he meant that the cultural centre of the world would be so alluring, he wouldn't be able to drag himself away.

One of my brothers finally went to London and tracked down his brother George, now in his dotage, and found out enough to acquire our father's birth certificate, and his actual name, and so we found out that the year of Dad's birth was curiously different from what we'd all variously thought.

I was still in my twenties – I told myself that I'd never had time to ask the real questions, to make the right deductions, though I'd had a whole long childhood – when my father's luck finally petered out. He had a heart attack so minor that going to hospital in an ambulance embarrassed him. He should've walked there, he said. It was hard to tell if he was blushing, with all the instruments on him, all the beeping. I never wondered why he asked so little for himself.

'I've got to get out of here. I've got a painting to finish,' he whispered to me. He didn't want the nurses to think he was ungrateful; they were going to so much trouble for him.

After his death, it took a decade – the death of my mother, a short-lived marriage and the birth of my daughter – to say his name again. It was my daughter who brought me back to life. I'd died with Dad.

My brother knew the address of George's second wife, our Auntie May, now widowed, now in a hospice. He hadn't been able to trace anyone else.

'You always wanted to know about Dad,' he said. 'You should go and ask her. But hurry.'

I told myself I had to go for my child's sake, so she could know who her grandparents were. I'd seen from my father's birth certificate that my grandfather had been a gardener, and I hoped he'd been a Capability Brown, since he'd had such an artistic son. Maybe there were landscapes I could show my daughter. Or maybe there was a house still standing, the family home, surrounded by a beautifully wrought garden. But my real question was – had my mother been right? Was it because of my drunken grandmother that he couldn't love me?

My Aunt was sitting up straight in a chair beside an impeccably made bed. There was a shock of white hair, strong and wiry, above her fragile face.

'You've come,' she said as soon as I sat down, 'because of what I said!'

I was astonished.

'What did you say?'

'To her. To your grandmother.'

A nurse came up.

'She's been very worried about your visit. Please don't upset her.'

I gazed between their faces.

'I wanted to know you, and find out . . .' as usual, I was struggling for words, 'who my father was.'

My Aunt, deflated, sat back in her chair.

'There you are,' said the nurse to her. 'I told you it'd be all right. Just a nice family visit. I'll get you both a lovely cup of tea, and your favourite biscuits.' She left, her white dress swishing against her stockinged legs.

My Aunt seemed energised by the promise of tea and biscuits.

'He was a good man, your father,' she said. 'George loved him.'

I knew that old ladies loved photos, so I thought it would please her if I asked for a photo of the family. My Aunt seemed taken aback.

'No, dear, there's none.'

'Where could I see my grandfather's gardens?'

The old woman struggled with this question too.

'Gardens? He was just a handyman, dear.'

And the house where they lived?

'Oh, the worst of the slums were cleared out in the thirties. There's good social services now but then—'

'Slums?'

'Your father spared you all this? Perhaps I should too.'

'No, please—'

I sighed, settled back in my chair.

'They didn't have a house, they just had a room.'

I laughed in disbelief.

'A single room! What, for all those children? It must've been a huge room – George and Frederick and Florence and—'

'Tiny. And of course, they were always being evicted, and so there'd always be a new room, if they were lucky.'

The nurse came with two cups of milky tea.

'See? It's all fine,' she said to my Aunt. 'You're having a lovely chat!'

'But there wouldn't have been enough space for all the beds—'

I was grabbing a biscuit.

'There was only one bed, dear, for Walter and Hannah. The children slept under it, on the floor.'

I tried to make light of this.

'Such a squash, five kids under a bed. They probably had such fun.'

'And there was a lodger, who worked night shifts, so he used the bed during the day.'

'A relative?'

'No, dear, people lived like that then. There was desperate, terrible overcrowding in the slums. George and your father would often sit up to scare the rats away. If they were lucky, there'd be one toilet for say, sixty people. Sewage littered everywhere. No furniture. Just rags and rubbish. Often they'd go for a whole day without food. And your grandfather often went without work – there were few jobs to go around, and they were almost unpaid. No unions then, of course. You couldn't have earned your way out of it.'

I gulped my tea. Under my Aunt's tutoring, I was sadly reconstructing my childhood image of Dad and his brother naughtily eating from the streets – I realised I'd always imagined the food they plundered as being contained in neat, Sydney-style garbage bins – and replacing it with a new image of ragged, shoeless, freezing and starving children, arms plunged in a rubbish pile up to their elbows, devouring scraps of mouldy food.

'So Dad was always hungry,' I said.

My Aunt cried out so loudly the nurse returned.

'You must not upset her or we'll have to ask you to leave!'

'It's not her fault – it's her father's – he told her nothing about the family!'

The nurse hesitated, then went away.

'They were starving!' she cried. 'And of course there was Hannah—'

I almost shouted: 'What was my grandmother like?'

My Aunt clanged the cup on the saucer.

'That's why I shouted at her! I had to take George's part!'

She saw my look of incomprehension. 'You've never been told anything, have you?'

She was exasperated that it all had been left to her.

'Most of the time—' she looked over her shoulder, bent her old white head towards me so not even Hannah's ghost would hear:

'I don't like to speak ill of the dead, but she took any money there was, and drank it. That's why the children hated her. There were some government programs for the deserving poor but because of Hannah, the family wasn't the deserving poor. And then – what she got up to when she was drunk!'

She slumped in her chair, deciding to spare me. But I didn't want to be spared, I had to know.

'Tell me.'

The old woman couldn't pollute the air.

'George often said that your father took the brunt of it.'

'But she was drunk – not in sound mind—'

'George often said that it was no wonder your father married a Spanish beauty. Not just because of her looks, which an artist would care about, of course, but she didn't look like his past, didn't remind him of that horror.'

I should've taken this as a clue, but I didn't, what with the old woman talking so angrily, reliving the past, and my fear that the nurse would return.

'Please, let's just chat about George. Tell me how you met.'

But she was wound up.

'George and Arthur went to work as soon as they could. But they had to hide their earnings, or she'd drink it. Till the end of his life George was proud that the two of them managed to make life easier for the younger ones. Jumpers, boots, food. The boys knew they could get killed in the munitions factory but dying was better than the family being thrown into those workhouses.'

'Then my father disowned them all to go to sea,' I whispered sadly, because I didn't want to stop believing in him.

'Never!' cried my Aunt so passionately that I glanced up to check where the nurse was. 'Whenever his ship came to London, he'd get word to George, and George would come to meet him at the docks. He'd hand over his wages to George, never to Hannah. He never saw Hannah again once the ship sailed away.'

My Aunt's words tumbled over each other.

'So one day I shouted at her – I just couldn't bear what she'd done. And then, after she'd died, after George had died, I met a distant cousin, and she told me about Hannah's childhood. I thought you knew that I'd lost my temper with her, I thought that's why you'd come. To tell me off!'

She paused with this old grief, and made folds in the quilt with trembling fingers.

'I knew nothing,' I said.

So she told me the story of my grandmother: Hannah had come from a mill family, working in the cotton mills of Scotland, the so-called Satanic mills. By the time she was ten, with no one in the world to help her, she'd nursed her sick father and then her sick mother to their slow, agonising deaths from consumption.

'In poverty, like Dad?' I asked, struggling to place it, to find somewhere in my heart for this hated drunkard.

'Worse. Scotland's poverty was worse, far worse. Hannah had worked with them in the mills since she was five.'

I was picturing a heart-shaped little face with tangled ringlets, but that was the face of my beautiful mother: my mother whose beauty was her only and useless passport. I had to adjust the image to a skinny, plain little girl, clothed in rags amongst the decay and stench that was her home.

'There would've been people helping her – they wouldn't have let a child struggle with that alone, surely,' I said.

My Aunt laughed.

'You still don't understand. No district nurses then for the poor. No doctor. No pills.'

'But neighbours—'

'It was a very infectious disease. Even if your heart was torn out for the child, you couldn't run the risk of going near her and infecting your own family.'

'What happened to her when her mother died?'

'No one knows. Apparently the mill wouldn't take her back – they thought she'd infect their workers. It beggars belief. Maybe she was selling her body – who knows? Ten years old! Word got around and her elder sister guiltily turned up out of the blue – she'd been keeping her distance at Pitlochry because she'd married well and didn't want her marriage ruined. That's how Hannah got to live in Pitlochry.'

'So at least they gave her a home.'

'Well, she'd discovered drink. The sister's husband was a caretaker and they were worried Hannah would lose him his job. So they married her off at fifteen to your grandfather and she went to London with him, out of the way.'

There were tears in our eyes.

'And I abused her! The poor woman. The poor child.'

We both cried amongst the toppling cups, we brushed each other's wet cheeks with our hands. We held hands. It's little comfort, holding hands, but it was all we could do. And my Aunt's were trembling.

'I'd have done what you did,' I said.

'Would you, dear?'

'Yes. Absolutely.'

After a while, something inside us both seemed to settle.

'Why didn't they tell the children?' I asked.

'People thought like that then,' she said. 'They believed that you shouldn't burden the young.'

'Telling would've saved a lot of pain,' I said.

We fell into silence. Then she broke it.

'George would never touch a drop. He was scared he'd take after her. Superstition, of course. Of all of them, he looked the most like her. The dead spit. He was scared, that since he'd inherited her face, he'd inherited her tendencies. If only George had known her story. He could've made up with her before she died. She died with all her children hating her.'

My Aunt was getting loud and agitated again. I said, to change the subject:

'Did George ever think of following Dad to Australia?'

The old woman sighed again. My ignorance was exhausting her. So she explained the last piece of the puzzle, the piece that without it, the rest meant nothing at all.

'George didn't dare.'

'Dare?'

'It might've complicated things for your dad.'

She was moving her old knees in her chair, preparing herself, as if she had to spring up. She hadn't had to work so hard for years, with this job of making me understand.

'I tried to give Dad a plane ticket back to see George,' I was saying. 'Dad wouldn't take it.'

'Your dad believed he wouldn't have got back in,' the old woman managed.

'In? To England?'

'To Australia! It's a wonder they never caught him,' the old woman continued, getting strength. 'His name would've turned up on official documents – he must've stayed ahead of them somehow.'

'His name? Which name?'

'He must've lived in fear all his life,' she said. 'There would've been such a fuss.'

Too late I remembered the word 'fuss', the word I never questioned.

'He didn't enter Australia properly,' the old woman said.

'He jumped ship – was that——?'

'George told him that there were amnesties but your father, with his background, probably wouldn't have trusted officials, or even registered what amnesties were, with all your family's strife going on.'

And so at last the old woman found the words to say it.

'He left England in a hurry – you know he was running away from Hannah – and when he got to Australia, he jumped ship. That was a criminal offence.'

I said, hotly, suddenly knowing as the words came out of my mouth that what had been an explanation for me and my brothers would've have been no explanation for the rest of the world:

'But anyone would sympathise – he fell in love with the Australian light!'

'He was an outcast in England because of the poverty, and an outcast in Australia,' the old woman cried.

I had forgotten the nurse. She was suddenly upon us.

'You'd better go – you're exhausting her.'

'I love her being here,' said my Aunt.

But I didn't want her exhaustion on my conscience.

'I'm so sorry,' I said to both of them.

We hugged a tearful goodbye, then she pulled away from me, tipped her white head on one side to gaze at me and said:

'It's been such a comfort, you visiting me. I'm so glad you came. It's been like having George back for a while. You know, you're the dead spit of him. Your father didn't tell you that either? The same red hair, the same blue eyes! I won't say the dead spit of Hannah, but you are, and I mean it kindly. The dead spit.'

Shame

Diana knew he'd be there, so she decided on her black, that's if she could still get into it. Of course he probably wouldn't remember it. She'd always known Bob's eyes swivelled over women's bodies – why hadn't she taken that as a warning? – and there'd surely be some wisp of memory left in him of her slender almost childish shape, the rounded belly almost gone now. But the shoes. They'd have to be heels, as high as she could manage, to set off the flattering folds of the skirt. The first heels since the baby. She'd be sitting down for most of the evening, in fact probably for the entire evening, apart from a walk across the pavement to and from the taxi, and for that she must be straight-backed and striding. There was the walk to the stage, but of course it was most unlikely she'd have that worry, given that her work was up against Bob's.

But when she fossicked at the bottom of the wardrobe, she found the heels of her good shoes, the ones other than the sneakers, had bits of leather hanging off like little streamers. Peter might be able to glue them down, but the sides were scuffed. Of course, the lighting might be low, but she should make an effort. Narelle had taught her that.

And the makeup, all her makeup was still in the bathroom cupboard where she'd left it before the baby, and her hair was lanky, a cut badly needed, especially the fringe. She'd use the curlers, curl the fringe and then brush it away from her face, and that would have to do.

Bob had been much older than her, twenty years, but one of those indestructible men, especially in a well-cut suit, and with such luminous vigour. When he entered a party, he'd hold up his arms high, waving them, inviting cheers, suggesting anything that had gone wrong in the room — snubs, teeth broken on the nuts, tiffs between friends, the best wine spilled, love affairs devastated — nothing would matter anymore, that was what his uplifted arms proclaimed. In his wake, she'd been a rocky little dinghy. She was an edger into rooms.

He'd said over and over again that Narelle was the most boring friend he had, and he was an expert, given his hundreds of friends — why, she was indisputably the most boring woman in the world. It was a joke, their shared joke; the phone would ring frequently at dinner time and he'd make a face and say: 'That'll be the most boring woman in the world – would you keep my dinner hot?' On the phone, he'd be yes, yes, and then he'd wink at Diana from time to time, yes, yes. Face turned partly towards her. Wink. Yes.

Bob was a comedy screenwriter and Diana found most of his work funny, and as for the rest, she blamed herself. It must be her mood, or her stupidity. Not that she thought herself stupid; in fact, she thought her mind was her best asset. On most points, Diana believed, she and Bob had the same views. About Narelle, she tried not to disagree.

Narelle was lonely though married, and unhappily married though painstakingly glamorous. Her loneliness was why they had to include her, though it didn't explain why she was always in exhaustingly tight skirts, and helplessly wobbling high heels. Diana on the other hand, despite her pretty face, slender body, dark eyes and red hair that blew behind her like a russet scarf, would prefer no one noticed her. She always wore loose shirts or trousers, or even, when she didn't think Bob would notice, track suits. She was a woman so careless of her appearance that often Bob would remind her as they got into bed that she hadn't brushed her hair all day. She'd guiltily promise that tomorrow she'd make an effort. But she preferred to be a bookish, serious person and surely that was sufficient, she thought. She worked at home as a literary editor and editing to her was setting things to rights, as important as bad governments being thrown out, or as death being cured. But, perhaps inspired by the manuscripts she read, it amused her to jot down odd thoughts of her own on anything handy – receipts, torn off cardboard, paper serviettes, tissues, even, on occasion, toilet paper – and stick all the bits on a nail that Bob had obligingly hammered through a piece of wood. It was kept on the kitchen counter in a dark corner under the kitchen clock, so that Bob could riffle through the bits and pieces and appropriate anything he liked for his own work. He was a proudly competitive man, the best in the business, he hoped, but in a good mood he'd say that his work stood out from the crowd because of her precious material.

'What's precious about it?' she'd asked several times.

'It has the ring of truth,' he'd always say.

Diana would shrug. The jottings came out of nowhere, and seemed dictated, almost as if she were their secretary, and that unnerved her. But she believed Bob treasured her for her mind, and she felt assured of his devotion when the bits from the nail turned up on television or film.

Then came a different phone call from Narelle. He faced directly into the phone. No winks. No glances. 'How terrible. He didn't! No! You poor thing. No! Of course, right away.' And afterwards, over the dinner they'd both forgotten to keep hot, came the news that Narelle's husband had brought home his mistress; no one had guessed there'd be a mistress, especially poor Narelle, poor Narelle! – despite her painted fingernails and thin silk blouses. So of course

Narelle had to leave him immediately, but how, and where, especially given her poodles, her five bouncing yappy poodles – he'd said he'd shoot them if she left them and what was she to do, they couldn't go with her to a hotel. Would Bob come around right now, this very minute, and help her work it out, her best friend, her most trusted friend? So Bob abandoned his dinner, which had already congealed, and he'd gone, by himself, of course, because he was the friend, not Diana, and he returned with a request from poor suffering Narelle. An unexpected request. Could they mind the poodles, yappy, bouncing, milling things that they were? asked Bob, not winking now because poor Narelle was really suffering. They were clean and not at all smelly; in fact, like their owner, they were always elegant, always off to the dog salon, curls high, brushed, sweet-smelling and snow white. 'Of course the poodles must stay with us,' said Diana, who'd always intended to make friends with Bob's best friend one day. The gates were tight, the garden was big, a quarter-acre block so the dogs wouldn't even need to be taken for walks. That would be the least she and he, in their happy union, could do for poor Narelle. Except that soon Bob was to travel to another old friend, this one two weeks off dying, the doctors said, and in distant Tahiti. Diana had a deadline, so she couldn't go with him. He, usually impatient with her deadlines, was sympathetic for once, even though it would be their first separation ever.

'The heart will grow fonder,' he said.

But Diana could manage the poodles, couldn't she, for him, for the sake of his old friend, for poor Narelle? Of course she could.

So the dogs moved in, along with a bag or two of dried dog food, and Bob left. And Diana bowed her head to her work and fed the poodles.

On the first day of his absence, her phone rang. It was under her papers and she didn't get to it in time, a blocked number, so perhaps an institution, not Bob, unless he was ringing from his friend's hospital – in fact, was he already in Tahiti? He hadn't rung her, which was odd. She went back to work but the phone rang again, and this time she scrabbled under the right papers and picked it up.

A doctor from the local hospital; she recalled his long, serious face, the way his wrinkled heavy upper eyelids had blinked, considering her uncertain future. He had thick, pale, purple lips that protruded in thought as she'd told him their grief; they couldn't conceive a baby and surely it must be her fault because Bob already had two daughters, now grown up, and she'd never been pregnant, probably never could be. *One can't ever be sure*, the long-faced doctor had said, *not till the test results are in*.

Now on the phone he was sympathetic. 'I know how you both yearned.' He had bad news. The tests. Oh she was fine, she hadn't been the problem after all. But Bob – husband? Partner – Bob, her partner. It was his sperm. Because of his age. 'Certainly he might have been fine twenty years ago. But now, no motility. What's motility? To put it in layman's terms, his sperm couldn't swim. Nothing to be done. No reliable medication. No surgery. Should he post them the written report?' It was easier to think about that issue. But Bob might open the letter, read the report, his hopes falling to pieces. She hesitated. The kindly voice said he could hold it at the front desk, she could pick it up anytime, he could do that at least for her. 'I understand your pain,' he ended.

The room was suddenly silent as if a fierce wind had blown out all the air, the dogs trooping outside as if they'd fled the news, clacking on the shining floorboards like shoeless ballet dancers with long toenails. But now she wanted their company and called them back. She didn't even know their names. She had lost touch with friends of her own, for Bob had thought them too bookish – like her, she suddenly realised with a thud. For a second, she thought of calling Narelle, Bob's oldest friend, but of course she couldn't, that would be an imposition, even a betrayal. After a while, she gathered herself up and wandered to the kitchen and watched the kettle boil for tea. How to tell him?

You're too old, I'm young and fertile, but you, you're past it. How could it be that such a determinedly vibrant man had sluggish sperm?

Perhaps she could claim she no longer craved a baby.

I've changed my mind, I've got cold feet, we can build another life, we'll be free, we'll travel.

But her baby craving had become so acute that when she saw a baby in someone's arms, she held a phantom one in her own, closer and warmer than her teddy bears in child-hood had ever been. She'd double over with sudden longing there in the street. Bob said he craved a baby too.

She woke on the second morning of his absence, fuzzy with worry about what to tell him. She'd ask the doctor to post the report then she wouldn't have to break the news to him. But she must. She must be the one to tell him. But how? Twelve days left before his return, in twelve days the right words would surely come, they must.

But on the third day, two of the dogs were sick, listless, whimpering, not interested in food rattling into their bowls, not yapping, both lying together in an umbrella of shade from a tree, two tails moving plaintively on the lawn, sending up little puffs of dried grass clippings, two noses in her hand begging relief, saying, *Make us better*. The other three dogs were quiet, coming insistently to sniff her when she opened the back door, encircling her to remind her of their companions, saying, *They're over here, see, waiting for you to make them better.*

She squatted, patting them. They'd been Narelle's silly pampered pets before but now they were fellow sufferers. She'd have to take them to the vet, but Bob had driven the car to the airport. Should she put them in a taxi? And which vet and where? She must call Narelle. Poor Narelle, staying in some hotel nearby, oddly not visiting her dogs. Of course poor Narelle could move into the house for a few days to tend to them, move in even for the length of Bob's absence – after all, despite tedious chatter, she was Bob's oldest friend.

By late afternoon the sick dogs were too weak to nose her hand, so she'd rung Narelle's office.

'She's not here,' a voice at the other end said brightly, the eager voice of someone in an office full of filing cabinets, glad of a distraction. 'Is anything wrong?'

Diana explained.

'Narelle can't help you,' the colleague said. 'She's away for a fortnight – no, eleven more days, ten days left tomorrow,' she corrected herself at a prompt from another bright office voice.

The thump at the pit of the stomach. Why, why the same number of days left?

The way time slows, like that time when she was in a car accident, the slow slide of time across the wet road, the slow slippery skid of time till the crunch. *Let there be no crunch.*

'Narelle's away sick?' she'd said, panting. The terrifying slide would, must, slow down, cease before the crunch.

'Not sick. On holidays,' said the bright voice.

What strange knowledge in her stomach made her voice say:

'In Tahiti?'

'You guessed Tahiti! How funny you knew! Lucky thing, isn't she?'

The shame, that's how Diana saw it. The horror. The shame.

The three dogs yapping at the back door even now, the ones who weren't sick, and the neighbours would surely complain. She had to end this shame, that's how she thought of it, that he'd preferred the most boring woman in the world to her with her good mind. She remembered the rat poison Bob had bought years ago, insisting on killing the noises in the night. It would still be in the laundry, surely, on a high shelf. She found the box – she'd pleaded with Bob not to use it and he'd capitulated and the rat had moved out – and leaning on the grey tub, she opened it. The powder was an evil shade of yellow and came helpfully with its own little plastic spoon. She'd swallow a heaped spoonful or two even, she must do the job properly. She worked it out like an equation: she'd put out the rest of the dog food so the barking wouldn't alarm the neighbours, then she'd take two spoonfuls of rat poison, perhaps three. The poison might take a while, and she mustn't be found too soon. A story by Raymond Carver popped into her mind, where a spurned lover had taken rat poison, and his gums had separated from his teeth, so they became like fangs. Was that in the published version, or was it in the unedited version written originally by Carver, the version that included the entire story of the old couple who were taken to hospital after a car accident and were left for dead, but they pulled through because of their love for each other? That story, surely a true one, had been excised from the edited version – how dare anyone remove a love story so obviously true – maybe all editing was wrong – maybe she'd never set things to rights at all, maybe all she'd done was destroy truth. Suddenly she was howling on all fours, with the dogs whining around her and nosing at her feet and her fingers, for the plan to die from rat poison was wrong, wrong, wrong – if she died, her shame would go on beyond her lifetime. Bob had chosen the world's most boring woman over her, and the preferred one would remind him all his life that her rival had died looking like a rat.

So she had to resign herself to shame, and the dogs yelped with her, running between her and their sick friends, watching her dragging herself around on all fours like a dying animal desperate to find a patch of earth kind enough to receive her.

Late in the evening, when they all were surely hoarse with howling, she thought to feed them or else they might howl through the night and a neighbour might come, even call the police. In the kitchen, the dog food packets were slumped against the wall, empty. Were the shops open? Could she go to a shop as if life hadn't ended? Could she be with her neighbours, whose lives were orderly, could she walk amongst neat rows of shampoo and baby food and cabbages, pretending that living was a reasonable act, and could she smile at a checkout girl who'd pass her the dog food packages and wish her a nice day?

She couldn't go alone, she needed someone to go to the shop with her, someone who'd hold her upright since she didn't seem to be able to do that by herself. A friend – but she'd neglected them all because Bob wanted her to himself, and she'd thought that was an assurance of eternal love. The kindly doctor of yesterday – it seemed last century but it was surely only yesterday – he'd said he understood her pain. He'd come with her and help her buy dog food. She found his number and clicked. It wasn't his voice but she told the voice, any voice would do, about sperm that aren't motile, and that rat poison is an evil shade of yellow, and that teeth could became fangs, and about Narelle's tight silk blouses.

'Have you eaten?'

A question so unexpected, she paused.

'I don't remember,' Diana said.

'Get in a taxi, come here,' the voice said.

In a nightie with a coat thrown over, dressed in the careless style she now saw that Bob despised, she'd gone out into the street, found a merciful taxi, and asked for the hospital. Bob hadn't cancelled their shared private cover, not yet – and she was led to a clean white bed, she was tucked in, and then she slept.

In her dazed state, she became the dogs, howling in a circle of shade, unable to lift her nose. She was given food, pills, and a fortnight to talk to doctors who nodded their heads and went away after a measured hour. She just had to endure the pain, the doctors said before their hour was up, and then one day it would be over. Last it through. It'll end.

Bob had gone completely, not even a goodbye note when she went back to the house. An unopened letter lay in the box – the letter from the doctor about Bob's sperm. So he'd never know. She ripped it up into tiny pieces like confetti.

Slowly, day by day, she went back to work, and begged her friends to forgive her neglect.

'You must feel so angry,' they said, themselves irritated by her long silence.

She agreed, floundering, not knowing how to explain the shame.

She spent hours gazing at walls. She'd never noticed before how unblinkingly, how scornfully, they glare.

She found all days lost to grief, but slowly, slowly, only some of her days were lost to it, and there were other days with mere patches of grief, like pools drying up in the sun. Maybe grief was coming to an end the way the doctors had said it would.

Her earnings had always been poor. She moved to a tiny flat of one room, and even that was more than she could afford. She was always falling behind in the rent, paying last month's rent with the new payment that should've bought her this month's food.

A year later, he rang. She scarcely recognised his voice. She was astonished to hear hers answering it. The sort of astonishment she'd feel if they'd both died and met on a gust of wind above their graves. His voice filled the room, its tiny space, and all the vast space inside her head. She could see his large body bulging with that voice, and her head bulged with it too. He asked if she was well.

'Fine,' she said, almost inaudible.

Was he ringing to ask her back?

But he hurried on. He was in charge of a new mini-series, and was able to choose the writers. She listened only because he might say he'd made a mistake in leaving her. There were two conversations going on – his, and the one inside her. *Say you're sorry. Say you prefer me.* He mentioned a name of a writer she knew – but would she also work with them?

She decided immediately.

'No,' she said. 'I want to leave things between us as they are.'

He laughed. She'd always been so adamant.

'It would be good for us both.'

'How would it be good for you?' she asked.

She wanted him to say he was bored with the most boring woman in the world.

'I'd get brownie points for discovering you,' was all he said.

She knew she should click off the phone.

'It's well-paid work I'm offering.'

She stirred herself. He'd always said the money she earned from editing was foolishly low. 'You make a stranger's writing look good and no one knows,' he'd said.

'I have no experience,' she said now.

He knew her well, knew she was weakening.

'But I have chosen you,' he said.

She moved to sit on a chair. She hadn't been the woman he'd chosen.

She managed a laugh, hoping it was ironic.

He ignored the irony.

'You're smart,' he said. 'The series needs someone smart.'

She knew that being smart didn't make her a writer. She said as much.

'You'd give us precious material,' he said.

Why hadn't he found her precious?

She said again she wouldn't live up to his needs, she'd disappoint both him and the other writer, she'd be a drag to them. He listened to her.

Then he told her the money he'd pay, a sum that would pay off her back rent and keep her alive for six months to come. Screenwriters got paid a lot. It was why he did it, rather than write real books, he'd said. One day he'd write real books, and she'd edit them.

'Tempted?' He laughed.

He'd known she'd be in financial trouble.

'Can I think about it?'

'I need a decision now,' he said. 'I've got to put the names to the producers.'

'I suppose I could have a go,' she said. 'Would that be okay, if I tried and failed?'

He was pleased to have his way, and rang off.

It was odd, the silence afterwards. As if the energy of his voice was like his arms held in the air, encouraging the world to turn in the way it should.

She put on the jug to make a cup of tea, hoping to understand his motives by the time she'd drunk it. It was too much to expect of a cup of tea.

The day they were to meet, she dressed in the usual loose clothes but brushed her hair till the curls slid into pretty places and, on the way, dawdled at a chemist shop to select a lipstick – the Summer Rose or the Cappuccino? The shop assistant helped her try both, painting her lips with a little brush and, stepping back, studying the effect. 'You're a natural for Summer Rose.' It seemed to beam light into her face, but shame was there too. Should she have taken this trouble with her appearance before he left? Could a little greasy stick of Summer Rose have saved her from such grief? Loss swept over her again, doubling her up so she was still staggering when she entered the office. He leapt up, hailing her with his arms held high as if to elicit cheers from her, and kissed her on both cheeks. But he didn't hold her gaze. And he didn't seem to notice the Summer Rose.

'Down to work,' he said.

They worked through the day, every day, never mentioning the past, never mentioning their lives. Together the three planned what would happen in the two episodes Bob allocated to each of them. It was to be a love story. They were to go away and write the episodes, and Bob would edit them afterwards.

There were moments when he paused after the other writer left – he was always leaving early, picking up his child from kindergarten – and Bob would take a breath. His eyes would sweep the floor, as if trying to gather a thought shattered there like glass. But then he'd speak and it was always about work. Their collaboration was supposed to take a week, and Bob ran their sessions like clockwork, so that they finished promptly on Friday at five in the afternoon.

When they were alone, Bob swept his eyes along the shattered glass again, vacuuming it up.

Is he going to ask me back?

And if he does, what will I say?

'How do you feel?' he suddenly broke his musing to ask.

Half a minute passed in silence. She struggled but decided that the question was only about work.

'I agreed to give it a try, so I will.'

She began packing up her computer and notebook, carefully putting the top on her pen, the pen in her bag, when he suddenly said:

'Don't.'

She froze, her hand in her bag, still on the pen.

'Don't go,' he said. 'I don't think you're ready for this,' he said.

It was hard to breathe.

But all he wanted was to sit together for another hour or so and work through some possible lines.

'But that's my job, you can't do my job for me.'

He insisted. She thought he might be playing for time, wanting to speak the words she most wanted to hear, so to give him time, she wrote down his suggestions. All the lines he suggested had the familiarity of lines from his old work that she knew so well, not the same words exactly, but the tone of them, the rhythm.

He petered out.

'That's it then,' she said.

She packed up her notebook again, her pen again.

All the time, he'd been facing her. Now he swung his body away.

It's coming.

'Look,' he said, almost over his shoulder, 'I had to leave.'

Somehow, she had to manage to respond.

'There are more decent ways to leave,' she said.

His body was still turned away so his neck twisted like a corkscrew. She saw for the first time the reluctant lines of age around his neck, tired little wrinkles spiking out from big creases. His neck would've been like that all the time and she hadn't noticed. Maybe she hadn't noticed much besides what was in her own head.

'It happened out of the blue. Narelle was so upset about her husband. She begged me to take her away from it all.'

'And you didn't imagine that I'd be upset?' she managed.

'I'm leaving,' she added. It didn't seem to be her voice.

'I'll get the scripts to you by the deadline, I'm good at deadlines – you know that,' the voice that wasn't hers said.

'It happened so fast,' he repeated.

She put on her coat and buttoned it around her tightly, even though the day wasn't cold.

As if speed had anything to do with it.

When she handed in her two scripts, she waited an anxious week. Had she failed? Surely she'd failed. Of course she'd failed, she was a rank amateur. Precious material can't take you far, especially when you've never felt responsible for it.

Then he rang.

He was delighted. Her work was as good as he'd thought it'd be. A few inelegancies, but that could only be expected, and would be easily fixed by his editing.

'A lot of it is yours,' she said.

'Your precious material. We're a good team,' he said.

So he had what he wanted: her mind, and company of the woman he preferred.

A year later, two lonely years later, just when the shining pools of grief had dried up to only a few minutes a day, and some days had none at all, she met Peter. A year later again, The Baby.

So the shoes. Peter minded the baby between breastfeeds while she rushed to the shops, just a kilometre away.

They still called her The Baby. She seemd a miracle. There were many miracles: meeting him after three lonely years, the love-making they'd both wanted almost as soon as they'd met, the night she'd sat up in bed saying in her sleep, *Someone is waiting to join us*, the more eager love-making to create the someone, the night his motile sperm burrowed into her longing egg – she claimed till the end of her life that she knew the exact moment, the face on the exact tiny fish. All through her pregnancy she wished she could meet it, this tiny fish. And then the pain beyond any, but only physical pain, the moment when the air around them fizzed like champagne, for there was The Baby, moving and spread-eagled on her.

'We've made a person,' he'd leant over and whispered into her eyes.

It was as if The Baby was teaching her how to live. One of the first lessons came on her first outing away from The Baby, as she strode down the pavement in her sneakers and track suit, pilled with white cotton wool. She'd been astonished that the air, unremarkable all her life till The Baby, now seemed to kiss her skin like sunshine and the sunshine warmed her rounded head so it glowed as if she were an angel. The blue sky sang above her, even the planes flying over hummed. But the lesson was that her arms ached, they had a heart of their own, a groaning heart, to hold

The Baby again. She couldn't be apart from The Baby. She nearly turned back. But Bob would report the state of her shoes to Narelle, or Narelle would be there to see, and how they would laugh, as Bob and she had laughed at Narelle. She was always pedantic. Inelegant. Awkward. The most awkward woman in the world.

The second lesson she learned was how difficult it was to let The Baby be minded by someone else. Peter could always stay behind with her on The Evening, but Bob, after he got the prize, would stride over to Diana and say, voice loud with generosity, that they were a good team. He hadn't thought that about their love. So a friend minded The Baby, an old friend who'd forgiven her.

'How are you feeling?' Peter asked her as the prize ceremony went on. For each category, one name was read out, the winner. The prizes weren't money, but metal objects too big to put in a drawer and too ugly to put on a table.

'I don't remember why we came,' she said.

Peter checked the program.

'You're in the last category,' he said. 'A long way to go.'

'My arms are aching for her,' she said.

To pass the time, she went to the Ladies. She did a pee and came out of the closet, and took her time washing her hands. Someone came out of another closet, and at the dryer, Diana saw Narelle. Perhaps Narelle mightn't look up. But there were big mirrors behind the taps and Narelle wasn't a woman to pass by a mirror. She met Diana's eyes. She started.

It was Diana who spoke.

'How are your dogs?'

'I had to give them up,' Narelle said.

'Oh, that's sad. Why?'

'Because of the child.'

'What child?'

'We had to let the dogs go. She thought she belonged to them, not to us!'

Even in her confusion, Diana saw the O that Narelle made to touch up her lipstick was heart-shaped.

'That must've been hard for you,' said Diana, confused. 'Losing the dogs, I mean.'

Narelle scrabbled in her makeup purse. Diana found herself peering into Narelle's makeup purse with her. It was crowded with broken brown and black kohl pencils and their shavings, crimson and vermilion lipsticks without their lids. The sides of the purse were grubby, the plastic lining torn.

'She was a premmie,' Narelle was saying as she searched, so her eyes were on the purse, not on Diana. 'I couldn't carry her the full thirty-nine weeks.'

'You never mentioned you had a child,' Diana said.

Narelle looked up uncomprehendingly.

'In the old days,' Diana stumbled.

'I'm sorry that you couldn't conceive,' Narelle went on, also confused but at last finding a blusher and applying it with deft strokes. A garden of roses bloomed on one cheek. 'Bob told me.'

Of course Bob would tell her, they were a couple, of course he'd tell her.

Narelle grew a garden of roses on the other cheek.

She slammed her makeup purse shut, and Diana noticed, in the way the mind snags at details, that the garden on one of Narelle's cheeks was far more prolific than on the other.

'It's not all beer and skittles,' Narelle was saying. 'I didn't want a child but Bob was longing to have one more. To prove his manhood.'

'But Bob can't . . .' Diana said, and stopped. Narelle was already out the door.

'He can't have.' She watched herself say it, but only her reflection was listening.

Something seemed to have gone wrong with the plumbing. The toilets wouldn't switch off. The cisterns were all constantly filling, each one at a different rate, some roaring, some high-pitched, some chugging, one coughing. It wasn't at all like being in a public bathroom; she seemed to be inside a cataract. And at the same time, astonishment was flickering, there in a bathroom with the cisterns going wild.

And then another woman burst open the door, bringing a blast of the ceremony she'd forgotten.

'They're still nowhere near your category,' said Peter. 'You were gone for ages. I'd thought you'd fallen in.'

She didn't sit down.

'Let's go home,' she said.

'You sure?'

'I'm sure.'

The next day, the phone rang just as The Baby, newly awake, was screaming in hunger.

'You won!' Bob was saying.

'Just a moment. I'll go outside,' Diana said.

She went out into the street.

Bob asked why she'd left the ceremony last night and, before she could think of an answer, he told her that as the team leader he'd been obliged to go up to the stage to accept her prize. She could tell from his voice what a difficult walk that had been, his arms not held high but flapping by his side.

'I said I'd mentored you,' he said. But he interrupted himself:

'Wasn't that a baby I heard? I saw you with a new man.'

She swallowed. She dreaded what this was leading to.

'You're cutting out,' he said.

'Sorry,' she said.

'Your new man – did he come already with a family?'

She fell silent.

'You're cutting out again. Who's your provider?'

He suspects Narelle. He'll abandon the child, just as he abandoned me. He's an abandoner.

'Jesus – couldn't she bloody get herself a decent provider?' she heard him shout, a man demented. Perhaps the hospital had sent two letters, and he'd picked up one.

Speech is slow, hindered by the unwieldy tongue and only eight muscles. The brain has a far greater advantage: a hundred billion neurons, each making thousands of contacts at any moment, so that their combined contacts exceed the number of elementary particles in the universe.

In the time that Bob's eight muscles took to utter those angry words, dozens of images had cascaded through Diana's mind: some: the slide of Narelle's brush painting pretend gardens on her cheeks; the wet slick on Bob's lips when he told her that, in Tahiti, his heart would grow fonder of her; her own arms raised with the pleasure of lifting high a knife, a spade, an axe at the man she now hates; herself shouting to the entire neighbourhood – not that he lived there – that his sperm couldn't swim; that his new child wasn't his, that he'd got what he deserved.

But then Peter came out and stood in the open doorway with The Baby screaming, still in her white wrappings, her angry arms flapping like the wings of a white cockatoo in flight, and in a new cascade of images, The Baby taught Diana the next lesson: a little child on all fours uncertain who she belonged to, of how she fitted in, of who she was; and then a memory: Diana about ten years old and looking up from her book in the school playground, furtively watching a group of girls playing skipping. A girl at each end turns the rope. The game is to choose the moment to run in – so you wait till the rope loops up into the blue sky, then, and only then you dash to join the jumping, giggling, chanting, hugging group, the ones who've made it to the centre.

Diana's new to this school, so she goes back to her book – she always carries two in her bag, in case of emergencies; but she looks up when there's a familiar loud sniff to see Gillian, an even newer arrival with a face as pale as the paper they write on, dreary grey hair of the wriggly sort where each strand refuses lie down with the other strands, and a perpetual sniff. Gillian is tracking the turning of the rope, pushing her spectacles into place on her nose. Sniff. Sniff. Diana feels a flash of impatience even with the girl: doesn't she know people like us have to hide in books? But the silly girl is clearly thinking that if she could only get to the centre of that turning rope, then she'd jump and giggle and chant and hug. Afterwards, someone would run upstairs to class with her, talk to her in class, look out for her, do homework with her, whisper to her, confide in her, walk arm-in-arm with her. Even Sally Tinsdale is jumping and giggling at the centre, Sally whose clothes are always dirty, and Barbara Fryer who never knows the answers and Wendy Thomas whose brother is in jail. It's worth risking a rope burn, Gillian's face says, to get to heaven.

Diana thinks of offering Gillian her spare book, but it'd look like friendship and someone might see.

She can tell Gillian's saying to herself: now the rope is about to thwack the ground – it'd be unsafe to run in now but you could do it now while it's looping high. Now – it's unsafe – now – safe. Unsafe – safe. Sniff. Sniff.

Gillian, arms flaying, feet kicking up behind her, launches her dash but she's thwacked, her back is thwacked by the remorseless rope. The girls at the centre, even the girls turning the rope, everyone heaves with laughter. Gillian tries again, she's lashed again. At her third attempt, she's tripped by her own feet; she's sprawled on the ground. The playground heaves with wicked glee. The rope keeps turning; Gillian's in its path, it'll lash her head, her ear is lashed, a terrifying spurt of red blood is in her hair and even her spectacles skitter away to gleam at her mockingly.

'Stop,' yells Diana against the noise but she doesn't want to be heard, and no one hears. Someone starts a chant and the skippers all join in:

'Out of the way. Out of the way.'

Lash. Turn. Lash. Turn. Lash. The bell to signal the end of lunch time clangs against the bright sun and the elation. The rope pauses mid-way through the blue sky and flops, the skippers meekly run for their bags, the rope's a mere circle bundled up by a turner, everyone runs to class, no one looks back.

Gillian and Diana inherit the playground. Only the birds sing now. Somewhere, a dog barks. Distant traffic hums.

Gillian stirs, sits up, feels around for her spectacles. She reaches out for them. Sniff. Sniff.

'Your ear – is it all right?' Diana asked, coming near, not too near.

Gillian is too busy dusting herself down and re-arranging her dress to answer. Streamers of red clump her grey hair. She attempts to put her spectacles on, but she can only use her good ear. They dangle uselessly down her face. She staggers to her bag, spectacles banging, she's sniffing, bloody-eared, bloody-kneed, round-shouldered, blind, cowed. Without a glance at Diana, she slouches out the playground gate.

Diana's brain explosions quietened; at last there was peace. Forever after, in idle moments, when she was carrying out the garbage or driving on quiet country roads, long, long after, she wondered if the thought that followed was what Bob might call precious material, or was it just the thought of a coward? The thought: that those of us who've somehow found a temporary place in this slippery whirling world must hold out a hand to those who haven't.

What she said:

'The Baby is Peter's.'

And she clicked off the phone.

With thanks to Tobias Wolff's 'Bullet in the Brain'.

Small talk

S he only knew the desert in her country from post-cards she'd find at markets or bookshops, and she'd send them overseas to friends to seem interesting and exotic.

This is my country, she'd write.

As if she belonged to it all, as if she knew what belonging to a country meant.

She was a child of migrants who'd settled here at various stages over a century, sheltering from who knows what deeds done against them. They'd been too traumatised to tell. She'd only lived in the Europeanised, Americanised cities on the coastal rim, crammed with new settlers, and longed to be with people who deeply belonged to this country, who'd belonged here forever, so that something of what they were might help her belong more. Might help her come home.

One day the longing became too great to bear. It so happened that she had a childhood friend who'd become a nurse for a tribe in the desert in the middle of the continent, hundreds of kilometres from the nearest town. In her twice-a-year emails, Pat would apologise for being so seldom in touch; she was just too busy. Once, she explained that she'd given up on her family and they'd given up on her, that she survived on Tim Tam biscuits from the bush store and that she wore the same clothes all week.

Diana told her friend she was coming to look after her.

'What language do they speak there?' she wrote.

Some weeks later a tape arrived in the mail, with no accompanying letter, just a note scribbled on the back of a torn envelope saying that the language on the tape wasn't quite the right language because it hadn't been written down yet, but this was more or less the same. Diana listened to the tape every night, surprised that in a desert where surely everything was just sandhill after sandhill, the people had evolved such a big vocabulary and a complicated way to speak. But she wasn't daunted. Then she took three months off work, bought a second-hand Land Rover and drove for ten days. She was like a woman possessed.

She knew she'd reached the desert when the ground turned from black to the colour of sunsets, blushes, apricots. She left the tarred roads behind, often stopping to consult a map. There was never anyone to ask. Behind her, dust rose like smoke. She camped at nights, lighting fires and heating cans of food. At first she was frightened of the heat, dingoes, snakes, spiders, axe-murderers. She'd never been a brave woman, but she became one now because she was in love with her mission. In early light the dust was mauve, the mulga trees were olive, the mountains were emerald green. By mid-morning the ground was red, the mountains Prussian blue. As she drove, yellow light moulded mountain ranges into hundreds of smaller hills, sometimes with gold outcrops that in another country she'd glimpse and think, Aha! That's a castle over there! But here there were no castles, no buildings, no sign that humans existed. Or were there? The thought crossed her mind that the people she was soon to talk to might be able to see signs invisible to her. Once, she stopped for a break at a dried-up claypan where there were hundreds, probably thousands of small, almost perfectly formed hexagonal clay clumps like pieces of a giant board game. She picked one up and beneath it was another, and another, and another, all the same shape. She crouched there alone in a space so vast and still that even a breeze seemed a dramatic act. After a while, she was ready to believe, like Pythagoras, that the purity of line of a geometric shape represents something fundamental and as yet undiscovered about the universe. Above her hung a low, intense cloud, itself like a phantom mountain. She drove on, but when she looked in her rear-view mirror, she saw that the dust behind her was now rising like uncertainty.

Another night it rained, sweeping, adamant rain that brought leaks to her tent. The next day was sunny and still again as if nothing had happened, but in a matter of hours, it seemed, there were William Shakespeare type neck ruffs of green lacy weeds around the roots of gaunt tree trunks so twisted with light they seemed as graceful and weightless as ballet dancers. Only the heat seemed to hold them down. By early evening of that day, she'd travelled beyond the mountain range and was in country so flat, with trees so low, that when she turned on her heel, she saw the entire circle of the horizon spinning by. She didn't put up her tent but lay under the dome of stars, watching the trajectory of the Southern Cross move directly above her toes, then above her stomach, above her chest, above her head. Until dawn, the black sky was spangled all the way down to the ground, all around her.

She felt herself become braver.

After many wrong turnings, she found a notice announcing her friend's community, and then she came upon a windmill pumping bore water, and now her heart was hammering with excitement. She came to a village that looked like any ordinary village, though the earth was the colour of ripe tomatoes. She passed naked black children laughing and shouting at a burst water main, their teeth startlingly white, and there was Pat at her gate, her once black hair now grey, her once slender body now chubby, her face like the face Diana remembered, but her wide toothy smile now disappeared into bulging cheeks and many chins.

'Look at you!' Pat said, for Diana was city slim and elegant, though her glossy skin was dusted with red. Their friendship used to be edged with competitiveness. There was a touch of envy in Pat's voice now, Diana noted with a small puff of satisfaction.

After they'd hugged and taken the bags inside the house and had a cup of tea, Pat said she was just about to drive around doing the evening delivery of tablets to people who might otherwise forget to take them.

'Isn't this after hours?' Diana said.

Pat laughed at the notion, and Diana saw that her old friend was full of an energy that seemed to bounce off her olive skin. Even her greying hair curled energetically.

'You can come but don't get out of the car,' said Pat.

'Why ever not?'

Diana was eager to be introduced, eager to begin talking.

'It's uncouth. Evening is family time. And don't look at them. That's uncouth too.'

'Looking is uncouth?'

'Just glance up, and look down again. That's their way.'

They drove around the ripe tomato streets, Diana sitting in the car trying not to look, but still peeking. The people were so dark-skinned that in the evening light they seemed like shadows or burnt tree trunks. They didn't seem to live inside their houses but around them, sitting in groups on gaudy blankets in the dust, women cooking over a small fire, men in other circles gambling, children sometimes playing with each other, sometimes sitting quietly with the women.

There were large flat boards set on flour drums she first took to be tables and looked around for chairs, but then she realised that the boards were probably beds. So the people slept under the stars as she had, she thought. Television sets were flashing colours and mumbling English in some yards, but they seemed like guests everyone ignored.

'Are people talking about me?' Diana couldn't resist asking as they drove to the next house.

'They notice everything,' Pat said. 'They seem to read people's bodies.'

That thrilled Diana. Surely they'd see how eager she was to talk with them.

She was ready to forgive the grubbiness of it all, the walls of the houses stained with greasy hand marks, the cars rusting and dismantled in yards, the litter of papers and plastic bottles blown against fences and trees. After all, she told herself to calm her nerves, they'd always been nomads and probably never had to think about cleaning up, just moving on to the next camp and leaving animal bones and seeds and chaff to the wind.

But when Pat drove down a street of partially demolished houses with the walls ripped off and only rusty framework left standing for years, Diana struggled with disappointment.

'Someone should clean this place up,' she said as they drove to the next house.

She felt Pat stiffen beside her.

'Not you, of course,' Diana added.

Pat grabbed a new batch of pills and slammed the door behind her, her back protesting. Diana, chastened, listened to the way Pat spoke simple English to the people, throwing in a few words of their language. Sometimes she gently touched the forearms of the women, and often she held their babies. When she returned from her next delivery she had softened, Diana saw.

'When a relative dies here, his house can't be lived in because of his cranky spirit. It must be destroyed and the family must move on,' said Pat, offering her this information in a conciliatory way.

She drove to the next patient.

'I know the mess is awful but the whites here who run the services do nothing. The headmaster, for instance, says these are the most degraded people on earth,' Pat said.

'Why don't the people have him sacked?' asked Diana.

'These are a gentle people,' said Pat. 'Not like a neighbouring tribe who wouldn't put up with it. These people put up with a lot. They don't do things white people's way. And they're preoccupied with family, huge families, all needy, all hungry. Rubbish is the last of their concerns.'

She swung into another street and laughed fondly.

'Though an old man yesterday complained that his yard was messy. He said he'd have to move house. I thought he meant the rubbish. But he didn't. They still track here. See how they're all bare-footed? He meant there were too many footprints. He couldn't tell who'd been in his yard.'

When she came back from her next delivery she said:

'I'm sorry, but you can't stay if you're going to criticise. You've got to look below the surface.'

'That's why I came,' said Diana. 'I want to.'

Pat smiled, and the tension between them eased.

'What are your plans?' Pat asked as they headed back to her house. 'Besides being my servant,' she added with satisfaction.

'I'm going to have real conversations,' said Diana.

For a difficult, frowning month, Diana kept house for Pat, shopping at the only store (she winced at the extortionate prices), beginning a vegetable garden because the store didn't sell vegetables, and relearning the language at the house of another white person, a Lutheran missionary, an earnest, patient man who spent long hours every day questioning people about exact meanings while he made them cups of black sugary tea. Diana had studied Italian and Greek at school and she'd learned the tape Pat had sent, but the local language turned out to be very different. She wouldn't let herself be deterred. This language was demanding, with multiple cases and unexpected detail – there was an entire page in the missionary's half-finished, often handwritten dictionary of the ways to say 'we'. She counted thirty ways. She discovered that much of the time when she wanted to say that someone did something, she had to split the verb open like a New York bagel and fill it with a number of other words chosen from scores of possibilities that revealed where the speaker was in the journey of the day – and only then could she finish the sentence. 'So,' the missionary said proudly, for he'd spent several years working this out, 'there were sixty-nine ways of splitting the word to hit. You split it to say you're hitting while you're going down a hill to home, hitting while you're going up a hill, hitting while you're walking away from the hearer, hitting while you're heading towards the hearer . . .'

His voice trailed on and on as if they were both dreaming.

'What if you're not travelling?' Diana asked, hoping for an easy way out. 'Can't you just miss out on all this?' The new linguistic complication might put off conversation for weeks. 'After all, there are lots of things you'd do when you were stationary – like cooking!' she told him.

'Even if you're sitting at a fire and talking about the kangaroo you caught,' said the missionary in triumph, 'you have to split the verb.'

To her it seemed like the way Latin might've ended up if the Romans had been nomads.

After another month, she visited Pat at the clinic and sat in the waiting room to try a conversation. A beautiful young mother with her breast bared for her baby smiled at her.

'What's your country?' the young mother asked in English.

'I usually live in Sydney,' Diana said in her new language and lurched to a stop.

She wondered if 'usually' ruined her answer.

'Your country is beautiful,' Diana said after she'd worked it out.

The woman fell silent, looked away.

Diana tried again.

'Your baby is beautiful too,' she said in the language.

The woman smiled again, caressed the baby's back, but still averted her glance.

Over dinner Diana tried to keep irritation out of her voice.

'I was trying to make small talk,' she said. 'She didn't help at all! I didn't have the slightest clue if she liked me!'

'They don't do small talk,' Pat said. 'They say, those white people, always talking.'

'That's all right,' Diana said, both to herself and to Pat. 'Really, I'm not interested in small talk. I want deep, meaningful conversation. Big talk.'

Pat smiled at the intensity of her friend. She'd always been like this, even as a child, insisting on her own way, refusing to play with other girls if they didn't play what she wanted. She'd refused sometimes to play with Pat.

'What's important to them is being together,' said Pat. 'Silent company. Marlpa, I've heard it called by another group.'

She saw how Diana's lips shut in a determined line.

One morning at the end of the second month, Pat ran up from the clinic to tell her that some people had asked to be taken out to a stand of bush oranges now in season. Diana was in the middle of watering the vegetable garden; she was enchanted with the willingness of the green sturdy leaves to shoot straight out of the red dirt.

'Almost as if the plants want to feed us,' she told Pat. She'd never grown anything before. Perhaps she could teach the people and turn them from a nomadic culture into an agricultural culture. It might be good for them and at least inspire them to modify those terrible verbs.

'Now,' said Pat, because Diana hadn't turned off the hose. 'They're ready to go now.'

'Won't tomorrow do?' asked Diana. 'It's going to be very hot soon. I was thinking of putting up some shade cloth for the spinach.'

'They don't plan ahead here,' said Pat, patiently. She was used to her friend. 'They want to go now. Not tomorrow.'

'They have cars,' Diana said. 'Why would they want me to take them?'

'There's no money for fuel,' Pat said, still patient.

'How far?' Diana asked.

'They must like you to ask you,' Pat said. 'Do you want to get to know them, or not?'

Pat filled Diana's car with people – a slender old man with a bare chest and a black plastic leg, his two wives, one much younger than the other, and his two sisters. One sister sat in the front and smiled and then looked away. Diana did the same. She cast around for something to say but all the words in her mouth seemed like small talk and they dried up like leaves in the sun. No one spoke, so she put off her meaningful conversation for a while and concentrated on driving. It had rained recently and the red road churned by recent cars looked like a child's finger painting. When they came to a fork in the road, she turned to her companion in the front seat. She had learned that the language didn't have left or right, but twelve points north, south, east and west and she wasn't exactly sure which way she was facing. But her companion didn't speak, she just indicated the way with a graceful, economical gesture, her hand stretched out ahead with the fingers clamped together and slanting to the right. Diana drove for another hour.

'Stop,' one of the wives at last called in English from the back.

Diana stopped. Her companion was gazing out at the mulga. In the back, everyone else gazed in the same direction. It's just undifferentiated trees, Diana thought impatiently.

'What are we looking at?' she managed to ask in their language.

No one answered her.

'Rubbish,' someone said at last, and in English.

'Rubbish?' repeated Diana.

'These bush oranges rubbish,' her companion said in English.

Meaning came to Diana slowly.

'They are not good?' Diana asked in their language. She had no idea of the word for 'ripe'.

Her companion didn't answer, but gestured onwards.

Diana drove. It was like city people going out for dinner to some distant restaurant because it's had good reviews, she told herself. After another eighty kilometres, one of the wives called again.

'Stop.'

Diana again saw only undifferentiated mulga, but her companion indicated with her hand that Diana should start the car again.

'Slow,' said the woman in English.

They pulled up underneath two trees that Diana hadn't noticed. She looked up. Green bulbous fruit hung high like Christmas decorations. Everyone clambered out. Diana, wanting to impress with her helpfulness, climbed up on the Land Rover's roof and threw the fruit down to waiting hands. This seemed to please everyone. When there was no more left to pick, she stood shyly amongst the seated group until one of the sisters patted the dusty ground. Diana sat compliantly, trying to cross her legs like them, though it hurt, telling herself not to fret over how she'd wash the red stains out of her trousers. She was glad they weren't her best cream ones.

The bush oranges were not like anything she'd ever tasted. They seemed layered in flavour. At the first bite they tasted like mango, and then, as she neared the seed, like marzipan without sugar, and then, she thought, an aftertaste of kerosene.

'Suck the seed,' said her companion in English, breaking a long silence. Diana obeyed. The seed was almost bitter but she pretended to like it. Perhaps it was doing her good. She even threw the seeds down on the ground like they did, stifling her impulse to bury them so they'd grow for the future. She reminded herself that this was a language without a future tense that extended more than a few days. Besides, burying the seeds might make it look as if she was trying to perform magic. She'd learned a little about their beliefs. She didn't want to do anything uncouth. Everything must aid her towards having a conversation.

'Beautiful food,' she said in their language when she could bear the silence no more.

Everyone laughed, and looked away.

So she put off conversation for later in the drive.

She was expecting to retrace their route but when they came to another fork in the road, her companion silently indicated a different way. Diana hesitated, then did as she was told.

'Stop,' one of the sisters called, after a while.

Everyone climbed out except the old man who had fallen asleep, and they bent over bushes at the side of the road, gathering handfuls of long fronds.

'What is it?' Diana asked in language.

'Bush medicine,' said her companion in English.

Diana wanted to help, so she found identical bushes on the other side of the road and gathered a big bouquet of fronds. Soon the back of the car was littered. Diana laid her own bouquet proudly on the dashboard for everyone to see. It might bring on a conversation.

'What's this for?' her companion asked in English about Diana's fronds.

'Your bush medicine,' said Diana, surprised.

Her companion reached over to the back, picked out from the pile one of the fronds and held it up to compare it to Diana' fronds. The leaves were different.

'No bush medicine,' said her companion.

Diana laughed in some embarrassment, and the woman smiled gently.

They drove again in silence.

'Stop,' someone called again.

Everyone clambered out except for the old man, who had taken off his black plastic leg and laid it across the back seat.

Diana again could see only mulga but the group was pulling at the trees and filling plastic bags with elongated green fruit.

'Bush pears,' said one of the wives in English to Diana, who stood watching.

Soon the women ranged out of sight, coming back every now and then with plastic bags bulging with green pears, which they emptied into buckets. Diana didn't want to walk away from the car. Her fears came back. What if there were snakes? The heat of the sun was beating on her head like a drum. She'd forgotten her sunhat.

She shaded her eyes and circled a few trees because she wanted to show her eagerness, but she could only find two pears. When one of the wives returned, bringing another bulging bag to the car and depositing it inside, careful not to disturb the old man or his leg, she touched Diana's arm and walked away ahead, some distance off. She lay down on the ground, patting it, indicating that Diana should come over and lie beside her. But Diana didn't want to rest. She wanted to be an impressive finder of bush pears.

'Come,' the woman called in English. Diana walked over reluctantly, half obeying the woman, half dazed by the sun. The woman patted the ground more emphatically. Diana sat down nearby, thinking that perhaps this wasn't the right moment for conversation. She wouldn't be able to split her verbs accurately, not in this heat. The woman banged the ground so hard that dust rose around her ample body. Diana didn't like to sit so close to anyone. She hesitated, then thought better of it and wriggled over. But the woman still wasn't satisfied. She insisted with her hand that Diana lie beside her rather than sit.

'My mother taught me when she was growing me up,' said the woman in English.

This seemed to promise a conversation at last, at least about childhoods, so Diana lay down. Only then did the woman raise her arm and point. Diana followed the direction of the point. At last, from that angle, with the breath of the woman on her face, she could see pear vines as they twined from one branch to another high up in the tree against the blue, searing, endless sky, and big green pears hanging from them.

From out of her pocket the woman fished a crumpled plastic bag and handed it to Diana.

'Get some,' she said.

The car by now smelled sweetly of plants but Diana barely noticed. She turned on the ignition key in a trance. Again she expected to retrace their route but again the woman beside her indicated another way. They drove cross country, far from the road, over spiky blond spinifex and deep watercourse ditches, beyond an outcrop of orange rocks and then, suddenly in front of them, smiling at the sky, gleamed a narrow stretch of water.

Her companion touched her arm lightly, indicating they should stop. The women burst out of the hot car and waded in, fully clothed. They submerged themselves and then beckoned to Diana, who'd paused at the edge of the water-hole, just wetting her feet.

'You too,' said one of the wives in English. Her smile was full of friendship.

She followed them in until she was waist-deep. The water was about the same temperature as the air, not cold as it would be on the coast, but she didn't mind. It was red with mud, but when she moved back to the shallows, her wet body discovered a breeze and almost sang in pleasure.

'Beautiful,' she said.

Everyone laughed and looked away.

She sank into the warm water then and let its soupy depths take the weight of her tired body. It was like yielding to a lover, the way it enfolded her. She turned luxuriously on her back and gazed at the torrent of blue sky and floated for a while in wonder at this unexpected turn of the day. She turned again and buried her face in the consoling wet warmth and almost slept. When finally she stood up, small animals brushed softly against her feet and legs but she didn't care. She felt no fear. The water and the women would look after her. Afterwards she saw that the red mud had stained her clothes, but she didn't care if her entire wardrobe got stained like this. Even her cream trousers.

She drove back into the community when the moon was so high it had drowned the stars. She took the women and the old man to their house. They disappeared into the darkness carrying their fruit and medicine fronds without saying goodnight or thanking her, but by now she knew that was their way. Greetings and thanks are small talk.

Pat had cooked dinner for once. It was waiting on the table, covered with a freshly washed tea towel. Diana slumped in her chair. She couldn't find the energy to speak, but she lifted her fork and toyed with the food to please her friend.

'You've had a good time,' her friend observed.

'The conversation I came for,' said Diana.

The Dancer Talks

Magdalena had developed a squint. In a performer, a squint is unacceptable, especially when accompanied with a wrinkled forehead. Dancing, as everyone knows, should look effortless. In the new photographs, Nadina, the other woman in the little troupe of four, danced with an absorbed look of quiet ecstasy, not as if she was solving a tricky mathematical equation. Magdalena's forehead showed itself to be furrowed asymmetrically, and her whole face was taut with concentration, with wrinkles making thorns around her squinting eye. The two male partners smiled through the performance, one passionately, the other enigmatically. Only Magdalena made tango seem arduous.

'What were you thinking about?' her dance partner, Greg, demanded. He was carefully amiable, and had such an air of certainty about him, he'd become the troupe's leader, aided by his readiness to stake up money for the troupe's performances. The photography, for a start, cost a lot.

Magdalena was in her early forties, and everyone said she was self-effacing and shy, but that was because she secretly but constantly heard the swishing of heavily winged arch-angels behind her back thundering down, to banish her forever from the earth. She felt doomed to appease them. Sometimes they wore hobnailed boots. She'd been pleased when she found out what hobnails are, with the pleasure of a chronically ill patient at last being diagnosed, however dire the illness. None of the medieval artists had painted angels with hobnailed boots. She didn't know if other people daily awaited the angry angels. She kept her fear to herself. Not that, if pressed, she really believed in angels. But certainly she believed in imminent banishment from life as she knew it.

Despite such beliefs, she led a normal life, more or less. There are no police sent to round up people who live in secret terror.

Now, in the matter of her squint, she waited more tensely than ever for the end of her world.

'I'm sorry,' she said to Greg, to the troupe, hoping they wouldn't notice her anxious blinking.

Greg acknowledged her apology with a nod.

The photographer had to be paid for another round of pictures. This time, Magdalena concentrated on not squinting but she was laggardly in her timing when they danced, there was no other word for it; when Greg, several metres away, had bowed his head to her in invitation, she hadn't acknowledged him, as a woman should, and hadn't even declined him.

'I was distracted,' she said.

'Distracted? By?'

She had to admit it:

'I couldn't see your face.'

Greg was ten years younger. She was painfully aware of this. When they stepped sideways together, long-leggedly sliding up the entire beat to arrive, the moment was as sweetly stretched as toffee. But soon, she feared, he'd see her as too old. To put off the moment, she'd doubled her daily practice time, already gruelling. The trouble was, she'd had a wasted youth.

'I'm sorry,' she tried again. 'My eyes have gone strange.'

'It'll be a cataract,' he said. 'Blocks your sight. My mum had one. They can be taken out.'

He often mentioned his mum. He'd been the adored only son of a wealthy widow.

Magdalena began to hear the usual clang of boots.

'Get your eyes checked,' he said.

An order, but his tone was, as always, amiable.

The eye doctor found a tearing in one of her retinas, and extremely dense floaters, together a rare condition but not unknown. His practice had done three of these in the past five years, he assured her, and though he hadn't done one himself, he'd assisted in all three operations. He ordered surgery the very next day.

It was hard for her to assert herself, but there were Greg, Nadina and Esteban to think about.

'We have a performance booked,' she said before she'd asked if it'd hurt, or was likely to be successful, the way other patients did. 'How long is the down time?'

'Two weeks.' He was sternly raised, young, slender and nattily dressed in a navy suit, white shirt and navy bowtie, which he wore with the ease of a man who always dressed. His mother was an elegant English woman whom he'd never seen in a dressing gown, his father Chinese and perpetually in suits. As a little child, the only son, he'd seldom played with other children, and the few times he had, he remembered not as events but as flashes of bright light with an explosion of joyous laughter, as if he were looking into a party through a keyhole from a dark outside. His parents had been proud that he preferred his books. His mother didn't glance at the Australian children in the sandpit, coarse grey dirt sticking to their clothes. She didn't understand the beach culture of Australia, she said, with all that sand.

'It's a fortnight before our next show. We need every minute to work. The surgery will have to wait,' Magdalena said immediately.

Dancing was frippery, he'd always known that, probably his parents had told him, though surely no one would've mentioned such an unremarkable subject. There were many subjects that were unremarkable. Dancing certainly was not work; nevertheless, he demanded, as he always did with difficult patients:

'Which is more important, your work or your sight?'

He was pleased, behind his set lips, that he'd shown such tolerance.

She paused. His patients didn't normally pause. He saw with surprise that she wasn't one to capitulate to what he'd assumed was a truism beneath consideration. In her pause, another man would have said she was beautiful, her black hair swinging forward in thought, the light carving out her face. Not a conventional beauty, you wouldn't notice her in the street, her face was long, her nose bony and slightly askew, but as she leaned into his question, she charmed even him. He had never been captivated by his patients, never yet by any woman. He was married to his fixing of eyes. Now, in this disturbing moment, his fingertips brushed his desk, new, blond, shining, orderly, bought for him by his mother. A desk was for him an affirmation of what was good and true, and even messaged him so, its certainty insisting itself on his fingertips. He wasn't going to be charmed any further by, of all things, a dancer.

But as the pause lengthened, his suddenly errant mind saw her slender body sculpting shapes like the wind does in grass and trees, and a memory silenced him – one that hadn't emerged for years – of his grandmother's house, windswept, somewhere in China beside a grey sea; a storm about to break, the grasses longing to flee; he must've been very young, surrounded by tall grasses rippling around him.

Though he knew he should run back home, he was mesmerised by the black clouds and the frantic grasses lit up from behind and fluorescing yellow. Then rain came, sheeting like a cloak, and he relished the way it obscured him, as if he was running away. When at last his grandmother found him and took him home to a warm bath, she couldn't stop him babbling in excitement. She insisted they keep his adventure secret from his parents.

'My work,' she decided.

She was so urgent, intent, ardent. It made him unbend a little.

'What date is this performance?' He tried not to put inverted commas around performance. It was like humouring someone demented.

She told him.

'I can't let them down.'

That made sense to him. He understood about duty – if anyone knew about duty, he did.

'I suppose your problem won't get significantly worse till my next surgery day, two weeks away,' he said.

The intensity left her face; it was like the ocean ebbing. He wanted it back. She became, as he watched, like an ordinary stretch of damp fawn sand. He knew to look down at his desk.

'Two weeks and one day.' She smiled, assuming his agreement. 'The show's in Singapore' – it was their first overseas booking, and they were all proud of it – 'and I won't get a flight back till the next day,' she added. She was always worried she was taking up people's valuable time by explaining too much, and so she never explained enough. She also knew that this man in his navy suit would never know about the clubs where her troupe performed, would never drink, eat and chat till two in the morning when the dancing began.

'Two weeks and three days. I only operate on Tuesdays and Thursdays.'

Of all his university class, he'd never lost a patient to blindness, though probably his fellow students hadn't met this particular challenge.

'Thursday, in two and a half weeks,' he said. At least that'd give him time to send for the notes of the previous patients and pore over them. Afterwards, he'd be able to write it up, a feather in his cap. He'd been behind this year in publications.

He consulted the diary on his shining desk. He named the date, glad to be firmly in charge of this at least, a man with days accounted for. He didn't take holidays, and never slept in after the dawn light crept under his blind.

'Tell my secretary.' A secretary was a reassuring functionary without resonances of secret storms, who inscribed his orders in an old-fashioned notebook with old-fashioned, neat handwriting. These could be depended upon.

He stood to farewell Magdalena, as he did all patients. Annoyingly, as if his mind had danced away on a solo of its own, he noticed that she came up to his heart. But only to his shirt pocket, he argued back. Where he kept only a pen, always at the ready. He wasn't a man for cravats or flourishes, though he did allow himself the navy blue pen bought from a leather shop, by his mother, the same shade as the bowties he always wore. He liked the adjective, navy. It justified the suit, the bowtie and the pen. No other colour so justified.

∞

Magdalena suggested Greg should bring Janette, his girl-friend, into rehearsals.

'An understudy,' she said. 'Just in case.'

'Because of a squint?' Nadina was quick to be alarmed for Magdalena.

Greg was also frowning. 'You're talking as if we could lose you.'

'It's just that the show must go on,' she said.

They all nodded then. They'd heard this all their dancing lives. The show must go on. As if the show didn't involve people, their hearts, their fears and tragedies, as if a show were a thing with its own life, independent of them. Of course, the show must go on. It didn't matter who the particular dancers were. Though that wasn't true either. Was anything true?

The troupe knew that the show couldn't go on without Greg's money or Nadina's dancing. Nadina had perfect posture and balance, after a childhood of somersaults and circus training, and could stand on the ball of one foot for eight beats or more while her free leg tossed around in the air, as defiant as a feather, stretching time while you held your breath in wonder. Then she'd flip that free leg so you'd laugh aloud at her cheeky freedom. She was partnered by Esteban, her mustachioed Argentinian husband, who had such a handsomely carved face that Magdalena was always taken by surprise when he spoke, or pontificated, rather. Esteban believed that Argentina had not been adequately acknowledged in the world. He taught English and American literature in a local high school, to fund, he said, his aid to Argentina.

'Tango is the truest music in the world,' he'd say. Magdalena would wonder exactly what he meant, but never liked to interrupt.

Esteban made them all learn Spanish, the language of tango, and was fond of pointing out that even an English poet, Robert Browning, had said about the lovely name of a flower in Spanish:

I must learn Spanish one of these days,
Only for that slow sweet name's sake.

What was good enough for Browning should be good enough for them.

Esteban was the DJ, which gave him rights, he thought, to pause the music if they referred to the steps in English. So there was no turn, only a *giro*, no eight described on the floor by the woman's foot stretched like an arrow, only an *ocho*.

'*Eso*,' he said when they conformed. '*Perfecto.*'

Magdalena guessed that at home Nadina, despite her cheeky free leg, would be helpless against his handsome face.

Esteban didn't permit them to dance to any but the music of the golden era of tango. Often at their performances, he irrepressibly gave a little lecture about the composer. Greg, behind the curtain, fretted that the audience would become restless, but they always adored him. Magdalena imagined the fate of a small country were Esteban its Prime Minister; the adoring citizens would follow wherever he led; warfare, massacre, extinction.

The troupe were averaging one performance request every three months, and they were all proud of this. Magdalena felt that of everyone in the troupe, she was the one who wasn't necessary, and that, any moment, the archangels would strike and someone would say:

'Why is she with us?'

'We'll be throwing in our day jobs soon,' laughed Nadina, who worked in a shoe shop, which enticed Esteban to talk about the virtues of Spanish leather, and how Argentinian leather made the world's best shoes.

For the Singapore show, he'd chosen his favourite composer.

The troupe held Esteban in such esteem, they dare not, especially Nadina, mistake their Miguel Caló for their Piazzolla. Magdalena had won his lifetime approval by mentioning that Caló's music made her want live up to it.

But when Janette, unafraid of anything, asked her what she meant, all Magdalena could manage was, 'Oh, all the sadness. The heartbreak.' She herself saw such swirls of meaning around words, she couldn't quite pick and choose between them. She got up and demonstrated with her feet, humming as she moved.

'See the anguish?'

Her concentration was so deep, the humming came out a little tunelessly.

'A true dancer,' said Greg, who, as leader, felt he should be the mouthpiece of the troupe in all matters not to do with Argentina. 'Explaining by dancing.'

Everyone nodded.

'I have trouble finding Caló's beat,' said Greg. 'But of course, I do in the end,' he added, conceding to Esteban but managing to sound heroic as well.

'1907,' Esteban said, turning his chiselled face towards Greg, 'was when the greatest music was born.'

'What happened in 1907?' Greg asked.

'Caló fell to earth,' said Esteban.

Janette was in her twenties and much prettier than either Nadina or Magdalena, with a cute snub nose and shining blonde curls, which she'd dyed black to look more Latinate. Nadina told Magdalena that Janette still didn't have the look of a dancer.

'What's the look of a dancer?' Magdalena asked, worrying that she didn't either.

'Fonteyn,' said Nadina. 'Dark, foreign face, hair pulled tightly back as if nothing was going to distract her. Janette won't pull her curls back for anything, and as for that nose!'

Magdalena was fond of Nadina, so all she said was:

'I think it's a cute nose.'

'I think it's a nose job.'

'Luckily, I take Magdalena's size,' Nadina told the dress-maker. Greg liked them to have new dresses for a new show, or at least what looked like new dresses, sometimes saving the budget by recycling the old dresses but with sleeves added, or with slits.

'I'm just bigger around the bust,' Janette added. 'But it's a cowl neckline, so that's not going to be a problem.'

The three of them were in the girls' bathroom, trying on the bras that the new dressmaker had sewn into the bodices. She'd said the bras would improve the line of the dress.

'But they're not the line of my body,' said Nadina when the dressmaker had left. 'My breasts are shaped' – and she sketched a sideways hyperbola in the air – 'and the bra is shaped like an ice-cream cone.'

Magdalena, who regretted coming to dancing later than the others, had never ceased to marvel at the way dancers considered their bodies rather like the way her carpenter father considered a tool, something that, with enough skill, could create a heaven on earth.

'Have you had implants?' Nadina interrupted herself, gazing at Janette, who, stripped to her skimpy panties, was admiring her body in the mirror, as if it were a bauble.

'Your nipples stick out,' Nadina added. 'Implants make your nipples stick out.'

'I've always had big breasts,' said Janette. 'Are you saying my nipples are a problem?'

'You're perfect,' said Magdalena quickly.

But Nadina asked, cheeky as her free leg: 'Always? As a kid?'

Janette didn't notice the cheekiness.

'Always,' she said.

Magdalena changed the subject: 'It'll probably infuriate Anna' – this was their dressmaker – 'but I'm going to do this' – she ripped out her bra. 'They feel like falsies. I hate anything false.' In actual fact, she suspected the archangels would.

'I will too,' said Nadina. 'You and I won't flop.'

Janette didn't notice this either.

Janette was a more athletic dancer than either of them, doing such high kicks Nadina muttered that one day she'd knock off her own nose. In front of them all, she practised the splits, to free her hamstrings, she said, inching forward on her bottom till her crotch almost touched the mirror. Caressed it, thought Magdalena, while Greg watched, nodding.

It came to her that Janette relied on her athleticism when she danced – and that she didn't seem to commune with Greg.

Nadina, standing beside Magdalena, seemed to sense her thoughts, for she said quietly:

'Janette doesn't form a passionate connection.'

'Why, do you think?

'There's a wall of chatter in her mind,' said Nadina. 'About Janette.'

Esteban put it another way.

'It's Magdalena who finds the spirit of the music,' he pronounced late one night after a performance. They were having a glass of wine, just one, all Greg would allow them, because he said, as dancers, they had to live like athletes. 'In fact, she is the spirit of the music.'

'My shyness gets in the way,' said Magdalena, unwilling to own this grandeur.

'Not at all,' said Esteban. 'It's what art does. It takes your weaknesses and uses them.'

'The way of what?' asked Greg of her.

'Caló,' was all Magdalena could think of to say.

'Her brain is in her feet,' Esteban reminded them.

Magdalena knew that from a dancer, this was a compliment, especially since Nadina squeezed her hand proudly.

But Greg was uncomfortable around talk of art.

'Come off it, mate, we're only dancing,' he said.

Esteban was never bested.

'Ironic, isn't it?'

Magdalena often idly wished she had Greg's self-belief. If she was with him, would his self-belief rub off on her, would she be surer of herself, and be able to banish the archangels?

Is that why they tormented her – because she was so unsure of herself?

Magdalena had come to dancing in an odd way – but then, she came to most things oddly, and knew this, and would've been embarrassed to explain herself to anyone, not that anyone asked. It can happen that way if your starting assumption is imminent banishment. Throughout her twenties, Magdalena had had too many men. She had lived alone, without family, and with very few friends. Apart from in her jobs – so far, dead-end jobs in shops – she'd made few acquaintances. She'd meet a man – anywhere – in the street, on a bus, in a shop. Because she was small and slender, almost pretty, obviously vulnerable and with downcast eyes, the man, if so inclined, and many were, would take his chances and begin to flirt with her, in case this day he hit it lucky. She liked sex, which isn't exactly true, as she was always disappointed and seldom reached orgasm, but she was excited by the hope of sex. She liked it that, before sex, the man's eyes went dreamy, as if he loved her, and after sex, there was the hope at least of being held for a while. She knew what she really yearned for was love, oh how her whole being yearned. In her loneliness, she'd ask herself how could one ever predict the end from the most unlikely beginnings? Wasn't it better to have a beginning, any beginning at all, just in case? So you have hope? Because she asked such abstractions into a vast silence, Magdalena had become a slut.

There would've been no way out of this but less attractive age or incapacitating illness, except that Magdalena discovered dance. As long as she possessed money for her lessons, she had somewhere to go that was lit and crowded with what passed as companionship. People nodded at her, made room for her at their tables, danced with her.

Esteban's pronouncements often had their kernel of truth, she mused. Because of her anxiety to please anyone at all, she'd spent her childhood and youth listening to people while guessing their thoughts. In fact, in every passing conversation, two lines of thought would be going on for her – the conversation in the air, and the other in her head.

'What did he imply by this?' she'd ask herself. 'What brought her to believe that?'

Since tango is an extemporised dance, in which neither of the partners knows where the music will take the leader, communing is essential, but not common. So Magdalena was considered by many of her partners to be something of a mind reader.

Once Magdalena had become competent in the demanding posture, basic steps and sequences of tango, she'd go to social nights and find to her astonished relief that she could dance with any competent partner as if they were no longer two people but had become only one, a four-legged beast joined at the heart, their arms in the embrace of lovers while they breathed together and thought the one thought. Occasionally, once she'd learned how to balance one-legged, her free leg, which for the length of the dance belonged to him, would apparently disobey him, but only to tease, to float and toss and weave patterns in the air, to say: *You'll have to wait till I come to earth. I'll do what you want, perhaps, but only when I choose.* And then it would become his again, surrendering.

∞

One day, Nadina, after some or other domestic tension, complained about the way women in tango always had to accept the man as the leader.

'Tango's caught in a time warp,' she said.

'It reflects Argentina's history,' said Esteban, deeply offended.

'It's good to acknowledge history,' said Magdalena because she wanted to smooth things over for Nadina, and she'd been struggling towards a concept in her head. She often felt like that, as if her mind was a dog sleeping in front of a fire, but her owner would come home and her mind would stir and leap up, barking.

The troupe gazed at her in surprise. 'We shouldn't modernise everything,' she went on. 'We'll blur over where we came from.'

Greg kissed her hand with a warmth that surprised her. 'I couldn't have put it better myself.'

∞

In the old days, she'd fall in love with each different partner, any partner at all, as long as he could move together with her and the gusts of violins and the anguish of the singer. Always the songs were about disappointed love. She'd be infatuated ten, twenty times a night, broken-hearted ten, twenty times a night, when afterwards she and her partner would disentangle themselves and walk to their separate seats, one ordinary, clumsy step after another, only awkwardly human after all. They'd sit apart in silence, awaiting the next moment of wild joy, hoping it would come again, this night, this lifetime.

One night a classmate, himself a competent dancer and deeply moved by her communing, came to sit beside her afterwards, and crept his arm around her shoulders.

'A kiss?' he murmured.

The music had long ago faded. There was only the jaggedness of chatter and a warm glass of water in her hand, with a disintegrating slice of lemon in it. For a moment her old life beckoned. It would've been so easy now that his face was nearing hers, his head tipped. But tango gave her the words of their teacher.

'All we were doing was dancing, 'she said. His head paused in its advance. It withdrew. His arm fell behind her.

'I've been inappropriate,' he said, looking down, chastened.

She was chastened too, for she felt responsible for everything that went wrong, including this stranger's temptation.

She repeated the teacher's mantra, as if to a child.

'The dancer is not the dance.'

'Of course not.'

In the plaintive music, which he felt to be as broken as he was, he'd forgotten that.

She laughed then, gently, because she felt she understood him.

'The music makes us feel we've at last found something we've needed for a long time,' she said.

They were silent for a while.

He indicated the dance floor again filled with embracing couples while violins sighed their heartbroken songs, 'This isn't the way one normally behaves with a stranger.'

She nodded. She longed to tell him her history, and how the music articulated the tumult she couldn't quite say, but she knew she must wait to tell him, that telling this, telling anything was too intimate. She'd like to tell him, one day. Perhaps, after all, he was the one she waited for.

But at that very moment, while she struggled for words, it came to him that she was too plain, her nose was too bony, her smile too sombre. In total, she was too intense, and he'd mistaken it as desire for him.

He left the tango hall soon after, and she never saw him again.

Magdalena suspected that her communing ways were why she'd been chosen for the troupe. But would it continue to be enough? Communing came so naturally to her that it didn't seem like a talent at all, and so she waited, as usual, for them to reject her. It was only a matter of time. Till then, she made the best of it. The passionate connection, as Nadina put it, was for all dancers a pose, but underneath there was a truth – that they were acknowledging together how tender are the possibilities with another human. She assumed Greg felt like this too, but she didn't know how to ask him.

She also knew, like any dancer knows, that the tango look was a culmination of simple, measurable physical things, such as the way she leaned her heart on his weightlessly, the way he rotated his chest from his hips upwards as smoothly as water swirling around stones in a creek, with her heart riding on it and her legs following his heart, his foot occasionally kicking up behind him in apparent exultation, while her stretched foot painted poignant patterns on the floor because she was grateful to it, the floor, the way it held her, how she loved the consoling way the floor nursed her foot when it finally landed.

As they rehearsed, Magdalena realised all over again it was going to be a wrench when she finally lost Greg to Janette, for no previous partner had moved with her like this. Once Janette took over, there'd be no more troupe for her, and she'd be alone in dance halls, and at risk again.

✂

Magdalena received an unexpected call three days before the Singapore performance and then the surgery, at home in her tiny apartment. She had been meditating, which she always did before shows. It was important she lose her self-consciousness, her sense of existential wrong-doing. Besides, Esteban had choreographed an unusual routine, and her memory of a particular sequence kept failing. Usually her memory wasn't required, for Greg danced a consummate lead and she sensed his every move almost before he even knew it himself, but this time Esteban required sequences that weren't led.

It was her brother's voice.

'Cheryl?'

It was the name she'd been born with. Magdalena was the name she'd adopted to forget her old life. Her heart always sank at the sound of Cheryl because Cheryl tethered her to self-destruction.

She hadn't spoken to her brother in years. He was a rich businessman with a wife almost identical to their other brothers' wives – blondes with high cheek bones. They all seemed to say the same things. Jim's wife had even said in her company that she didn't know what to say to Cheryl, and Jim wasn't able to tell her for he'd never known either, even when they were children sucking green ice blocks outside the corner shop and licking up sticky drips from their hands. Her mind had always seemed somewhere else.

'I'm ringing about your operation,' Jim said.

She'd been soaking her feet in a mixture of witch hazel and warm water, to clean and soften the skin, so it'd seem less wrinkled. Another sign of age. She'd had to step across the carpet to reach her mobile. Her wet footprints had made tracks on the grey carpet, like an explorer's footsteps in the desert. But she lived by herself, and there was no one to complain.

'I've had the same,' Jim said. When she was quiet, he prompted: 'Operation. I heard you were having it.'

'The same,' she repeated. She and her siblings had nothing in common. Only strands of DNA and of memories.

He began to talk about himself and his operation, relishing the details. How difficult, how delicate. He always had been one eager to talk about himself, especially into the silence that was his sister.

'We seem the only ones who got the germ. The mutation. It must've been a mutation.'

She'd asked the young doctor in the navy suit what had caused the eye problem. He hadn't known.

'So I'm saying, it's genetic,' said Jim. She wasn't sure what he expected of her, with their sharing of this mutation. It wouldn't give her more to say to him, she reflected. She walked back with the phone to her dish of warm water, but it had cooled.

'May I just put the jug on?' she asked, not thinking about the expense for his phone while he waited.

She didn't stay for his answer, just padded to the kitchen, filled the jug, turned it on.

She couldn't hear his voice above the noise of the jug.

When she could hear, he'd rung off.

She wondered if she should call back, but didn't. She was trying not to think about the operation. She poured the jug into her dish. She laid the mobile on the sofa beside her. This time when it rang, she didn't lift her feet out.

'I thought you'd be glad to know, you can survive it.' He laughed.

'I'm glad you're fine now.' She added, trying for a laugh: 'So it's not dangerous?'

'I had the best doctor.' He named a doctor. 'You should use him.'

'I trust mine,' she said.

'Your sight matters,' he said. 'Go with the best.'

She had a moment of panic until she remembered Jim always believed that whatever he'd chosen to do was the best, and whomever he'd chosen to do it with.

She changed the subject to asking how he'd found out about her operation. It turned out that the connection was the photographer, the one who'd complained about her squint. Jim owned a successful real estate business, and the glamorous houses he sold needed photographers who emphasised grandeur.

'Do you want my doctor's name?'

She thanked him, but no. She was a little in love with her own, though she didn't tell Jim this.

'Ring me when it's over,' he said.

When he rang off, she had her first moment of terror.

If it's true that in the moments of drowning, you review your life, Magdalena in those next few days before the operation became a drowning woman. She didn't know where the last ten years had gone, except into the dance. Dance had taken up all her time, her hope of a settled, domestic life, a family, a career. Tango wouldn't always last, couldn't, not for a woman, old men don't invite old women to dance, she'd always seen that, but she'd committed herself to the dance when she was still young enough to believe she'd never get old, not this old, not old enough for her eyes to fail. What is old age, she suddenly had to ask herself, but the body dying, part by part, the body that had brought her this salvation?

The only person Magdalena usually talked to was Rashmi. For her day job she now wrote instructions for an online publishing company website. Greg, a computer programmer, had helped her get it. After her waitressing and dress shop jobs, a friend of Greg's needed assistance and was willing to overlook her lack of formal qualifications because he didn't have to pay her so much. She was required to answer authors' questions about their digitised manuscripts. It was anxious work, for while she was fine with some questions, she didn't know the answers to technical ones, and relied entirely on the advice of Rashmi, the digitising expert in India. They talked every day on Skype, and only Rashmi knew how much help Magdalena needed. Rashmi never seemed to mind, and often showed her photos of her little daughters, the matching dresses an aunt had made, the ringlets she'd put in their hair. Magdalena enjoyed this but shared nothing about her own life. She didn't even mention she'd be absent from work, for fear she'd burst into tears and that would be difficult for Rashmi.

So that last afternoon, before Singapore and before the operation, they simply said goodbye as always. When the Skype call clicked off, Magdalena stared for a while at the blank screen. She thought: If I die under the knife, she'll never know who I was.

Afterwards, she didn't remember much about the flight from Sydney with the troupe, the hotel in Singapore, or the city itself because of her fear. But in the performance, all that filled her was the music, though she'd heard it a thousand times, every time they'd rehearsed. Sometimes, as they moved together she wondered where she ended or where Greg began, what was feminine or masculine, who was the leader and who the follower – at which point in space was that boundary since their bodies and minds had melted into one? Dancing with him in that performance was a damp, mossy, cushiony dark fern-like swaying, as if they were beings other than human.

In the last embrace, his head bowed against hers, holding the pose for five seconds before he straightened and gently set her down, in that moment, a thought came to her, almost bulged all the way down from her head and through her body: *This is the only world where I am myself.*

They all slept in the next day, the girls in one room, the boys in another. She wondered why Janette hadn't shared a bed with Greg as planned, but didn't comment. Only Magdalena was going home, and Nadina soon after to pick her up from the hospital: the others were going to stay in the city for a few days, being tourists. Greg had been invited to teach men's classes and Janette would accompany him. Janette couldn't hide her excitement as she fussed over what dress to wear, and whether she'd wear the blue suede shoes or the black patent, trying, Magdalena noticed, not to gloat over this lucky turn of events.

'Oh, it'll be nothing like your triumph last night,' she said to Magdalena over and over.

Greg insisted on accompanying Magdalena to the airport. They rode in a rocking train, and he took her hand. She couldn't explain this to herself, until he asked:

'Are you frightened?'

And she'd answered:

'I won't worry till the moment I walk into the hospital.'

She felt him exhale a deep breath.

It was another of their maxims about performing: put off the worry till it's over. They all did. But this time it wasn't true.

He changed the subject:

'Who's taking you there?'

She blinked in surprise, and pointed out that the hospital was a short taxi ride from her apartment, and she could get there as easily as she could the day she first went to the surgeon.

Greg was unsurprised at her answer. 'I wish Janette was as independent as you,' he said.

'She has other qualities.'

In a way, in the face of the drama of her operation, the doings of her ordinary life seemed so simple. She suddenly wondered why she'd always found them worrying. Why, all she'd needed to do, she now thought, had been to be happy. How simple it all could have been!

'No one dances like you in the whole world,' Greg blurted unexpectedly. 'If things were different, I'd ask you to marry me.'

He smiled ruefully. She didn't.

'There's a complication,' he said.

'If things were different,' she repeated in a murmur. They said little else, but he kept holding her hand.

He held her against his body for a long moment as they said goodbye, the way they always held each other as they danced. Even longer. This was unexpected too.

She also remembered little about the surgery, except that she seemed to swim into consciousness several times, as if she'd dived into a pearly lagoon and was rising occasionally to break the shining stillness of its surface. At one moment, she heard a doctor or nurse exclaim over her vitreous fluid, how packed it was with floaters.

Her surgeon replied:

'They are meaningless.'

And Magdalena wanted to exclaim: 'But they might be the end of my dancing!'

Of course she didn't, because her mind was diving again into the pearly lagoon.

Afterwards, she remembered the comforting presence of Nadina holding her, Nadina nodding as the clinic people told her to ring immediately if there was any sign of trouble.

'What sign of trouble could there be?' Nadina asked.

'Severe pain,' the nurse said.

Magdalena wondered what severe meant, but didn't like to bother anyone with the question.

Nadina had arranged a roster of tango friends to stay with her for those first days. There was a sequence of different touches, soft touches, and gentle voices. Magdalena, without a contact lens in her good eye, had always had poor vision, but enough to see shapes and colours. She was not up to putting a lens in her good eye now and she didn't like to ask anyone's help.

It was on the fourth day that Nadina's roster failed. It happened, as these things often do, on a Sunday. Someone thought someone else was taking a shift with Magdalena, and Magdalena didn't like to ring Nadina when the friend failed to turn up, even though Nadina had lovingly inscribed her mobile number in huge letters on a bit of paper on the fridge door, and underneath it, the doctor's emergency number. As luck would have it, or perhaps fate, an ache that could've been called severe started above Magdalena's right eyebrow. Magdalena was determined not to panic. She stumbled to the fridge door and, though she didn't like to worry Nadina, by all manner of squinting she made out the doctor's number.

But then she remembered it was a Sunday. Magdalena felt she couldn't ring the emergency number on a Sunday only because of a headache. Why, people had headaches all the time. The pain got worse in early evening, but still she didn't ring. Ringing on a Sunday evening was worse than ringing on a Sunday.

The weight of the pain was exhausting. When she woke, the flat was dark but someone had left the radio beside her, so she switched it on. There was music playing, and the combination of music and pain made her doze off again. She woke again to the fanfare of a news broadcast and still she waited for the time to be announced: ten thirty. Could she ring a doctor at ten thirty on Sunday evening, if she couldn't ring him in the afternoon? Shouldn't she sleep now, and if the headache continued in the morning, ring him then on a proper working day, on a Monday?

This madness would've continued but suddenly her phone rang. It was Greg.

'I'm sorry if I woke you,' he began and then they both said together:

'Is everything all right?'

'That's what I was ringing about,' he said. His voice seemed high and tight. 'I had a feeling – probably silly – of dread. As if you were calling me . . .'

There was a long silence, so that Greg kept saying: 'Are you there? Are you there?' In that silence, Magdalena, who'd never imagined that Greg would commune in ordinary life, wanted to cry, except that somehow her headache wouldn't allow it. So she told him about the pain.

'It's like a warm animal shifting around in my head.'

Telling him that seemed to cross some boundary. All she'd ever done was move with him, and never in all that time had she talked about her feelings.

He made a sound of surprise, for talk about having animals in the head made her seem like someone who could listen to the strangeness that he feared was inside him.

'It's one thing to be independent, but I'll get Nadina to ring your doctor,' he said. 'I doubt he'll be happy about this warm animal.'

Her doctor rang within minutes.

'Come immediately,' he said. 'You must not wait. Why did you wait so long?'

Of course she took this to mean he was angry because she'd woken him, and she apologised for the late hour.

She got herself into the apartment lift by feeling her way along the walls, and pressing every number of every floor until she reached the ground floor, and stumbled out into the street, which seemed full of flashing lights. Her phone rang but she assumed it was Greg and promised herself she'd ring him as soon as this nightmare was over. She put up her hand every time she heard the noise of an approaching shape, and soon one appeared with a blur of light on its roof. She gave the address of the surgery, for that had been emblazoned on her memory since she'd first gone to the doctor.

The taxi pulled up at the row of buildings. A shape was hovering there. The shape came over.

'Come in, come in,' her doctor's voice said, leaning in her window. 'Where's your carer?'

'I can't pay the driver,' she said.

She showed him her wallet and he picked out the right note, paid the driver and helped her out.

'I came alone,' she said, expecting a reprimand.

There was none.

She tried to glance at him, but she could only see a shape.

He said nothing, but as he ushered her inside, he explained that the pain was caused by pressure inside her eye, and if the pressure was high for too long a time, the eye would go blind.

'Has it been too long?'

'We'll see,' was all he said.

He led her to his room, sat her down, put drops in her eye, waited, then tested it.

'The pressure is very high,' he said.

'Can you save my sight?'

He said nothing, tipped her face back and put more drops in her eye, waited, put more drops, waited, put more drops.

'We'll try,' he said. 'But the structures of your eye are tight. You do a lot of exercise?'

'I dance,' she reminded him, reminded herself.

'Of course, the dance. There's not much . . .' He hunted for an ordinary phrase. 'Not much room in your eye. So you are at risk.'

He let her face drop. He paced around the room and fiddled with files. They waited. The minutes did not merely creep by, they seemed to stop. She tried to distract herself by thinking of Singapore and the performance, and then of Greg, but there was only a blank where her thoughts should be.

He tested her eye again. She could see little of his face, but because she was used to communing, she sensed that his anxiety matched hers.

'Is the pressure coming down?' she asked.

'If it's going to, it'll take its time.'

He made her sit there for another half hour and wandered in and out of the room. There was a clock ticking some-where, measuring her terror, perhaps their shared terror. The ticking faded when he left the room, and she realised that it must've been the sound of his watch.

Eventually he tested her again.

'Is it coming down now?'

'A little,' he said. There was no relief in his voice. 'But it may shoot up again.'

'What will I do?'

He bundled up four bottles of drops, all with different coloured labels, and wrote down in huge letters how often she should take them through the rest of the night.

'Can you read that?'

'No, but say it again. I'll remember it.'

He went over it several times, with her repeating it.

'You must do exactly what I say. Go home and sleep now. You must relax. I won't give you a sleeping pill because you might sleep on the wrong side. I operated on your right eye so you must sleep on your left.'

She didn't think the nurse had told them this, but she so didn't like to say so in case it sounded like an accusation.

She tried to think about him, rather than her fear. There was a blur of brown in front of her eyes. Perhaps he wore a brown suit at night. He was altogether too formal to wear pyjamas at any time.

She said: 'Do you ever sleep? It's as if you never stop working. I hope you sleep nearby.'

They were both standing, her glossy head level again with his breast pocket, now without its pen.

She managed again:

'Why—do you care so much about a total stranger?' She was waving her hands in the air, to take the place of words.

She watched his brown blur rise to its full height, an almost military drawing up.

'I am,' he said, 'a retinal surgeon.'

Between them, there seemed nothing more to say.

'Thank you,' she said, holding her hand out in front of her.

He was surprised at how smooth a hand could be, like, he imagined, holding a downy bird with fragile bones.

'Call me if the headache doesn't go,' he said. He led her out of the surgery and opened the street door. 'Tell me immediately, this time. Any hour. I'll get you a taxi.'

He propped the door open, leant her against the building as if she were a doll, crossed the footpath and hailed an approaching light.

'Lucky,' he said.

He opened the back door of the taxi, shut it when she was safely inside, and waited till she'd given the driver her address.

She gave the doctor her wallet again, and he leaned in towards the driver, and pre-paid him, including a tip.

'Please escort her right to her front door,' he said in his clipped voice. 'She cannot see, and falling could blind her.'

The driver kindly helped her open her apartment door, and reached his hand inside to switch on the light.

'It's no problem, no problem,' he kept saying. Magdalena was astounded that he should bother.

At twelve thirty a.m., the headache hadn't abated. Should she have more of his drops? How much more? Should she ring him? He'd given her his mobile but how could she see it? Your sight is at stake, she thought and the chill came over her.

Then the phone rang.

'Cheryl? Doctor Liu. How is the headache?'

Again, the difficulty of words. She tried to describe the animal in her head, the way she'd described it to Greg. She blushed. She wished she could see things in the way other people seemed to. Her description didn't make much sense to him. An animal inside the head? He wanted a number out of ten to rate the pain. She couldn't tell him that, her mind didn't seem to work anymore. He brought the discussion onto more reliable ground.

'Not better?'

'I don't think so.' She wanted to please him, but her sight was at stake.

'Not worse?'

'No.'

'We may have stabilised it.'

They both made a sound that could be described as a sob of relief.

'Take more drops. Have you got someone to give them to you?'

'No.'

He sighed. This case was proving to be far more difficult than he'd imagined.

'Then I'll talk you through it.' And step by step, while she obeyed, he instructed her how to angle her head, how to hold the little bottles, how to squeeze the tear ducts, how to keep her head back afterwards.

'Okay?'

She couldn't say yes, not this time, despite not wanting to be a nuisance.

'What if I've given myself just half a drop?'

'Did your eye feel full of liquid when you took them just now?'

'I think so.'

She couldn't trust any apparent certainty.

'Then the pressure will start to go down soon.'

'How will I know?'

'The headache will ease.'

'That's the measure?'

'That's the measure. Lie down and sleep now.'

She lay down on the sofa as soon as he rang off, forgetting for the first time in her life to be grateful.

She woke at three a.m., the headache still so insistent the small animal inside her forehead was now shuddering. Should she take more drops? Had she been truthful when she'd said her eye felt full of liquid? Had she just wanted to please him?

The phone rang.

'Cheryl—Doctor Liu. How's the headache?'

She had to admit it.

'The same.'

She worried that it sounded like a complaint.

'Take more drops. The same way. Do you want me to tell you how to do it again?'

'Yes.'

'Do it while I talk you through it.'

She obeyed. Slowly, one by one, the drops were administered.

'Lie down now and go to sleep.'

Like a child, she obeyed again and slept.

At dawn, she woke alerted by a sudden stillness inside her head. It was as if the animal had left, padding back to the cave where it belonged.

She slept again, and woke in bright sunlight to the phone ringing.

'Cheryl, has the headache gone?'

She was unable to keep the joyful sunlight out of her voice.

'Completely!'

'Ring me if it comes back.'

'Anytime?'

'Anytime. This is important.'

Despite himself, he shouted:

'We've saved your sight!'

At nine in the morning, he rang again.

'Cheryl—How's the pain?'

'It's gone.'

She was beginning to like the sound of her own name, the soft way he said it.

'Good. I want you to get a relative to sit with you. A cousin, a sister.'

'I live alone.'

'You must not fall. Find a neighbour, anyone.'

'I'm a dancer, I don't fall.'

'At the moment, you might.'

She always said later that she meant to ring Nadina to tell her that she was alone, but Greg rang again.

Later, she considered why, in tango, the woman always seems to be about to fall but it's an artifice; in reality, she's completely balanced by her own strength. Magdalena had seemed about to fall ten thousand times. Her partner on the dance floor always seemed to catch her. It was just a pose.

When she heard Greg's voice, she was unusually assertive.

'Greg! Could you come and sit with me? I must not fall.'

He said without a pause:

'I knew it. I'm leaving for the airport right now.'

'Oh – I didn't realise – you're still in Singapore?'

He'd already rung off.

When she woke, it was dark again. There was a line of light under the bedroom door, a light on in the kitchen. She stumbled out. Nadina was making dinner and told her to go back to bed.

'I'm filling in till Greg gets here. Why didn't you tell me you were in trouble?'

'I didn't know I was,' said Magdalena, holding on to the bench. Somehow she couldn't summon up the energy to apologise. There had always been so many apologies inside her and they'd never required energy to slide out before.

'Why are you all so kind?' she managed to ask.

'You just need to ask for help,' said Nadina.

'Help,' said Magdalena.

Nadina led her back to bed so gently.

The next thing she was aware of was Greg's face bending near hers, peering at her. He was sitting on her bed, making a dip in it. He seemed glossy with airports and importance.

'You're awake,' he said. 'I've been longing for you to wake up. I have something to tell you.'

She fought her way through a fog in her head, in the room.

'I'm so hungry,' she said. The dip in the bed was making her fall towards it.

'Nadina left dinner for you.' He passed a plate over from the bedside table. 'Want me to feed you?'

She grabbed the food with her fingers, unable to do anything but behave like an animal, like the animal that had been in her head.

'I've broken it off with Janette.' Greg was talking as if she were of sound mind. 'On the train I mentioned a complication. I'd made a promise to her mother.'

'Don't sit up,' he interrupted himself because she was doing just that so that she could swallow. Her hand was sticky with gravy, but she didn't know how to tell him.

'I'm not going to keep that promise. I want to marry you.'

All she could do was wipe her hand surreptitiously on the sheet.

'Could you make me a cup of tea?' she asked after a pause.

'Oh—' and he was off, clattering in the kitchen. He imagined that she wanted time to think. She knew he'd think that.

But in those few minutes, she couldn't think. Later, she remembered that her mind seemed to be looking at white sheets stretched out on a washing line, like the sheets

Nadina had tucked her into. Stretched rectangles of white-ness. Like a long side step when your body makes the beat never end, time never end. She just existed between beats. Think, she commanded herself: Consider. But there seemed nothing to consider.

Greg returned with a rattling tray.

'I remembered you like sugar,' he said, pleased with himself.

She murmured a thanks. She never took sugar.

'When you flew out of Singapore, it was as if the bottom dropped out of everything,' he said. 'The spirit. When we're dancing together, you take me deeper than anyone ever has. I glimpse depths in myself, depths that I had when I was a child, that I've lost. You give me back my real self.'

He stirred his own tea. He always had two teaspoons of sugar, always stirred ringingly to emphasise his thoughts.

'That's why I was frightened about this. I thought, if I lose you, I'll lose that, and I might never find it again. The only way out is to marry you. So I'll never lose it at all. Do you see?'

The stretched sheets of whiteness.

'That last dance showed me how deeply I felt for you,' he said, himself stumbling now, because she wasn't helping at all.

She wanted to murmur that it was the dance, not the dancer, but it took too much effort.

A word came up out of the depths.

'Caló,' she reminded him.

'I know. It was Caló who made me realise this. Because of Caló, I've come a long way. And you, of course.'

She realised he meant emotionally a long way, not the distance from Singapore to Sydney. She was quite proud to have made this deduction. Perhaps her mind was returning. They sipped their tea. She liked an ice block in hers to cool it down, but asking seemed impossibly difficult.

'I've always had that feeling with you but I didn't realise it till this happened,' Greg's voice was going on. She might've fallen asleep during a pause, but he didn't seem to notice.

'I got you into the troupe, you know, because I wanted that feeling when I dance with you. You can thank me for your inclusion.'

He took a gulp.

She thought a thank you was demanded, but couldn't manage more than a nod.

'This last performance, the last song, the feeling took over me, so strongly, it was . . .' He was lost for words. 'And then, you abandoned me to go to hospital—'

'Abandoned?' she repeated, knowing something was expected of her and pleased that at least she could repeat the sound.

'I lost my mum like that, under the knife.'

Understanding shot through her like a torchlight, that this was the proposal she'd imagined she'd wanted, in what seemed an aeon ago.

They drank their tea in silence. Magdalena noticed there were little sluicings and burbles from behind his lips, so she could imagine the silver saliva bubbling between his teeth around the pink gums. She'd have liked him to open his mouth so she could see this interesting sight, but of course, even if she asked, she would be able to see very little at all.

'Should I leave you to think about it?' The gloss of importance had fallen off him.

She reached out and held his hand.

'Me,' she managed. 'Not me.'

He paused.

'I thought you had feelings for me . . .'

She managed a whole sentence:

'I love dancing with you.'

'But not being with me?'

'It's the dance.'

'Are you saying no?'

'Yes. No.'

There was no ambiguity in her voice. He knew her well, of that he was sure. The only thing she was sure of, was that he seemed blind. Perhaps he'd always been blind.

He rose, defeated, as he'd seldom ever been, except when his mother had died.

Then anger came, and rescued him.

'It's your damned independence. Look at you – it nearly cost you your sight. You couldn't bear being dependent on a man.'

She paused and inclined her head up and down what she hoped might be a nod and in indecent haste fell back to sleep.

She never knew when Greg left.

In the next fortnight, if Greg had quizzed her on who she'd prefer to him, Magdalena would've nominated the surgeon. Not only did the surgeon prove to have no interest in her, just in her retina, but, as she recovered her sight, she realised that that was the only interest they had in common, and that interest was fading. She seemed to have no attraction to or for anyone else.

Magdalena recovered her sight, but she left the troupe because Greg had immediately married Janette and Janette insisted he partner her. Magdalena kept dancing and didn't go back to her old ruinous ways. Instead she sat in dance halls and began to talk to other women between dances. She didn't quite know why, except that Nadina had shown such kindness, and perhaps more people were kind than she'd thought. It was difficult at first, like learning to tango. She dropped in at Nadina's shop when her boss was out and they tried on the most expensive shoes. They found out that they both had uneven feet, so they both needed shoe sizes 6 and 7; while Nadina needed a size 6 on her left foot and a size 7 on her right, Magdalena's sizes were the other way round.

'Why didn't we notice this before?' said Magdalena.

'We're made for our friendship,' Nadine said. For her lunch break, they sat on a nearby park bench, eating sandwiches and sharing a soft drink.

'We're all missing you,' Nadina said. 'No one's like you.'

Magdalena threw a crust to a seagull.

She said she didn't know what Nadina meant.

'Exactly,' said Nadina.

At work, Magdalena made herself tell Rashmi why she'd been absent.

'Why didn't you tell me this before?' Rashmi said. 'I thought we were friends.'

Magdalena heard her distress.

'I'm sorry. Can I make up for it now?' she asked.

After that, there was less work done, or maybe it still got done. No one complained.

In a year, Janette had left Greg for another dancer, and the troupe insisted Magdalena return.

'I made a mistake,' Greg said, apologetically.

She would've thought coming back to the troupe was the answer to all her hopes, but something more important had happened, something immense that changed everything. She wasn't entirely sure when it happened, for you don't always know when these things come, and certainly you don't know why, but one dawn you wake up and you realise that you're lighter, easier, you're untied somehow, you walk out into the kitchen for a drink of water and you lean on the sink, cold against your sleepy nightie, and watch the plummet of silver water from the tap, and as I do that I suddenly realise that sometime recently the archangels have flown away, without even a tremble of air, and now I know they will never come back to me.

The Last Taxi Away
From Here

I must admit it now, I tell myself, as I ride in the back
seat of a taxi to my friend's apartment: I came to this
city for love.

I had no right to the yearning. I'd known forever that
my dull life was my own fault for gazing out the window
in school rather than concentrating on what my teachers
were saying. I was always being accused of daydreaming,
which was true, though what the daydreams were about,
I couldn't have said, even then, except that I was impatient
with ordinary things, as if I wasn't ordinary. Oh, I knew
my life was ordinary, my looks were ordinary, and clearly,
judging by the way my teachers viewed me, my mind
was as well – though I wasn't really convinced, and that
was the problem. I felt everyone was ignoring something
mysterious and incandescent that slipped behind the
shadows and under the surfaces. If they knew it was there,

they pretended it wasn't. To me, anyway. If they knew this secret, they hadn't bothered to tell me.

My home life seemed mired in the practical. My father owned a milk bar, where I had to serve behind the counter and worry about getting the change right. However, when he died, my brother inherited it and made it into a restaurant, where I became the kitchen hand. Then he was suddenly killed in a car accident and I inherited it, along with his half-grown children. Ironically, for all my daydreams, I had no choice but to become a practical person.

I loved the children, and despite me the restaurant prospered; I should've been reconciled to my lot.

But I wasn't. I secretly wanted more. I came to think of it as the wanting that you feel when a piece of music ends and something seems left out. The notes end in mid-air, lopped off. And because they're not finished, you have a hole inside you. A hole in your soul.

I never knew how to ask people what they did about this hole. At the restaurant, we talked about how to make a custard fragrant – I'm very knowing on this matter – or the best method for mussel soup – I'm an expert on this too – and at home, children, even when they're grown up, need cossetting and comforting, and there's no time for thought.

Next door to my restaurant was a public library that had a foreboding school-day air, but one morning, especially needy, I passed through the doors – and stopped in my tracks. Thousands of books glared at me. A librarian smiled up at me from her desk. She was one of my regulars, unwisely partial to deep fried seafood and cheesecake. 'What are you looking for?' she asked. A name from school popped into my head: Shakespeare. Hot with foreboding, I followed the clipping of her heavily laden shoes to a whole cabinet of shelves. I wished she'd leave me there, so I could sneak out the EXIT. But she smelled my desperation. 'Here's his cure for unrequited love,' she said, as if she thought I needed that. She reached for a book, flipped it open, and read aloud in a high voice:

'*"Why, what would you?"*' That's one lovelorn character needing advice about winning a heart,' she explained. 'And the other replies' – and now she was reciting but in her normal voice though suddenly more passionate:

> *Make me a willow cabin at your gate*
> *And call upon my soul within the house . . .*
> *Halloo your name to the reverberate hills*
> *And make the babbling gossip of the air*
> *Cry out 'Olivia!' Oh, you should not rest*
> *But you should pity me.*

A man jumped to his feet, a blush crept from her neck up her face, and they gazed at each other. I fled.

I tried church, but the faces of the congregation and the priests were round with silent satisfaction. At three o'clock in the morning in my lonely bed, my lopped-off feeling grew like a potato plant under thick black soil, until one Christmas in the cathedral, during the reading from the Old Testament, a poet who'd lived thousands of years ago spoke to me as if we were kindred souls. 'How beautiful on the mountains are the feet of those who bring good tidings,' he'd written. It wasn't exactly a whisper, read as it was by the priest's voice, as fat and thick and gold-trimmed as his rich garments, but the line leaped through the air in a shiny bubble like the ones the children used to blow, bubbles slicked with rainbows. Good tidings, I thought. About the secret. It seemed a line from a fellow yearner.

For the first time ever, I said to my confidante, my old, rheumy dog – a puppy when the children first arrived – somewhere else in the world there must be yearners like me – and surely they'd know what to do with this emptiness. And just at this time, a customer mentioned his apartment in Florence.

'Florence is a place of the spirit,' he said.

I'd often confided in my dog, also a yearner, though easily satisfied by a strip of bacon. I showed her pictures of Florence I'd found on the internet.

'Look,' I said to her. 'All of them, the statues and paintings, the decorations and the curlicues – what are they saying? Look at the naked cupids reaching out to something, look at the holy men turning their pale, shining faces to something, look at the Madonnas with closed lips barely suppressing their joy about something, not to mention those ragged shepherds and no doubt smelly stable-hands – they're all openly yearning, they're not ashamed of the holes in their hearts; indeed it seems an assumption amongst the artists who created them that there's a hole in everyone's hearts. Surely the people there know what to do about holes in hearts.'

I didn't exactly speak those words to my dog, but I sent my thought to her, the way the poet had sent his thought to me. She licked her old, droopy jowls. The next day, she died.

I told my customer I needed a break and asked if I could rent his apartment in Florence. He imagined I wanted a rest. But, though I'd been busy, I'd rested, in a way, all my life.

So, after I buried my dog, I left for Florence.

I wandered through galleries and cathedrals, amongst a noisy mob of fellow yearners oddly clad in spotted sun frocks or loose yellow shirts patterned with palm trees, as if they weren't pilgrims at all. But they, too, responded to Florence's yearning all around us, it was yearning along with us: all the statues, the altar pieces, the very walls, they all unashamedly, even flagrantly yearned along with us; there were meandering narrow streets with buildings almost toppling into them, such was their yearning. Why, even at night the river Arno coiled with a pleading light through the darkened city; it didn't hurl itself in a drench of sand and sunshine like our toiling oceans. Once, in a hushed cathedral, a man in the congregation began to sing of his desire, and it was just like mine. I wanted to go up to him and hold his hand and sing with him but of course I didn't, I can't sing and I didn't know the words, there never seem to be the right words, and his pleading gusted like a wind through the empty spaces inside us as we stood with upturned faces waiting for the vaulted arches to crack open and give us – what – what would yearning give us? For the first time in my life I was with soul mates, and from then on in Florence I trod more stoutly.

I can never go home, I thought. I must stay here with soul mates. But time was running out, my friend needed his apartment back; my restaurant and the children needed me back.

Then, one muddy afternoon on a bus back to the city from Scandicci, I found a ridiculously simple solution. A Florentine man, surely with yearning rampant in his blood, in his very DNA, a man with palely lidded orange eyes – I'd seen those pale eyelids without eyelashes a hundred times in medieval paintings – directed his gaze at me. It came to me, his gaze, in a fierce beam of orange light. That's how it felt, twin torches burning orange light through the grey, slippery day. When I met his gaze, he stepped out of the frame of the Renaissance painting, pursed his lips into a kiss, lowered his eyelids as if he were swooning, then rolled his eyes back into his head, and entered what seemed to be a state of bliss.

I looked behind me to see what god or goddess had occasioned this. There was only the dismal afternoon falling away against the fogged window glass. I counted to seven, a sacred number according to one of my guide books, and turned back. His gaze was still on me. He went through the act again, then unpursed his lips and smiled. So I had no choice but to admit the impossible.

He was suggesting bliss to me. Sexual bliss.

Of course, you'd think it obvious, the notion that yearning could be fulfilled by sex, but it hadn't occurred to me. If a man in my country had done what he had, it would mean nothing but his wish for sex, he'd be just a disappointing predator. Not that I'd had many of those, I'm not a pretty woman that men notice, I am what used to be called large-boned, with a long, thin face, close-set eyes and a prominent nose. Against my better judgement, my heart gave a little lurch of joy at being noticed – but more, noticed by a Florentine, surely a fellow yearner.

I dared another look. He was shaven-headed, ear-ringed, leather-jacketed – cream and black leather, far too fancy for a man in my country. Even his jacket set him apart, suggested he was a man from the land of the yearners. There were no lines on his face, no sags under his eyes.

A matron rustled her plastic shopping bag and in the sound I came to my senses. All the warnings my mother had given me, that I've given my brother's children: never trust strangers, always run from them, especially strange strangers.

I wriggled off between the soft matronly bodies to the far end of the bus where I held on to a pole near the driver, my skin wrinkling around the base of my fingers like a tide ebbing out past gnarled rocks. As the concrete apartment blocks slid by, I struggled to accept that there were, after all, compensations in my life: the children remembering to ring me up every so often; the customers staying back after hours serenading each other and sometimes me; the camaraderie with my chef, who's a friend from schooldays; our little experiments with recipes. And then, unbidden, there popped into my mind the new regular who'd prop a book against his wine glass and catch my eye whenever I emerged from the kitchen to see if the diners were pleased – as if he was waiting for me. His face, with its muscles and crinkles, broke into many surfaces when he smiled, so for me it was like crushed velvet. I'd never stopped to chat with him because I was intimidated by his constant books. He'd find out I meant to read but didn't. He always left his dog tied up outside and many times I'd wondered if I should put a bowl of water out for it, but what if all the diners took it into their heads to bring their dogs? The restaurant would be ringed around with dogs. My brother would turn in his grave.

Suddenly there was a firm male body pressing against me. I had forgotten male firmness. It came back to me from my youth, when I'd sometimes danced with men in the town hall that has now become a disco. I'd had few partners, only boys who knew my father and were obliged to do a round with me. Apart from a few unsatisfactory sexual encounters, soon over, I hadn't known men.

A large, olive-skinned hand gripped the pole I was holding, and slid down onto my fingers and covered them, and then the hand slid down to become a bracelet on my wrist. Or a handcuff. I swayed to the rhythm of the bus, not moving my arm, not looking up. The world narrowed. There was only the old man's catarrh of the motor and the warmth encircling my wrist. There were no tumbling cupids or upturned faces lit by a beam from a crack in the heavens, but nevertheless the circle of sexual warmth stilled my thoughts.

After a long while – funny how time's arrows suddenly cartwheel, and could that mean I was already experiencing the timelessness of ecstasy? – something, perhaps politeness, demanded I follow with my eyes the man's arm, the bunched up shoulders of his cream and black leather jacket, the cheeky diamond in his ear, and, when I dared, his orange eyes. I didn't free my hand.

I'm the one who can give you what you seek, said his orange eyes.

If the soft-bodied matrons pursed their lips in scorn, if they made faces to each other of contempt, I didn't see, as the Madonnas nearing a state of bliss in paintings don't see. Their eyes accept the exalted moment. So I saw nothing, nobody, only him, for his eyes were repeating: *I am what you came for*.

It couldn't last. He took his hand away, and suddenly my wrist was damp and cold. He turned, the cream and black jacket crackling. My hope got off the bus.

I had no choice. I plunged between the women and the plastic bags and the children, and with the superhuman strength of the stricken, I forced open the closing doors, so I could get off too.

He strode down a street. I walked behind. A café beckoned relief, all bright lights and gleaming glasses, just like my restaurant back home. Home washed over me, the warm bathwater of ordinariness. I remembered the curious sense of harmony when we get the menu right, so we'd begin to think what we do has an importance beyond feeding people; I remembered the orderly lines of tables just before we opened for the evening, with the plates the paleness of peace; I remembered the face of the new regular whose dog waits outside for him. He's not my sort of man, being small and spindly, but there's something accepting about his gaze. Perhaps he senses something about me, something that speaks to him – perhaps he'd understand what I can't put into words. And if that's true, he may not mind that I don't read books.

I turned like the dumbly respectable person I am, and went inside the café, leaving behind this wild Florentine and my foolish moment. I sat at a table. After all, I told myself – and I still sent my thoughts to the ghost of my dog, though I was trying to give up that habit – it's just envy making you desire what you haven't had, what you weren't meant to have.

I hailed a waiter.

But it was the Florence man who loomed. He stood gazing down at me, while I could only gaze down at the table top. He sat opposite.

'Come to my home,' he said in perfect English, overly perfect.

Then the waiter appeared. 'Madam?' he asked.

There's never anyone handy to advise you what to do.

'A short black,' I said.

We sat in silence for several minutes until my coffee arrived.

I broke the silence.

'I didn't come to Florence just for sex,' I managed to say.

He shrugged.

'I'm after,' I said, stumbled, and then suddenly I found the words, 'someone who knows what this city is saying. So I can hear it too.'

He sat up so straight, proud and tall, his shoulders could have lifted the entirety of the chandelier-hung ceiling.

'I am a man of this city,' he said. 'You are with the right man.'

I could scarcely look at him then. When I managed a glance, to my surprise he wasn't looking into a mysterious distance, he was only examining the bar with its array of fine bottles.

I wondered if I should suggest a drink, but no, he was our leader.

He said:

'Shall we go?'

'First,' my voice said, playing for time, trying for decorum, though decorum so far hadn't stood me in good stead but at least there was dignity in decorum, perhaps even nobility – this voice of mine didn't belong to me anymore, it was high, silly, almost a squeak – for my secret had been revealed. He knew what I was searching for as nobody anywhere in the world had known, it was clear to him; why, even the waiter slopping my expensive water on the table knew of my emptiness. They were, after all, from Florence.

'First,' this thing, my voice, squeaked, 'we must have three meetings.'

I hoped that in three – again a propitious number – I'd be able to explain to him that despite my acceptance – perhaps – of mere sex, I was actually seeking out what Florence knows. The sacred knowledge that yearners share, and receive.

He bowed his head. It seemed like assent.

I went back to my friend's apartment, and pondered what to do. One moment my pondering told me to go home before anything happened and that seemed the right solution, and then, after I'd gone for a coffee in the sunlight on the piazza, my pondering told me to take this chance, and that seemed the right solution as well.

On the first two of our outings, we scarcely spoke. It was not the fault of my stumbling Italian, learned largely from recipes, nor of his perfect English, with even an Oxford accent, because he'd been sent away by his mother many times to stay with a family in London. 'The family was as chilly as the country,' he said in an unusual burst of loquacity, 'but they spoke well. Families do that here, send their sons to get the right accent.'

That hung in the air, against the screams of an espresso machine. Clearly my Australian accent wasn't right.

Sitting across from each other in little cafés, he was as preoccupied as a philosopher working on a conundrum. I was awed by his silences. Dozens of times in my head I composed a speech to further explain myself, but the speech became smaller and smaller until it was a crouching, curled-up speck he could flick onto a dusty floor.

During both meetings, I'd announce, over the dregs of our coffees, that I must go home. It was the only moment I became an authoritative person who knows what's what, someone who's on top of things. He'd suddenly come to life, ringing a taxi for me on his mobile, speaking in Italian too rapid for me, joking with the man on the other end of the line. He always forgot my address, or perhaps he assumed I had no fixed address.

'To—?' he'd ask again.

I'd say it again: 'Via del Paradiso.'

He'd repeat it to the taxi company, but in English, laughing.

'She is bound for the Street of Paradise.'

I felt absurd even about the name of my street.

At the third meeting, we went to a movie in a cinema, but he pulled at my hand just after the opening credits.

'It's time,' he said.

I stood up. I didn't complain that I still hadn't explained myself. This affair, I now knew, was not about words. I whispered to the ghost of my dog that he seemed too refined to be a murderer, and besides, isn't this what I'd longed for? Hadn't I sought the bliss his clumsy pantomime had suggested – by now I could admit that it had been clumsy – and was my life at home ever going to give me what I needed?

He strode impatiently through streets I didn't know. Again, I followed, though I comforted myself by promising that I'd turn back here at the statue, I'd turn back there at the fountain. I broke my promises.

'My home,' he announced at last, slowing down so I could catch up. We were in a piazza. On two sides were expensive shops that in the day would've glowed in gold and crimson like the frescoes in the cathedrals, but now they were ominous shadows, as if the sacrament was over forever. On a third side was a church spire that poked around hopefully at a starless sky. And on the fourth was a grand house with a porch, crowded with a beggar and his dogs.

'Give him nothing,' my lover said when he saw me looking. 'Let's not encourage them.'

There were five dogs, the largest, a collie, at one end, and a little dachshund crouched under the beggar's feet. Two dogs lay on either side of him and my favourite, a mongrel, balanced on his chest, its front paws nestled at the man's chin, its little body rising and falling with his breath. It was the hour of the *passeggiata,* and the dogs smiled at the elegantly dressed crowds in a stately way as if they weren't beggars at all. I didn't say it to my lover, but the dogs made it more possible for me to follow the cream and black jacket inside. Behind his back, I flung them a secret smile. I was only visiting a friend's house, my smile said. But then I wondered, would they hear me if I screamed? Yet, like a woman deranged, I followed him.

I felt no lust. I certainly felt no love. All I felt, like the suck of a tide I couldn't begin to fight against, was a dull thud of determination. I must see what might be given.

The street door opened directly onto a vast white room that in earlier days might've hosted grand ceremonies, but now there was only the man and I, and a deep stillness under the forbiddingly beamed ceiling. It was as if the room's past was with us, observing me, half-knowing I'd disappoint it. Over in a shadowy corner was a heavy, ornate wardrobe that was already mocking me, and a bed that perhaps he'd made up for my arrival, with a dark blue velvet cover and blue cushions stamped with an important gold crest. Perhaps someone else had made up the bed. He wasn't the bed-making sort.

'Our family,' he said, seeing me look at the crest. 'From the thirteenth century.'

There were three doors in the room, I noted, suddenly aware I might have to escape – one, the street door through which we'd come; another, a small modern door:

'The bathroom,' he said. 'My mother permitted an ensuite.'

But the third. The third door was ornate, surrounded by a wide oak frame on which half a dozen snarling lions competed for my terror.

'A portal,' I murmured, for I'd heard the term and remembered that they're often the entrance to exalted places.

'It goes to the rest of the house,' he said.

I struggled with disbelief.

'Who lives there?' I asked.

'Just me and my sister.'

I should've noticed the way his voice thickened. My voice never thickens when I mention my brother.

I should've asked further. But all I said was:

'And your mother?'

He shrugged.

'Away.'

On the wall above the bed was a patch of faded fresco. He followed my gaze.

'When my mother is gone, I'll have it painted out,' he said. 'I'm bored with age.'

'But you're a man steeped in this city,' I said. It came to me that he might be one of a race of interlopers who had nothing to do with the grand passion of Florence.

But he certainly wasn't a new arrival.

'This is my great-great-great-great-great grandfather's house.'

To be honest, he listed so many greats, I lost count.

'When my mother dies, the house will be mine.'

'Will it belong to your sister as well?' I asked.

He didn't answer.

Undressing seemed called for. I went to a dark corner so I wouldn't bore him with my age as I pulled off gloves, scarf, thick coat, trousers, tights, woolly jumper, skivvy, thermal singlet, bra. But I didn't need to hide from his gaze. He was too busy shedding skins of his own, throwing them off so they skidded across the russet tiled floor, making splashes of unwanted colour like stains.

Then he was lying on the bed. Against the blue velvet, his orange eyes startled me all over again. To escape them, I lay down beside him.

'Just one moment,' he said. He swung his muscled legs off the bed, strode across the floor and threw open the portal.

'Why?' I asked.

'The heating is overpowering,' he said.

'But your sister might come in. Is she in the house?' I asked.

He ignored me.

I asked him to touch me the way I liked but he didn't seem to understand. Perhaps the family who'd perfected his English didn't talk about such matters. He worked on me for a minute or two his own way, but it was to prepare me for himself. Afterwards, I was only my disappointing self. Perhaps patience was required. But as I lay there I realised that the imposing room was silent in the way memories make rooms silent, so that there's almost a whirring in the air of memories, on the other side of silence. Just beyond and above his face, itself a sculpture, was the patch of fresco that he'd have painted out. It depicted an angel, not an entire angel, just one angelic shoulder with one white wing jutting out. The shoulder was like his, the same sharp almost right angle, no gentle curvature down to the arms.

'Was your great-great-great-great-great-great grand-father the model for the shoulder?' I asked when he woke.

He corrected the number of greats, but that was all. When I shut my eyes again, I had an after-image of angel's wings.

We made love for ten nights afterwards, always on the blue velvet under the snarling lions. We'd meet first, eat dinner in a little restaurant nearby, always the same restaurant, then we'd go to his house, always entering his room from the street door. We never went through the house from the other side, though every night the heating irritated him, he said, and he'd fling open the portal that was turning out to be no portal at all.

Once, during our lovemaking, it seemed to me that we were wrapped around with the angel's wing. I tried to tell him this because it might be a sign, though I knew not of what, but he wasn't interested in signs.

Each time, more and more, I saw the angel's wing the way he seemed to, as something that added nothing to the city's passion, just a dreary, drooping thing stuck on a shoulder in a desultory, almost sulky way, bereft of visible feathers, somewhat similar to the machine-like wings in da Vinci's *The Annunciation*. But da Vinci, I remembered, had believed in the possibilities of angelic flight. When da Vinci was painting it, if his brush had wandered a little further, the wing might've become a helicopter. Whereas the artist employed by the great-great-great-great-great grandfather – I still couldn't get right the number of greats – judging by the wing, believed in neither the flight of the soul nor angels. He'd been pleased, I could imagine, to have his model turn side on so he didn't have to bother with a second wing. Perhaps his patron had required as much, not wishing his left shoulder to be immortalised. Perhaps that left shoulder had been wizened by an illness forgotten by us now, something that reminded the great aristocrat of his ordinariness. Perhaps it had been ruined in battle. However, the good shoulder could've supported a dozen magnificent wings. The painter seemed not to believe in wings, only in shoulders.

I asked, after one of our nights of love – still disappointing but I was still too polite to show it – if I could see the rest of the house.

'Why?' he asked.

'To understand you more,' I said.

There was a long pause.

'My house,' he paused again, 'is irrelevant to us.'

I was comforted that he said Us. It kept me returning a little longer.

Perhaps I'll achieve it next time, I said to myself, though by now I had no idea what 'it' was. I just seemed to be waiting like the room, without will or mind, waiting on the desires and needs of another. Nothing in my life had told me how to be other than someone who waits.

On the sixth night, over dinner, I asked the orange-eyed man what he did during the day.

'I look after the library,' he said.

'Which library?' I asked.

When he said nothing, I added that it might be one that the guide books had recommended.

'My family's library,' he said. 'My mother pays me to do this.'

I told him that I have a shelf full of books, old recipe books given to me by my customers – *Keys to the Pantry, When Mother Lets Us Cook*, *A Cook Book of American Negro Recipes*, *Fine Old Dixie Recipes*, *Favourite Recipes of Famous Musicians*, and a well-thumbed old *Commonsense Cookery* of my brother's with a quaint emphasis on milky recipes for invalids and an underlying belief in the healing power of onions.

He said after another silence:

'Our library is exclusively manuscripts. Illuminated manuscripts from the fourteenth century.'

On the seventh night I asked where his sister was. We were having dinner in the usual restaurant. I was comforted at how we'd developed a routine. At the mention of her, he became unexpectedly vivacious. He told me that she works, like me, in a restaurant – till well past midnight, he added quickly. She sleeps till lunch and then visits friends until she's due at the restaurant.

Talking about her eased something in him. His skin glowed as if it had been basted. I wanted his vivacity to continue, so I tried to encourage more talk.

'What does she do in the restaurant?' I asked.

A wrong move. He paused. His willingness to talk ceased.

'Women's work,' he said. 'She feeds.'

I was curious to see and hear her, to observe what they'd both inherited from their grand ancestors.

'Let's go to her restaurant,' I urged. 'Tomorrow night?'

'Perhaps I can't find it,' he said.

On the tenth night, from deep in the ancient house, I heard . . . what did I hear? Was it an ancestor, breathing so close? Was it the grandfather of the magnificently squared right shoulder? I held my breath, to hear again. But my lover contrarily didn't hold his. He breathed heavily into my ear. He shouted in his orgasm, and subsided. Afterwards, there was only silence, the sound of a house settling into night.

'Was it good for you?' he asked.

He was always a man for the ceremonies.

He fell asleep before I could answer.

On the eleventh night, while I sat on the bed waiting for the taxi, I asked him:

'Do you have a pet?

His orange eyes, as he lay on his blue velvet, swivelled to me.

'No,' he said.

'Nothing at all?' I asked.

'Why these questions?' he said irritably. But because the taxi took its time, he eventually answered:

'My sister has a fish.'

He became animated.

'It comes from the Red Sea, it's called a lion fish, although it's small and white. It has many flowing fins behind it, like trailing wings. In the Red Sea it would grow huge, but here in her small fish tank, it will never grow.'

'Should you set it free?' I asked.

He didn't answer.

After a while, he added: 'I bought it for her. Neither of us care about it. But that's fine. She was offered a dog but I wouldn't let her take it. It would possess her. Take her love away from me.'

I felt I was moving to the heart of the matter.

'You're very close, your sister and you?'

'At times,' he said.

Then tonight, on my twelfth night, after I'd lain down beside him, he turned to me and took off my watch. It had been my father's watch, overly large on my wrist and with cranky angles that are always catching in things, and it needs winding every night, but I'd worn it since the day of his death. It times my life: when I get up, when I open up the restaurant, when we close it, when I sleep. I thought he would ask me about the watch, and then I could've told him at last something about my life, but he just pushed it under a cushion. I felt bereft.

He got up and strode to the portal. We were back to the usual ceremonies. Just then, the angel's wing fluttered — no, that's not possible, it was the fluttering of something else in the room, a movement that seemed like sound. My mind stood on its toes and pointed out at last what I should've seen all along — that the artist had painted such a poor, perfunctory wing because the great-great-whatever grandfather had had a fine shoulder but no soul, not even one perforated with emptiness like mine, and only a soul can support a wing.

At that moment, I stood too, and snatched at my clothes. They were tangled, turned upside down and inside out, and I buttoned them up wrongly but I didn't care. I reached out to grab my father's watch as I rang the taxi's number on my own mobile.

'Why?' he asked, startled.

I pulled on my coat, grotesque with its bunched gloves bulging the pockets, and headed for the street door.

'Why?' he asked again.

'The sound I heard was weeping.'

He said nothing.

'It's your sister!' I said. I was only guessing, hoping I was wrong, but he blinked and as the orange lights momentarily dimmed, his spell over me broke.

'Your sister is in the house. She's been here every time.'

He had the grace to look down, twisting the royal blue coverlet between his fingers, holding on to it.

'That's why you picked me up.'

I wanted him to deny it, but his breathing seemed to quicken.

'To torment her.'

He wasn't someone to be accused.

'Every summer,' he said, louder than usual, 'you tourists come here like pilgrims. Then you go home with nothing.'

'You've done this before, many times, haven't you?' I said. 'Picked up a woman, to torment your sister.'

I let myself out the street door.

'You know why? Because there is nothing,' he called after me. He repeated 'nothing' because it was important to have the last word.

By that hour the piazza was deserted except for the wind whisking ice-cream wrappers into the chilly air. The taxi lights illuminated the sleeping group of the beggar and his dogs wreathed in black plastic bags. I tucked money into one of them, and the mongrel, my favourite, opened an eye like a pleased old man, and wriggled its tail up and down, encouraged.

Now, as I think about all of this, the taxi turns onto the Ponte Grazie, to cross the Arno. The waters seem to dawdle there, accumulating a silent strength underneath, before they can tumble over the weir, and return to black silence.

I wind down my window. The driver turns around and shouts that I must shut it. But I need air, space, my country, the smell of rustling gum leaves in the midday sun, the silky steaminess of a damp Australian summer. I hang my head out into the air but it's the wrong air, the wrong temperature, the wrong smells. Then a full moon slides out from behind a cloud and lights the river, which flashes and winks.

Go home, says the winking river to me. *Take your yearning home.*

The driver, swerving dangerously, reaches back and winds up my window himself. But the ancient river keeps talking through the finger-smeared pane of glass, talking as it must've done over the years to many bewildered pilgrims.

Go back to your restaurant, it repeats. *Ask the new regular about his book when he looks up. And give his dog a bowl.*

The List-maker

D ear P,[1]
How do I explain to you, my only friend, my reaction when he touched my breast? – such a tiny incident in the scheme of things, since to most observers I manage my life as well as any other, though constantly fearing that someone will find me out. In the meantime, I'm making the best of it, for as they said all that time ago in the hospital, I must live like anyone else, as if It hadn't happened. I was living alone – for who would there be to cope with me? – in a pocket-sized apartment in Stanley

---

1   This is an extract from the personal papers of the highly-honoured author; these papers have been held by the National Library under a caveat that made them unavailable until her recent death and the death of her husband, for reasons that will become apparent in the text. However, less apparent is the identity of P.; to date it has been, as I argue, inadequately, even salaciously considered, without due reference to her juvenilia, published here for the first time.

Street in Darlinghurst, then lined by thin, dark houses, like long and decaying teeth. In its midst there was an apartment block towering high over its neighbours, once a proud hotel built in the 1930s with the graceful and geometric grandeur of Art Deco, now broken and shame-faced like me except my breakage occurred, unlike the hotel's, in my early years. I must insist I'm here not because of what they said I must do, but because I couldn't bear ordinariness.

Though Nan's a woman querulous about life, especially about being saddled with me, she never thinks of her life as ordinary – what with the embroidery still glowing vermilion and emerald and yellow and sea blue on the trousseau serviettes, tablecloths and bed sheets after sixty years of scrubbing; what with the enormous pumpkins she grows, almost big enough for her to be put in, Snakey the neighbour laughs, darting his shiny prehensile head towards her; what with the glossy furniture bought for her wedding to the handsome man who even on that day pulled his hat over his eyes (she still assiduously picks up bits of veneer and saves them in a matchbox for the day he'll return to mend everything, her broken heart as well); what with the mauve-shadowed milk that cascades under her knobbly hands every morning from the ten softly nuzzling cows that she calls by name; what with the way the dozen hens, nameless because one day they'll be dinner, produce eggs far bigger than city eggs in cardboard boxes, eggs coloured like their feathers, brown, beige, fawn and chocolate. Nan's a woman world-famous – she says – for knowing how to draw eggs out of hens, even though Hen Number 9 periodically flies off in a huff and an eddy of glittering feathers, then in mid-air flaps frantically above her own cloud of dust, reels backwards at the sight of the big world beyond, and slumps ruefully in the nearest tree, skulking back to her own perch when no one's looking. You'll be like that, Nan laughs at me, more a cackle, really, her thin body creaking over her joke. Oh, how I hated her then.

It so happened that history conspired with my determination. At a particular moment in the century, the politicians and authorities, moved by a sentiment that isn't relevant here, permitted the deserving poor, the brighter students, including girls, to sit in the great halls of the universities along with the more genetically deserving, the children of the rich. Though, like a person displaced not only by this stroke of destiny but by my previous history, I listened always but spoke seldom to girls and boys astonishing for the glow of their money and their assurance about the future, I had a sense of being found out on that chilly day when I stood in front of the notice board in the university quadrangle and read that I'd come first in the final examinations.

Gotcha! Nan would've cackled.

I'd walked home that day to my tiny shared room where my only territory was my bed and, relieved to find my roommate gone shopping, I crawled fully-dressed under my sheets and blankets, and trembled. What should I do now that the protecting university had finished with me? I couldn't amuse Nan by skulking back to the perch. Teaching was an obvious answer but I was terrified to face children, for children have such knowing eyes. My professor in the struggling department of Asian History had invited me to become his research assistant, but I'd declined because the stipend wouldn't be enough to keep a roof over my head, not even the peeling ceiling of the tiny flat I aspired to in the once-grand hotel a few streets away. The real estate lady, a girl of my age but with a strawberry birthmark from her forehead to her mouth, as if an autumn leaf, the sort you'd hold to feel its fire, had blown onto her and she couldn't peel it off—she'd intimated that she'd seriously consider me for the flat if I found immediate employment.

Gotcha! again.

I could no longer put off the dreadful moment. On my bed I frowned over the Saturday newspaper advertisements for work, and made stammering phone calls. So I found myself across a gleaming desk from Maria, a stern but, as I was to find out, furtively kind European who must've seen her own displaced self in me, for she hired me in preference to the other young graduates yawning on a line of black chairs outside her office.

✄

It's the early days of a television channel that shows foreign films needing translation. The translators adept at their own languages write subtitles in English that themselves need translating. It's shift work. So I travel to my new life on an ashtray-smelling bus that coughs its way through the city traffic carrying dark-suited men who rustle newspapers with such importance that I'd forgive a poke in the eye from the unwieldy pages of print – and women who, dressed in suits with tight skirts and shoulders enough to carry a sheep, clack knitting needles on the stuttering journey just like Nan does in front of the fire, though it's true that they consult intricate patterns from glossy magazines pushed back into handbags on the neat creases of their laps, whereas Nan's knitting never varies from one line purl, the next line plain, the next purl, the next plain, the next purl, plain, purl, plain, purl, plain, purl, plain, purl, plain, purl, plain, purl, plain, purl, plain, purl, plain . . .

It's my work to sort out the subtitles, partly by silent puzzling, partly by checking with the movie on my monitor, partly by questioning the translators, and – the part I like the best – partly by conferring with my colleagues. That's because I confer with Simon.

It's the first day of winter, I wake up to hear heavy rain, a wall of sound. I'm irritated by my own clichés for there must be millions of individual pear-shaped drops pulled by gravity to sparkle and drench the particular metre of earth between my window and the building next door. But no matter how hard I listen, it just sounds like a wall of sound. When Nan woke to such a sound she'd be delighted and, despite the cold, she'd run in and wake me up like a child at Christmas who can't bear not to share her toys, but I've left the farm and her behind and merely grizzle to myself about the stoutness of my shoes in the rain, the only pair I own.

Then I remember I have no shift today. In a break in the rain I rush to take in the washing up on the roof. I like riding in the lift to the top floor. Even though it's only ten floors up, it feels important, and in case someone gets in, I carefully arrange the straw washing basket on the jut of my hip in the stylish way I saw in a movie, not like Nan who'd hold it in front of her stomach like a wheelbarrow. The roof garden – Nan would cackle at the name – is no garden at all, only a few weeds in pots – no, today there's a new pot, and I can tell it's spinach, with thick tempting green leaves. I don't see Irene waiting in ambush while I glance between other people's pillowcases and sweatshirts, already weighed down and sullenly sodden. But I mustn't take them in; the Manager warned me last time that's being suspiciously over-friendly. I look over beyond Hyde Park to the city beneath me and beyond, to a rectangle of Harbour lying like a puddle between the buildings. In the foreground there's the little island where starving convicts screamed in agony but now we pretend that screams from people like that didn't matter; why the screams held in those stones were probably no different than the screams held in any other. Beyond the buildings, the puddle of harbour will spill and spread like a tipped-over 44-gallon drum all across the roundness of the planet.

Irene emerges from her chair under the little canvas awning where the rain's been plopping.

You see how well my spinach is doing?

She's been watching the rain too – and me. I blush. Did she read my thoughts? Often I allow myself to wonder if the thoughts of others might be contagious because they come as a fluorescent green line unbidden into me, ready-made, it seems. Do mine go like that into other people's minds? You'd know these answers, P.[2]

Irene launches into instructions on how I should've pegged the shirts so the peg marks don't show – you must place the pegs at the armpits – and she pokes at one of shirts in case I don't know where an armpit is. She lives in the city, not out in the sticks – and she thinks about this? Then she tells me how I should always shut a door so everyone in the corridor isn't disturbed – and since I don't like to walk away, she's holding the handle of an imaginary door, pushing it open only a gap, slinking her feet, hips, stomach, shoulders, head through it like a fat mouse sneaking through a gap in the floorboards, and *voilà* she's on the outside. Her smile even makes the roof garden glow.

---

2 Some scholars have read this, and other such utterances, as a plea to a lover, the supposed P. – but I suggest this is a whimsical reading.

I'm not sure if I should clap.

I see, I say.

Before she insists I do it with her, I flee.

I try to write to you in the roof garden when it's not raining, but my thoughts fan out like striped butterflies over the city. Did you ever see this astonishing city? Over the roof gardens where lonely dogs pace up and down, I flutter over the building tops and land, quivering on thread-like legs on ugly grey air conditioners, then I fly off over the dome of the Queen Victoria Building that was once gleaming copper but now is poignantly aged with streaks of blue and green verdigris, lumpy and crumbly beneath my quivering thread-feet. Now my thoughts ride in straight lines on the long red noisy train crossing the Harbour Bridge, but I'm swallowed in a gulp by the black tunnel.

Day two of rain: I will count the days of rain because, as Nan would gloat, this rain is settling in. It's a shift day, and I'll wear my only pair of thick jeans, thick jumper, thick woollen coat. I'm cursed with big motherly breasts, already pendulous, so I'm square shaped, maybe the shape of a bar fridge, especially in this coat. On the bus to work, I'm a bar fridge on legs.

My desk is pushed next to the desk of the handsome Simon. I like to think that we puzzle together. When I haven't interrupted him for a while, I consult with him, but never with what's-his-name, an afterthought when the Channel was forced to accept they needed a third editor, and what's-his-name's desk was set up apart from mine and Simon's, and in the way, really, so you have to walk around it just to go for a cup of tea. What's-his-name is an afterthought man, even his face is a mess no one got around to organising, a wide nose and hair that only kindness could call brown. He's more the one colour all over, he's a dirt-coloured blur, I decided when I was in the tea room while he took such a long time to stir sugar into his cup that I considered snoring.

Or at least saying: Did you know sugar is highly soluble?

It's a good thing I'm shy. I could do damage with my tongue.

Day three of rain: when someone sits near you for every eight-hour shift, you think you know more about him than anyone else would, you know every burp, fart, arm scratch, belly scratch, crotch scratch, every stroking of the chin and whether he's a sporadic throat clearer or a rhythmic throat clearer. You'd know what he ate from the snack machine (not that he'd use it, he wouldn't be seen dead with a Wagon Wheel or a Milky Way).

His lips turn up right at the corners and his red hair recedes from his face, already an admission of mortality, though he's only twenty-five, but there's a heart-rending copper lock that falls over an eye and he has to flip it back. And my heart flips. There's a scrubbed quality to his almost transparent skin, as fine as a woman's, so that I want to stand him against the window light to find out what handsome men are made of. But there'd be nothing sullied inside.

A month ago I came across a photo of him in the Sunday papers, and he'd won a poetry prize. It was a shock to see his face on the table under my plate of toast crumbs, his face all angles but charming in the way it comes together, his patrician nose, his velvet eyebrows, his heavily eyelashed eyes – not that you could make them out in the picture, but as his neighbour I count and slide down his eyelashes – and the perfectly placed lines that guard his mouth. When we talk – and he graciously talks to me from time to time – I study his face for no reason and to guard my heart against him, I rearrange his nose and eyes to make him ugly, more ordinary. But to be honest, I haven't guarded my heart.

Beside him in the picture posed a sweet-faced woman, named as his wife, a woman with her own jewellery business, and holding a little wrapped-up baby. I wondered that in our conversations, he hadn't mentioned a word about his wife, the baby, the prize or his poetry. I have to admit that we haven't talked personally at all. As soon as I had a few shifts off, I went to the library and tracked down anthologies that included his poetry. I've been borrowing them from the library ever since. I could see the poetry's ingenuity but I was relieved that I wasn't so very impressed – otherwise, I'd have lost my heart entirely. Not that I'm a great one for poetry, but being a poet, that's far from ordinariness. Imagine going back to Nan with him on my arm and telling her I'd married a poet! But much of the poetry felt like clever contrivance. However, every now and then, a bit snagged at me. It was like walking across a paddock in the dark and being caught by blackberry brambles. Not the whole poem, just a line or two, when he'd leaned on a word so it broke like a twig and shot out of the grass.

> *Waves scurried like crowds in a subway,*
> *Heads down not daring to stop*

I wondered about that.

Last time I found an excuse to consult, I asked him would he use the subjunctive in the film I was watching or did he think it required less formal English? I showed him a couple of scenes on my monitor. He accepted the offer of my headsets, intimate since they'd been on my ears, but he'd have had to go to the trouble of reaching back behind the machines to unplug his own. I liked the way he thanked me by ducking his perfectly rounded red head as if he was bowing. He watched, grunted amicably, pulled off the headsets and announced that the subjunctive would be too formal. Since he'd been interrupted, he unexpectedly asked:

What's your attitude to the dash?

Caught off-guard, I always take a while to think. My lower lip trembles. It's annoying, but if I covered my lip with my hand, it'd look worse. He had to repeat his question before I answered.

I talked about em dashes and whether he'd want to emphasise the parenthesis or to keep it subtle.

Depends, he said.

We both laughed.

Everything always depends.

I bent to my work, flattered all over again that he sought my opinion. We both know that when he talks to me he's only sweeping off what's at the very top of his mind. There's a lot more going on, deep down, surely, to write that poetry. He'd reveal his depths to his pretty wife, whisper about it to his baby. He's always courteous. He probably learned courtesy at his grammar school, and it's become natural.

I come from generations of people uncomfortable if someone gazes at us. Even in my dreams I still finger the cracks in my hands that could be grubby with dung.

We talk about our fellow editor – Liam – that's his name! – about Liam's sideways grin. Simon says it was caused by a childhood muscular paralysis. Liam's family were very poor, he says. No one ever searched out the right medical attention.

Peasants, he spits out, almost angrily. I'm stabbed with fear that he'd find me out.

Many of the European films we subtitle have sympathetic peasant characters. It's made me feel safe, but I see now it's a false security.

I must speak.

I came from peasants too, I say.

Oh of course we were all peasants, generations back, Simon says. I come from the dirt.

But you're not a peasant?

My father, he says – irritated that I don't know – is a lawyer.

So I don't tell him about Nan.

To see the sky, I have to kneel on my office chair, wobbling because of its wheels, and crane up into the space between the buildings, to a sky bloated with rain.

It'll go on all day, I report to Simon. He grunts deep in thought.

At lunch break, I put down my pen, stand and pick up my handbag in a slow, deliberate way. I want him to know I'll be out of his way.

Sometimes his eyes fix on mine, unblinking, not seeing me but deep in his poet's thoughts.

I won't come with you, he says, charming as always.

When the vast room is empty, or nearly so, he'll make it bulge with the thoughts that poets think and so he'll make this space immortal, like John Donne's bed, like John Keats' meadow.

On the way out I pick my coat – dry now – from the rack, pick up my umbrella from the drip stand and leave.

In this tiny, unremarkable, unremarked way I want to help him — might I be in love with him? I've never been in love. Maybe I just like to have something or someone to look after? At least Simon's a warm presence in my mind, someone to spoil as I was never allowed to spoil Nan's hens. I'd like to have a cat but Irene would find out and tell.

I usually eat sandwiches from home on a little strip of lawn outside the office, for there's no knowing what city shops mean by butter. 'Butter on your bread?' and then they reach their knife into yellow fat. I feed my crusts to an edgy group of seagulls who eye me with the friendliness of snakes. My bench was donated by someone whose blackened name on a brass plate is now illegible, but I like you, unknown person, bequeathing a park bench so even when you've become illegible, you still give pleasure. Today I need a café out of the rain and slosh my way to one I've seen from the bus a street or so away from the office. I pass a dress shop — and despite the downpour, I admire a lace dress on the manne-quin in the window but decide it would make me more vulnerable, a hardware shop where I'm tempted by a set of wooden spoons with little dolls on the handles but decide I don't want a Nan-type kitchen — and then a shop that seems full of ice-cream pink and pale green paper.

Waves scurried by like crowds in a subway, heads bent.

Simon again, he's always in my mind.

Waves scurried by like crowds in a subway, heads bent.

This isn't the tight-lipped Simon I know. This is unrestrained, a linking without contrivance, as if waves and rushing crowds are, to him, already superimposed on each other. Are they?

Today's list

I feel unlocked in my mind by the connection of waves and subways, as if I've burst out of a dungeon into the air. Do other people feel like me?

Is there special thinking that poets do, that artists do? But not only them: what about tens of thousands of years ago, when someone amongst my distant kin had, in the blur of swirlingly disparate sensations – dog worm bird man flower dolphin bud spider child – walked over to a tree and scratched an entirely new mark: one.

Is it a special mind? Special muscles? A special gland? Special paths of thought? Streams of green fluorescent light so he sees lines between disparate things that no one else has traced? Now I'll never see waves without a scurrying crowd.

Can anyone make those connections? Can I?

And are you allowed to say that? But who is there to give permission?

Those times when I was little, lying in the spare paddock, nose so deep in the grass it tickled, thinking about you,[3]

---

3   Further to my argument on the identity of P.; our subject seems to have known P. even as a child on a remote farm.

thinking about the smell of dirt, ant piss, then nothing – that was when I was happy. Strange things came into my mind. Does Simon lie down – not in a paddock, of course – and strange connections come into his mind?

I'm so deep in thought, I step into another puddle and then on the footpath, my shoes squelch, making puddlets of their own. Will the shoes dry out overnight? What will I wear tomorrow if they're still damp?

I order sandwiches and coffee, and reach for a free newspaper someone's left on a nearby chair, but Simon keeps invading me.[4]

The new Left Brain Right Brain theory might be a clue – Simon knows to use the creative side of the brain – but many scientists are scornful of the theory. It doesn't feel that my brain is divided but the mind tricks us, making us believe that what we feel is what is. And should I be saying brain not mind? Are the two different?

People say creative brains buzz with ideas all the time, but my nose-in-the-grass times didn't come with a feeling of buzziness. Just a sort of dreaminess. I heard about a scientist who said that creative people's brains go more still than

---

4 Not pertaining to the identity of P., but the reader may forgive me for mentioning small matters, for details in research may count for a great deal. Our juvenile author was actually in a café when she wrote this, evidenced by a coffee stain with some flecks of powdered chocolate and a circle of a cup on the right-hand corner. Her writing about her home life only refers to the drinking of tea. This adds veracity to the detail when in a state of shock she makes herself a cup of tea. Whether the state of shock is warranted is another matter.

normal.[5] I wish I could ask Simon but I'd have to admit I'm stalking him and ruin everything – and maybe he wouldn't even know.

---

5   The reference will probably be unfamiliar to most readers but our author flirted with the work of the neuroscientist Colin Martindale.

    As an artist she was often asked where her inspiration for her stories came from. Rather than answer with an ecstatic 'I'm channelling the universe', and rather than tell the truth – but more of that soon – she liked to put on an imaginary scientist's white coat and flirted with the work of the neuroscientist Colin Martindale; let me assure those readers that his early papers were plausible but his later work became problematic. In *The Clockwork Muse: The Predictability of Artistic Change*, Martindale argued that the time artistic genius appears in the world is predictable in the same way as one can predict the outcome of a toss of a coin; and he argued, somewhat self-indulgently in my opinion, that this timing could be formulated in the equation (where PC is Primordial content) $PC = 2.73 - .37t + .01t \, 2 - .32PCt - 1 - .36PCt - 2$.

    No doubt our author saw herself as one of his geniuses who'd been born just at the moment required by the equation. But, ironically and pertinently, in the above book Martindale revealed himself as a believer in the degenerate theory of the artist, along with the great though now sadly overlooked Hans Eysenck; the theory posits that the artist shares with psychotics and felons a weakening of higher, inhibitory brain centres, and therefore a 'shared proclivity to disinhibition'. Such disinhibition is exhibited in a number of tell-tale traits listed by Eysenck, and it is relevant that the reader have some familiarity with the list, to see its startling relevance to our author:

    'morbid vanity' – so greedily ambitious was our author that she constantly published 'her creations' despite my excellent advice as an editor that she work further on them.

    'a loss of a moral sense' – the reader will see evidence of this in the extract!

    'isolation' – to say the author is isolated is speaking the obvious.

    'inability to focus and to differentiate the relevant and irrelevant' – the extract evidences this.

    'exaggerated verbosity' – no doubt the reader will heartily agree.

    Most in evidence is Eysenck's listed trait of 'over-emotionality', with the author's absurd over-reaction to what is merely an ill-advised gesture, a hopeful touch in circumstances that were ambiguous. I have often pointed out that female fiction authors should never be tempted to use the first-person narrator; the writing inevitably descends to the hysterical.

    This constellation of traits are known to be part of the personality of the felon. More of that in the following pages.

The rain so heavy it weighs down thought. I'm bogged down with Simon. I almost wrote bedded down. I wish I'd met him before his wife came along but of course peasant stock wouldn't rate.

I watch cars plough through the wet streets like tractors, sending fountains that spangle people, or bedew them; there's new but uneasy camaraderie as people cower together on damp porches, considering a dash between the buildings, eyeing the passersby like me who hold umbrellas self-righteously, not offering to share.

I hide from the rain, from thoughts of him, in the pastel paper shop. It has a heavy-panelled, old-fashioned green door. I push it open, and the doorbell tinkles into a hush of pale colours, I put my dripping umbrella in a stand. A woman, a thin streak of black dress behind the counter, looks up in a preoccupied way and smiles doubtfully. My spirits plummet for the shop sells only gold embossed journals, spiralled notepads with marbled edges, note paper decorated with flowers. The well-mannered pastels, the ice-cream pinks, blues, and peppermint greens and even the fleshy thickness of the paper insist that this paper must not be smeared with the dirt of the unguarded. This is not the shop for poets.

I turn to leave and almost knock over a display of coloured inks in little bottles with a human shape of shoulders – almost like a Minoan female sculpture. When I tip the bottles back and forth, ink flows and lingers, and the glass is stained, this one with crimson, this one with emerald, this with purple, this with turquoise. They're my glossy bared shoulders I'm imagining, and it's Simon tipping the bottles. Am I in love? Of course not – it's just natural to imagine the poet tipping the ink like that while he thinks his unrestrained thoughts, his brown eyes with eyelashes as long as a cow's, tracking the turquoise, purple, emerald, crimson ink flow past the bared shoulders and up the slim neck, and back again.

Can I help you? The shop assistant, the elegant black figure.

The colours, I say to the woman. I can't say more, with the light blazing through them. My voice chokes. For no reason at all, there are tears in my eyes.

They come in a boxed set of four, she says.

I'm relieved to talk about boxes and sets and how many.

Oh, four is too many. Just three.

Because a plan is forming. If he wrote in these inks, maybe he'd be more often unrestrained. I would be, I know.

I take risks with the traffic in side streets, partly because I want to keep as dry as possible, but also because of my thoughts about Simon, not thoughts exactly, I couldn't call them that. Just nudgings of thoughts.

Is he thinking about me right now? A green stream of blazing light?

I carry the bottles back to my office in a little plastic bag so the white boxes stay new. But a rogue gust of wind blows my umbrella inside out, the spokes bend in the wrong direction like bony elbows. I turn into the wind as a sailing boat might, hoping to catch another gust – but it's useless, I give up, run through the rain like everyone else.

By the time I pass my park bench, I regret the emerald ink. Simon wears serious, scholarly colours, brown sweaters and trousers, navy blue cardigans and black trousers. How can I have been such a fool? By the time the lift arrives, I'm regretting the purple ink. And by the time I enter the workroom and see him chatting to Sarah, the Italian translator, in her cubicle, leaning his elegant, slender body against the board that divides her from her neighbour, and swinging his coffee mug back and forth, I know the scarlet is ridiculous.

I'm weak with jealousy – perhaps he's talking to Sarah about poetry, about what goes on in his mind – is it Sarah's greyhound body that has elicited the talk I'll never have with him? Oh how foolish, how foolish I've been. Chastened, I put the inks in my drawer, along with the dust, the stapler, the large orange scissors, the bent paper clips I refuse to throw away. All three inks are inappropriate. What if he shows them to Sarah? What if she says: That fat girl's got a crush on you! Watch out! And he'll say in his boarding-school way: What could she have been thinking of?

This afternoon, tomorrow, next shift, I'll just mention I've seen his photo, I'll admit I know he's a poet. That'd be better, that would make it the right moment to give them to him. Wouldn't it?

But when he comes back to his desk, he sits without looking to left or right, his handsome head constantly bent to his work, and I can't stop myself, I interrupt him to ask his opinion about using 'whom' in a conversational setting, and he seems to drag himself out of a deep pool of reflection.

I won't say anything now.

Day four of the rains: The rain has eased and I'm so pre-occupied with rehearsing what I'll say, I forget to buy a new umbrella.

I'll say I was in that card shop down the street and fell in love with this little bottle of ink but I'd never use it – would you like it? I'll show him just one, the turquoise.

Would you like it?

I go over and over it. I must get the tone exactly right: indifferent, wry, confessing to a foible.

As always when you don't take an umbrella, it starts pouring again.

I haven't found the right moment but it so happens that we finish our shifts together. Just as I pack up, the rain becomes a wall of sound again. He hears my gasp. At least, that's how it seems.

I've got a car and an umbrella, he says. You need a lift?

The old hotel has a flight of twelve marble steps sweeping in a blaze of white around a corner and marching up to the lobby. Pieces of marble have fallen off the outside corners of some of the steps but the staircase remembers being grand, with Art Deco lamps shaped like tulips of light. Simon insists I must go up first, and he's assiduous about protecting me with the umbrella. At the top of the steps, now hidden by the curve of the handrail from the footpath below, I stop to fish my key out of my handbag, and I turn to say at last:

I was in that card shop down the street

but his lips are open on mine, his mouth, the poet's mouth, only it's a cavern full of teeth.

He pulls away.

All you're interested in is pleasure, he says.

The words take their time to untangle, they're in a language I don't speak. I reel, steady myself, wait for the whirling to stop.

He puts his mouth back on my open one, breathes words into me, dirty words, he's got peppermint on his breath, my mind stupidly snags on details, it says that he never sucks peppermints.

And then, The Ceasing comes: my cells of jelly: my cytoplasm cytoskeleton endoplasm lysosomes mitochondria plasma ribosomes; they all jolt together, clang, collide, change shape, mill, murmur. My wits fail.

The Ceasing, as it always happens, has always happened since the terror.

His voice, his teeth-filled cavern, his peppermint-breath words, more dirty words I won't tell you, don't want you to ever know, you my better self.[6] And then to prove I'm who he says I am, he reaches under my skirt and between my legs.

Why don't you run shout kick scream bite punch, you've been trained, they taught you, they said Don't just stand there.

But I'm always eleven years old, the years have crashed away, down the broken white marble steps, I'm eleven and unable to run shout punch kick scream bite punch.

He thinks my stillness is saying yes, they always do. I become aware his palm is making a crescent moon of heat under my breast.

And more heat – oh, don't, don't let him notice, don't let his hand know – my panties have a flood of warmth, I'm losing control, I am eleven years old and terrified and urinating and they'll know, they'll smell.

He'll find me out. He'll know others have been here before.

A bone in him, oh his penis of course swells and hardens against my belly.

I should yell but I scream the way I do when I'm asleep, a silent scream.

Heavy feet on the steps – not high heels, full feet – a man's feet? Who cares, man or woman? – the creak of an

---

6   I have argued that 'P.' was a childhood companion. Our author was by the time of writing this in her twenties but P. is still 'her better self' – this would indeed argue for a very long-term admiration.

umbrella being closed, a big one, rain-laden one, heavy plastic folding. The dearest sound.

It'll be okay. Soon.

His penis softens. I'm rescued, rescued, the madness of The Ceasing stops, my wits return, I pull his hand from my breast as I jump away.

Irene looms, face warm comfortable ruddy round, and now I see she has a kind koala face with a bush of hair over each ear despite her accent from Europe. I beam at her, my friend, my teacher, my rescuer.

Ah, you've got a key, she says. I thought I'd be shivering, waiting for someone to come.

If she sees Simon, she doesn't acknowledge him. I put the key in the grate and push. I keep my back to him through the slow slide open of the jangling old wrought iron. Irene walks with me, shaking rivulets of rain on the lobby tiles.

Thank you! she says.

At least that's the order I hope it happens in.

Footsteps, penis softening, my hand detaching both of his, we part, Irene appears.

However, The Ceasing always muddles me. It could've been

Footsteps, penis softening, Irene appears, my hand detaches his, we part

or even

Footsteps, Irene appears, my hand detaches his, penis softening, we part.

∽

The doors close, he's locked out. He turns on his heel and dashes straight out into the downpour, not waiting to put up his umbrella. He's ducking his head against the rain in a useless way, as if he could escape its wet flaying.

While Irene goes to check the letter boxes on the wall, I hold the lift door open.

You went to work without an umbrella? she says.

Silly me, I manage. I'm panting.

I long to tell her, to cry in her arms – but what is there to tell? God knows what she's gone through. From now on, I'll peg my clothes under the armpits. I'll squeeze mouse-like through doors.

And then, without warning, she hugs me.

Did my thoughts go into her mind in a green sizzling line?

Thank you, she says, and releases me.

Your skirt, she says.

The Ceasing returns. Isn't it over yet, the torment? My legs – my very bones have dissolved and all that's left are threads. Did he come on my skirt? His semen? But his penis wasn't bared, his fly never opened.

I look down.

My skirt?

Wet through, she says. This shocking rain.

Shocking, I repeat, nodding hard. Shocking.

I'm still saying shocking shocking as the lift doors clunk-choong behind me.

∞

Safe in my apartment, I double lock the door and put the chain on. I hold myself up by the walls, I feel my way to the kitchen counter, and for no reason except that its ordinariness is comforting, I turn on the jug. Its familiar humming stirs up a little courage in me, enough to pull my shoes off, put on the heater, set them in front of it. Enough to take off my shamefully sodden pants, now chilly, and throw them into the wash basin, and take off my skirt wet only in patches. Enough to wash my hands, to put a teabag in a cup, to fill it with boiled water, to warm my hands. I put on music to drown my shame. I turn into the cushions, to drown in shame.

You must care for yourself, they trained you to care for yourself, you must remember it, you must do it now.

But they couldn't train me for there wasn't a me, how can I care for myself if I've ceased?

That's my defence. My heart has imprinted on me its own way to defend me. Cease, it says. Cease.

I failed to do what I should've done. I weep with shame.

After a while, I put on my pyjamas and get into bed. I wake hours later, the milk has congealed. But the rain has stopped.

I ring Nan too early in the morning, though she's always up early for the chooks and she'll be swearing at her old stove for the first cup of tea. I ask if she's fine.

Have you forgotten, I've got the hillside, she says.

Even her cackling sounds like home.

Her flooded neighbour, Snakey, says it's wrong she got the hillside when all she does is run a few cows on it.

I'm in the city, I'd forgotten the rain.

You sound like you're moping, she says. When are you coming back?

In all the welter of words between us, I've never really known if she loves me.

I try to think about Simon: all this time has he been furtively observing, noting my every breath, tremble, swallow, twitch, gulp – oh god have I farted in deep concentration? He'd know my farts as I know his – was he noting them down in his lonely lunchtime while I was imagining him writing poetry? I thought I knew him but I knew only a bit of him, like my dentist knows only my teeth. Knowing someone suddenly seems as hard as learning every silver drop of rain.

And then, as always, the Blaming, just as if I was eleven all over again: Was it my fault? Did he guess my thoughts?

Today's list
Dearest P.,

It's true I want sex, wild, uninhibited sex, not one but a group, three men, all panting for me, though not just wanting sex but wait – they must first know who I am, know my fears, they must understand The Ceasing.

Though that's a lot to ask of blokes at an orgy.

It's true I want sex.

I want love.

I want people around me who love me.

I want home, shelter, belonging, continuity.

I want to think clearly, clear as water, but I want more.

I don't want Nan's life. I want my life to be extraordinary.[7]

There's so much to fear.

I must not hate myself.

I hate myself.

I must not hate myself.

What do you like doing? They asked.

I like writing lists.

Then write lists, they said.

Up to this moment, we all pretend there's a me.

I can't, I said. There's no me.

Day five of the rains: It's an act of bravery to rise from my narrow bed.

My face blotchy, my eyelids red from crying, broken vessels in my left eye.

I must find a me, even though there's none. I'll paint on a face as if there's a me. I scrabble in a drawer and there's a

---

7 Please note that when she writes to or about 'Nan', it's never 'my Nan'. So in my considerations about the identity of P., I began to suspect a shared 'Nan'.

broken kohl pencil and I sharpen it with the kitchen knife. It makes the red eyelids worse. I rub it off.

I'm anxious now to go to work for the buzz of company. I leave with a half hour to spare before my shift so that I can stop at a chemist and choose a lipstick. I've been meaning to get one for a while. A lipstick will put an outline around a me.

In the chemist as the shop assistant, a girl a little younger than me with a pure, shining face, considers the exact shade I need. She doesn't laugh at me, or reject me. The subject of my lipstick has gravity.

To go with your outfit? she asks and I realise that I've pulled on what I took off yesterday and thrown on the floor, my baggy brown jumper knitted by Nan. Today, however, too late for safety, I thought to wear my jeans.

My skin, I say and I blush again in case the girl suspects that the lipstick needs to go with what Nan would call my birthday suit.

Find your anger, they said.

They'd be pleased to know that as I go in the office doors, I get angry. I'll tell him off, I won't raise my voice, I'll speak as if I have practised manners from an expensive boarding school.

Who do you think you are? I'll say.

What a bastard, I'll say.

You are a shit, I'll say.

I see his chair the moment I enter the office. His chair stands out, as it never has before. His chair is empty.

❦

By mid-morning, I know that he's not going to come in today. By mid-afternoon, I plead to go home early, claiming I've got a chill. It's true, my heart is chilled.

I hope you're not going down with this flu, Maria says when we meet in the tea room. We won't get these programs to air. I'm afraid you'll have to stay till the work's done.

It's only then that I notice what's-his-name is also absent.

Must be the rain, I say.

We'll warm you up, she says. Someone's sure to have something warm. She rummages in everyone's drawers. If she went to my drawer, she'd discover the inks for the poet I used to love.

She holds aloft someone's big thick cardigan. She brings it over, and bundles me into its warmth.

No excuses now, she says.

For a moment I feel like telling her, but what is there to tell? I steal a look at her face, laughter around her eyes, grief around her mouth.

I work a double shift, and Maria allows me a work taxi home.

Thanks for helping out, she says. She leans towards me and my heart thumps. But all she does is confide:

Why don't you grab some woollies from the shops before your shift begins tomorrow? Thick woolly underwear. I depend on it myself. You can still look glamorous on top.

I laugh, almost in tears.

I get out of the taxi at the shops. At the front of the vegetable shop, there's a big display of mushrooms, large, palely topped but dark and secret underneath. And I'm dizzy with memory, the cold morning I'd disobeyed Nan and walked to school, the bumps that had landed overnight in the neighbour's paddock and surely were mushrooms, and I scrambled through Snakey's barbed wire fence with spikes that could scrape out my brains. If you'd been there, you would've held out the barbed wire in a diamond until I was safely through and running.

I'm through and I'm running towards them and I smell them before I get to them, the sweet armpit smell of mushrooms, I'm plucking them out between the wet blades of green grass, that one's poisonous, that one's all right, not that one, yes that one.

And then, the bang on my skull and I'm on my face in the spiky grass and they're holding me down and the pain and the pain and the pain and then, The Ceasing.[8]

Today's list
Ways to love myself

Leftovers in the fridge promising there'll be tomorrow.

Feeling the towels on the washing line, still damp in parts, but in a few hours, if the sun stays, they'll be dry.

An empty washing basket thrown on my carpet.

The fat bulge of my teapot around the spout.

Folded hen-coloured jumpers plain purl plain purl folded in a drawer – the fat neat piles like little homes.

---

8   It is of interest that if 'P.' had been present at the intended mushroom gathering, our author assumes that he or she would've helped her through the fence. It seems that 'P.' was already absent in her eleventh year.

Making lists.

I'm proud so proud of my list.

Day six of the rains:

Full house today, Maria says cheerily as I enter the office.

Get yourself a nice warm cuppa first.

I spot Simon immediately above everyone's bent heads as I come out of the tea room: I'm ready to shout at him you bastard you shit. I haven't Ceased, I'm a list-maker and I'm alive – but he's standing at Sarah's cubicle.

I don't know how to think – what will I say?

Nothing of course.

I always say nothing.

I Cease.

I cast my eyes down, pretend absorption with walking carefully holding a cup of tea, with not spilling my tea. I'm a person who does not spill tea. I walk past him. He's still at Sarah's cubicle.

I've nearly passed him.

I glance into Sarah's cubicle, I don't know why – the streaming green blaze of thoughts, his thoughts, her thoughts, mine? She's sitting at her desk, he's standing close. There's something unexpected glimmering in the light and shadow of the video that flashes on her monitor. It's the top roundness of a pale breast. Her breast. She's unbuttoned her top, she's exposing herself. She's exposing her breast to him.

Or he's unbuttoned it.

Her gaze is on him, enthralled, exhilarated, questioning. His back is to me but I know, oh how well I know that his eyes would've climbed like an explorer's over that glimmering hill, memorising its curvature, telling himself about that breast being proffered to him, about its promises offered him, telling himself it will balloon onto his cupped hands, the same hands that only a matter of hours ago imprinted a crescent moon of fire on my breast and on the lips between my legs. I will know till I die those crescents of heat.

I almost stumble. I don't stumble.

I should say: Oh, what is there I should say?

I say nothing.

I trudge, I don't know how long I take to get past them, how long does it take to pass her breast and his body, how many years to cross that huge continent and in all that time, during all that trudging, the breast keeps glimmering and he keeps gazing.

My legs moving one after the other, as if nothing has happened and indeed nothing has. Eventually the corridor of cubicles ends and I'm out into the open space of the editors' section, then my pretence falls away and I stumble, catching hold of a desk.

A deep voice says:

Are you okay?

Is the voice inside me, or in the room?

I look up. A pale wave of milky tea is flowing towards a pile of papers. It's what's-his-name's desk, Liam — I suddenly remember his name, he's lifting papers up in a comical way as if a spill of tea is of no concern, and he's fishing out from his pocket a dirty but large handkerchief, and stemming the tide.

I'm okay, I say.

For the first time ever I look at him. His eyes.

I'm not, actually. Not okay.

I think I say that.

Want me to go and refill your tea? he asks.

It seems the kindest question anyone has ever asked. All I can do is nod.

He gets up, takes my cup. I go around the desk and sink into the warm hollow of his chair. I don't normally like sitting where someone else's bottom has warmed, but now I'm in the barn, do you remember the barn, the flanks of the cows, their warmth that enters you on chilly mornings, their dear warmth?[9]

Liam is heading to the tea room, passing those two, not knowing to look into the cubicle, not knowing to look away. If anything, he seems preoccupied by the grey rain lashing the windows. And suddenly I'm bereft, like a puppy, wanting people to pat me, wanting him to pat me, wanting to be in his warmth.

This is the way to care for yourself. Not karate not kick-boxing not yelling. Maybe not even making lists, but finding kindness.

I stand up, I don't look in the cubicle, I don't look their way, I head towards kindness.

---

9   Another reference to an early childhood shared by P.

In the tea room, with the jug already humming, he nods at my arrival, doesn't probe, looks only at the jug as if its humming is talk enough.

And it is.

The humming stops. He fishes a teabag out of his pocket, two teabags.

My favourite tea, he says glancing at me. Special occasion.

He pours the hot water and we wait for the tea to steep. I lean on the counter, he glances at me, and I know that his glance, despite its rapidity, takes me in, takes in my distress. He's sophisticated. He comes from a quiet, unassuming people who read weather, birds, animals, people. He wipes his mouth as if to silence himself, he turns his attention to the windows, streaked with rain.

He asks have I noticed the rain has different sounds? I say no.

Apparently you can tell by the sound if it's falling on gutters, on roofs, on footpaths, on plants, on dirt paths, on the sea. It patters on cement footpaths, it sloshes on guttering, it makes an echoing sound on canvas canopies over doorways and shops, it plops lightly on the gardens on suburban verges, it drops sweetly on the petals of pansies, and thoughtfully as it weighs down the spikes of grass.

Rain's not just a wall of sound! I say.

I had to stay in bed a lot when I was a kid, he says. It makes you notice things.

He goes over to the cups, takes out the teabags and throws them in two neat arcs into the bin. They don't even drip.

I dreamed of you last night, he says suddenly. You were in trouble and came to me. But I want to know, he continues — if you're psychic, and sometimes I am — why don't you sense when something important is going to happen? Why do we know only the trivial? Or is it trivial? Don't we know what's what?

I watch him get the milk from the fridge. He doesn't ask how much, of course he matches the milky spill on his desk. He's a peasant like me but there's a natural grace about him. It's like an aching absence, that I'm too awkward to have this grace, it's like a tooth that my tongue has just noticed is missing and must probe again and again. I wonder if it's too late to learn this grace, and to learn it from him.

We stand watching the rain and sipping our tea. I'm thinking of Nan on her hillside, and how she'd always told me that she'd chosen the hillside. Grandpa had wanted a farm in the valley, but that was in the time of the droughts, and she guessed that one day there'd be floods. Suddenly I realised that she hadn't been doomed to her life, that she'd chosen it, and she'd been, in her own way, remarkable.

My cup's empty. I turn to Liam, to thank him. He says:
What are your plans?[10]

---

10 There is one last irony I wish to bring to my reader's attention, given the 'degenerative theory' underpinning Martindale's work, as explained in the earlier pages in which, as you may remember, the creative disposition is linked to that of the

felon. You may remember that our author often speculated aloud about the origin of artistic inspiration. But this, dear reader, was a ruse. While artistic theft is not commonly considered felonious, such was the ambition of our vaunted author that she committed many thefts, often beguiling such as me in apparently innocent conversations but furtively recording them either by a machine concealed in a pocket or in her shrewd memory and afterwards rendering them as if they were her creations. Her 'work' is littered with my life: I will try your patience with just one such telling instance. Witness the oft-quoted funeral scene in which the grieving daughter is required to kiss her father's dead cheek, but instead snatches up his small, shrivelled corpse and runs away with it and has to be pursued by the law across the land. I recounted this and many other experiences from my extraordinary life to her and would have in time penned them myself or at least told them to my admirers – but once she'd written them, I was met with calls that I was the plagiarist. I confess I was lost. What is one, without one's history? To her works, I have donated my identity. I grieve for it.

But I am a generous scholar. To return to the caveat: amongst the personal papers and the bottles of ink (crimson, turquoise, emerald and purple, I'm sure you remember) was a small, apparently unremarkable paper, worn to tufts along its folds. It proved itself to be an invoice from the North Shore Crematorium for the cremation of her brother Paul in his infancy and in hers. I contend that Paul was 'P.'

So my contention is that our author communed to her dead brother Paul all her childhood, and through her youth, but gradually, as she found her voice, she reached out to real, live readers.

To return to the degeneration theory – Eysenck pointed out that withdrawal and isolation are traits of this particular personality type, and in her juvenilia this is clearly apparent, for who but the truly isolated would talk continually to the dead?

And here, I must allow my finer feelings free rein.

Some have unkindly suggested that this, my brief article, is an attempt to bring my name and grievance before her vast public. Far from it; it is this, her juvenile addressing of the dead that makes even those as mightily wronged as I have been to remember one's softer feelings of humanity. We realise that even the mighty are puny, the unassailable are vulnerable, even the felons are needy.

My discovery of the identity of 'P.' has led me towards forgiveness of her, and it insisted that I reveal to you my investigations.

Professor Amelia Broughton,
Central and Southern University
2016.

Acknowledgements

WILLY: How can he find himself on a farm? Is that a life?
A farmhand? In the beginning, when he was young, I thought,
well, a young man, it's good for him to tramp around, take a lot
of different jobs. But it's more than ten years now and he has yet
to make thirty-five dollars a week!
LINDA: He's finding himself, Willy.
WILLY: Not finding yourself at the age of thirty-four is a disgrace!

From *Death of a Salesman*, Act 1: Arthur Miller

I'd written these stories before I realised that, like Biff in
Death of a Salesman, and though much older, I am still trying
to 'come of age'. How do other people arrive so fast? All
the women in the stories – and one man – are trying to find
themselves at what Willy would say was a disgraceful age.

Stories too sometimes take a long while to find themselves; some here have been published before, but in other
forms. 'Small talk' was published in *Southerly Magazine* in
2007 in more or less the same words but 'The Last Taxi
Away From Here' was published in *Text Journal* in 2013
and before that, as 'The Last Taxi Ride' in *Acts of Dog* (ed
Debra Adelaide, Vintage Press 2003). It's taken years for

me to find the story's heart. 'Her Laughter Like a Song of Freedom' was published in *Wild Minds: Stories of Outsiders and Dreamers* (Random House 1999) but I've tinkered with it because after publication, Gerard kept arguing against his own ending; Gerard in fact went on to live a second life as Owen in my novel *The Secret Cure*. 'Passport' was published as a short memoir 'The True Story of My Father' in *A Country Too Far* (ed Thomas Keneally and Rosie Scott, Penguin 2013) but is now almost completely re-written after a previously unknown distant cousin in the UK found me and solved a family mystery; why my Scottish grandmother lost her family and her life to alcohol.

Apart from 'Passport', all the other characters and their doings in all the other stories are entirely fictional, and if they bear any resemblance to anyone living or dead, that is purely coincidental.

I'd like to thank Linda Funnell, who I hope will always be my first editor; Larissa Edwards, Roberta Ivers and Anna O'Grady of Simon & Schuster Australia, and Kim Swivel, who showed a unique belief in the short story and lavished care and attention on mine. I'd also like to thank my agent, Rick Raftos, for advice so good I dare not follow it, and my friend Libby Hathorn for spending several mornings at a café poring over 'The List-maker'. Nothing would be possible without the quiet encouragement of my life partner and fellow-writer Gordon Graham, and my daughter Kitty.

Sue Woolfe

More About the Author

Sue Woolfe has worked as a teacher and lecturer, TV subtitle editor, documentary maker and cook. She is the author of the bestselling novel about mathematics and motherhood, *Leaning Towards Infinity: How My Mother's Apron Unfolds Into My Life*, published in five countries and described in the *Baltimore Sun* as 'the deepest novel of ideas in years', and by Fay Weldon as 'glorious'. It won the Christina Stead Prize for Fiction in 1996 and was shortlisted for many other prizes, including the Commonwealth Prize and the prestigious US TipTree Prize, and she re-wrote it for the professional stage.

Her novel *Painted Woman*, about a woman coming of age as an artist, was first published in Australia in 1989, and in translation as *Ici et à jamais* in France in 2008. It has also been produced twice as a play, and also as a radio play. *The Secret Cure*, a novel concerned with a mother's determined search for a cure for autism, is currently being adapted to an opera by Woolfe. Her most recent novel, *The Oldest Song in the World*, is set in the Northern Territory in an Indigenous community, after Woolfe lived there for over a year.

Woolfe has also co-authored with Kate Grenville *Making Stories: How Ten Australian Novels Were Written* in 1993, and in 2007 she wrote *The Mystery of the Cleaning Lady: A Writer Looks at Creativity and Neuroscience*. She has written one script for TV, a comedy that won an AWGIE (1985).

Woolfe teaches at the National Institute of Dramatic Art (NIDA) and at annual writing retreats overseas, emphasising what neuroscience tells us about creativity. She writes in a hideaway on the Hawkesbury River in New South Wales, which she shares with her partner, playwright Gordon Graham, but most evenings in the city, she dances Argentine Tango.